D1034257

HD 7105.45 .U6 C56 2000

Clowes, Michael J., 1942-

The money flood

DATE DUE

NEW ENGLAND INSTITUTE OF TECHNOLOGY
LIBRARY

THE
MONEY FLOOD

Other Books in the *Wiley Investment* Series

THE
MONEY FLOOD

How Pension Funds Revolutionized Investing

Michael J. Clowes

NEW ENGLAND INSTITUTE OF TECHNOLOGY
LIBRARY

John Wiley & Sons, Inc.
New York • Chichester • Weinheim • Brisbane • Singapore • Toronto

10\05

43109763

To Ellen, John Paul, Molly and Jeffrey

This book is printed on acid-free paper. ∞

Copyright © 2000 by Crain Communications Inc. All rights reserved.

Published by John Wiley & Sons, Inc.

Published simultaneously in Canada.

No part of this publication may be reproduced, stored in a retrieval system or transmitted in any form or by any means, electronic, mechanical, photocopying, recording, scanning or otherwise, except as permitted under Sections 107 or 108 of the 1976 United States Copyright Act, without either the prior written permission of the Publisher, or authorization through payment of the appropriate per-copy fee to the Copyright Clearance Center, 222 Rosewood Drive, Danvers, MA 01923, (508) 750-8400, fax (508) 750-4744. Requests to the Publisher for permission should be addressed to the Permissions Department, John Wiley & Sons, Inc., 605 Third Avenue, New York, NY 10158-0012, (212) 850-6011, fax (212) 850-6008, E-Mail: PERMREQ@WILEY.COM.

This publication is designed to provide accurate and authoritative information in regard to the subject matter covered. It is sold with the understanding that the publisher is not engaged in rendering professional services. If professional advice or other expert assistance is required, the services of a competent professional person should be sought.

ISBN: 0-471-38483-6

Printed in the United States of America

10 9 8 7 6 5 4 3 2 1

Contents

Acknowledgments

The following gave generously of their time to share their knowledge about the evolution of pension fund investing:

Gil Beebower, SEI Corp.; Theodore (Ted) Benna, The 401 (k) Association; Gordon W. Binns, General Motors Investment Management Co., retired; David Booth, Dimensional Fund Advisors Inc.; Peter Bowles, Fiduciary Capital Management; Robert Brehm, formerly A.G. Becker Funds Evaluation; Roger Brown, formerly A.G. Becker Funds Evaluation; Ed Callan, Callan Associates; John Carroll, GTE Investment Management, retired; John Casey, Rogers, Casey & Associates; Tony Cashen, TMP Worldwide, formerly A. G. Becker; Budge Collins, Collins Associates; Michael Costa, Alliance of Fiduciary Consultants; William Crerend, Evaluation Associates Inc.; James Dunn, GTE Corp., retired; Charles D. Ellis, Greenwich Associates; Robert Evans, TCW Asset Management; Michael Fisher, Barclays Global Investors; William Fouse, Mellon Capital Management, retired; Elliott Gartner, Pfizer Corp., retired; Gary Glynn, U.S. Steel and Carnegie Pension Fund; Michael L. Gordon, Attorney, Washington, D.C.; Jeremy Grantham, Grantham, Mayo, Van Otterloo & Co.; Helane Grill, The Frank Russell Co.; William Gross, Pacific Investment Management Co.; Graham Harrison, U.S. Steel and Carnegie Pension Fund, retired; William Hayes, Walter Frank & Co.; John Hobbs, Jennison Associates; Robert Kirby, Capital Guardian Trust; Bennett Kopp, Sentinel Pension Institute; Ian Lanoff, The Groom Law Group; Dean LeBaron, Batterymarch Financial Management, retired; Ray Lilleywhite, Alliance Capital Management; John Mabie, A. G. Becker, retired; Maury Maertens, New York University Endowment; Katherine Magrath, ValueQuest Ltd.; Terry Magrath, ValueQuest Ltd.; William Marshall, Copper Beech Capital Services Inc.; Richard Mayo, Grantham, Mayo, Van Otterloo & Co.; Meyer Melnikoff, Prudential Insurance, retired; Jeffrey Miller, Provident Investment Counsel; Frank Minard, Plan Sponsor Network; Robert Monks, LENS; James Muzzey, Pacific Investment Management Co.; Chris

Nowakowski, InterSec Research; Russell L. (Rusty) Olson, Eastman Kodak; Robert D. Paul, Martin E. Segal Co., retired; Ron Peyton, Callan Associates; Henry Porter, General Mills, retired; Norton Reamer, United Asset Management; W. Allen Reed, General Motors Investment Management Co.; Tom Richards, Richards & Tierney Inc.; Barr Rosenberg, Rosenberg Institutional Equity Management; Claude Rosenberg, RCM Capital Management; George Russell, The Frank Russell Co.; Dallas Salisbury, The Employee Benefits Research Institute; William Sharpe, Stanford University; Robert Shultz, Pinegrove Asset Management; Rex Sinquefield, Dimensional Fund Advisors; Madelyn Smith, The Frank Russell Co.; Ron Surz, Roxbury Capital; David Tierney, Richards & Tierney; Dennis Tito, Wilshire Associates; Jan Twardowski, The Frank Russell Co.; Karl Van Horn, Arlington Capital Management; Harvey Young, Metropolitan Life Insurance Co., retired.

Introduction

In May of 1973 I accepted a job as executive editor of a startup publication, *Pensions & Investments*. The publication's mandate was to report news on all aspects of pension fund investing. When I accepted the job I knew nothing about pension funds, but as I began talking to people involved with the funds—executives overseeing the investment of the assets and investment managers making the actual investment decisions—I discovered I would be reporting on an exciting, burgeoning, rapidly changing field. In fact, I would discover later, I had been covering a financial revolution.

In my first few months, I learned pension funds were an important area of economic and investment activity that had been largely ignored by anyone not intimately involved with it. The funds had assets of more than a quarter of a trillion dollars invested in stocks and bonds. This huge treasure trove was largely unknown not only to the general public, but even to most sophisticated Wall Street executives and virtually all politicians. That would change briefly within a year of the launching of *Pensions & Investments* when Congress passed, and President Gerald Ford signed into law, the Employee Retirement Income Security Act. This law, known as ERISA, set new standards for funding pension promises and for investing the accumulated assets.

But soon after ERISA became law, pension funds again dropped off the radar scope of most politicians and the general public. Although pension funds continued to grow rapidly and to change how they invested their assets, only those in the field paid much attention, even after assets passed $1 trillion. No one noticed how powerful pension funds had become until, in the mid-1980s, they helped finance a few headline-grabbing leveraged buyouts, where pension fund and other money was used to return to private ownership such large, prominent companies as RJR-Nabisco. Since then pension funds have been regularly in the news and, for a time, in the sights of politicians trying to close the federal deficit.

From October 1973 on, I was involved in directing a staff reporting on all events involving the investment of pension assets. Executives at leading corporations had been changing the way they managed their pension funds' assets since the early 1950s, but in the early 1970s the rate of change accelerated as new money management firms or new investment vehicles or approaches were created, tried by a few pioneers, and then were widely adopted.

For most of the period, however, my staff and I were reporting on the growth of the trees and missing the impact of the spreading forest. The growth of the nation's pension assets and their redirection out of (mostly government) bonds into stocks, real estate, venture capital, leveraged buy-outs, and international securities had dramatic effects on the nation's capital markets and, through them, on the economy. The executives who directed these revolutionary changes were no less pioneers than those who opened the American West. They may not have risked their lives by charting new courses for the investment of the assets for which they had responsibility, but they often risked their jobs and their livelihoods.

This book is the story of these executives, the changes they wrought in the way pension assets were invested for the benefit of both the sponsors of the pension plans and those whose benefits were secured by the assets. It is the story of the impact of pension funds on the U.S. economy. It identifies those executives and funds that were the first to adopt new ways, the first to react to new information. These were the executives who turned new ideas into trends and then into accepted practice. This book is the result of interviews with more than 60 industry veterans who helped make the history. Many of them are mentioned in this book, but the memories and insights of those who are not were also invaluable in the writing of this story. Unless otherwise noted, all quotes in the book are from those interviews, which took place between February and July 1998. In addition, many of the events recounted were culled from the pages of 25 years of *Pensions & Investments* issues.

Special thanks are due to Robert (Bob) Shultz, Pinegrove Associates, Robert (Bob) Evans, TCW Asset Management, Carl Van Horn, Arlington Capital Management, and Michael Costa, the Alliance of Fiduciary Consultants, for their personal stories and insights, as well as for reading the manuscript and suggesting many corrections and improvements. Special thanks also to George Russell, the Frank Russell Co., who brought Russell veterans from around the country to Tacoma, Washington, so that I could gather their recollections of the beginnings of the industry, and to Professor Jay O. Light of Harvard Business School who provided hard-to-get case studies on the General Mills pension fund. I should also thank Dallas

Salisbury of the Employee Benefits Research Institute, Washington, D.C., for making available EBRI's research library.

Thanks are due also to William T. Bisson, publisher, and Nancy K. Webman, editor, of *Pensions & Investments* for their support in this project and especially to my wife, Ellen, who supported me continuously during the writing, and who, on a long drive from New York to southern Ohio and back, patiently read me stories from back issues of *P&I* and made note of the ones I wanted to refer to for this book.

Mike Clowes

Chapter 1

Revolution

A revolution has occurred in the United States in the past 50 years, a revolution that has reshaped investing and in the process changed the U.S. economy, the role of the federal government, the financial security of individuals, corporations, and financial institutions—including insurance companies—and the capital markets not only in the United States but also worldwide.

And yet this revolution has gone largely unnoticed by most of those affected by it. It occurred quietly, without bloodshed and with minimal disruption of lives. Like most revolutions, this was a revolution of ideas that swept away old thinking and old ways of doing things. Unlike most revolutions, the payoff was almost immediate and each step produced a positive return.

Also unlike most revolutions, this one was directed and driven by those generally considered among the most conservative in the nation, the nation's bankers, insurance executives, money managers, corporate executives, and state and local government officials. It was powered not by aroused passions, but by a flood of money released, inadvertently, by a decision, made by a federal government regulatory agency—the National Labor Relations Board (NLRB)—which oversees negotiations between companies and unions. The NLRB ruled in April 1948 that pensions had to be included in contract negotiations between an employer and employees, if a union wished. Until then, pension provisions had been set unilaterally by the employer. Afterward, union demands for pension benefits sparked rapid growth of pension plans and resulted in employers pouring money into pension funds to finance the promised benefits. The employers could no longer simply pay the benefits out of earnings; they now began to contribute additional amounts each year to meet future obligations.

As they stepped up their contributions to pension plans, the employers also began to search for better, more efficient ways to invest the accumulating assets. Better investments could produce higher returns, and higher returns could reduce the burdens of the pension obligations. The result of the search was a revolution in the way the nation's retirement promises are secured and the retirement savings are invested for the future, a revolution that continues today. This revolution affected every investor, institutional and individual, and through them, most aspects of the economy.

In 1949 the nation's pension assets totaled only $14.3 billion[1] and were, in effect, preserved in insurance company general accounts or locked into government bonds. They were not truly invested for growth. At the end of 1998 the nation's pension assets totaled more than $8.7 trillion,[2] more than 600 times what they were in 1949. They were larger than the national debt and growing faster. They were also larger than the nation's gross domestic product. That is, they could buy all the goods and services produced by the nation in one year and still have money left over. The pension assets were invested in a myriad of ways that financed true growth in the economy—that is, financed the growth of that gross domestic product.

This flood of money effected radical changes in financial institutions in this country and even internationally. The institutions overseeing pension assets in 1948 managed the assets according to a conservative interpretation of the old common law doctrine which stated that a trustee should invest the assets under his care with the care, skill, prudence and diligence that a prudent man, acting in like manner, would exercise. This doctrine was interpreted by the courts to mean that each individual investment must be prudent. If one investment turned out to be imprudent, the trustee could be found at fault, even if a dozen other investments were judicious and productive. Over the next 50 years the concept of prudence, indeed, the concept of risk, changed, and with it the investment practices of the nation's financial institutions.

Dramatic Changes

By April 1998, 50 years after the NLRB decision that unleashed the money flood into pension funds, the world of pension investing had changed completely, and it had changed the financial world. Fifty years ago almost all of the pension assets backed defined benefit plans that promised a specific monthly pension benefit when employees retired. By 1998 almost 25% of pension assets backed defined contribution plans for which the sponsor promises only to make a specific contribution into an account on behalf of each employee. No specific pension benefit is promised. Rather, the employee receives at retirement the value of the assets in his or her account. In addition, in 1948 both the asset allocation decision (that is, how much would be invested in stocks and bonds) and the portfolio management decision (which particular stocks and bonds would be bought) were made by perhaps 1,000 executives at a dozen major insurance companies and fewer than 100 major trust banks in the United States. A few pension executives at public employee pension funds and a handful of corporate funds were also involved.

By 1998 the asset allocation decision was made by more than 40,000 pension executives for defined benefit plans and by 35 million employees for defined contribution plans. The executives overseeing defined benefit plans, both corporate and public employee, influence the ebb and flow of almost $4 trillion of assets invested in the world's stock, bond, real estate, venture capital, and private equity markets. They decide how much of their funds' assets should be invested in each of these asset classes.

Through their selection of investment managers and the amount they give each manager to invest, they also influence the kinds of stocks or bonds or real estate in which the assets are invested. They decide, for example, how much money to give to a large-cap growth stock manager to invest in established growth companies—companies perceived to be growing faster than average; or how much to give to a manager specializing in a different kind of stocks; or how much to give to a venture capital manager or a junk bond manager to invest in small, less creditworthy but promising companies. Moreover, they are, for the most part, long-term-oriented investors. Their decisions affect the allocation of capital among companies and the cost of capital for different kinds of companies. The availability of capital and its price can affect the success or failure of a company, and ultimately the well-being of the whole economy.

Individual Control

The 35 million individuals directing the allocation of their own defined contribution plan investments are similarly influencing the flows of almost $2.2 trillion in assets.[3] These individuals, though not as familiar with the theory of investing as the professionals, have generally received some investment education from their employers. Many have learned about the relationship between risk and return. They have discovered that over the long run stocks have far outperformed bonds and other conservative investments. Many are now able to match their investments with their own financial status, future financial needs, and risk tolerance. They themselves decide how much they will invest in growth stocks or value stocks, large-cap or small-cap stocks, bonds, or guaranteed investment contracts through their decisions about how much to put into which mutual fund options offered by their employers. These employees have become investors, and some are becoming long-term-oriented investors as their investment pools increase.

Portfolio management decisions—decisions about which stocks, bonds, real estate property, venture capital deals, and so on to invest in— are now made by almost 10,000 highly educated investment executives at money management firms and at mutual fund companies. They are backed by an equal number of security analysts whose job it is to identify the stocks and bonds offering the best investment return prospects over the next few years. Thus, many more people, with many different decision-making processes, concerns, and needs, are involved in the investment decision process today than in 1950, when a relatively small group with similar concerns and backgrounds were involved. As a result of these changes, the capital markets, especially the stock market, have become more efficiently priced. Because so many people are looking, it is difficult for any single investor to consistently discover stocks that are wrongly priced in the market and buy them before others also discover them and act. Mispricing may occur briefly, but it is quickly eliminated by the actions of investors who recognize it and attempt to take advantage of it. Studies have shown that it is incredibly difficult for anyone, even these professionals, to outperform the market on a risk-adjusted basis over any significant period of time. As Charles D. Ellis of Greenwich Associates said in his seminal book, *Winning the Losers Game:* "The problem is not that professional managers lack skill or diligence. Quite the opposite. The problem with trying to beat the market is that professional investors are so talented, so numerous, and so dedicated to their work that as a group they make it very difficult for anyone of their number to do significantly better than the others, particularly in the long run."[4] Pension executives spend millions of dollars each year employing money management firms in search of returns in excess of the market. For most of them this is a futile exercise. Yet, if they did not all engage in that pursuit, if money managers weren't constantly evaluating the future prospect of companies in search of those most likely to prosper, if there was no contest of investment ideas and insights in the market, the capital allocation by the market would be far less efficient. Pension funds and their sponsoring organizations are paying the bulk of the cost for that efficiency. Even the bond market, though there are far more bonds outstanding than stocks, has become more efficient through a similar process.

This market efficiency has a very important consequence for the economy. It means that capital is being allocated efficiently across enterprises. If that were not so, if capital were not flowing in appropriate amounts and at the appropriate cost to the companies that could make the best use of it a very high percentage of the time, some investors would be able consistently to discover the fact and profit from it to earn returns in excess of the market as a whole. The economy as a whole benefits from that efficient allocation of capital. It can grow faster and at lower cost.

In 1950, in one of the most fortuitous developments in the U.S. economy since World War II, companies began seriously to fund their pension obligations, and they most often handed the assets over to investment professionals for investment in diversified portfolios of stocks and bonds. Many large companies limited the proportion of their pension fund assets that could be invested in their own stock, usually to 10%, even though there was no legal limit at that time. The companies wanted the pension funds protected from any difficulties that might strike the companies or their industries.

This was a fortuitous development because it channeled the pension fund money out of the companies, many of which were mature and in mature industries, into the capital markets. There, all companies competed for that capital on an equal basis. The institutional investors (eventually mostly the managers of pension assets) set stock prices; that is, they established the price for equity capital. Those companies perceived to have the best long-term return prospects were able to raise equity financing at the lowest cost. If the companies sponsoring the pension plans deserved the capital, they got it at reasonable cost; otherwise not. This was a strong positive for the U.S. economy, as we will see.

Investments Changed

The people making the decisions about investing pension assets have changed since 1948 and so, too, have the investments they use. Fifty years ago more than one-third of the assets of the nation's $14 billion in pension assets was invested in insurance company annuity products. Behind these annuities were portfolios of long-term bonds, mostly governments, which were simply held to maturity. More than 80% of the remainder was also invested in bonds, almost 50% of that in Treasury bonds. Less than 5% was invested in corporate equities—common and preferred stocks.[5] Most of the money in corporate equities was in the stocks of a few hundred large companies. There was no investment by pension funds in startup companies through venture capital or junk bonds; no investment in companies outside the United States; no investment in real estate, except tiny positions in mortgages. Nor was there any use of derivative securities such as options or futures to hedge risky positions. In 1950, there was no clear understanding of the nature of investment risk—how the risks of securities could compound or offset one another, or how risk and return were connected. Pension funds were the first investors to adopt new theories, approaches, and tools developed by academics and others.

The pension investment picture had changed radically by late 1998, 50 years after the NLRB decision. By then, large U.S. pension funds, both defined benefit (financing a plan where the company promises a specific retirement benefit) and defined contribution (where the employer promises only to make a specific annual contribution to a fund on behalf of each employee), had more than 60% of their assets invested in equities and only about 30% in fixed income securities. The remainder was in real estate and other private (i.e., nonmarket-traded) investments.[6] This surge of money into the equity market, in particular, helped lift the prices of stocks. The 1950s bull market that began when the threat of a postwar recession faded and continued until the late 1960s was reinforced by the growth of company contributions to pension funds and the movement of more and more of those pension assets out of bonds into stocks. In 1949 corporate pension funds had only $586 million invested in stocks.[7] A year later that figure had doubled. The amount had climbed to $3.1 billion by 1954,[8] to $16 billion by 1960,[9] and to $76 billion by 1970.[10] Pension funds had replaced individual investors as the drivers of the stock market. During the economic booms of the 1950s and 1960s, this flood of pension money into stocks helped lift stock prices, and the increase in stock prices reduced the cost of equity financing, helping hundreds of thousands of small companies go public and financing new plant and equipment for thousands of others.

A second surge of corporate money into pension funds, and hence into stocks, developed after the Employee Retirement Income Security Act (ERISA), the pension reform law, was passed in 1974. In 1975 corporations contributed $37 billion to their pension plans. By 1980 that total had climbed to $66 billion. By 1985 it was $95 billion. At least half of the contributions went into common stocks. During 1974–1980 private pension fund holdings of equities increased to $235 billion from $63.6 billion, a 19.7% compound rate of increase, while the stock market was climbing at a still healthy 9.9% compound annual rate.

Just as the corporate pension fund move into equities peaked and leveled off in the mid-1980s, public employee pension funds sponsored by state and local governments began to surge into equities. Their ownership of common stocks increased from 26% of their assets in 1980 to 60% in 1999. The equity holdings increased from $44 billion in 1980 to $1.5 trillion in 1998. The surge into equities during this period helped to lift stock prices even further. This surge in prices, by reducing the cost of capital, helped the U.S. economy restructure during the late 1980s after the energy crises of 1974 and 1979 had exposed much of U.S. industry as uncompetitive. Companies didn't respond immediately to the recovery of the stock market. High inflation and fear of recession slowed their reinvestment in plant and equipment until almost the mid-1980s, until inflation subsided and the cost of capital fell far enough for investment to become irresistible. But by the mid-eighties the restructuring was underway, and the results became apparent as the nineties began. The rising stock prices also helped restore individual investor confidence in the stock market, confidence that had been seriously eroded by the 1973–1974 bear market which cut the level of the Dow Jones Industrial Average, the most widely recognized stock market index, in half. In the wake of the bear market, individual investors had fled the stock market.

Reinventing America

Massive reinvestment in the U.S. economy was needed if the country was again to be competitive with the likes of Germany and Japan, which had now taken the economic world lead. In 1985 the U.S. economy was considered a basket case. U.S. chief executives were being urged to copy the German and Japanese corporate models. Harvard University economists argued that U.S. companies should seek their financing from institutions with which they had long-term relationships, not from the stock and bond markets. By the early 1990s, however, with the aid of pension fund capital, the U.S. economy had reinvented itself and was the most efficient, most resilient, and strongest in the world. As a result of the more competitive, more efficient, highly innovative economy, 15 million jobs have been created in the United States since 1990, and two-thirds of those have been jobs paying above the median wage. That is, they were not hamburger-flipping jobs, as some have alleged.

The huge flows into corporate equities and bonds from pension funds—private and public—helped finance that reinvestment. The largest funds were also major contributors to economic growth and the drive for efficiency through investments in venture capital or leveraged buyout pools. These funds reported more than $17 billion in venture capital investments and more than $49 billion in buyout pools at the end of 1999.[11] The total amount invested in both by all pension funds was far larger, perhaps as much as $100 billion, since many companies refused to disclose these "private" investments. The venture capital pools provided the resources necessary to get startup firms to a size where they could go public. The rise of Silicon Valley and the U.S. high-tech industry that leads the world parallels the growth of venture capital investing by U.S. pension funds. Without the pension fund assets, the U.S. high-tech industry might not now lead the world, for many firms would have been starved for vital capital or might have paid too a high price for it to permit success. Venture capital may be considered akin to rocket fuel for the economy, and pension funds provided much of that fuel.

Similarly, pension funds invested in leveraged buyout (LBO) pools that provided the financing for managements to take their companies private when they believed they could manage them more efficiently out of the public eye. LBO pools also provided the financing for outsiders to buy up the outstanding stock of companies and get rid of poor incumbent management which was not earning a competitive return on the assets. The leveraged buyout deals received bad press during the mid- to late 1980s, but in fact the threat of a takeover often shook up a sleepy management and stirred it to improve a company's efficiency and return on assets. Many completed LBO takeovers improved the performance of the company because the new management had to cut costs and improve efficiency and profitability in order to meet the debt repayments. As Christopher Farrell wrote in *Business Week* magazine: "For every leveraged buyout or hostile takeover, a dozen corporate chieftains got the message: Take risks, or lose your job. In other words, restructure your workforce and start breaking down barriers; refocus on core competencies and shed peripheral businesses; tie executive compensation to the stock market, work your capital smarter, and add to shareholder value. If you don't do it, we'll do it for you."[12] For too long, top managements at many companies had run them as their own private playgrounds, often at a cost to the investors. The improved management of America's premier companies prompted by the LBO movement was good for investors and good for the economy.

These changes were not without negative aspects, especially in the large numbers of employees laid off by companies heavily burdened by debt. The cost to these employees should not be overlooked. But the layoffs and downsizing were necessary as companies adopted new technologies, and the result was a fitter, more efficient, more competitive economy.

The LBO movement of the 1980s and 1990s could not have occurred without the financial support of the nation's pension funds. Individuals did not have sufficient amounts of money, and banks and insurance companies were, by and large, too conservative and risk averse. Pension funds were willing and able to provide billions. Through both leverage buyouts and venture capital vehicles, pension funds contributed to the growth and improved efficiency of the U.S. economy. In addition, the pension surpluses that built up, largely as a result of good investment returns in the early 1980s, often allowed companies to downsize humanely as they strove to become more efficient in the late part of the decade. They were able to use the surpluses to offer early-retirement incentives to long-term employees, preserving the jobs for hundreds of thousands of younger employees who otherwise might have been let go.

The flows into the bond markets as inflation subsided also helped lower interest rates and make fixed income financing affordable so that companies could finance the plant and equipment they needed by issuing bonds. So great was the flow of money and the desire for investment return to offset burgeoning pension costs in the 1970s and early to mid-1980s—driven largely by ERISA's provisions—that pension fund executives were willing to take additional risk, even in normally conservative fixed income investments, in search of higher returns. The result was the emergence of the junk bond market for bonds issued by companies rated below investment grade, or not even rated, by the rating agencies. Like the LBO phenomenon, the rise of junk bonds was criticized in the late 1980s; this was largely because of the perceived excess influence of Michael Milken, the investment banker who virtually invented it, and because junk bonds financed some poor deals. But the junk bond also had a positive effect on the economy: It made recovery possible for some sick companies and growth possible for companies too small or immature to raise capital in the stock market and not glamorous enough to attract venture capitalists. The emergence of this market was supported by pension fund bond managers and, to a lesser extent, by insurance companies and others.

The largest pension funds also contributed greatly to the building boom in the United States in the 1980s and 1990s that was an essential ingredient of the country's spectacular economic growth. At the end of 1998, the 200 largest pension plans had $79.8 billion in equity investments in real estate[13]—in office buildings, factories, shopping malls, warehouses, apartments, and hotels—compared with almost nothing in 1974. Sometimes the pension flows contributed to an oversupply of buildings and returns tumbled. Usually, however, the surplus was absorbed within a few years, and investment returns rebounded as continued economic growth increased demand for real estate of all kinds.

Looking Overseas

Pension executives also looked overseas for investment opportunities. Of the assets invested in equities, just under 10% was invested in non-U.S. equities in 1998. This flow of money not only helped develop the capital markets in many countries, but also helped finance economic development in those countries. Without the flood of U.S. pension money seeking investment opportunities, for example, the stock markets in Hong Kong, Singapore, Indonesia, and China would have been far slower to develop. Some pension funds invested in private investments in China before a stock market developed there, but most required the liquidity and transparency a stock market provided before they would agree to invest.

Large, defined benefit pension funds led the way into international investments, first into the developed markets of Europe and Japan and later into the emerging markets of Asia, the Pacific Basin, and Latin America. For example, at the end of 1998 the 200 largest pension funds had $253 billion invested in non-U.S. equities and $46 billion in non-U.S. bonds.[14] Of the assets invested in non-U.S. equities, $27 billion was in the stocks of companies in emerging markets, those underdeveloped countries, particularly in Asia and Central and South America that were most in need of additional capital. The largest amounts of funds flowed to those countries that had stable political systems, welcomed foreign investment, and seemed to be able to sustain economic growth, such as the major European countries. Mutual funds then followed, giving individual investors the opportunity to diversify their investments outside the United States as well.

Yet some money, seeking higher returns, flowed into less developed and more risky economies and markets. Some of the countries proved unable to sustain the economic growth, and some of the political systems proved less stable than the investors had thought. As a result, some pension funds saw their emerging market investments suffer losses when the emerging markets collapsed in late 1997. Others got out quickly. The pension fund flows were a two-edged sword. When they flowed in, they lifted stock prices; when they flowed out, prices crashed, as many nations have discovered since 1997. And they flowed out when the fund managers lost confidence in an economy, a market, or a political system. The $27.4 billion in emerging-market equities at the end of 1998 was down from $35.2 billion just a year earlier.[15] Nevertheless, assets flowing from U.S. pension funds through investment management organizations into these foreign markets helped finance accelerated change and growth in dozens of countries around the world. The pension funds also paved the way for the development of stock markets through which individual investors may also invest in developing economies in search of higher returns.

A Costly Lack

The absence of a well-funded pension system in other developed nations around the world has no doubt retarded their economic agendas. In Japan, for example, that country's inability to pour capital into the equity markets and direct that capital to the companies that could use it most efficiently, greatly hampered its efforts to restructure and regain competitiveness with the United States after it fell into recession in 1989. Although major companies in Japan made some effort to fund their pension promises, the pension fund contributions generally flowed into insurance companies and trust banks associated with the sponsoring companies. Then the assets were often invested back into the stock or bonds of those companies or their subsidiaries. They did not flow through independent money management firms and the stock market into the stock of the most promising companies. The capital remained trapped, often in inefficient old-line companies, leaving little for the financing of startup companies. In addition, pension assets in Japan financed virtually no venture capital industry, and the country experienced no LBO or corporate governance movement to shake up sleepy managements.

The German and French economies have also been far slower to restructure and become more efficient than the U.S. economy, in large part because they both lack funded pension systems and the strong, efficient, flexible, and diversified capital markets such funds demand and support. Without the pension funds providing the capital flows for the capital markets to direct toward uses promising the highest risk-adjusted returns, there was no lubricant to facilitate change. In Germany, most corporate pension promises are secured only by an IOU carried on each company's books. That is, the German equivalent of the money that U.S. corporations put into their pension funds to be invested in diversified portfolios of stocks, bonds, and so on, remains trapped within the sponsoring company. That company may be the least efficient possible user of that capital. German companies that need additional capital go to the major banks for loans, and German bankers are noted for their conservatism.

In France, there is almost no private pension system, not even the German book-reserve system, so again the capital markets there are small compared with those of the United States. In neither France nor Germany are the venture capital or LBO markets as highly developed as in the United States. It is therefore more difficult for entrepreneurs to raise capital to start firms to exploit a new idea. As a result, far fewer small businesses are started in those countries than in the United States. And far fewer of those that are started grow into huge, successful companies like Intel or Hewlett-Packard or Microsoft.

The pension fund money flood was not the sole cause of the U.S. economy's outperformance in the 1990s. Although there were many other causes, without it the wheels of change would have ground more slowly, and perhaps come to a halt, as they have in Japan.

Academic Support

The changes in the investment practices of U.S. pension funds were driven by the need to invest the flood of money from the funding of existing pension obligations or from new or growing pension plans. They were greatly accelerated by the work of academics in the nation's great universities who had begun to wrestle with the economic and financial implications of the capital markets. The research gave rise to a whole new avenue of economic research and a whole new branch of economics called *financial economics*. These academics, Harry Markowitz, William Sharpe, Fischer Black, Myron Scholes, Merton Miller, and Robert C. Merton among them, studied the stock, bond, and options markets to see how they actually worked. They examined what investment returns had been delivered by stocks, bonds, and cash equivalents in the past; how stock, bond, and option prices were actually set by investors, and how those prices could be calculated; and how investors actually chose, often subconsciously, between stocks and other assets; and how they created portfolios of stocks. In addition, these economists developed ways to measure the risk of a stock, a bond or an option, or a whole portfolio, and theories about how risk could be reduced. This new branch was finally recognized in the 1990s with the award of Nobel Prizes for economics to Markowitz, Sharpe, Scholes, Miller, and Merton. Fischer Black was excluded solely because he had died.

The findings of the academics led to new investment approaches and new techniques. Pension executives and their money managers were the first to adopt these new approaches, but later mutual fund managers and other investors also adopted them. Pension executives and money managers were able to structure portfolios to meet specific levels of risk and could measure the amount of risk taken to achieve a particular return. They were able to examine the results of money managers in detail to determine how and why the managers outperformed or lagged the markets or why one manager outperformed another. They adopted risk measures that individuals now use in selecting mutual funds to meet their risk tolerances. The findings of the academics also led to the development of index funds, funds that are designed to exactly match market performance and that now form the core portfolio of most large pension funds. Index mutual funds are also the fastest growing vehicle for individual investors.

A New Industry

The revolution in pension fund investment created a new industry—*institutional investment management*—whose purpose was to provide sophisticated, professional, long-term investment management for the assets of pension funds and other large, tax-exempt institutions such as charitable foundations and college and university endowments. The industry involved parts of the banking and insurance industries, but the executives from those industries came to think of themselves as part of the new industry, not the existing industries of their nominal employers. It involved the mutual fund industry and powered exceptional growth for it. It also involved whole new institutions, known as *investment counseling firms*, or *investment management boutiques*, which sprang up solely to manage the assets of pension funds.

These new institutions developed new ways to identify the stocks and bonds likely to provide the best investment returns and began to combine them into portfolios. Over time the companies often specialized. First there was *specialization in asset class*, with managers moving from managing balanced portfolios of stocks and bonds to managing portfolios composed only of stocks or bonds. Then there was *intra-asset class*, or *style*, *specialization* in which managers specialized in different types of stocks, growth stocks or value stocks. And then there was *specialization within style*, for example, large-growth or small-growth stocks. Again the pension funds and their managers led the way that mutual funds and individual investors would follow a decade later. Some managers specialized in real estate investing, whereas others focused on venture capital on leveraged buyout investing, or investing in non-U.S. stock and bond investments. They were swamped with money. At the beginning of 2000, a money management firm overseeing "only" half-a-billion dollars was considered a minor player. This was an industry, as Jan Twardowski, president of Frank Russell Securities, commented, "that money rained upon."[16] Mutual fund companies, which at the beginning of the pension fund revolution came in just one or two varieties, increasingly adopted one among the multitude of investment approaches pioneered by pension funds, so that individual investors now have virtually the same choices of investment as pension funds.

Disciplining Government

Whether in the United States or in other countries, U.S. pension fund managers could and did act as brakes on government actions. In the United States, bond managers in particular could frustrate government policies with which they disagreed, and particularly after the inflationary period of the late 1970s, they often did. The bond managers had been burned by the high inflation and demanded higher interest rates to offset that inflation. But higher interest rates on new bonds slashed the value of the bonds already in their portfolios. As a result, bond managers tended to view government economic policy actions with suspicion, especially the actions of the Federal Reserve Board. If the government attempted to stimulate the economy with a loose monetary policy designed to bring down interest rates, and the bond managers thought the policy was likely to stimulate inflation, they demanded higher interest rates before they would buy government or corporate bonds. In the end, the government wound up with higher rather than lower interest rates. The higher rates would likely hurt corporate earnings and slow corporate expansion, causing stock prices to fall, consumer confidence to drop, and the economy to slow further.

Until the early 1980s, when pension assets flooded into institutional money management firms willing and able to move assets into and out of the stock and bond markets, the Federal Reserve had virtually a free hand. As pension assets grew, the Federal Reserve's hands became less free and its tools less effective. In addition, unwelcome fiscal policies could also trigger negative feedback from the stock and bond markets, which could sometimes counter the intended effect. Foreign governments hoping to raise money in U.S. markets or from U.S. pension fund managers had to tailor their securities offerings, as well as their economic policies, to the demands of the money managers; otherwise, the managers refused to buy the offerings.

Besides disciplining the government, the pension funds and their managers also disciplined the managements of corporations when those companies appeared to be underperforming and using assets inefficiently. They did this first by helping to finance change through leveraged buyouts and second by using the power of the shareholder vote to push management to do better, even forcing some chief executive officers from their posts when companies continued to underperform. This approach became known as the *corporate governance movement,* and U.S. pension funds even exported the concept to other countries.

Government Meddling

The flood of money into defined benefit pension funds, together with the strong growth of the assets from investment gains, of course tempted the government to meddle. The very success of defined benefit pension plans, the rapid growth of assets, led the government to take a series of actions that not only halted their growth, but eventually put them on a path toward extinction. The first of these actions, the passage of pension reform legislation in 1974, was driven by the need to correct some abuses in pension plans and to set clear rules for pension funding and investing. For example, some companies had been using pension assets for their own purposes, such as building factories or warehouses. Others had channeled pension assets to friends for investment and found ways to deny long-term employees their promised pensions. Initially, the law strengthened pension funds and contributed greatly to the money flood by requiring companies to fund their pension promises over 30 years.

Some companies, however, found the increased regulation under ERISA too burdensome and terminated their pension plans. Except where a pension plan is part of a negotiated union contract—a minority of cases—companies are free to terminate a pension plan at any time. Other, later government actions were driven by the fear that exempting company contributions to pension funds and the investment earnings of funds from taxation was keeping too much tax revenue out of government hands. The Congress's steps to reduce that leakage of tax revenues weakened the interest of corporate managements in pension plans, especially defined benefit plans, which are the most expensive plans for companies to maintain.

Finally, thanks to Senator Howard Metzenbaum, companies were effectively prevented from recapturing any surplus assets that might accumulate in their pension funds through accidental (or deliberate) overfunding or through excellent investment returns. Corporate executives saw little reason to continue to support defined benefit plans when the company was stuck with the cost and risk of funding a long-term obligation without any possibility of benefiting if it did a good job.

Defined benefit plans have been replaced at many companies by defined contribution plans, particularly 401(k) plans. Defined contribution plans relieved companies of the long-term liabilities of defined benefit plans, replacing them with the short-term obligation to make contributions matching those of the employees. The employees inherited the investment risk from the employer. On the other hand, the growth of 401(k) pension plans has led employers to offer investment education to their employees. Now many individual investors are far better prepared to make investment decisions than they were even 10 years ago.

The surging growth of defined contribution plans has further complicated government economic policy making. Workers' pensions are now directly tied to the performance of the capital markets. If the government tightens fiscal or monetary policy, or both, and provokes a bear market, those policies will permanently damage the retirement income of hundreds of thousands of workers who retire during the bear market, or who lose their jobs and have to cash out their pension assets at much reduced prices. If an employee retires in a bear market, his or her retirement income will be smaller than if retirement had taken place during a bull market. When the nation's pension funds were mostly defined benefit plans, an employee's retirement benefits were not hurt if he or she retired during a bear market brought on by tight monetary or fiscal policies. That is because the pension benefit was guaranteed by the employer. If the employer was unable to keep the promise because of financial difficulty, the Pension Benefit Guaranty Corporation (PBGC), a government corporation established after the passage of ERISA, guaranteed the payment. The PBGC does not guarantee anything for 401(k) or other defined contribution plan participants.

The United States has not experienced a sustained bear market since the growth of 401(k) plans. Therefore, 401(k) plan investors have not experienced a significant loss in their balances in any year since they joined the plan. How they will react in the event of a bear market is unknown, but those who have to retire or cash out of their plans during a bear market will no doubt make their unhappiness heard in Washington. As a result, the federal government and the Federal Reserve Board will have to be far more careful in their economic policies in the future. Although in the past recessions caused employees to lose their jobs for a time, they could recover after the recession was over. Retirees who cash out of the market while it is down will have suffered a permanent loss of wealth.

The Winners

Who have been the winners of this revolution? Certainly those 50 million-plus employees covered by a private or state and local government pension plan. First, a far higher percentage of such workers is covered by pension plans than in 1948. Second, the pension promises made to those employees are far more secure today than those made 50 years ago because of the growth of pension assets largely through investment. Whereas pension promises were poorly funded in 1949, most large corporate pension plans today have more than sufficient assets to pay their pension obligations, and most public employee pension plans are also almost fully funded. In addition, many of these employees have direct daily control over their pension assets. They can decide how they should be invested, how much risk to take, and how much return to seek.

In addition, every taxpayer has been a winner. The growth in gross domestic product, financed in part by the flood of pension assets and their efficient investment, has helped raise the nation's standard of living far above what it would have been without pension funds. In addition, the improvements in corporate efficiency that pension fund investments helped finance have helped create or preserve jobs and keep prices lower than they otherwise would have been.

This book tells the story, up to 1998, of this flood of money and the revolution it powered. It describes the first companies to recognize that the money flood had been unleashed and to begin to prepare for it; the pension executives who pioneered new ways of investing the burgeoning pension assets, often at the risk of their jobs; the money managers who left large, stable institutions to start new organizations to manage the assets and try new investment approaches; the Nobel Prize-winning academics whose research and insights showed pension executives and money managers better ways to invest and to control risk; the evolution of the various techniques and asset classes that have been developed to cope with and direct the flood; and the bureaucrats and politicians who, for better or worse, attempted to influence the direction flood's course. Finally, it raises the issue of what will happen as the flood of money changes direction and inevitably begins to dry up.

The revolution is 50 years old, but it is a continuing revolution and so remains unfinished. In a paraphrase of Winston Churchill's words: We are not yet at the end, not even the beginning of the end. But it is, perhaps, the end of the beginning.

Chapter 2

The Way Things Were

Like a dynamite charge exploded at the bottom of a dam, a National Labor Relations Board ruling on April 12, 1948, triggered a flood of money into the capital markets. The NLRB ruled that Inland Steel Corporation must negotiate with its unions on pension issues. As a result, companies with unionized workforces were soon confronted with union demands that they offer pensions to their blue-collar workers, or if they already had such a pension plan, to improve the promised benefits and set money aside to guarantee them—that is, they were being asked to fund the pension promises. Previously, many companies offered pensions only to white-collar employees. Those that did offer pensions to union employees offered only modest plans, and often the promises were not well funded. The United Steel Workers Union filed its grievance with the NLRB in 1946. Specifically, the union challenged Inland Steel's policy of compulsory retirement at age 65, claiming that the policy constituted a breach of a provision in the union's contract with the company concerning separation from service. Inland Steel refused to negotiate the matter, claiming that compulsory retirement was an essential part of the company's pension plan, the provisions of which did not fall within the scope of collective bargaining. It could not foresee the gargantuan impact of its refusal to negotiate the issue with the union.

The members of the NLRB rejected Inland Steel's position and declared that pensions "lie within the statutory scope of collective bargaining." A year later in 1949, the U.S. Supreme Court in effect upheld the NLRB's decision by declining to hear an appeal of a Seventh Circuit Appeals Court decision which had supported the NLRB. The Supreme Court's refusal opened the flood gates of pension plan formation in the United States, and soon after, money began to pour into pension funds to back the promises the pension plans made. This flood of money sparked a financial revolution in the United States, which has continued unabated for 50 years and has spilled over to many other countries.

The first pension plans appeared in the United States just after the Civil War. At the time there was no thought of funding them—that is, building a pool of assets to ensure that the promised benefits could be paid in the future. The U.S. government provided a pension for disabled veterans after the war and later extended it to all elderly Civil War veterans. Since the pension was backed by the taxing power of the government, no fund was deemed necessary.

The first private pension plan in North America was offered by Canada's Grand Trunk Railway in 1874, and it was followed in the United States by that offered by the American Express Co. in 1875. The Grand Trunk plan was partly funded. Employees contributed 2.5% of their salary and at retirement received one-sixtieth of the final salary for each year of employment, to a maximum of two-thirds of the salary. The company matched employee contributions and guaranteed any shortfall up to 50% of total employee payments. However, the Grand Trunk plan covered only white-collar workers. It was a way of keeping trained clerks and managers from leaving as the promotion pyramid narrowed and their chances for promotion waned.

The American Express plan, on the other hand, covered all employees but with a lower level of benefits—a maximum of 50% of final pay—and the benefits were paid only if an employee were injured or "worn out in service." The American Express plan, however, was unfunded, as were most of the plans established in the next 25 years. The promised benefit payments were made from company earnings on a pay-as-you-go basis, and no fund was built up to guarantee their payment.

The Pennsylvania Rail Road established a contributory pension plan in 1886 but soon converted it to a noncontributory plan with benefits paid out of operating revenues so that the company could have a free hand with regard to employment and retirement practices. Many other railroads, which were among the earliest adopters of pension plans, followed its lead. Once again, there was no prefunding. The railroads were growing, and their owners and managers believed they were strong enough to pay the promised benefits out of future earnings. They probably also believed that if the burden became too great, they could rescind the promised pensions, or at least reduce them.

Many pension plans were established between 1890 and 1920, but their benefits were not very generous: 1% of pay per year of service was common, and the normal retirement age was 70. In addition, a worker typically vested only at retirement; that is, workers were not entitled to a pension unless they remained with the company for their entire working lives and retired from the company. The retirement liabilities were generally unfunded or minimally funded. Even the American Telephone & Telegraph Co. did not begin to fund its pension obligations until 1927, and then it did what many other corporations did—it contributed company bonds to the fund.

The pension plans were usually established for a variety of motives. In some companies, as at the Grand Trunk Railway, the pension plan was designed to retain skilled middle managers. It was an early form of "golden handcuffs," though they were not so golden. In other companies, it was a way to humanely get rid of employees who were too old to contribute. Many employers, especially large ones, gradually realized that they could not throw elderly workers on to their families or to charity when they could no longer work. The numbers were just too great. Before industrialization, people normally worked on the family farm or in the family enterprise until they could no longer work, and they were then taken care of by younger family members. After industrialization, however, there were no longer family farms or enterprises to support most workers.

By 1919, more than 300 pension plans covering 15% of the nation's workforce had been started. In 1927, 90,000 retirees drew $55 million in pension benefits, and 9 of the top 10 and 87 of the nation's 200 largest corporations had pension plans.[1] Pension outlays for these companies generally rose inexorably in the 1920s as the first wave of pension-eligible retirees began to leave the companies. Even though not all employees stayed with companies long enough to receive the pension, the burden on companies' finances was still enormous. Managements found themselves faced with large, intractable costs that they did not know how to forecast with any precision and that did not decline when business slowed and profits dropped.

Advance Funding

In the early 1920s, a pioneering actuary, George Buck, devised a funded pension system for New York City, which showed that pension costs could be estimated using actuarial principles and therefore could be funded in advance. At almost the same time, Metropolitan Life Insurance Company entered the pension business, offering to sell to employers, on a group insurance basis, single-premium deferred annuity contracts as a way of funding their pension obligations. The product allowed employers to make a contribution each year for each employee towards an annuity that would be paid to the employee upon retirement. The contribution, and the ultimate annuity, were based on each employee's salary, with the insurance company pricing the annuities based on a very conservative estimate of its general account investment results and the mortality of the workers. The employees received a certificate each year indicating that the employer had made a contribution toward a retirement annuity for them.

Metropolitan Life's single-premium deferred annuity contracts offered a relatively simple way to fund the pension promises, and by 1927 Metropolitan was managing more pension plans than all other insurers in the world combined.[2] Most converts to insurance-funded plans were medium-sized firms, however. The large companies thought they could rely on their own financial strength and did not need an insurer. Many of them therefore continued to finance their pension benefits on a pay-as-you-go basis.

As a result of the burgeoning pension burden and economic pressures, by 1929 almost two-thirds of corporations with pension plans, excluding the railroads, had begun funding them and about one-quarter of them were funded through insurance companies. However, according to Steven Sass in *The Promise of Private Pensions*, funding was often more apparent than real as almost one-third of those that reported funding their benefits used balance sheet reserves as the funding. Others funded the plans by investing the funding contributions in the company's own bonds—in effect, lending the money back to the company.

The Depression had a devastating effect on many pension plans. At least 10% of plan sponsors terminated their plans; another 10% continued their plans but severely cut back the already meager benefit levels; and still others switched to contributory money purchase plans run through insurance companies. Surprisingly, many new plans were started in this period, mostly by small companies that had somehow survived the economic crisis. Most of these new plans were also money purchase plans funded through insurance companies. The Depression thus accelerated an emerging trend for companies to switch to schemes funded through annuities purchased from insurance companies over an entire working career.[3]

During the late 1930s, as a direct result of the failure of many companies and many pension plans, unions changed the direction of the debate over the role of the Social Security System, seeking to make it more protective of lower-paid workers. This led, in 1939, to amendments that tilted Social Security in favor of low-paid workers at the expense of higher paid workers. At the same time, the New Deal taxed incomes of more than $100,000 per year at a 70% rate. As a result, there was renewed interest in pension plans as higher-paid workers sought to avoid the higher income taxes and make up for the redirection of Social Security benefits away from them. And once again, most of these new plans were funded through insurance companies.

More Plans

World War II's prohibitive personal and corporate income tax rates further stimulated interest in pension plans. Besides increasing the tax rates, the government broadened its reach. Whereas in 1939 only 6% of the nation had paid an income tax, by 1945 75% paid it. So tax avoidance became important to the general workforce. In addition, government wage-stabilization policies during the war led companies to offer pension benefits in lieu of increased current wages to keep or attract scarce workers. By 1945 pension plans covered 6.5 million workers, up from 2 million in 1938.[4] However, the rate of plan formation declined after the war as workers became more interested in current wages to keep up with inflation than in future pension promises. The inflation rate for 1945 was only 2.3%, but in 1946, after price controls were lifted, it surged to 18.2%, and though it declined to 9% in 1947, auto workers, scared by the inflation, actually rejected a contract with a pension provision at Ford in 1948 in favor of one with no pension but more cash. Ironically, the inflation rate in 1948 was only 2.7%.

Nevertheless, at year-end 1949 the pension promises of corporations and state and local governments were backed by $14.4 billion in assets.[5] State and local government funds had assets totaling $4.2 billion,[6] largely managed internally because state laws generally required it. Of the $10.1 billion in private pension plans, $4.8 billion,[7] almost half, resided in insurance company annuities. Noninsured private pension plans had $5.4 billion in assets,[8] partly managed internally and partly trusteed by banks. Of that $5.4 billion, $2.24 billion was in Treasury securities and $1.86 billion was in corporate bonds (often the sponsoring company's own bonds).[9] Only $586 million (10.8%)[10] was in corporate equities, and these were often the equities of the company sponsoring the plan. Of the combined $9.5 billion in noninsured private plans and state and local government plans, only $606 million, 6.3%, was invested in common stock. The bulk of the assets, 47%, was invested in U.S. Treasury securities, with smaller amounts in corporate and state and local government bonds.

When inflation suddenly declined in 1948, union interest in pensions suddenly was reborn. Almost immediately after the Supreme Court rejected the appeal of the NLRB ruling in the Inland Steel case, more unions began to negotiate pensions and funded final pay pension plans at that. The unions no longer were willing to rely on the health of the sponsoring corporations to secure pension promises; they wanted real money set aside. Because of their recent experience with the effects of inflation on the purchasing power of wages over time, they wanted final pay plans.

Companies such as Ford, General Motors, U.S. Steel, and Inland Steel, many of which had plans for their white-collar employees, soon found themselves negotiating the pension benefits for their hourly workers, benefits they had totally controlled in the past—if they offered them. They began to increase the funding of their pension plans, stepping up the annual contributions, and they sought ways to get more out of those contributions. They rejected the idea of funding the plans through insurance annuities as too expensive and too inflexible. They were willing and able to take more risk in search of higher investment returns than insurance companies, hampered by insurance regulations, could take. These industrial companies relied on trusteed plans, which allowed alternative funding methods. In a trusteed plan, a legal trustee, usually a trust bank, is appointed to ensure that the legal provisions of the plan are adhered to, that the assets are kept safe, and that any investments are prudent. A trustee may or may not actually invest the assets, though generally bank trustees insisted they be given the assets to manage. Public employee pension funds often appointed the state or city treasurer or comptroller the trustee, and they hired a bank only as a custodian of the assets. Sometimes the treasurer or comptroller also served as custodian of the assets.

Managing the Assets

In the wake of the contract negotiations of the early 1950s, U.S. Steel chose to manage its burgeoning pension assets inhouse. Ford, General Motors, Chrysler, and many other industrial companies gave the assets to banks to manage as trustees. Often these banks provided them with financing and generally were allowed to invest the assets in a mix of stocks and bonds in so-called balanced accounts. The banks at least implied that they would move some of the assets from stocks to bonds when they thought stocks were likely to underperform, and vice versa. They, together with the companies sponsoring the pension plans, had noted that stock prices had begun to rise as the economy responded to the release of pent-up consumer demand from the war years. They wanted to take advantage of those rising stock prices. As the banks shifted more and more of the growing pension assets into stocks, the increased demand helped push stock prices up more steadily. This attracted still more pension assets to the banks. By the mid-1950s the pension fund management tide had begun to flow in favor of trust banks and against the insurance companies.

Not all companies began to fund their pension plans immediately; many did not, or they took minimal steps toward funding. Moreover, not all of those who decided to fund began immediately to invest in common stocks. Many remained committed to insurance company annuities, especially among smaller companies, and many large companies continued to invest in bonds, especially U.S. government bonds. But a movement had begun that would gather speed and power over the next four decades. Like a flood, it would sweep away the old ways of securing pension promises and, in doing so, would change the trajectory of the U.S. economy.

Chapter 3

The Flood Begins

Early in 1950, Anders M. Voorhees, chairman of the finance committee of the U.S. Steel Corp., one of America's largest corporations, realized that the U.S. Supreme Court's decision on Inland Steel had expensive implications for U.S. Steel and other major corporations with large unionized workforces. Obviously, U.S. Steel would soon face contract negotiations with the United Steel Workers Union in which pension benefits would be determined. No longer would the company be in sole control of the level of pension benefits or under what circumstances they would be paid. The union would now have a say in the benefit structure. And whatever pension improvements the union negotiated for its members would inevitably flow across to the nonunion white-collar staff. Costs would rise, probably rapidly.

The U.S. Steel pension plan was one of the oldest in the country, having been started in 1905 by Andrew Carnegie, the industrialist founder of the Carnegie Steel Co. which later became the United States Steel Corp., and funded by Carnegie with a gift of $4 million in bonds. It was a defined benefit plan, specifying how much an employee would get in pension benefits after so many years of employment. In 1911 the U.S. Steel Corp. contributed an additional $8 million in U.S. Steel bonds to the plan, and in 1914 the U.S. Steel and Carnegie Pension Fund was established as a nonprofit corporation. Over the years the company made additional contributions to the fund, and by 1949 it had assets of $149 million which were kept at J. P. Morgan & Co. Inc. and First National City Bank in New York. The two banks managed portfolios that were invested primarily in utility bonds, railroad bonds, government bonds, and some preferred stock. But there were no common stocks.

Voorhees realized that, in the wake of the Inland Steel decision, simply investing in bonds and holding them until maturity would not suffice.

The pension liabilities, he realized, were about to surge, and a better way of funding them was urgently needed. Voorhees, unusual for his time, believed common stocks offered better investment returns than bonds and so offered the best chance of funding the coming tidal wave of liabilities. Although many were still traumatized by the devastation wreaked on common stock investors in the Great Depression, Voorhees was not. Voorhees was far more concerned about inflation and its possible impact on pension liabilities than he was about another stock market crash. Inflation, he realized, could do as much damage to the pension fund invested in fixed income instruments, and through it the U.S. Steel Corp., as another market collapse. He was able to bring the U.S. Steel Board to his view, and to persuade it that the company should manage the money internally. This was no mean feat of persuasion, for it meant taking the money away from the Morgan Bank, with which there was a historic relationship. However, the bank was retained as trustee and custodian. The decision to manage the money internally was driven by the view that the company could do a better job, especially since banks in those days were resistant to common stock investing and could do it at lower cost. Once he had approval, Voorhees went looking for a talented investor to join the U.S. Steel and Carnegie Pension Fund and to guide its move into common stock investing.

He found this person in Harvey Molé, a vice president specializing in bank and insurance stocks at the Bank of New York, whom he hired as vice president of investments to oversee the fund. The move into equities was funded by contributions of $100 million a year made by the company until 1955, when the contributions were increased again. Molé hired a staff of two other investment professionals to select the stocks in which the fund would invest, using what today would be called a classic value or Graham and Dodd approach. He insisted on thorough fundamental analysis backed up with company visits. Given his background in bank and insurance company stocks, the U.S. Steel portfolio, under his leadership, also had a heavy weighting in those stocks. The timing of the move into the stock market could not have been better, for between the beginning of 1950 and the beginning of 1960 common stock returns grew by 17.5% compounded annually as investors of all kinds reacted to the booming economy as consumers made the purchases they had postponed during the war. The 17.5% compound annual return meant the assets would double every four and a quarter years. In 1950 alone the value of stocks, on average, jumped by 31.7%. In 1954 they grew an astounding 52.6%. By 1955 the fund had grown to $900 million from the contributions and the returns of the stock market, and it was approaching a 50% allocation to equities.

Molé was not content to invest only in U.S. common stocks. He encouraged his staff to seek common stock investments overseas as well; they found some in Japan, investing first in a Hitachi convertible issue in 1958. The fund invested in similar issues by other Japanese companies until the Interest Equalization Tax was imposed in 1963. Molé also pushed the fund into real estate investments through sale-leasebacks to major corporations beginning in 1957, and pioneered in pension fund investment in timberland investing the same year, buying timberland in the southeast from Federal Paperboard Corp. and Consolidated Can Co. and leasing it back to them. By 1965 the U.S. Steel and Carnegie Pension Fund had grown to $2.5 billion in assets invested in domestic and international stocks, U.S. bonds, real estate, and private investments.[1] Except for two factors, it could have served as a prototype for other major U.S. pension funds. First, it was totally internally managed (and still is to this day), and most corporations were unwilling to build and compensate a large enough internal operation to use this approach. Second, it was relatively secretive about its investment activities. As one official noted, the company would not even have revealed the size of the fund in 1955. As a result, most pension executives except a favored few at very large, generally internally managed funds with whom U.S. Steel fund executives compared notes, were unaware of the fund's activities and experience and could therefore not learn from it.

Nevertheless, the activities of the U.S. Steel fund were indicative of what happened at most large corporations in the wake of the Inland Steel decision. Executives at other companies realized that pension plans were serious enterprises which implied significant long-term costs and liabilities, and their current ways of funding the plans were inadequate. Some, who had been funding their plans through contributions of company bonds or, occasionally, company stock, realized this method was costly and began to look for a better way. Others who had been investing their pension contributions in bonds, largely overseen by trust banks, also realized that the low returns on those instruments would be insufficient. Some who had been funding their plans by buying deferred annuity contracts from insurance companies such as Metropolitan Life realized that their method was very expensive. The real return on the assets given to insurance companies was at best zero and in some cases negative. A fourth group of companies, which hadn't been funding their pension benefit obligations at all but had instead been paying them out of company earnings each year, quickly realized that the liabilities were likely to explode. Corporate earnings weren't likely to be able to keep up, and the companies began to set aside money to meet the future obligations calculated using the actuarial methods pioneered by George Buck and others.

The spectacular returns of the stock market in the early 1950s caught the attention of companies suddenly confronted by militant unions negotiating for pension benefits and often for final-pay plans rather than career-average pay plans at that. When companies controlled the pension benefit and funded it through insurance companies using deferred annuities bought over an employee's working career, the pension benefit was, in effect, based on the employee's average salary over that entire career. But unions, fearing inflation, wanted no part of that. Instead, they wanted pensions based on the last few years of employment, when earnings would likely be at their highest. This formula greatly increased the cost of pensions. In that environment, the fact that the stock market produced a return of less than 18% in only one year between 1950 and 1955 (−1.0% in 1953) and produced returns of more than 30% in three of those years[2] quickly caught the attention of more and more corporate managements.

At the same time, trust banks, which had long envied the insurance companies' hold on the pension business, began aggressively marketing their investment skills. The banks had long managed the trust assets of wealthy Americans according to the wishes of the clients, the Prudent Man Rule, and often, a legal list of investments. Usually, the assets were invested heavily in bonds that were bought and held until maturity and then replaced with other bonds. Sometimes, if the client desired, the portfolio also invested in some common stocks, usually the most conservative, dividend-paying stocks available. At first the trust banks offered corporate pension plans investment accounts that also were mainly invested in fixed income securities. As the bull market surged, however, they included more and more equities in their portfolios to take advantage of the stock market returns. They quickly found receptive ears for their message that the high returns available in the equity market could make the increased pension costs palatable. They offered what were known as "balanced accounts," accounts that would be invested in a mix of stocks and bonds, with the amounts in each varying with the outlook for each asset. When stocks looked best, the portfolio would hold more stocks, and when bonds looked best, the portfolio would hold more bonds. As the bull market continued, however, the balanced accounts came to hold more stocks and fewer and fewer bonds.

Ford and General Motors

In early 1950 Ford Motor Co. found itself negotiating a defined benefit pension plan for its auto workers, and in July it began funding the plan. Unlike U.S. Steel, Ford did not set out to manage the investments internally. The United Auto Workers (UAW) Union insisted on trusteed funds, putting the assets into the hands of a bank or trust company, as the safest option. Ford hired Guaranty Trust Co. (later Morgan Guaranty Trust Co.) and Chase Bank (later Chase Manhattan Bank) as the two initial trustees.[3] Like U.S. Steel, Ford began funding its pension plans aggressively, and by 1971 the assets of the salaried employees' plan had grown to $729 million and the UAW plan to $737 million. The salaried plan had four trust banks as managers, whereas the UAW plan had three.[4]

General Motors Corp. also negotiated a pension plan with the UAW in 1950, with an official starting date of October 1, 1950. GM management had seen the writing on the wall in the wake of the Inland Steel decision and early in 1950 had engaged the actuarial consulting firm, the Wyatt Co., to help design and cost the plan. By the time the five-year contract specifying the pension plan was negotiated with the UAW, GM management had committed itself to 30-year funding of the unfunded past service liability that would be created by establishing the plan and had begun to plan for the management of the assets.

At the same time it established the UAW plan for hourly workers, General Motors also set up a new noncontributory plan for salaried employees. The company had an older plan established in 1940 for salaried workers, but it was contributory and available only to employees earning more than $250 a month. Although this plan now covered many salaried workers, thousands more were not covered by it. It was managed by three insurance companies—Metropolitan Life, Prudential Insurance Co. of America, and Aetna Life and Casualty. The new 1950 salaried employees' plan covered all salaried workers, but to get the highest level of benefits an employee also had to contribute to the older plan.

GM management decided that the two new plans would be managed identically in separate trusts using the same managers and that they would not be insured. GM, anticipating that the assets would grow rapidly, hired seven trust banks as managers, becoming one of the first funds to employ multiple managers. These banks were J. P. Morgan, Guaranty Trust Co., First National Bank of Chicago, First National Bank of Boston, Mellon Bank, Chase Bank, and National Bank of Detroit. The number was reduced to six when J. P. Morgan and Guaranty Trust Co. merged in 1959, and Bank of America was added at that time.[5]

GM also decided to permit and to encourage the banks to invest the assets in stocks. Initially, there was a limit of 35% of assets in common stocks, excluding the stocks of banks and insurance companies. Another 15% of the assets could be invested in bank and insurance stocks and in preferred stocks. During the 1950s and 1960s the investment experience was good, and by 1971 the Hourly-Rate Employees Pension Plan had assets of $1.46 billion, whereas the Retirement Program for Salaried Employees had assets of $938 million, not including the insured contributory plan.[6] Between 1950 and 1967 the GM plans had total returns exceeding 8% compounded annually, compared with which a 6% interest rate assumption looked conservative.[7]

The Bell System

The American Telephone and Telegraph Co.'s manufacturing arm, Western Electric, established one of the first corporate pension plans in 1906. It was noncontributory and offered low benefits. The entire AT&T system adopted pension plans in 1913, but no funds were accumulated to meet benefit payments to retirees until 1927,[8] in part because they were so few. Only 982 employees in the entire massive Bell System were collecting benefits in 1926.[9] However, a pension trust was established in 1927, and at the end of that year the Bell System funds, including Western Electric and Bell Laboratories, had assets of $12.1 million.[10] The funds were overseen by Bankers Trust and, until the late 1930s, at the direction of the company, were invested only in AT&T securities. Thereafter they were invested in a broad range of mostly fixed income securities, still with Bankers Trust. Even though the assets were all at Bankers Trust, they were in separate plans, one for each operating division and one each for Western Electric and Bell Labs. The assets of each plan were invested identically by Bankers Trust, though they could, in theory, have been invested differently if the operating companies had so chosen.

By 1949 the Bell System pension funds had grown to just under $1.1 billion; by 1960 they had reached $3.4 billion; and by 1970 they totaled $8.1 billion.[11] Such asset growth could not be ignored, and executives at the Bell System realized the assets could not remain with one institution, even one as large and strong as Bankers Trust. Between 1968 and 1970 the

Bell System operating companies were encouraged to hire other institutions to oversee the assets of their specific plans. They first selected local banks. New York Telephone kept its plan, with $733 million in assets at the end of 1970, with Bankers Trust. AT&T, with $363 million at the end of 1970, hired the Bank of New York and Chemical Bank. Illinois Bell, with $389 million, hired Harris Trust & Savings Bank, Chicago. New Jersey Bell Telephone Co., in Newark, New Jersey, with $231 million, hired Fidelity Union Trust Co., Newark, and so on.[12] These banks were encouraged to invest in stocks as well as bonds.

Between the end of 1950 and the end of 1951, the pension assets of companies not using insurance company annuities increased by $1.1 billion to $8.177 billion. The next year they climbed by $1.7 billion, and the year after that by almost $2 billion. Since the value of equities in these funds had increased by only $253 million, $485 million, and $549 million, respectively, in those years, clearly most of this growth came from booming contributions. The money flood had begun. By the end of 1960 these assets had surged to $38.1 billion, having grown at an 18.3% compound annual rate. By 1970 they had reached $110 billion, of which $67 billion, or 60.9%, was invested in equities.[13]

During the same period, corporate pension assets being managed by insurance companies increased at only a 12.8% compound annual rate— from $5.6 billion to $18.8 billion. Between the end of 1960 and the end of 1970, pension assets with insurance companies grew by only 8.1% compounded annually to $41.1 billion, while noninsured private pension assets grew at an 11.2% compound annual rate to $110.4 billion.[14] Thus, at the end of 1949 noninsured private pension assets were only 10% larger than insured pension assets, but by the end of 1970 they were almost three times as large.

As can be seen from the asset figures, the pension business of the insurance companies did not completely dry up. They had large sales forces across the country selling the concept of pension plans to businesses of all sizes, but especially medium- and small-sized businesses. Pension plans could help these businesses remain competitive for employees at a time when the postwar economy was booming and unemployment was low. The insurance company could take care of everything for the employer, from the actuarial work in establishing the plan to the investment of the assets and the payment of the benefits to retiring employees. In addition, even large companies often bought annuities for large groups of retiring employees to dispense with the administrative burden.

New Products

The insurance companies tried to fight back with new products. At first, these were merely variations on the old deferred annuity contracts, often offering more flexibility and lower costs. Still the insurance companies were not competitive, restricted as they were to investing in the general account and prohibited from investing significantly in common stocks that were turning in amazing investment returns. Only if they could somehow get the freedom to invest in equities could they hope to compete with the trust banks in the pension area.

One insurance company executive decided to try to do something about it. Meyer Melnikoff, a veteran actuary and pension executive at Prudential Insurance, had noted that in 1952 Teachers Insurance Annuity Association, a pension management organization for people in higher education which was organized as a private insurance company, had won for itself a change in law to allow it to invest in equities. Melnikoff soon decided to try to win similar legislative changes for Prudential, though it would require changing the law in every state in which Prudential operated. Melnikoff knew Prudential had to be able to invest in stocks to be competitive, and he won the support of Carroll Shanks, then the chief executive of Prudential, for the effort to change the insurance laws.

Melnikoff had begun his career with Prudential in 1939 as an actuarial trainee and from 1941 on, except for three years in the military and two years in Pru's Planning and Development Department, had worked in the pensions area, becoming deeply versed in all its aspects. He needed all his expertise and all of his tenacity to win the approval, starting in Prudential's home state, New Jersey. He even had to fight competitive insurance companies. At one hearing on the proposal before the New Jersey Assembly, after Carroll Shanks testified on Prudential's behalf in favor of the requested changes in the law, Fred Ecker, president of Metropolitan Life, testified against the changes. Pru won. The testimony of the out-of-towner Met Life against the change requested by the local insurance company, Pru, may have swung the vote in Prudential's favor. In 1959 New Jersey allowed insurance companies to offer variable annuities and separate accounts investing in common stocks, but only to pension funds. The equity-based products could not be offered even to other tax-exempt organizations such as college endowments or charitable foundations.

New Jersey was just the start, and it took Melnikoff and the Pru team another 10 years to win similar changes in the other states, with help from other insurers. In New York the battle was led by Equitable Life Assurance

Co. and was finally won in 1962. In Massachusetts it was led by John Hancock Mutual Life Insurance Co. Pru's first equity separate account was offered in 1962. A few years later Melnikoff had the satisfaction of winning an equity-based variable annuity account assignment from the New York City Teachers Fund when Teachers Fund officials learned that the other contender, Met Life, had opposed the equity-based variable annuity contract a few years before and had tried to sabotage the whole product.

Even after they had won the right to invest in common stocks and set up other kinds of separate accounts (e.g., for real estate), the insurance companies continued to develop new kinds of annuity-like products, culminating in the early 1970s in the Guaranteed Income Contract, or GIC (also sometimes known as a guaranteed investment contract and guaranteed interest contract). In a GIC the employer handed money over to an insurance company for a specified period and the insurance company guaranteed a return for a specified period. In effect, the GIC was a bond issued by the insurance company, but it was backed, not by the earning power of the insurance company or its assets, but by the earning power of its general account. Initially, the contract could run as long as 10 years, but some insurance companies were badly hurt by long-term high-interest rate guarantees in the late 1970s, and from that time on the guarantee periods became shorter. The GIC was eventually a successful product for the insurance companies, but it was not available in the 1960s and so their market share continued to decline. While insured pension assets grew at an 8.9% compound annual rate between 1960 and 1972 to $56 billion, noninsured assets grew at a 12.4% compound annual rate to $156.1 billion.[15] However, new opportunities were just over the horizon for insurance companies, opportunities arising from developments that would damage the banks and change the structure of pension fund investing once again. That was in the future.

Public Funds Follow

Meanwhile, public employee pension plans were not immune to the pressure of the Inland Steel decision. If pension benefits were negotiable for unions and employers in the private sector, they were negotiable also for unions and employers in the public sector. As a result, public employers also began to pour contributions into funds to back their pension promises, though at a slower rate. The assets of public employee pension plans totaled $4.2 billion at the end of 1949. A year later they were $674 million higher, and at the end of the next year they had grown by an additional $760 million. By the end of 1960 public employee pension fund assets had climbed to $19.7 billion,[16] a 15% compound annual rate. In the 1960s some of the public employee pension plans also looked to outside management to enhance their investment returns, and some even began to flirt with equity investment, though at a slower rate than corporate plans. In 1949 only $20 million of public fund assets, less than half a percent, was invested in corporate equities. Ten years later the amount in equities had increased to $500 million, or 2.8%, and 20 years later, in 1969, assets had reached $53.2 billion, but the percentage in equities had climbed to only 13.7%.[17]

Public funds trailed corporate funds in moving to equities for several reasons. First, they were ultimately overseen by state or local legislators, or the state or local treasurer, all of whom were concerned about political exposure if the funds lost money in investments. In the words of veteran public fund executive, Ray Lilleywhite: "You can be sure they didn't want to be caught losing any money. If they didn't make money, that was alright. There was no, or not that much, criticism, they thought. But, if a headline came out that they had lost money on an investment…" This fear of political exposure, combined with fairly recent memories of the Depression, encouraged public fund officials to invest in the most conservative investments, often Treasury and state government bonds, and even municipal bonds. In 1949, for example, state and local government pension funds had 53.9% of their assets invested in Treasury securities, 32.3% in state and local government bonds, and 9.6% in corporate bonds. Public fund officials were encouraged in this conservatism by the natural risk-aversion of the actuaries, who had influential advisory roles with most state and local government funds, and by the bankers who served as advisers to, and custodians for, the funds.

A few public fund executives, like Lilleywhite, attempted to modernize public fund investing. Lilleywhite began his career as executive director of the Utah State Teachers Retirement System in 1937, immediately after graduating from college, soon after the system was established. He remained with it until 1952 when he was recruited to become executive secretary of the Wisconsin State Teachers Retirement System. Lilleywhite had been impressed by TIAA-CREF's development of the equity-based variable annuity in 1952. With the help and encouragement of Mark H. Ingraham, dean of the School of Arts and Sciences at the University of Wisconsin and chairman of the Wisconsin Teachers' Retirement Board, Lilleywhite set out to develop a similar variable annuity for the Wisconsin Teachers' System.

Lilleywhite and Ingraham gathered the necessary law books, and with a pile of writing pads and pens, they retired to a woodstove-heated shed behind Ingraham's weekend cabin overlooking the Wisconsin River. There they wrote a draft statute amending Wisconsin law to allow a variable annuity program for the teachers. Participation was to be voluntary, and specific limits and safeguards were included. The draft was quickly passed into law in 1957, giving Wisconsin Teachers a vehicle with which to participate in the stock market.

In 1963 Lilleywhite moved on to become the assistant director of the Ohio State Teachers Retirement System, which at the time had assets totaling almost $600 million and was less than 10% in stock. Again he set about trying to relax the very conservative investment restrictions. In 1967, by which time the assets had grown to more than $1 billion, Lilleywhite became executive director of the Ohio State Teachers Retirement System and focused intensively on trying to raise the statutory limit on equity investments to 45% from 25%. He was opposed by the state auditor, who argued that the risk in common stocks was too great and that the fund needed the security of bonds. Lilleywhite countered that staying in bonds was as dangerous as taking the money to Las Vegas because bonds do not grow and lose value to inflation, "so at maturity we've lost buying power."[18] He lost the argument that year, but shortly before he retired from the Ohio system in 1970, he had the satisfaction of seeing the very conservative legal list of investments replaced by the Prudent Man Rule. In addition, the fund hired three investment management firms—Capital Guardian Trust, Los Angeles, the Bank of New York, and Stein Rowe & Farnham, Chicago. Soon after he retired, however, the Ohio State Teachers Retirement System let the managers go and returned to internal management, hiring an investment staff headed by Lilleywhite's successor, James Sublett. At the time, most public funds were still locked into bonds, and it was several more years before the trickle Lilleywhite helped start became a flood.

At the same time Lilleywhite was working to increase the Ohio Teachers fund's commitment to equities, the treasurer of Oregon, Robert Straub, was fighting a similar battle. Straub had campaigned for treasurer on the issue of pension fund investing, telling the voters that investing the $1 billion fund solely in bonds was costing them money, and that if elected he would work to change this rule. Upon his election, he began campaigning to get the state legislature to change the law, and he succeeded in 1967. The legislature established the Oregon Investment Council to oversee the investments and voted to allow both the investment of 10% of contributions each year in equities and the hiring of outside managers to run the equity portfolios. Over the next few years the legislature raised the equity allocation first to 25% and then to 35%. At the same time it established a variable annuity fund for employees whereby the employees could put up to 75% of their own contributions into equities.

In 1969 the Oregon Investment Council hired its first three outside equity managers—Capital Guardian Trust, Transamerica Investment Counselors, and Fayez Sarofim & Co. Four more managers were added in 1971 when the equity allocation was raised to 25%. During the bear market, the move to equities came in for heavy criticism when the fund reported declines of 15% and 20.75% in 1973 and 1974. Some members of the state legislature called for returning to all-bond investment, and they were backed by editorials in the state's newspapers. The storm was weathered by then Governor Straub and treasurer Clay Myers who remained convinced of equities' role. Straub pointed out to critics that the state had hidden losses on its low-yielding bond portfolios. The calls to return to bonds faded when the fund reported gains of 23.3% and 20.8% in 1975 and 1976, respectively.[19] Other public funds would travel similar paths in the coming years, though they would remain perhaps a decade behind corporate funds in adopting some investment approaches.

Chapter 4

The Rules Change

Just three years after the Inland Steel decision was confirmed and pension assets began to burgeon, Harry Markowitz, a young University of Chicago Ph.D. candidate, published a short article in the *Journal of Finance* in March 1952 which would radically change the way those assets were invested. Markowitz's initial paper, simply titled "Portfolio Selection," for the first time presented a method by which risk could be overtly recognized in investment decision making. Previously, investment theory dealt with ways to value individual stocks and identify those with the best prospects. Risk, if it was considered at all, was considered subjectively because there was no recognized way of identifying, measuring, and controlling it. Markowitz's paper, as its name implied, focused not on individual stocks but on how to build efficient portfolios—efficient in terms of earning the highest possible return per unit of risk taken.

Markowitz knew nothing about investing, but casting about for a Ph. D. dissertation topic, he met a stockbroker who had suggested he write about how people should select stocks. After discussing the idea with his adviser, Markowitz researched the subject and realized that according to the equity investment theories of the time an investor should identify the one or two stocks with the best return prospects and put all of his or her money into those stocks. He also realized that few investors put all of their money into one stock. Instead, most spread it around over many stocks. Obviously, they were concerned about more than return, and Markowitz soon realized that they were also concerned about risk and were dealing with it by spreading their eggs across many baskets. As Peter L. Bernstein wrote in his book *Capital Ideas*, "Markowitz's key insight was that risk is central to the whole process of investing."[1]

Markowitz made risk an equal consideration in an investment decision with expected return, and for the first time he provided a concept of risk that allowed it to be measured quantitatively. His concept of risk was *variance*—distance from an average. A stock's riskiness, he wrote, is measured by how much its returns vary from year to year. Or, taking the stock market as a whole, its riskiness is measured by the variance of its returns over a number of years—that is, how much they bounce around. For the decade of the 1950s, the period in which Markowitz was writing, the compound annual return of large stocks in the market was 19.4%, but the annual returns were as low as −10.8% in 1957 and as high as 52.6% in 1954, with lots of different returns in between.[2] These numbers suggest why stocks are considered risky: An investor can't rely on a steady return from year to year and can even experience losses in some years.

Markowitz developed his concepts more fully in his Ph.D. thesis, which he completed in 1955 but which was not published until 1959. He argued that risk could be reduced by diversifying the investment across a number of securities, that is, by buying lots of different securities, as investors had indeed been doing. But naive diversification, he said, might increase risk because of what he called *covariance*. That is, some stocks are moved in the same direction by the same economic or market forces. For example, all airline stocks are affected in the same way by higher fuel prices or by a recession. Combining such high-covariance stocks in a portfolio does not reduce risk but increases it. To reduce risk, the investor has to combine stocks with low covariance of returns, he said. It is possible to put together a portfolio of stocks that are very risky individually, but that have low covariance and as a result produce a low-risk portfolio. That is, it is possible to put together a portfolio of stocks whose price movements offset one another to a large extent. For example, oil company stock prices rise when oil prices rise, while airline stock prices will decline in response to rising fuel prices. In addition, Markowitz observed, to produce an efficient portfolio, the investor must buy those stocks that have low covariance as well as those that have the highest expected returns. Markowitz's approach became known as *mean (average)-variance analysis*.

Although it was a great theoretical advance, Markowitz's dissertation did not cause a ripple, neither when he presented it to his examining committee of University of Chicago academics nor when it was published in 1959. One member of the examining committee, Milton Friedman, the famed economist who would eventually win a Nobel Prize for Economics for his monetary theory, gave Markowitz a difficult time, not over the graduate student's reasoning, but over whether it deserved a Ph.D. in economics when it was neither economics nor even finance! The Nobel Prize

Committee had no such concern when they honored Markowitz with the Nobel Prize in Economics in 1990, along with William F. Sharpe, whose own work built on Markowitz's theory, and Merton Miller.

Nevertheless, Markowitz's dissertation marked the start of an incredible 30-year period of academic research into the workings of the capital markets. Interestingly, Markowitz did little of this research himself as he moved into other fields, first with the RAND Corp. and later with IBM, among other things, developing computer languages. Only in the late 1980s did Markowitz return to the field of finance, teaching courses at Baruch College in New York and consulting with a number of investment management organizations.

The great problem with Markowitz's mean-variance approach to the construction of an efficient portfolio was the enormous number of calculations required. The covariance of every stock in the available universe of stocks had to be calculated. In the 1960s, with the limited and expensive computing power then available, a full run of the Markowitz model on all available stocks would be prohibitively expensive. (Today personal computers have the power to run Markowitz's full model quickly and inexpensively.) Into the breach stepped William F. Sharpe, a young doctoral candidate and teaching assistant at the University of California at Los Angeles.

When Sharpe's faculty adviser rejected one Ph.D. dissertation topic, the adviser, a fan of Harry Markowitz's work, suggested Sharpe talk to Markowitz, who soon after became Sharpe's adviser on his dissertation. The new topic decided upon was a simplified, and hopefully more practical, version of Markowitz's mean-variance model. Markowitz himself had pointed the way to the simplified model when he had noted that when the market as a whole rises, the prices of most stocks also rise. Sharpe theorized that the returns of all stocks are related through common relationships to some basic underlying factor. If that single factor could be identified, rather than calculating the covariances of all securities with each other to develop an efficient portfolio, the investor could calculate the covariance of each security with the common factor, a far simpler problem. Sharpe published his paper, "A Simplified Model for Portfolio Analysis", in 1963 but continued to work on the concept, producing the Capital Asset Pricing Model (often shortened to CAPM, or "cap-em") in 1964. CAPM states that the single underlying factor connecting the prices of all securities is the stock market itself. Sharpe used the Standard & Poor's 500 Index, the best index then available, as his proxy for the market.

Sharpe introduced the concept of beta as a measure of risk. Beta is a measure of the volatility of the price of any stock relative to the volatility of the market as a whole. The beta of stocks can be combined to derive a portfolio beta. For example, the market is assigned a beta of 1.0. If a stock or portfolio rises (or falls) the same amount as the market, then the stock or portfolio has a beta of 1.0, the same as the market. If, however, the stock or portfolio rises (or falls) 12% when the market rises (or falls) 10%, then the stock or portfolio has a beta of 1.2 (i.e., it is 20% more risky than the market as a whole). A stock or portfolio can also have a beta of less than 1.0, meaning it is less risky than the market as a whole. This concept alone helped revolutionize portfolio management. First, it allowed pension executives to specify the level of risk they were comfortable with. Second, it enabled portfolio managers to tailor the risk level of a portfolio to a level specified by the pension fund client. Third, it allowed pension executives and their consultants to compare not just the absolute performance of the pension funds' portfolios, but the risk-adjusted return with both the market and the risk-adjusted returns of other portfolios. As both Markowitz and Sharpe made clear, investment return is a function of how much risk is taken. Every day now individual investors use the concept of beta to compare the riskiness of mutual funds, but pension funds led the way.

One of the most significant pieces of research for pension funds in the early 1960s was the examination by Lawrence Fisher and James Lorie of the University of Chicago of the long-term investment returns produced by common stock investments. Fisher and Lorie found that $1,000 invested in the stock market on January 30, 1926, and held to the end of 1960, with dividends reinvested, would have grown to $30,000, a compound annual return of 9% in spite of the impact of the crash of 1929 and the Great Depression. This total was far higher than anyone expected and far higher than an investor could have earned in bonds or savings deposits in that period. Fisher and Lorie updated their study to 1965 and confirmed the original findings. Their work provided another chisel chipping away at the rock of resistance to equity investing by pension funds.

Late in 1965 another seminal study, as important in its way as Markowitz's dissertation, was published in the *Financial Analysts Journal*. This study, by Eugene Fama, then a young assistant professor of finance at the University of Chicago, was called "Random Walks in Stock Market Prices," and it concluded that stock prices are not predictable. Fama was not the first to reach this conclusion. Other academics had studied the available evidence and had come to the same conclusion. But Fama's paper expanded on all the previous work and argued that there are so many security analysts and investors searching out companies selling below their intrinsic values that prices adjust "instantaneously" to eliminate any such discrepancy. Fama described the market as "efficient"; that is, it digests new information with minimal friction or delay, so it is difficult for the average investor to consistently get an edge on all other investors. Studies of mutual fund performance over long periods of time have tended to confirm Fama's theory, known later as the Efficient Market Hypothesis. At the time, however, Fama's ideas were rejected by most practicing investors, including most of those overseeing the investment of pension fund assets. Nevertheless, the belief that the markets are efficient laid the intellectual foundation for the later development of index funds. A few academically attuned institutional investors among the money manager and pension executive ranks had heard and absorbed Fama's message, and later they would make their presence felt. The work of Markowitz, Sharpe, Fama, and several others became known as Modern Portfolio Theory, which laid down new rules for institutional investing.

How Are We Doing?

At about the same time, pension fund executives, actuaries, and academics were focusing on efforts to determine how well the investments of a pension fund were performing. This was a natural consequence of the amount of money the companies were pouring into the funds. They naturally wanted to know if they were earning a decent return on the asset classes in which the contributions were being invested. Companies needed a way to calculate performance for different purposes. First, they had to know how well the total fund was doing and what kind of return on investment it was earning because the investment return was key in calculating the contributions needed to fund the plan over the long term. In addition, if the return on the fund could be increased by one percentage point long term, benefits could be increased, or contributions needed to fund the future payments to retirees could be decreased by 20% to 25%. Second, pension executives needed a reliable method to compare one fund manager with another. Two fund managers might produce identical returns, but one might perform far better than the other because he or she might have taken far less risk in achieving that performance. The most efficient portfolio, according to Markowitz's and Sharpe's work, is that which achieves the highest possible return for a given level of risk or achieves a target rate of return at the lowest possible level of risk.

For many years, however, there was no agreed-upon method of measuring performance. The performance reports issued by money management organizations, mostly banks, could only be described as perfunctory. The most common approach at the time was simply to divide the annual income from interest and dividends by the total cost, or "book" value of the assets, in order to calculate a "yield" on the assets. The method ignored the market gains or losses, realized or unrealized, of the assets. Another method added realized gains into the yield or subtracted the market losses, often over a number of years, but still ignored unrealized gains or losses.

In the early 1960s a number of people began working on these two problems independently. The Martin E. Segal Co., an actuarial consulting firm in New York, was asked by the Air Line Pilots' Association to develop a way of measuring the investment performance of its money-purchase pension plan. The pilots in the plan needed to know how well their investments were doing because it was a defined contribution plan. Their retirement income depended in large part on the investment return. The Segal Co. developed a dollar-weighted rate of return measure, based on market values, which included the unrealized appreciation as well as the size and timing of cash flows. For a defined benefit plan it is the return most appropriate for comparison with the assumed rate of return used in calculating the employer's annual contribution to the fund. A dollar-weighted rate of return below the assumed rate of return for any significant period would lead to increased contributions.

In 1966, the National Foundation of Health, Welfare and Pension Plans, Elm Grove, Wisconsin (later the International Foundation of Employee Benefit plans), put together a research committee to examine the issue of performance measurement. The goals of the committee were to develop methods for measuring and reporting performance, as well as for comparing and appraising investment performance, and to discuss the implications of past investment performance for both future investment policy and the benefit levels of multi-employer plans. The ability to measure investment performance, particularly for stock portfolios, would make all investors more comfortable with equity investments.

The committee, composed of eight leading investment practitioners from major New York investment institutions, noted that the then prevailing "yield-based" measure of performance "produces only a 'snapshot' of the fund at a particular moment in time, and an estimate of the income which would be produced by that fund for the next 12 months if the fund remains frozen into the position that we find it when the 'snapshot' is taken, and if no dividend rates are increased or decreased."[3] At the end of its considerations, the committee, like the Martin E. Segal Co., concluded that the best measure was a dollar-weighted rate of return measurement system.

A dollar-weighted return methodology also was developed by the A. G. Becker Co., a Chicago-based investment banking and brokerage firm that specialized in commercial paper underwriting. Through its commercial paper operations, the company had a lot of contact with corporate treasurers, and conversations with those treasurers began to turn more often to the pension funds, their size and their performance. The treasurers of some (but not all) of the leading companies in the country expressed strong interest in whether the resources they were pouring into the pension funds were being well handled by the trustees. The treasurers were working hard with their commercial paper underwriters to squeeze basis points out of their costs, but they had large pools of assets into which they were pouring ever larger sums without any clear knowledge of what was happening in terms of investment performance. In 1965, a group of A. G. Becker executives, headed by Roger Brown, head of institutional sales, John Mabie, vice president of sales, and David Peterson, vice president, Funds Evaluation Group, an ex-consultant from Booz, Allen & Hamilton, began a study with a group of 16 corporations, among them General Tire & Rubber Co., Textron Inc., Container Corp. of America and several utilities. The purpose was to determine if it was possible to develop a database of the actual investment performance of pension funds. The study had arisen from a sales call Mabie had made weeks earlier on the Whirlpool Corp. when the treasurer of the company was examining the results the bank trustees had achieved for the Whirlpool pension fund. "Look at these results," the treasurer said to Mabie. "I think they're doing a lousy job. What do you think?" Mabie declined to venture an opinion on a cursory examination but agreed to look more closely at the results.

The more he thought about the treasurer's request, the more convinced Mabie became that it was a dilemma faced by corporate treasurers across the country who oversaw pension funds, and the more convinced he became that it offered a business opportunity. He took the idea to Roger Brown, who supported him, and they hired Dave Peterson to head the Funds Evaluation Group, in part because of Peterson's quantitative background. Mabie recruited the first 16 funds to participate in the survey. The companies either supplied whatever data they had on the asset values, dividends, yields, contributions, and payments on their funds, or they directed the managers, virtually all major trust banks, to turn over the records. At first the banks were reluctant to turn over the records, even at company direction. They were the legal trustees, the fiduciaries, and while they were sure they were fully responsible for the assets, they weren't certain they could or even should turn over the records to a third party. One of the most reluctant was Morgan Guaranty, ironically, because it was found to have very good performance.

At the end of its study, the A. G. Becker executives decided that the performance measurement of pension funds was a potential business in its own right and might also open the door to other business opportunities for the firm. For a start, companies could pay for the service by telling their trustees to direct trades through A. G. Becker, which would expand Becker's regular brokerage operations. It might also open the door to more commercial paper and other investment banking business. Becker decided to commit resources to further develop the database by collecting five years of data and to put together a group to extract the data by plowing through trustee reports and calculating rates of return. After very quickly realizing that the product could not be sold by the firm's regular brokers, it formed a marketing staff. The first product, the Corporate Funds Evaluation Service, was launched in 1965, followed soon after by the Institutional Funds Evaluation Service, which reported to the money management institutions how well they were doing with the assets under their control. A big breakthrough came in 1966 when Standard Oil of New Jersey (now EXXON Corp.) agreed to participate in the survey. Vince Motto, then assistant treasurer of Standard Oil who oversaw its fund, had his own comparison system because it had 10 of the nation's largest trust banks overseeing its various pension funds (for salaried and hourly workers). But Motto told Mabie that he would participate because he wanted professionalism brought to investment management and performance reporting, and A. G. Becker was doing it correctly. Motto therefore turned over the data on his trustees to Becker.

When Morgan Guaranty was still reluctant to make the information available, John Morrow, financial vice president and treasurer of Continental Oil, whose fund was trusteed by Morgan, insisted that the bank cooperate, providing the data to Becker and directing brokerage business to pay for it. "Once it became evident to people that we were not going to go away, that we were going to be there and the corporations thought we were right, the reluctance factor went down on the part of the financial institutions," said Tony Cashen, former vice president of sales for the Funds Evaluation Group.

As A. G. Becker collected more and more data from more and more pension funds, the credibility of its database grew and helped attract even more clients, though some corporate treasurers were still reluctant. Some were afraid of offending the banks, on which their corporations often relied for financing. Others simply had no interest in knowing how the pension fund was doing—that was the trustee's responsibility. With these executives, "It was like selling to a wall," observed Roger Brown. "Some people didn't want to disturb anything, and if they had a problem they didn't want to know anything. Some treasurers thought their job was to keep their banks happy. Sometimes we got into top management or the board of directors, and they went down and asked the treasurer, 'why don't we get this service?'" By 1970, however, the dam had broken, and corporations were calling A. G. Becker to have their funds included in the database. Typical was Allied Chemical Corp., which had established a pension fund in 1964 and the first year contributed $20 million to it. It had contributed each year up to 1969 when company executives realized they had no idea how the fund, managed by five New York banks, was performing. As a result, the company hired A. G. Becker to look at the fund's performance from 1964 to 1970. The Allied board of directors got the bad news in April 1971. The fund's compound annual return for the period was less than 2%. The money would have been as well off in a savings account. In 1972 the fund hired two investment counseling firms and fired one of the banks, began examining the performance of the managers quarterly, and retained Becker to do the performance measurement. Public funds, trailing behind the corporate funds, also began to request inclusion in the Becker universe, and a public pension fund service was added in the early 1970s. At one time A. G. Becker's data crunching needs were so great that it was renting time on a NASA computer in Ames, Iowa. By the middle of the 1970s, more than 3,000 pension funds were having their investment performance monitored by A. G. Becker, and had begun to manage their funds on a performance basis, though in a rudimentary fashion. They had begun to compare the returns of their funds with the Standard & Poor 500 Index or, less commonly, the Dow Jones Industrial Average. The development of the A. G. Becker funds evaluation universe was a major step in developing professional management of pension funds because it told executives overseeing the funds what returns their bank trustees were earning on the assets, and they could compare these results with the results of the S&P 500 Index.

Time Weighting

When pension funds used only one money manager, the dollar-weighted rate of return was sufficient. However, when they started using more than one manager, as General Motors did in 1950, and a few others followed in the early 1960s, they needed a way to compare the managers because the size and timing of cash flows to these managers would rarely be identical. Because the size and timing of the cash flows could significantly affect performance, a different measure of performance was needed. The first approach to providing a comparative measure of performance was published in 1966 by Peter Dietz, a professor at Northwestern University, as his doctoral thesis. Dietz had become interested in the problem when he noted that most pension plans measured how well they were doing based on original cost. They ignored unrealized gains or losses, and they took realized gains or losses into the rate of return over an extended period of time. Only a few, he noted, evaluated performance on a market-value basis.

Dietz's book, *Measuring Investment Performance*,[4] provided a formula for measuring what became known as the *time-weighted rate of return*. The time-weighted rate of return eliminates the effects of cash flows, allowing the performance of portfolios managed by different investment managers, or using different investment approaches, to be compared. It also became possible to compare the performance of the different portfolios with an index, initially the Dow Jones Industrial Average for equities, but later many other indexes. Two years later the Bank Administration Institute, Park Ridge, Illinois, released its own study, "Measuring the Investment Performance of Pension Funds for the Purposes of Interfund Comparison," which blessed the time-weighted rate of return as the correct methodology and provided a way of calculating it, which was similar to Dietz's method. By combining time-weighted rates of return with beta, the risk measurement, pension fund executives could compare the efforts of their various money managers.

In 1968, shortly after the release of the Bank Administration Institute report of performance measurement, Merrill Lynch Pierce, Fenner & Smith Inc. decided to offer a performance measurement service of its own. The group, headed by Jack Treynor, one of the most original thinkers in the institutional investment arena, who had edited *The Financial Analysts Journal* for many years, hired Bill Sharpe as a consultant and in 1969 began to offer not just performance measurement but also risk-adjusted performance measurement of pension fund portfolios using time-weighted rates of return and beta. Soon after, measurement of alpha, the return in excess of that to be expected from a portfolio's risk level, was also offered. Alpha is a measure of the value added by a portfolio manager. However, Merrill Lynch, unlike A. G. Becker, did not hire a separate sales staff for its performance measurement system but instead relied on its registered representatives calling on institutions. Often these brokers were out of their depth when calling on pension funds, so Merrill's system was not as successful as the A. G. Becker product, peaking at about 1,000 clients. In addition, because Merrill was a powerhouse in equity research and trading and received commission flow from many different sources, it was difficult to identify the commission dollars generated by the performance measurement service, while it was easy to identify its costs. This problem would bedevil other consulting operations located in brokerage firms and cause many of them to break away and become independent.

Now What Do We Do?

The 1967–1969 period was in many ways a watershed in pension fund and institutional investing. In 1967 the institutional investment industry was recognized as an important sector of the whole securities industry when Gilbert Kaplan started *Institutional Investor* magazine to report, analyze, and comment on the personalities, institutions, and trends driving it. A year later the first *Institutional Investor* conference was held in New York, attracting almost 2,000 money managers, analysts, and pension fund executives. Also during that period, the first investment consulting firm and several of the most successful and influential nonbank investment management organizations were launched. The investment consulting firm was the Frank Russell Co. The money management firms started in the period included Capital Guardian Trust Co., Miller, Anderson & Sherrerd, Jennison Associates, and Batterymarch Financial Management Inc.

The Frank Russell Co. stepped into a vacuum A. G. Becker Funds Evaluation left behind after it had delivered its performance reports in the familiar green books. Russell was prepared to recommend changes in money managers to pension executives whose fund managers were underperforming. Often the pension executives, seeing the underperformance, were left with the question: Now what do I do? A. G. Becker had consciously decided to be in the data analysis business, not the advice business, so its representatives were not prepared to suggest alternative managers. Not until 1975, when other consulting firms were well established, did Becker change its mind about consulting.

The Frank Russell Co. was originally a financial counseling, insurance, and mutual fund company based in Tacoma, Washington. In 1958, when George Russell Jr. joined the company, it had two small mutual funds with $300,000 in assets, 175 customers, and 14 investment counseling clients. But two months after Russell joined, his grandfather, Frank Russell, who had started it and ran it, died suddenly. That's when George Russell Jr. did his first manager search. "I didn't know what to do with the 14 clients he was buying and selling stocks for. So I looked in the yellow pages of the Seattle phone book and found three money managers that were at that time in the yellow pages and wrote them down on 14 pieces of paper because at that time we didn't have a Xerox machine. I gave those names to the 14 clients—their average account was $50,000—and wished them luck. So that was our first manager search." Eleven years later Russell invented investment management consulting with investment manager selection advice for pension funds as its primary business. For those 11 years, however, Russell kept the firm alive selling a combination of term life insurance and the family's mutual funds. During that period he began thinking that mutual funds should be a useful product for pension funds at the million dollar or higher level because at the time most mutual funds had high initial sales charges. If one could get to $1 million, however, the sales charge was 1%, which made it more acceptable to larger investors.

In the summer of 1969 Russell attended a Harvard Business School conference in Seattle at which James (Jim) Ling, chairman of Ling-Temco-Vought Corp. (LTV), was a guest speaker. Russell found himself sitting beside Ling's executive assistant. Their conversation turned to LTV's $150 million pension fund, and the assistant told Russell that the fund was losing its internal manager and wanted help finding another manager. Russell suggested that the company use mutual funds rather than hire another fund manager. A month later he flew to Dallas to sell the idea to Jim Ling, accidentally leaving his dress shoes at home and arriving in Dallas with only the tennis shoes he was wearing. Arriving in Dallas after normal shopping hours, Russell found a shoe store with a light on and persuaded the shopkeeper to open his shop and sell him a pair of dress shoes for his early morning presentation to Ling. Russell was given six minutes to make his pitch for mutual funds. Ling bought the concept, and within three months Russell had sold $50 million in mutual funds to LTV, General Telephone & Electronics, and Textron. In the process Russell found that the pension executives really didn't want mutual funds; they wanted to understand about money management.

Soon after, Russell, cold-calling for business, made a phone call to Kenneth Axelson, the CFO of J. C. Penney Co. Inc., in New York to try to set up a meeting. Axelson was not in and the call was referred to Paul Kaltinick, the treasurer, who six months earlier had been put in charge of the J. C. Penney pension fund. Just a few days before Kaltinick had walked into the office of Robert Evans, assistant treasurer at J. C. Penney, and declared: "We need to look into what's going on in the pension fund," so he was ready for help. Kaltinick invited Russell to New York and showed him a list of 19 money management firms he was interested in for the Penney fund. Russell took the list, and three weeks later, after visiting all 19, he delivered a report to Kaltinick which said that three of the firms were worth keeping but the others were not. Russell also told Kaltinick that there were good managers not on the list who ought to be considered. Kaltinick soon hired the Frank Russell Co. as J. C. Penney's investment management consultant.

A few months later, on Kaltinick's recommendation, Park Davidson at Burlington Industries also hired the Frank Russell Co. as that company's investment management consultant. This initial success convinced Russell that investment management consulting could be a viable business, and he began traveling across the country selling the concept, scheduling 35 meetings in five cities in five days. Between 1969 and 1974, Russell signed up 38 more clients for his pension consulting service, and during that time he sold off the insurance and mutual fund business. He also began collecting performance figures on the managers—not that he understood how to use them at that point. Russell was asked to consult to the Penn Central Corp. pension fund soon after J. C. Penney and Burlington Industries hired the Frank Russell Co. At the first meeting Russell was asked: "How are you going to measure performance?" Russell remembered that a few weeks before someone had mentioned to him Peter Dietz's work on performance measurement. Russell responded: "We use the Dietz method." Penn Central hired him, and when he got home on Saturday, Russell set out to locate Dietz. He found him teaching at the University of Oregon, interviewed him on Monday, and hired him as a consultant to the Frank Russell Co. on performance measurement. Dietz later joined the Frank Russell Co. full time, heading the research department for a time, and later he opened Russell's Tokyo office.

Russell quickly learned that it was impossible to identify successful managers based only on their previous performance. Something more was needed, so he hired a staff of researchers to visit the managers to try to learn all it was possible to learn about their investment philosophy and how they selected the stocks they invested in. Russell hired Helane Grill as his first researcher and set her up in New York. The first Russell office in New York was a furniture storage closet rented from C. J. Lawrence Inc. Grill had joined A. G. Becker's New York office out of college as a secretary, hoping to become a broker, and was familiar with Becker's performance evaluation service. Although she knew nothing about researching money managers (nor did anyone else), Russell knew how to research stocks. Applying the same concept to researching managers, he developed the 4-P approach: people, philosophy, process, and performance. First find out about the *people* in the money management organization. Who were the owners? Who were the other members of the staff? How long had they been with the company? What were their backgrounds? What were their ambitions? Second, what was their investment *philosophy?* How did they define investment value? Third, what was their *process?* How did they construct portfolios, including how much diversification did they seek? And finally, what was the firm's *performance?* Grill wrote down the questions Russell developed and had them in front of her as she conducted her first interviews. Soon she was able to throw them away and developed additional questions of her own. In 1971 Russell hired another researcher,

Madelyn Smith, a Seattle housewife, who was ultimately responsible for developing Russell's style classification of investment management into large- and small-cap growth and large- and small-cap value managers.

During 1969–1973, a bull market for large-cap growth stock managers, the Frank Russell Co.'s manager recommendations performed very well. But these managers and most others fell out of bed during 1973 and 1974. Russell analysts looked at the managers they had recommended and realized they were all "high-beta" managers—that is, they all had above-market risk. "So we told our clients, don't worry, they went down 20% more than the market, but when the market turns they'll go up 20% more than the market," said Madelyn Smith. "Then when 1975 came along, the high-beta managers went up about 80% of the market while other managers went up 20% more than the market. We said, wait a minute, we've got to really examine these different portfolios." Russell analysts examined the managers' portfolio characteristics, beta, return on equity, yield, price/earnings, price/book, perhaps 10 characteristics, and found consistent performance patterns. At times managers buying large-cap growth stocks did best, at other times managers specializing in small-cap growth stocks did, and at still other times those buying large-cap value stocks or small-cap value stocks did best. This observation gave birth to the classification of managers by investment style. Today the styles defined by the Frank Russell Co. are used to classify not only pension fund managers but also mutual fund managers. In this way investors can diversify their roster of managers or mutual funds by investment style.

The Frank Russell Co. was the first specialized investment management consulting firm designed to help funds select better investment managers, but just by a nose. Early in 1970 John Casey, then a young broker with Paine Webber in Chicago, became involved in helping Consumers Power in Illinois select a money manager for its pension fund. Casey had become interested in the stock market when he graduated from college and had joined a broker training program at Harris Upham & Co. in 1967. Two years later he had joined Paine Webber and had become interested in the investment management world. Following the Bank Administration Institute report on performance measurement, Casey suggested to his superiors at Paine Webber that there might be a business opportunity in helping pension funds select managers. In the New York office of Paine Webber, Dick Corrington, the partner in charge of the institutional business, asked Bill Crerend to check out the concept.

Crerend had begun his career with Equitable Life in 1955 but left in 1962 to become controller at the National Foundation, where his responsibilities included overseeing the pension fund. In 1969, in need of more money to support a growing family, he had joined Paine Webber in New York and became Corrington's assistant. Crerend was not impressed at first, finding that Casey and a colleague had spent substantially more on the project than they had generated in revenue. But Corrington urged Crerend to keep an eye on the idea, and Crerend read all he could about institutional investing and money management. Soon after, Crerend attended a conference in New York on how to select a money manager and found himself volunteering answers to questions from the floor when the panel was stumped. Afterward he was approached by an executive from the brokerage firm of Dominick & Dominick who was impressed with his knowledge. The executive told Crerend that Dominick & Dominick wanted to get into the manager selection business and asked him to join the firm to help start it. After Crerend told the story to Corrington, Corrington told Crerend and Casey to build the business for Paine Webber, both on commission. "The first month I remember making $500, and the sixth month I made $15,000. I don't remember how much John (Casey) made, but it suddenly became apparent to Corrington that this was a big thing."

Paine Webber's first pension consulting client was Itek Corp., an optics firm in Lexington, Massachusetts. At Crerend's recommendation it hired Jennison Associates to manage its pension fund. By 1976 Crerend's department, by then named Corporate Financial Services, had become so successful that it was causing a problem for Paine Webber. At the same time Paine Webber might be trying to sell a private placement to one of the major trust banks, Crerend's department might be encouraging a pension fund to fire the bank and move $1 billion in pension assets elsewhere. That didn't help Paine Webber's sales efforts. James Devant, chairman of Paine Webber, told Crerend: "The more successful you are, the worse this [problem] is." He asked Crerend to buy the unit from Paine Webber. As a result, Crerend and three other employees bought it for a percentage of revenues for five years and named it Evaluation Associates. In the following years it became one of the top investment consulting firms in the nation. Meanwhile, Casey had moved on to another pioneering consulting firm, Callan Associates, and a few years later was a co-founder of another top firm, Rogers, Casey & Barksdale Inc.

Edwin Callan, who in 1973 founded Callan Associates, first ran into the manager investment performance question in the late 1960s when he was selling research for the San Francisco brokerage firm of Mitchum, Jones and Templeton. In 1968 he was in Pittsburgh trying to sell the research to Mellon Bank when he called on an old friend at National Steel Corp. The friend told Callan that he had no use for securities research because the company's $100 million pension fund was managed by trust banks, but the company didn't know how the fund was doing. "I heard some people are measuring that," the friend said. Callan realized that here was information someone would pay for, if he could deliver it. He approached the Martin E. Segal Co., which had done the study for the Air Line Pilots' Association, about providing the performance figures for companies he might gain as clients, and after some hesitation, Segal agreed. Callan then called several friends at corporations with his idea for the performance measurement service, received encouragement, and began to market it. He quickly picked up several clients. At this time, however, the New York Stock Exchange ruled it was not appropriate for a member firm to buy outside research (i.e., the performance figures from Martin E. Segal) and to resell it for directed commissions. That led Callan's firm to hire a staff to gather the data and calculate the returns internally. Soon his department, through consulting fees, was generating about one-eighth of the trading volume of the brokerage office.

In 1969 Callan conducted a study of the performance of Bankers Trust for the Pacific Lighting Service Co.'s $110 million pension fund. Unfortunately, the bank's performance was poor for one, three, and five years. Pacific Lighting therefore fired Bankers Trust as its manager, and Callan helped the executives select new managers. Soon after Callan did a manager review for International Paper, which then also decided to drop Bankers Trust as its pension fund manager. Unfortunately, the bank was doing business worth $1 million with Mitchum, Jones and Templeton at the time, while Callan's study delivered only $15,000 in fees. Since this was not a healthy tradeoff for the firm, it directed Callan to stay away from Bankers Trust. Callan, in effect, had the same problem as Crerend at Paine Webber and even A. G. Becker had. As a result, Callan broke away from Mitchum, Jones and Templeton in 1973 to establish Callan Associates as an independent investment management consulting firm.

Also in 1969, a young MIT and UCLA graduate, John O'Brien, joined the Los Angeles-based Oliphant and Co. from Planning Research Corp. to try to market a new performance service for pension funds based on Sharpe's Capital Asset Pricing Model. When O'Brien had joined Planning Research Corp. in 1967 as a systems analyst, the firm had a profit-sharing plan run by a bank. Although the bank told the company that everything was going well, company executives asked O'Brien to do a performance analysis of the fund just to make sure. When O'Brien looked into the literature, he noticed that Sharpe was doing interesting work on risk and return, and so he hired Sharpe as a consultant to the fund. In effect, it was a $500 contract for Sharpe to give O'Brien a private tutorial on the Capital Asset Pricing Model. As a result, O'Brien and Sharpe built a CAPM-based risk measurement model to help Planning Research understand its fund's investment performance. Then O'Brien suggested that Planning Research market the model, and Aerospace Corp. became the first client. Soon O'Brien and his associates developed the first book of betas for stocks, again using Sharpe's methodology. Unfortunately, Planning Research was trying to sell its product for cash, and all the prospective customers wanted to pay for it in commissions, so the business did not grow.

O'Brien soon was asked to join Oliphant & Co., a brokerage firm that was looking for products and salesmen for its San Francisco office, and began selling books listing the betas of stocks and risk-adjusted performance measurement. O'Brien also developed simulations of how different portfolios would behave in different market environments. For the latter service, most of the big clients were investment managers, including almost all of the banks in New York and many of the banks in California, anxious to understand their portfolios better.

O'Brien also recruited a strong staff for the department. Among them were Dennis Tito, who had worked on the U.S. space program at the Jet Propulsion Laboratory, Gifford Fong, who later started his own fixed income consulting firm developing fixed income analytical tools, and Gil Beebower, who later joined A. G. Becker and wrote a number of groundbreaking research papers on investment returns and diversification. However, in 1972 Oliphant & Co. decided to go public and wanted O'Brien and Tito to trade in their partnership percentages for stock ownership. When they resisted, Oliphant & Co. fired them and locked the doors of the operation over the weekend. O'Brien and Tito rented office space on Wilshire Boulevard and started O'Brien Associates (which became Wilshire Associates in 1975) to continue to develop and market the services. Most of the staff, including Beebower and Richard Ennis, joined them. The team expanded the portfolio measurement service, created what they believed to be the first asset/liability modeling product for pension funds, and produced the O'Brien 5000 Stock Index, which is now known as the Wilshire 5000 Index.

The asset/liability model allowed pension funds to play "what if?" with the pension fund. What will happen to the pension liabilities if the stock and bond markets behave in various ways? It allowed pension executives to see how vulnerable the pension fund, and the pension plan sponsor, whether a corporation or a state or local government agency, would be if the markets stumbled for several years, allowing for likely contributions and withdrawals and each plan's own demographics. One of the first big clients for the asset/liability model was the New York Telephone Co. pension plan, overseen by Robert (Bob) Shultz.

By 1970 the first phase of the financial revolution powered by the money flood was drawing to a close. Pension funds had grown rapidly during the previous 20 years and now totaled $212 billion. Only $41 billion of that was in the hands of insurance companies, while most of the remainder was managed by trust banks. The new assets from increased contributions to existing plans, or from contributions to new plans, had been more heavily invested in equities. Now 45% of the assets not in insurance company hands was invested in the stock market, largely through balanced accounts managed by the trust banks. That $77 billion flowing into the stock market had helped push stock prices up during the 1950s and 1960s. But directing increasing amounts of the pension fund flows away from insurance products and bonds into the stock market was only the first timid step. Pension executives, encouraged by the new pension consultants and bolstered by the academic research, would push forward to change the financial markets by investing in new and different ways and new and different investment vehicles. Many of the basic tools used today by pension managers and individual investors—manager-style classification, beta as a measure of risk, alpha as a measure of a manager's true ability, and diversification—had been developed and were being implemented by more and more pension funds.

Chapter 5

New Players Enter

Banks dominated the investment management world of the 1950s and 1960s. Having built on their reputations as both conservators and managers of the trust assets of wealthy individuals, they won market share from the insurance companies in the pension fund management area. During the bull market of the 1950s and 1960s they had performed well, as far as anyone could tell. Many had become focused on rapidly growing corporations such as IBM, Xerox, Polaroid, and Avon, the so-called Nifty Fifty. They were also known as "one-decision" stocks. The only decision an investor had to make was the buy decision because the companies were so good that the stocks would never have to be sold. At least, that was the theory. The bank portfolio managers, as well as some mutual fund managers, kept buying more of the same stocks, no matter how high their prices rose. But the banks' very success in gathering pension assets had attracted the attention of other institutions, primarily the mutual fund companies at first.

Scudder, Stevens & Clark, a Boston-based old-line mutual fund company, began to pick up pension clients in the early 1960s, in part because of its excellent fixed income investment record and in part because of its contacts with wealthy individuals. These pension clients, however, were still generally purely advisory clients; that is, Scudder advised the officials of the institutions what and when to buy but could not act independently to buy or sell for them. On the other hand, the Putnam Management Co., another old-line mutual fund company started in 1937, established the Putnam Advisory Co. in 1968 specifically to pursue institutional, full discretionary accounts from pension funds and other institutions such as college endowments and charitable foundations.[1] Putnam hired a separate portfolio management staff for the Advisory Co., and its first institutional

client was part of the Brown University endowment. This facilitated Putnam's efforts to win pension clients. David L. Babson & Co., another old-
line Boston firm, picked up a few pension clients in the late 1960s, as did
Loomis Sayles & Co., also of Boston, Lionel D. Edie, a New York-based
investment counseling firm, T. Rowe Price & Co., a mutual fund company
based in Baltimore, and Stein Roe & Farnham in Chicago.

Capital Guardian Trust Emerges

On the West Coast, Capital Research & Management, a mutual fund company, also decided in 1968 to enter the institutional investment management business, albeit by chance. The company initially planned to enter
the investment counseling business serving wealthy individuals, and to
make its offering more attractive to such individuals, it registered a private
trust company subsidiary—the Capital Guardian Trust Co. The trust company was headed by Robert Kirby, a Harvard MBA whose first job was with
a small Los Angeles brokerage firm where his responsibilities included
sweeping the sidewalk in front of the office each morning. Kirby later
joined Scudder, Stevens & Clark as an analyst and later portfolio manager.
He left Scudder when his superiors objected to his weekend hobby—racing
sports cars. It was Kirby's idea to form the trust company, rather than just
an advisory firm registered under the Investment Advisers Act of 1940,
because he thought having trust company status would be a strong selling
point with individual investors.

Soon after the trust company was established, however, Kirby received
a phone call from an executive overseeing the General Mills Inc. pension
fund asking if Capital Guardian Trust would be interested in managing a
pension fund. When General Mills hired Capital Guardian Trust to manage $50 million of its fund, Kirby realized there was more potential in man-
aging $50 million pension accounts than even $5 million accounts for
wealthy individuals. Therefore, Cap Guardian was soon in the pension
fund business. Capital Guardian's business really took off when General
Mills' hiring of Capital Guardian and several other managers was reported
in *Fortune* magazine. As a result, when the Common Fund, was formed to
provide professional management for college endowment funds, it, too,
hired Capital Guardian as one of its initial managers. Capital Guardian
Trust's performance was strong in 1967, 1968, and 1969, and, in the words
of Bob Kirby, "money poured in." But in 1970 the performance turned
down. Kirby had avoided the "Nifty Fifty" because he believed they were
overpriced, and the stocks he was in were clobbered beginning in 1970. "I

dreaded coming into the office on Monday morning because I knew the phone was going to ring about four times and there would be four clients who quit," Kirby said. Capital Guardian's business declined for several years thereafter.

Batterymarch Begins

At almost the same time that Kirby was founding Capital Guardian Trust, Dean LeBaron, a portfolio manager at Keystone Custodian Funds in Boston, another mutual fund company, was assigned to look at how Keystone should enter the investment management business. Upon graduation from Harvard Business School in 1960, LeBaron started work as a security analyst with F. S. Moseley & Co., a Boston brokerage firm. After three years there he moved on to Keystone Custodian Funds as director of research and later was the portfolio manager for the K-2 Growth Fund. He proposed that Keystone start to use some of the ideas about the market coming out of academia and to make greater use of computers, rather than simply relying on the latest hot portfolio manager. When Keystone rejected the ideas, LeBaron, with two Keystone colleagues, Jeremy Grantham and Richard Mayo, together with financing from a venture capitalist, established Batterymarch Financial Management in 1969. Batterymarch, named after the street on which the offices were located, offered an active strategy involving small stocks which LeBaron, Grantham, and Mayo believed were inefficiently priced and undervalued because brokers' research departments were not following them. The brokers ignored small stocks because there was little or no trading activity in them. Later, Batterymarch became a pioneer in the development of index funds. Batterymarch gained its first client, the $2 million pension fund of Instrom Co., a small Massachusetts-based instrument manufacturer, in 1970, but it was a struggle and by the end of 1970 the company managed only $25 million. By the same time, Capital Guardian Trust had $430 million under management, despite client withdrawals.

Jennison Associates

Like Kirby and LeBaron, Richard E. Jennison was a visionary. He was president of Auerbach, Pollock and Richardson, one of three prominent Wall Street investment research boutiques at that time (the others being Donaldson, Lufkin & Jenrette, and Faulkner, Dawkins & Sullivan). He believed that asset management was going to be a good business, just as he had foreseen there was a place on Wall Street for research boutiques. He thought an asset management firm independent from a brokerage firm or a bank trust department or mutual fund companies would be attractive to investors, though he didn't foresee pension funds as the natural clients.

Jennison proposed an investment management firm that would do nothing but asset management and have no other sources of revenue but management fees. If it was to succeed, it would have to do so on the basis of its investment results. Aided by an old friend, William (Bill) Armstrong, Jennison started Jennison Associates, recruiting experienced investment talent from among people they both had known, especially from Waddell & Reed, a strong Kansas City investment banking and brokerage firm. Top hires included John Hobbs and John Hagler, each of whom would later serve as president of Jennison Associates. The firm was launched on April 1, 1969.

The firm succeeded more quickly than even Jennison and Armstrong anticipated. Most of the investment staff they hired had contacts with presidents and chief executive officers at major corporations because of their work as directors of research or portfolio managers at major firms. "We thought we would run a variety of different types of assets," said John Hobbs, chairman of Jennison, "and it turned out, to our surprise, we had pretty good success getting retirement assets from corporations, based on the relationships with them that we had developed as researchers." Jennison's first pension account was Litton Industries, and it was followed in quick succession, all within two years, by Abbott Laboratories, Upjohn Co., Hughes Aircraft, and Gulf Oil Corp. It now found itself in the corporate retirement business. Jennison started as a growth stock manager and had good investment success from 1970 to the end of 1972, when it had $600 million under management. Like many money management organizations, however, it was about to undergo what John Hobbs described as "a chastening experience" as 1973 approached.

Even more of a visionary than Jennison was Fayez Sarofim, who formed a professional individual money management firm, Fayez Sarofim & Co., in Houston in 1958. Until then, and for a few years afterward, personal or institutional investment management was dominated by half a dozen trust banks in Houston and Dallas. Born in 1929, Sarofim arrived in the United States from Egypt in 1948. After graduating from the University of California at Berkeley and Harvard Business School, he returned to Houston to work for the Anderson Clayton Corp. Not long afterward, Sarofim decided to set up his own investment counseling firm. According to Texas legend, when he told his mother of his plans, she responded: "Well, I suppose you may be right, but I really don't see the need."

Sarofim opened his doors with three clients: a personal trust, an endowment fund, and a corporation. Twenty years later the firm had $3.8 billion under management, much of it from pension funds, for it was perfectly placed to take advantage of the disillusionment with the banks, even Texas banks, after the 1973–1974 bear market. Indeed, Fayez Sarofim, with a 10-year record behind it when pension funds first started to add investment counseling firms in the late 1960s, was a popular choice for pioneering funds. The firm continued to grow by producing investment returns better than the banks and most of its independent peers, helped by some timely industry bets, such as that on the oil industry shortly before oil prices shot up in the late 1970s.

Fayez Sarofim & Co. spawned another early entry among investment counseling firms, Eagle Management & Trust Co., which also became successful. The founders of Eagle were brothers, Monroe and Homer Luther, who had been vice presidents at Fayez Sarofim & Co.

Rosenberg Capital Management

In 1970 another investment counseling firm, which would become very successful later in the decade, opened its doors on the West Coast—Rosenberg Capital Management, based in San Francisco. Its founder, Claude Rosenberg Jr., had begun his career in 1954 as the first official security analyst with the San Francisco investment banking and brokerage firm of J. Barth & Co., after graduating from Stanford and serving in the Navy. At the time, institutional research houses were just starting to offer buy, hold, or sell opinions on stocks, and Rosenberg got in on the cutting edge. In 1960 he became the head of institutional research at J. Barth. He realized that if his company could produce an institutional-type research team, it could dominate the West Coast. In 1961 he wrote A Stock Market Primer, an introduction to stock investing for the average investor who found Graham and Dodd's classic Security Analysis too daunting.

Most investors at that time bought stocks for income, for until the late 1950s yields on stocks were greater than yields on bonds. Rosenberg thought it logical that if an investor could buy companies that were growing earnings rapidly, the compounding of those earnings would be to the investor's advantage over time. This led him to growth stock investing, and in 1970, when J. Barth was taken over by Dean Witter, he left to start his own firm with one account, a $20 million jointly trusteed (union–management) pension fund. By 1972 the firm had grown to $110 million under management, and by 1974 it was at $170 million. In 1973 Rosenberg saw inflation growing, and he warned one of his clients that it was in a danger-ous position because it had a heavy position in long-term bonds. The client turned the bond portfolio over to Rosenberg, and Rosenberg Capital Man-agement was suddenly also a fixed income manager. Rosenberg quickly reduced the average maturity of the client's portfolio to less than three years, saving it a lot of money as inflation and interest rates soared in the late 1970s and early 1980s.

Brokers Too

Brokerage firms on Wall Street began to establish investment counseling arms; those firms that already had them began to focus them on the grow-ing pension fund area. Other advisory firms which had been established to provide investment advice to wealthy individuals also began to discover the pension fund flood and to market toward it. Bear Stearns, a brokerage and investment banking firm on Wall Street, established Bear Stearns Capital Management. Merrill Lynch had Lionel D. Edie & Co., and Smith Barney & Co. established Smith Barney Advisers Inc. Although in 1971 some of the investment management and investment counseling sub-sidiaries of brokerage firms reported advising on large amounts of money, only a small portion was managed for pension funds. Lionel D. Edie, for example, reported $5 billion in assets under management in 1971. How-ever, much of that was in mutual funds, some in advisory services to indi-viduals, and some to pension funds.

Even the rating agencies entered the investment management busi-ness. Standard & Poor's Inc. started Standard & Poor's Counseling Inc. and S&P Carter Doyle & Co., while Moody's Inc. started Moody's Investors Services. S&P/Carter, Doyle & Co., started in 1972, was proba-bly the first investment counseling firm to specialize in active bond man-agement—a new field. It was headed by Andrew M. Carter, whom many regard as the father of active bond management. Carter graduated from Harvard University in 1968 with honors in English and physics. Soon after, he started at Irving Trust in New York in the credit department, heading teams that analyzed the collapses of American Express Field Warehousing (the "salad oil scandal") and Atlantic Acceptance Corp.

Although Carter had wanted to be involved in stocks, when he heard in 1964 that the Harvard Endowment was looking for an assistant bond manager, he did some research and found the bond market was bigger than the stock market. He flew to Boston and interviewed for the job, at the end of the interview telling Paul Cabot, the treasurer of Harvard, that he really wanted the job. When he didn't hear anything after several days, he called and reiterated his interest. Still there was silence. He called and asked to be interviewed again. After the second interview he reiterated his interest. Again silence prevailed. Finally, Carter called again and said: "I really, really, really want the job." John Thorndike, assistant treasurer at Harvard, responded: "Andy, you've been our second choice all along, but you're so persistent, the job is yours."

After he settled into his new job helping manage the $500 million bond portfolio of the Harvard Endowment, Carter suddenly found that everyone on Wall Street wanted to share their knowledge with him. "Gus Levy, senior partner of Goldman Sachs, called me every morning, as did Cy Lewis, senior partner of Bear Stearns," said Carter. "Bill Simon, then head of treasuries and municipals at Salomon Brothers [and later U.S. Treasury secretary], gave me a two-week training session on his trading desks in New York." Carter recognized, of course, that this was because of the large bond portfolio he managed, not because of his sparkling personality. One of Carter's first correct calls occurred soon after, when interest rates reached the apparently lofty 4 1/4%. Although others thought that interest rates were now likely to decline, Carter thought they were more likely to go higher because Lyndon Johnson had launched the War on Poverty and the country was slipping into the Vietnam War. As a result, Carter kept $100 million of the endowment's assets in cash. This kind of analysis would later be called *interest rate anticipation* and become a staple active bond management approach.

While at the Harvard Endowment, Carter noticed that on many occasions apparently identical bonds from different issuers were selling at different prices. That is, for example, bonds issued by two subsidiaries of AT&T might have identical ratings, almost identical maturity dates, and identical coupon yields but would be selling in the bond market for different prices. Carter realized he could sell the higher-priced bond and buy the lower-priced one and pick up significant yield to maturity. This was the start of active bond management. Previously, bonds had been bought and held to maturity. Carter realized that returns could be improved by actively managing the portfolio, by actively positioning it in terms of maturity, by swapping one bond for a similar but lower-priced or higher yielding one, and by moving up or down in quality when there was an opportunity to profit. In 1968 Carter left the Harvard Endowment to join Thorndike Doran Paine & Lewis, a Boston-based money management firm. Thorndike Doran managed $200 million in equities, but no bonds, and within four years Carter was managing $500 million in bonds for the company, including fixed income portfolios for Sears Roebuck, the Borden Co., and the Ford Foundation. It was not long before others noted what Carter was doing and began to use the same techniques; a few other bond managers had also been moving in the same direction as Carter independently. Most bond managers today, whether managing pension assets or mutual funds, use the active bond management techniques pioneered by Carter.

In 1972 Carter left Thorndike Doran to start S&P/Carter, Doyle. Carter also helped develop the first bond index when he proposed to Salomon Brothers that they develop such an index and suggested how it might be done. The result was the Salomon Brothers High Grade Corporate Bond Total Rate of Return Index, known for many years simply as the "Salomon Index." It provided a yardstick against which to measure the performance of a bond manager. In 1975 Carter joined Jennison Associates, where he remained until 1992. While he was there, Jennison's bond assets grew from less than $100 million to more than $10 billion. During this period, the bond swapping and interest rate anticipation techniques of active bond management that Carter pioneered became accepted and widely adopted by other fixed income managers..

Needed: A Phone Book

One great problem for money managers wishing to prospect for pension fund business was identifying which companies had worthwhile funds, who was the person in charge of the fund, where were the public employee pension funds around the country, and who was overseeing them. The first step in filling this information vacuum was taken in April 1970 when Thomas A. McQueeney and Thomas L. Robinson Jr. published the first edition of the *Money Market Directory*. McQueeney and Robinson had gathered information on pension funds and money management organizations for a fledgling pension consulting operation that never got off the ground. To reap some reward for their time and energy, the two formed Money Market Directories Inc. to publish the data they had gathered in book form.

The first edition, which contained information on 1,100 pension funds with assets of $135 billion, was an instant success, and so it was that McQueeney and Robinson were in the publishing business. The second issue, published in 1971, reported on 2,450 pension funds with assets totaling $160 billion. It also had information on 600 U.S.-registered investment advisers, 600 banks and trust companies, 550 insurance companies, 100 Canadian investment service providers, and 300 foreign banks. By the

1974 edition, it profiled 7,993 tax-exempt funds with assets of $362 billion, the great majority being pension funds, and 4,094 money management organizations with $888 billion under management. The *Money Market Directory* included not only the names, addresses, and phone numbers of corporations and state and local government arms sponsoring pension plans, but also the names of the people overseeing the investments, the size of the assets of each fund, and the names of the institutions managing the assets. It was, in effect, a prospecting guide for anyone seeking pension fund investment management business, especially the have-nots, the investment management companies. It was also a prospecting tool for pension funds seeking investment management organizations. No longer did prospecting rely solely on personal references or on tips from brokers or actuarial consultants. Now there was an encyclopedia that made the task easier. It came along at exactly the right moment, as investment counseling firms were beginning to battle the banks and insurance companies for a share of the booming pension fund investment business. Finally, it provided a phone book through which pension fund executives could easily find the names and phone numbers of their peers so that they could compare notes on strategies and investment management and consulting organizations.

More information was needed, however, before a money manager, consultant, or custodian could make a successful sale. The service provider needed to know the needs of the potential customer, as well as how his or her firm was perceived by the potential customers. How did the pension funds feel about different products and different organizations, and what could the organizations do to meet the needs of the clients and modify those perceptions where necessary? Into the breach stepped Charles D. Ellis and a firm called Greenwich Research Associates, later Greenwich Associates. Ellis had graduated from Yale with a degree in art history and philosophy in 1959 and a year later entered Harvard Business School. Graduating in 1963, he "lucked into" the opportunity to work for Rockefeller Brothers Investment Management, managing the personal assets of the Rockefeller family and the endowments it had set up, including that for Colonial Williamsburg.

Needing a job that paid more than $8,000 a year to support his family, a few years later Ellis joined Donaldson, Lufkin & Jenrette (DLJ) and spent five years in institutional sales. He also spent time with the polling and research firm of Louis Harris & Associates, then a subsidiary of DLJ, and when Harris was not interested in expanding into research on the institutional market, Ellis decided to set up his own firm in 1972. Greenwich Research Associates started with Ellis and one other employee, whose key responsibility was to answer the phone. Ellis drew up the survey questions and got together the target list of interviewees, but he subcontracted the actual survey work and tabulation to another firm. The first survey targeted 800 pension executives on their activities, interests, and attitudes for half a dozen institutional money management organizations. Many of those management organizations were surprised when the survey revealed pension fund executives thought investment performance was important and that fees did not matter greatly. This was at a time when a bank fee of 25 basis points was considered high.

Besides surveying attitudes, Ellis also offered consulting to money management organizations on opportunities for the firms and ways to fix any problems the pension executives perceived with the firms. Greenwich Research Associates provided an avenue for greatly increased information flow between pension executives and money management organizations. In addition, the company distributed the summaries of its research into the interests and activities of the pension funds it surveyed to all participants so that they could see how their activities compared with those of the average and median fund. In 1973 Ellis warned pension executives that they should rid themselves of the euphoric market expectations of the 1960s. The "go-go" markets of the 1960s were a "winner's game," he said in speeches, as well as in an award-winning article in the *Financial Analysts Journal* in 1975 and later in his 1983 book *Winning the Loser's Game.*[2] By the 1970s, he argued, the markets had become dominated by institutional investors, each with teams of analysts searching for the best investment opportunities. A loser's game, he said, was one in which increased activity leads to errors and increased losses. The strategy for winning the loser's game was to make fewer errors than the opponent. That, he maintained, was also the key to winning in investments.

Funds Reluctant

Most pension executives at corporations and public funds were slow to leave their bank or insurance company managers. In 1971 most of the largest pension funds still had only bank managers, and many only one bank manager. The 1971 *Money Market Directory* showed that Morgan Guaranty Trust Co. of New York was the single most popular fund management organization; it was employed by 129 companies or public employee plans. Next came Chase Manhattan Bank with 114 clients, and Bankers Trust Co., New York, with 106. Most of the other plans were overseen by local trust banks. In the Pittsburgh area, Mellon Bank was the dominant pension fund manager. In Chicago, Harris Trust and Savings Bank and First National Bank of Chicago dominated. On the West Coast, Bank of America, Wells Fargo Bank and Trust, and Crocker National Bank fought it out. Companies generally employed the banks from which they received their financing. Nonbank investment counseling firms had made very little headway by the end of 1970. The most successful in terms of the number of funds advised was Moody's Alliance Capital Management which had 14 clients. Next were Scudder, Stevens & Clark and Loomis Sayles, each with 10, while Capital Guardian Trust and Lionel D. Edie each had eight.

The 1971 *Money Market Directory* identified only 10 pension funds that used two or more investment counseling firms: American Greetings Corp., the Budd Co., Hewlett-Packard Co., General Mills Inc., General Telephone & Electronics Corp., Inland Steel Co., International Telephone & Telegraph Corp., Scott Paper Co., the Oregon Public Employees Retirement System, and Upjohn Co. (for its savings plan but not its retirement plan). The most adventurous of these firms were American Greetings Corp., General Telephone & Electronics, International Telephone & Telegraph, and Oregon Public Employees. American Greetings used J. M. Hartwell & Co. Inc., New York; Putnam Advisory, Boston; and Scudder, Stevens & Clark Inc., New York, for its $11 million pension fund. General Telephone used Berger-Kent Corp., New York; Putnam Advisory Co., Inc. Boston; and Fayez Sarofim & Co., Houston, as well as two banks, Bankers Trust Co., and First National City Bank, now Citicorp, both of New York, for its $432 million fund. International Telephone used Fidelity Management & Research, Boston; Jennison Associates, New York; and Tsai Investment Services Inc., New York. Tsai was the firm formed by Gerald Tsai, one of the hottest mutual fund managers of the late 1960s who had left Fidelity Management after successfully managing one of its mutual funds to set up his own firm. In addition, ITT managed some assets internally and used seven banks scattered around the country for its $1.025 billion pension fund. Oregon Public Employees Retirement System used Capital Guardian Trust, Fayez Sarofim, and Trans America Investment Counselors as its three managers for its $339 million fund, eschewing the use of any banks.

Pioneering Pension Funds

At the time the investment counseling firms were being formed by portfolio managers and analysts leaving mutual fund companies, bank trust departments, and brokerage firms, pension executives were beginning to try to identify which of the new firms had the best investment talent and which to hire. Eventually, the consulting firms such as the Frank Russell Co., Callan Associates, and Evaluation Associates would be able to help by doing much of the research and analysis, but until then pension executives had to depend on seat-of-the pants learning. One of those in the forefront of the learning process was Robert Greenebaum, treasurer of Inland Steel Co., who oversaw the $300 million pension fund. Greenebaum decided, soon after he became treasurer on July 1, 1968, that a change was needed, that the fund should diversify its managers, and that better results could be achieved than were being delivered by the First National Bank of Chicago. He therefore hired three investment counseling firms in 1969: Capital Guardian Trust Co., Endowment Management & Research, and Standard & Poor's/InterCapital Inc. He gave the new equity managers 50% of the assets and left the remainder with First National of Chicago to manage mostly in fixed income. However, the roster didn't remain unchanged for very long.

The first change was the dropping of Capital Guardian Trust in 1972. The assets were being managed by Bob Kirby. "He was sticking with what we would now call mid-caps, but then they were small-caps," said Greenebaum, "and they weren't going anywhere when the Nifty Fifty were plowing ahead. And pretty soon I called up Kirby and said, you know Bob, it's gotten to the point where it's your job or mine, and in my position, it's yours. And he said, you know, I don't blame you." By 1974 the Boston Co. Institutional Investors and Putnam Advisory Co. replaced Capital Guardian. Not long afterward, Endowment Management & Research was dropped, in part because of performance.

Another fund in the forefront was the International Telephone & Telegraph pension fund. The ITT fund was overseen by William A. Hayes, director of pension fund investing. Hayes had begun his career with the investment department at New York Life Insurance in 1960 but left in 1963 to join the Wall Street specialist firm of Marcus & Co. as assistant to the director of research. In 1969, however, he was recruited to join ITT to oversee its $1 billion-plus pension assets. A key reason for joining ITT was that shortly before he had had an interview with William (Bill) Donaldson, one of the founders of Donaldson, Lufkin and Jenrette, and had asked Donaldson where he thought the future was. Donaldson replied that the future in investment lay with pension funds. The thought of running a $1 billion pension fund therefore intrigued him.

When Hayes arrived at ITT, the fund used Fidelity Management and Research and Tsai Investment Services, as well as the banks. He reported to Lyman Hamilton, a creative treasurer willing to try different approaches who had put parts of the fund with Fidelity and Tsai. Tsai and other "go-go" stock managers bought seemingly "hot" stocks, rode them for a short time, and then sold them and moved on to the next "hot" stock. Today they would be called *momentum managers*. Hayes added Alliance Capital Management, Dreyfus-Marine Midland Inc., and T. Rowe Price Associates to the roster of nonbank managers by the end of 1972. In addition, ITT under Hayes managed part of its equity assets internally. By the end of 1973, Tsai Investment Services was gone, victimized by poor performance after the go-go stock era ended in 1969. Less than a year later, Bill Hayes himself was let go as the 1973–1974 recession accompanying the worst bear market since the crash of 1929 took its toll on ITT earnings and executive ranks were slashed. Hayes, however, moved on to run the Hughes Aircraft Co. pension fund in California and later joined the Wall Street specialist firm of Walter Frank & Co.

GTE

The General Telephone and Electronics (GTE) pension fund was overseen by the assistant treasurer, James Dunn. Dunn had joined the company in 1963 as budget coordinator at a time when GTE was buying many small regional telephone companies. A few years later John Douglas, financial vice president of GTE, was scheduled to give a speech to a group of financial executives on how to make an acquisition when, shortly before the speech, GTE was sued by International Telephone & Telegraph (ITT) over an acquisition. Clearly, Douglas could not speak on acquisitions while the suit was pending, so Dunn, who had been concerned about the performance of the three managers for GTE's pension fund, suggested he speak about how to run a pension fund professionally, as a profit center instead of a cost center. Douglas agreed and told Dunn and his staff (including William Marshall who would later run the fund) to research the subject and prepare the speech. The resulting speech prepared the way for the changes Dunn wanted to make. However, before making any changes, Dunn had Bill Marshall gather data on the performance of the managers and compare it with the Standard & Poor 500 Index. Then Dunn hired Tony Cashen at A. G. Becker and Peter Dietz at the Frank Russell Co. to provide additional performance data to back up Marshall's figures. That way there could be no dispute as to their accuracy.

As a result, GTE took away half of the money managed by Bankers Trust Co. and some of the money managed by Chemical Bank and First National City Bank, and split it between Putnam Advisory Co., Berger-

Kent Corp., New York, and Fayez Sarofim, Houston. As Dunn explained it to Douglas, it was like great baseball manager Branch Rickey going to his farm team for some new talent to shake up the team and improve results. "I had warned Bankers Trust several times that if their performance didn't improve I would take money away from them," Dunn said, "but they didn't believe me. We'd had a long relationship with them and they were our transfer agent, and it was quite a shock when I did it."

At the same time, Dunn increased the equity exposure of the fund to 60% of the assets. He believed that equities were a must for several reasons. First, unions were going to be demanding higher benefits, so the fund had to earn higher returns. Second, the company, as a utility, couldn't go to the public service commission for higher rates unless it could show it was getting the best possible returns from the pension fund to keep funding costs low. Finally, since GTE was largely a regulated utility at the time, its cash flows were more predictable than those of most industrial companies, and it therefore could take more market risk than most industrial companies. "There was no question we were underperforming," Dunn said. "The question was could we select managers who would perform better. I was convinced we could." Dunn was also comparing notes from time to time with Bill Hayes of ITT. In 1972 GTE added Jennison Associates and Wells Fargo Bank to the roster. The GTE fund prospered in the first two years of the 1970s but like so many others suffered in the 1973–1974 bear market.

Delta Airlines

In 1971 Delta Airlines joined the ranks of pension fund pioneers who were moving toward an investment structure using multiple pension asset managers, often a mix of a few banks and more investment counseling firms. The banks brought conservatism and steadiness, while the investment counseling firms seemed to offer flexibility and new ideas. The first hirings were often based on little more than guesswork and good vibrations between the pension executive and the managers, and little effort was made to select complementary managers. But the pension executives and the consultants who were emerging to help them find the best money managers were learning and pushing the revolution forward.

Jim Howell, fund administrator at Delta, began a review of its $200 million pension fund, which was managed at the time by First National City Bank (then in the process of changing its name to Citibank), and Citizens & Southern National Bank. In the course of the review, Howell interviewed about 40 managers, cut the list to 20, and then studied them more closely. Finally, he selected six nonbank managers: the Boston Co. of the Southeast, Jennison Associates, Montag & Caldwell, Fayez Sarofim & Co., Schroder Naess & Thomas, and Thorndike, Doran, Paine & Lewis. First National Bank of Atlanta, which had been managing a separate trust for Delta, began to manage some of the pension money. Howell observed that the review of managers was prompted by improvements in Delta's benefit programs and "the only way we could afford them was to be more aggressive in our money management."[3] In 1973 Delta added Batterymarch Financial Management and George D. Bjurman, a small Los Angeles-based firm.[4]

Public Funds Too

Even public pension funds were making changes. Like most public funds, until the mid-1960s the New York City Employees Retirement System funds were invested mainly in the city's own debt. When Abraham D. Beame began his first term as New York City controller in 1962, 57.7% of the $3.2 billion in assets belonging to the city's five plans was invested in city bonds. Another 14% was in low-yielding long-term U.S. government bonds, and 26.7% in corporate and other bonds. One of Beame's first steps was to begin investing the assets of the funds, which were generally managed identically, in common stocks. In 1964 he hired a commercial bank to carry out the equity investing. In 1969, however, that bank was replaced by First National City Bank and the city funds' first investment counseling firm, Alliance Capital Management. Two more banks were added in 1971, the Bank of New York and the U.S. Trust Co. By then common stock had climbed to almost 15% of the funds' assets.[5]

Like many public funds, the State of Connecticut pension funds were managed internally and were heavily in fixed income securities until 1972. However, that year three funds were pooled: the Connecticut Mutual Equity Fund of $190 million, the Connecticut Mutual Fixed Income Fund of $463 million, and the Mortgage Fund of $3.7 million. Also at that time, four outside equity managers were hired: David L. Babson & Co., Connecticut Bank and Trust Co., Putnam Advisory Co. Inc., and Standard & Poor's Counseling Group. In January 1974 Standard & Poor's was replaced by Capital Guardian trust and NN Investment Services Inc. of Minneapolis. In a unique move for a pension fund, the Connecticut pension fund bought a seat on the PBW Stock Exchange in Philadelphia so that it could do its own equity trading and control trading cost. After one year, the $10,000 investment in the seat had earned the Connecticut Fund about $124,000.

A Case Study: General Mills

General Mills Inc. had the most innovative and thorough approach to nontraditional pension management. The company had long since moved away from a bank trust department as the sole manager for its pension assets, and it had done so in a very methodical way that served as a model for no fewer than three Harvard Business School case studies developed by Professor Bertrand Fox. The company's financial staff, headed by vice president of finance and treasurer Henry H. Porter Jr., had realized early in the 1960s that pension funds would in the future make ever larger demands on the company's financial resources. The staff therefore began a search for better methods to manage its pension funds, realizing that better investment returns on the more than $100 million funds could be translated into a better bottom line for the corporation. In 1966, on comparing the performance of Bankers Trust, the sole bank trustee for the fund, with the returns of the Standard & Poor's 500 Index in the years between 1959 and 1965, the staff found that Bankers Trust had underperformed the index by three percentage points, returning 8.3% per year versus 11.4% for the index. Furthermore, the executives found that an average of growth mutual funds had compound annual returns for the same period of 14.9%. The recently released Fisher and Lorie study of long-term stock market returns showed that from 1926 to 1960 stocks returned, on average, a compound annual return of 9.03%. These rates of return appeared to be substantially higher than the rates returned by bonds.

Porter and his staff had decided that a manager or managers other than the bank could achieve a better return, that the company should take the responsibility for achieving that return, that the bank should be relieved of most of its investment responsibilities and become largely a directed trustee and custodian, and that more aggressive investment in common stocks would enhance returns. The first change it decided to make involved the $136 million fund backing the plan for salaried employees. It became one of the first funds to develop a three-part process, which later in the light of the pension reform law and capital market theory would be significantly revised to consider risk also, but which was a good first step. The General Mills model was later adopted by many funds.

First Porter's staff developed a statement of investment objectives and policies. A primary objective of the fund was to achieve above-average investment performance while providing assurance that it could still meet all required payments even in the most extreme conditions. The executives were mindful of the 1929 market crash and how long it took equity values to recover, as well as the impact of the subsequent Depression on the company's earning power. They proposed to provide that insurance by establishing a $7.5 million liquidity reserve made up of high-grade corporate and government bonds sufficient to meet benefit payments for 13 years. This was to be managed by Bankers Trust. After the liquidity fund was established, the staff proposed that $89.5 million should be invested in order to obtain long-term returns 30% better than the S&P 500 Index. The remaining $39 million would be managed somewhat more conservatively. Its objective was set as a rate of return 10% greater than the S&P 500 Index, with fluctuations no greater than the index.

The second part of the process was the selection of appropriate investment organizations to achieve these investment objectives. Since the Frank Russell Co. and other consulting firms had not yet been started, the staff had to do its own homework. For a year the staff examined more than 30 investment organizations as potential investment managers, including major trust banks, insurance companies, brokerage firms, and investment advisers across the country. Ten organizations were invited to make formal presentations to top management in Minneapolis. Four of them were then selected for their different investment philosophies and to achieve diversification of assets. Capital Guardian Trust Co. was selected to manage the more conservative equity assets, and these were the assets that put Capital Guardian Trust into the institutional investment management business. The more aggressive assets were split between three East Coast firms: Brokaw, Schanen & Clancy, New York, and State Street Research & Management and Thorndike, Doran, Paine & Lewis, both of Boston. Porter and his staff had pioneered an approach that would later be reinvented and advanced by George Russell.

In the third part of the process, Porter and his staff established strict investment guidelines for the managers. For example, the portfolios could include no General Mills securities or assets in which General Mills had either a direct or an indirect interest. A maximum of 10% of the assets under management could be invested in the securities of any one issuer. No foreign securities could be bought unless they were listed on the New York Stock Exchange or the American Stock Exchange. The managers could not lend assets to General Mills or individuals. Nor could they invest in commodities or commodity contracts (even though General Mills was thoroughly familiar with such commodity futures). Selling short or purchasing on margin was prohibited. Some of these restrictions later appeared in the Employee Retirement Income Security Act (ERISA) passed in 1974 to improve the administration of the nation's pension plans. In addition, Porter proposed that the treasurer oversee the investment managers and report twice a year to the board. The General Mills approach was a prototype of the model adopted, with modifications, by many pension funds. The key modification, adopted as Sharpe's Capital Asset Pricing Model became known more generally, was the inclusion of risk limits and controls in the investment guidelines.

The new structure at General Mills performed well in 1967 and 1968. Capital Guardian Trust, the manager of the more conservative portfolio, had outperformed its target return rate comfortably, and two of the three managers of the general account had also beaten their targets. The overall return on the fund, despite the underperformance of one manager, was well ahead of target and the market as a whole, and also far head of the funds backing the General Mills nonsalaried employees plan which were still managed by the bank trustee. For 1967 the General Mills fund ranked first out of 44 funds in the A. G. Becker Funds Evaluation Service universe, up from twenty-seventh out of 42 in 1966. In 1968 the General Mills fund ranked third out of 45 funds.

As a result of this strong performance, the company's overall top management decided to increase benefits and to refund employees' contributions to the plan, making it noncontributory. These two moves combined to reduce the margin of safety offered by the liquidity reserve. Porter and his finance staff recommended more changes. The company established the Voluntary Investment Plan (VIP) in which salaried employees could invest all or part of their refunds of their previous contributions to the retirement plan. In addition, employees could invest additional amounts, up to 5% of salary, in the VIP, and the company would match these contributions to the extent of 25 cents on the dollar. The employees could choose between an equity fund and a fixed income fund. The VIP plan thus took the structure of what is today a 401(k) plan, though the employee contributions were on an after-tax basis, whereas 401(k) contributions are pretax. At the same time, General Mills decided to commingle all of the equity funds—those of the pension fund general account, the VIP account, and the appropriate segments of the retirement funds for nonsalaried employees. In effect, the company set up a large pooled fund or internal mutual fund managed by the outside managers, in which the various plans bought shares—that is, it was an early master trust.

By June 1970, a fresh review was called for: the 1969 and early 1970 returns had been so poor that the market value of the pooled equity fund had dropped from $160 million at the beginning of 1970 to $97.8 million as of June 30 that year. Moreover, for the three and a half-year period through June 30, 1970, the compound annual return was -8.9% compared with 1.4% for the S&P 500. Though no one really understood it yet, a bear market had begun, which hit the stocks of small and medium-sized companies first and hard, while leaving the Nifty Fifty growth stocks unscathed for a time. In fact, the resilience of the Nifty Fifty in this period convinced many investors that they were truly different, truly recession proof, and that increased their attractiveness.

Not all money managers believed the Nifty Fifty would grow forever. Many considered their prices far too high and so avoided them. As a result, their investment performance suffered in the 1968–1974 period. One of those so affected was Capital Guardian Trust Co. General Mills found its belief in equities sorely tested but reaffirmed it in the 1970 review. However, the finance staff noted that interest rates had risen so much that "bonds presently offer a viable alternative for investment." In addition, the staff turned its attention to real estate, stating: "Real estate is a more complex medium with a wide range of return and risk and differing cash flow characteristics." The fund did own some shares in real estate investment trusts, but the executives observed: "Unlike equities or bonds there are no apparent investment managers competent in all aspects of this medium."[6]

The Real Estate Answer

The General Mills staff did not know that Meyer Melnikoff of Prudential had a possible answer to their real estate wishes near at hand. Melnikoff began thinking about real estate as an investment for pension funds early in 1967 when he sought ways other than stocks or bonds in which pension funds might be invested. He was looking for investments that would have different return cycles from stocks and bonds and would therefore provide stability of return while yielding a return close to that of stocks and bonds. During a Prudential staff retreat that year, Melnikoff spent some time talking with two officers from Pru's real estate department, and he began to wonder whether real estate might be a good investment for pension funds. Prudential had been investing in real estate since 1875, first in residential mortgages, but after World War II it had expanded into business properties and apartments, and even into property development. In his research into real estate as an investment, Melnikoff found the written record very sparse, but by chance he heard about the Pension Fund Property Unit Trust of London. After he made contact with the managing director of the organization, his suspicions were confirmed that PFPUT, as it was known in England, was a pooled fund for real estate investment by British pension funds.

After much correspondence, and drawing on the British experience, Melnikoff began to structure his pooled real estate fund, to be known as

Prudential Property Investment Separate Account, or PRISA. The first task was to make sure it would work under the insurance laws of New Jersey, New York, and other states, that it would not run afoul of any requirements of the Securities and Exchange Commission, and that it would satisfy federal tax laws and IRS regulations. When it cleared all these hurdles, PRISA was activated on July 31, 1970, receiving its first assets from the Retirement Plan for Prudential employees. Unbeknownst to Melnikoff and his Prudential colleagues, Wachovia Bank and Trust Co. of Winston-Salem, North Carolina, had established a commingled real estate fund for pension funds in 1968, but except for Wachovia's own pension clients, its existence was virtually unknown.

Melnikoff soon began criss-crossing the continent marketing his new separate account and found the going tough. The top investment person at one of the nation's major pension funds asked Melnikoff how much leverage PRISA would use. Melnikoff answered that PRISA would not create any debt and would limit the leverage to that resulting from buying mortgaged properties. The pension executive countered that he would not be interested in PRISA unless it leveraged up 400% to 500%. That kind of leverage was not unusual in real estate investment trusts at that time. Melnikoff did not know it, but real estate investment trust (REIT) leverage would cause him problems in the reverse way two years later. In the meantime, PRISA gained its first client, Robert Greenebaum's Inland Steel pension fund, in March of 1971. By September 30, 1971, PRISA had 20 clients and total assets of almost $50 million.

No one foresaw what was about to hit the U.S. economy, the U.S. stock and bond markets, real estate investment trusts, banks, insurance companies, investment counseling firms, and mutual funds. The country was entering a prolonged recession, broken temporarily and tentatively in 1972 and early 1973, while inflation began a dramatic rise, interest rates climbed, and the stock market stumbled, first the high-flying go-go stocks such as National Student Marketing, then most other stocks except the Nifty Fifty, and ultimately the Nifty Fifty themselves. During the late 1960s, the median equity exposure of pension funds monitored by A. G. Becker rose from 55.4% when the service began to 82% by 1974. As a General Mills finance staff report of 1974 pointed out, the institutional share of trading on the New York Stock Exchange had risen, along with the increase in equity exposure, to 60% of the shares traded from 31% and to 68% of the dollar volume from 39% between 1960 and 1971.

The market was being dominated by institutional investors who were putting to work the increasing flow of pension contributions. A new era was beginning in which most bank trust departments would be driven out of the investment management business, most of the active investment of equities would swing to investment counseling firms, and insurance companies would be left struggling to find products that would keep them competitive.

The real estate investment trusts which were highly leveraged were soon in trouble, and many were liquidated with large losses to their investors. This development jaundiced many pension funds against real estate investing just as Melnikoff was attempting to market PRISA. He had to spend a great deal of time explaining why PRISA was not like a REIT, especially the REITs that had failed. It was not the underlying properties that had caused the problems in such REITS, Melnikoff stated, but the leverage, the debt burdens at a time of rapidly rising interest rates.

Melnikoff did not know it initially, but he had an ally in the Frank Russell Co. In late 1970 George Russell had made a speech to the Treasurers Club in New York at which he urged the treasurers to consider investing pension assets in real estate and international equities. Though they laughed at him for those suggestions, in June 1971, Russell hired Blake Eagle, a real estate developer, as head of the newly formed real estate consulting group. At the time, Russell estimated that pension funds had less than $500 million invested in commercial real estate equity. It would take time, but by 1975 PRISA was on its way to success, and other insurance companies were rushing to develop and market their own real estate separate accounts. Other real estate management firms would soon emerge. Pension funds had begun pouring their assets into real estate, and the very size of those flows would change the industry.

Chapter 6

Accelerated Change

At the beginning of 1973, the move away from banks toward investment counseling firms was still only a trickle, but over the next three years it was to become a flood. That flood would power a new stage in the financial revolution—the development of a whole new sector of the investment management field. It led to the growth of independent investment counseling firms, a few of which had begun to seek to manage pension assets, and they in turn pioneered new ways of deciding which stocks and bonds to invest in. The investment counselors were, in general, more competitive than the bank trust departments, whose trust officers considered themselves too genteel to compete for business. Generally, business came to them from personal or corporate relationships. The investment counselors competed with one another on the basis of investment performance, and they competed against market indexes. They had twin goals: to earn higher returns than their peers and thus win more clients, and to provide an investment return in excess of the return of the average stock in the market, as measured by stock indexes, particularly Standard & Poor's 500 Index. This intense competition for the best investment insights, the search for the most promising stock or bond investment strategy, and the best individual stock and bond investments, greatly increased market efficiency. Eventually, the investment counseling firms, and with them their pension fund clients, broadened beyond market-traded stocks and bonds into private investments such as venture capital. But that was in the future.

As 1973 began, more pension funds had added investment counseling firms to their manager rosters, but generally only one or two, and generally alongside their bank managers. American Airlines, for example, in 1970 used only two banks, J. P. Morgan and Old Colony Trust, to invest the

$353 million assets of its five pension plans; at the start of 1973, it used three banks, one insurance company, and two investment counseling firms.[1] In 1970 Standard Oil of New Jersey had eight banks managing its almost $2 billion in pension assets; by 1973, when it had become Exxon Corp., it had dropped one bank and added two investment counseling firms.[2] Illinois Bell, which had used only Harris Trust & Savings Bank in 1970, had added three banks and four investment counseling firms by 1973.[3] A few had gone further. International Harvester Co. used only Bankers Trust Co. and Harris Bank in 1970 for its $327 million in pension assets; by 1973 it used five investment counseling firms, four trust banks, and three insurance companies.[4] At the beginning of 1973 the 100 largest corporate pension funds used 113 money managers, 62 of them trust banks and 51 either insurance companies or investment counseling firms. In addition, 19 were internally managed, either wholly or in part. The most commonly used manager was Morgan Guaranty Trust, which had 27 top 100 clients, followed by Bankers Trust Co., with 18, First National City Bank, with 15, and Chase Manhattan with 14. The investment counseling firm most used by the 100 largest corporate funds was T. Rowe Price & Associates, which had 11 top 100 clients, followed by State Street Research & Management, with eight, Putnam Advisory, with seven, and Capital Guardian Trust with six.[5]

There were several reasons for the slow pace of change. First, trust banks often provided financing to the companies, and companies were reluctant to endanger what they regarded as a vital relationship. Second, many companies had not yet begun to focus on the size of their pension assets or liabilities, and, as a result, the pension fund was often an afterthought. Frequently, the investments were overseen by a financial executive who was near retirement and had been "put out to pasture." The pension executive of one New York-based corporation was also in charge of janitorial services. Finally, there was as yet little swapping of information among pension executives.

Nonetheless, the trend was definitely against the banks. More and more pension executives were reaching the same conclusions independently. The banks had done a poor job, and a number of banks decided to fight fire with fire by pulling their institutional investment management operations out of the trust departments and setting them up as independent investment management subsidiaries. There, freed from bank rules, regulations, and bureaucracy, they might be more flexible and successful, and more attractive to clients. One of the first to use this approach was Citizens & Southern Bank in Atlanta. It formed C&S Invesco in 1971, headed by Charles Brady. The new subsidiary managed not only pension assets, but also the bank's own trust assets. Ultimately, Invesco would leave the bank and become truly independent, and one of the world's largest money management organizations.

Similarly, Chase Manhattan Bank set up Chase Investors Management Corp. in 1972, while in the same year United California Bank set up Western Asset Management as its investment subsidiary. Over the next few years, many others followed, including Chemical Bank, which set up Favia, Hill and Associates; First National City Bank, which established Citibank Investment Management, much later to become Chancellor Capital Management; Crocker National Bank, which started Crocker Investment Management Co.; and Bank of America, which formed BA Investment Management Co.

The success these subsidiaries achieved seemed to be determined by how far they were able to separate themselves from the bank trust department model. This involved reducing layers of bureaucracy and increasing flexibility and speed of decision making. For example, Chase Investors Management Corp. moved far away from the trust bank structure, setting itself up as a boutique investment management firm, even moving itself from Chase Manhattan Bank headquarters in the Wall Street district to a midtown location. Chase Investors became one of the success stories and was ultimately sold to the Union Bank of Switzerland to become UBS Asset Management. Favia Hill and Associates, on the other hand, was ultimately a failure. Two years after it was established, a pension executive who had just visited the firm responded when asked what he thought of the supposedly new firm: "If it walks like a duck and quacks like a duck it's still a duck." The only things the firm had changed from its days as the trust department of Chemical Bank, he said, were the floor it was located on and the name on the door. It was still in the same building as its parent, and it employed roughly the same number of people as it had when it was the trust department and, as far as he could tell, used the same bureaucratic investment process.

The trigger for the sea change that eventually swept many of the banks out of the pension management business was the culmination of the bear market, which had begun in 1969. It hit small-cap stocks and go-go stocks first. That year small stocks declined 25.1%, followed by a 17.4% decline in 1970. There followed a 16.5% gain in 1971 and a 4.4% gain in 1972.[6] This lulled many investors into believing it was just a blip, especially as the Nifty Fifty growth stocks were unscathed and marched confidently onward and upward. But losses of 30.9% and 19.9% for small-cap stocks followed in 1973 and 1974, respectively. Large company stocks had a more modest 4% loss in 1969, followed by gains of 4%, 14.3%, and 19% in 1970, 1971, and 1972, respectively. But large company stocks were clobbered along with small company stocks in 1973 and 1974, losing 14.7% in 1973 and 26.5% in 1974.[7] So between the beginning of 1969 and the end of 1974, small-cap stocks lost 58% of their value, on average. In the same period large-cap stocks, despite having positive returns in 1970, 1971, and 1972, lost almost 19% of their value. In 1973 and 1974 alone they lost 37% of their value.

The bear market began in January 1973 for many large-cap stocks and hit the Nifty Fifty in July. The bank trust departments, heavily weighted in those large-growth stocks, generally rode the stock prices down. Often they could do nothing else because their cumbersome investment committee-based structures did not allow for quick reaction to changing conditions. Portfolio managers often needed investment committee approval to significantly increase, reduce, or eliminate a position in a particular stock. And the stock could not be sold until a suitable replacement stock had been identified, for significant cash in an equity portfolio was not acceptable. In addition, many banks, such as J. P. Morgan, held such large positions that they had little flexibility. They could not quickly or easily sell them to build cash and cut their losses because selling would drive prices down further and faster. Insurance companies performed no better than bank trust departments in their equity separate accounts in 1973 for many of the same reasons. They, too, had been enamored of the Nifty Fifty and other large-growth stocks and held large positions, and their decision-making processes were often as cumbersome as those of the banks.

Although investment counseling firms were not immune to performance problems and also lost clients in the bear market, many suffered less than the trust banks. Whereas investment counseling firms generally had more in small-cap stocks than the banks, and small caps suffered worse than large caps, most cut their losses more quickly than banks and retreated to the sidelines with their cash reserves. They generally had no investment committees to discuss and approve each proposed sale or purchase and slow the decision-making process. Since they were smaller in terms of staff and assets under management, the portfolio managers and analysts could meet informally at any time to talk over buy and sell decisions. In addition, since their positions were generally far smaller than those of the large trust banks, they were more easily liquidated. Moreover, the portfolio managers generally had more discretion and more freedom to act. Jennison Associates, for example, allowed its cash position to build up during 1973 as it cut its losses and eliminated stocks it had lost faith in, so that by mid-1974 it had between 25% and 30% in cash. Then, in July, before the end of the bear market was clearly in sight, Jennison began to redeploy the cash, buying growth stocks that had been beaten down so far they were clearly bargains, according to John Hobbs.

Evidence that the pension funds were getting restless late in 1973 came from the first issue of a new biweekly newspaper aimed at the institutional investing world, especially pension funds: *Pensions & Investments*. *P&I*, as it quickly came to be called, reported in its first issue that International Harvester had dropped Harris Trust & Savings Bank as a pension fund manager, ending a more than 20-year relationship.[8] International Harvester also dropped Capital Guardian Trust, whose performance had trailed during the 1970 through 1972 period because Bob Kirby stayed away from the Nifty Fifty growth stocks, and Brokaw, Schaenen, Clancy & Co., another 1968–1969 vintage investment counseling firm. As Keith Potter, senior vice president at International Harvester, told the publication: "It was a performance problem."

The same issue of *P&I* reported on the hiring of Montag & Caldwell, an Atlanta-based investment counseling firm, and Supervised Investors Services, a Chicago-based investment counseling subsidiary of Kemper Insurance Group, to replace First National Bank of Miami in managing the $60 million equity portion of the City of Miami's pension fund. Bankers Trust Co. of New York was hired to manage the $20 million fixed income portion. Similarly, a few weeks later, the Budd Co., a maker of auto body parts, hired T. Rowe Price & Co. and F. Eberstadt & Co. to manage part of its $85 million fund, replacing First Pennsylvania Bank and Smith Barney & Co. They joined Girard Bank of Philadelphia and Scudder, Stevens & Clark. By the end of the year Chase Investors Management Corp., the investment management subsidiary of Chase Manhattan Bank, reported it had lost almost $1 billion in pension accounts during the year, including a $500 million portfolio of Western Electric Co.[9] Other large banks could have reported similar client defections. *Pensions & Investments*, with its reports on the hirings and firings of money managers and its reports of other steps leading pension funds were taking, helped accelerate the pace of change by disseminating information to less innovative pension executives and pension oversight committees. It showed them that they didn't have to accept things the way they were. Many of the pension funds were unhappy with the performance of the banks and were ready to try something new. Change was bubbling just under the surface. As the investment results for 1973 and 1974 were reported to pension funds by A. G. Becker and Merrill Lynch, and the new consulting firms, change became inevitable, especially when Congress passed a pension reform law.

Pension Reform

Pension reform legislation was on its way. President John F. Kennedy had ordered a study of the private pension system as far back as 1962, and federal pension reform legislation had been in gestation since the collapse of the Studebaker Corp. in 1964, which had left many long-term employees without pension coverage. The company had been funding its plan since 1950, contributing normal annual cost for benefits earned each year and paying down over 30 years the huge costs it incurred for benefits earned for service in the past (its past-service liability). Studebaker had met its funding obligations each year, and it had invested its pension assets as wisely as any other company at the time. There was no malfeasance, no one absconded with pension assets. Unfortunately, the company was unprofitable and simply did not stay in business long enough to fully fund its past-service liability. The situation was worsened by the fact that with every contract negotiation the union negotiated improved benefits and Studebaker's past-service liability increased, often fast enough to offset its funding. In fact, the year before the company failed, the union negotiated a pension increase at a time when both labor and management must have known the financial future of the company was in serious doubt. "The Studebaker pension plan was one of the best in the country at that time, but incredibly it was still no good," said Frank Cummings, a lawyer for Studebaker in its bankruptcy who later went to work for Senator Jacob K. Javits (R-New York), who spearheaded reform efforts. "It wasn't the people who were evil. They were just doing what everybody else did."[10] Theoretically, Studebaker could have funded more vigorously, but through the 1950s the company was struggling, and higher pension contributions might well have brought about its collapse even sooner.

According to the terms of the Studebaker plan, the first claim on the fund's assets went to retired workers and to those over 60 years of age with at least 10 years of service. There were 3,600 of these claimants, and $21.5 million of the fund's $24 million in assets provided full benefits to them in the form of annuities bought from an insurance company. The next 4,000 participants, those who had been employed long enough to have vested rights in the plan, received payments worth, on average, only 15% of the value of their vested benefits, sums ranging from $200 to $1,600. Another 2,900 employees who had not worked long enough to become vested received nothing.

The plight of the employees vested but not eligible to retire, whose average age was 52, was especially upsetting to the public and the Congress. In the years following the Studebaker collapse, Congress held a series of hearings on the state of the pension system and the need for reform. It heard cases of employers who did not fund their pension promises at all; of others investing the assets in corporate assets, such as warehouses and office buildings at unfair prices; of employees having to meet almost impossible vesting requirements, such as 30 years continuous employment, before winning the right to a pension; of employers firing employees immediately before they were due to vest to avoid paying pension benefits. Some of these issues were also highlighted in an NBC television documentary on the private pension system, "Pensions: The Broken Promise," aired in September 1972, which highlighted abuses and pension plan terminations by employers. The push for reform was also helped along by reports that the trustees of the Central States Teamsters pension fund had made loans of fund assets to reputed mafia-connected figures building casinos in Las Vegas.

The U.S. Senate had passed its version of the pension reform bill in mid-September 1973 after months of wrangling between the Senate Finance Committee and the Senate Labor Committee over which should have jurisdiction and whether the Internal Revenue Service or the Labor Department should oversee the law when passed. The Finance Committee argued that since pension funds were tax-exempt, tax issues were involved, and therefore it and the IRS had jurisdiction. The Labor Committee argued that since pensions were employee benefits, and often negotiated for by unions, it and the Labor Department should have jurisdiction. Both committees made compromises, agreeing the IRS and the Labor Department would share oversight, and the 300-page bill was approved unanimously and passed on to the House of Representatives. However, the House Ways and Means committee made it clear it was not about to rush to accept the Senate version of any pension reform legislation. A jurisdictional battle soon broke out in the House between the Ways and Means Committee and the General Subcommittee on Labor.

At the same time, debate in the pension industry about the prospective pension reform law was heating up. A study by Robert Taggart, a George Washington University economist, which suggested that greater pension regulation by government, as proposed in the pension reform law, could lead to a stunting of pension plan growth, was pooh-poohed by government officials drafting the law.[11] Much later Taggart was proven right, at least as far as defined benefit plans, then the largest and most important of pension plans, were concerned. At the same time, companies were voicing concern about a proposed government agency to insure pension benefits for workers of companies that went out of business. The proposed Senate bill, for example, left companies responsible for the liabilities of a terminated pension plan up to 30% of the net worth of the corporation. Critics of the legislation declared that such a provision would cause companies to terminate fully funded plans to avoid the possibility that the plans would ever become underfunded. Others warned that the proposed funding and fiduciary standards would impose costly burdens on pension plans and their sponsoring corporations. Meanwhile, a number of states, despairing of federal reform efforts, were preparing their own pension reform legislation. At the end of 1973 Massachussets, New Jersey, and New York were all working on their own pension legislation.

Go to Cash

By the end of 1973, with the Standard & Poor's 500 Index down 14.7% and many managers down much more because small stocks had declined 30.9%, pension fund executives were getting nervous. Money managers were getting calls from clients urging them to lighten up on their stock holdings and to build up cash. Some clients even suggested that the managers buy bonds. "I think it's been generally true in talking to our clients this year that there has been questioning—including by ourselves—if purchasing bonds at perhaps 8.5% offers a competitive return," Samuel R. Callaway, chief investment officer at J. P. Morgan, told *Pensions & Investments* in December. Jim Howell at Delta Airlines was looking to add two more managers to the pension fund's ranks. He was considering adding smaller, more flexible managers who would swing significantly to cash when the outlook was unfavorable. During 1973 Delta's managers moved only tentatively into cash, not enough to satisfy Howell. "It's the down draft that clobbers long-term performance," Howell said at the time.[12] The pension executives' nervousness was driven not only by the recession and the bear market, but also by the energy crisis which had begun in November as Middle Eastern nations cut supplies to the United States.

In its first issue for 1974, *Pensions & Investments* identified and profiled the 100 largest corporate and union pension plans, ranked by their assets a year earlier. The Sears, Roebuck & Co. Savings and Profit Sharing plan was the largest with assets of $4.2 billion, followed by the General Electric Pension Plan, $2.3 billion, and the U. S. Steel & Carnegie Pension Plan, $2.2 billion. The assets of the 100 largest totaled $52.3 billion, up 10% over the previous year, and companies contributed $4.5 billion to the plans in 1972.

Pensions & Investments' second issue of 1974 caused a stir by reporting the investment performance of the commingled pension funds of 21 of the nation's largest banks. The figures were generally not made public, but a member of the *P&I* staff had heard that the banks swapped the figures quietly between themselves. By asking bank A how bank B did and then asking bank B how bank A did, he was able to piece together the figures for the New York trust banks and then follow a similar strategy with banks outside New York. Only two banks, the Bank of New York and Philadelphia's Girard Bank, managed returns better than the 14.7% loss of the Standard & Poor's 500 Index. The Bank of New York's fund was down 11.2%, and Girard's was down 14.1%. The three most-used trust banks, Morgan Guaranty, Chase Manhattan, and Bankers Trust, were down 20.8%, 17.9%, and 28.4%, respectively. Similar figures were not available for investment counseling firms because they did not pool their accounts, and they refused to reveal the performance figures for individual accounts. The *P&I* data caused a stir, being reported later in both the *New York Times* business section and the *Wall Street Journal*. A few weeks later *P&I* reported similar data for the insurance company equity separate accounts, and the insurance companies rejoiced that their performance figures were no worse than those of the banks. One bright spot: Prudential's real estate separate account, PRISA, reported a return of 9.2% for the year, in large part because much of PRISA's assets were invested in short-term securities while the company sought suitable real estate for investment.[13] Never before had these performance figures been made public, though funds subscribing to A. G. Becker's Funds Evaluation Service or hiring one of the consulting firms like the Frank Russell Co. or Callan Associates would have received some of the data. In those cases, however, the identities of the managers were coded, and only the consultants knew which managers were which. Publication of the data became another blow to the reputation of the banks (and insurance companies) as money management organizations.

Index Ahead

Meanwhile, a development was emerging that potentially threatened trust banks, insurance companies, and investment counseling firms—indeed, it threatened all managers whose goal was to provide investment returns greater than the market as a whole, or "to beat the market." This new development was the *index fund,* a fund that would not try to beat the market returns but would exactly match them, either up or down. The index fund concept had its genesis in Fama's Efficient Market Hypothesis, but probably the first effort to implement it occurred in 1969 when William

(Bill) Fouse tried to persuade Mellon Bank in Pittsburgh to start a fund that would track the market—an index fund. Fouse graduated from the University of Kentucky with an MBA in 1952, took a job as a management trainee with Mellon Bank, and ended up as a security analyst in the research division of the trust department. After a few years, Fouse decided he wanted to know how the recommendations of Mellon's analysts worked out, whether the portfolio managers' implementation of those recommendations added value, and whether Wall Street's recommendations contained any useful value. In his spare time he began tracking these things in one of the bank's computers.

At about the same time Fouse became involved with a group of like-minded young analysts and portfolio managers interested in using quantitative techniques in investment analysis. Before long the group had concluded that the traditional approach to security analysis and portfolio management was, in Fouse's words, "intellectually bankrupt." The information out of traditional security analysis, he decided, was random. Out of his discussions with the members of the quantitative group, which included Jack Treynor and, occasionally, Bill Sharpe, Fouse got the idea for an index fund—perhaps, he admits, from some comment by Sharpe or Treynor. He was certainly the first practitioner, however, to try to put the concept of the index fund into action. Lloyd Peterson, head of the trust department at Mellon, rejected the idea. Fouse had also been experimenting with a dividend discount approach to investing—trying to forecast corporate earnings out five years, then determining how much the companies would pay in dividends over those five years, and discounting the value of that stream of dividend payments back to a present value to determine the proper value of the stocks. His testing of the approach seemed to give very good results in terms of valuing stocks, so Fouse took the idea to Peterson. Again his idea was rejected with the words: "Dammit, Fouse, you're trying to turn my business into a science." At that point Fouse realized his 18-year career at Mellon Bank was over.

Through his contacts with the quantitative group, Fouse found a job in the management sciences department at Wells Fargo Bank in San Francisco, headed by John A. McQuown. When Fouse arrived at Wells in the Fall of 1970, the management sciences department was early in discussions with the Samsonite Corp., then a family-owned corporation, which was interested in a new approach for its pension fund. Keith Schwayder, a member of the family that owned the company, had attended the University of Chicago, had been exposed to Modern Portfolio Theory there, and thought it offered possibilities for the about $6 million pension fund that had been invested in mutual funds. Through Bill Sharpe he had been connected with the Wells Fargo group. The management sciences team came up with an index fund based on the equally weighted New York Stock Exchange Index—the very first index fund. It proved a nightmare to manage because keeping the portfolio equal-weighted in line with the index as some stocks moved up and others declined in value required heavy trading and thus incurred high trading costs, particularly in that era of fixed commissions. Next, Wells Fargo developed the Stagecoach Fund, a portfolio of low-beta stocks leveraged up so that the beta of the portfolio was 1.0; that is, it had the same risk as the market.

After almost two years of marketing, however, only $30 million had been committed, and the breakeven was $100 million. As a result, in October 1973 the fund was dropped (the fund's demise was reported in the first issue of *Pensions & Investments*) and replaced with an S&P 500-matching index fund. Since the S&P Index was capitalization weighted, tracking was much easier and costs were much lower. A small part of the bank's own pension fund had been managed using the S&P-matching approach since early 1973, and a few of the funds that had subscribed to the Stagecoach fund told Wells they were interested in doing the next best thing. Wells executives offered the S&P index fund. The first client to actually commit money to the Wells Fargo index fund was George Williams of the Illinois Bell System pension fund, which had assets of $600 million. Williams told Wells that if the bank would increase its commitment, Illinois Bell would match Wells's total in the fund, and they each committed $10 million. After the index fund was up and running, Fouse installed the dividend discount approach to portfolio management for nonindexed accounts and also installed a risk control approach that forced portfolios to be diversified by beta, growth, and capitalization.

In September 1973, American National Bank and Trust Co. of Chicago began running a $20 million market index fund tied directly to the S&P 500 Index—probably the first publicly marketed S&P 500 Index Fund. The bank converted a commingled pension fund into the index fund from an active approach and received no objections from the clients. The index fund used a technique called *stratified sampling* which bought a statistically weighted sample of securities in each segment of the S&P 500 Index. As a result, its performance almost exactly matched the performance of the index, and its beta was almost exactly 1.0, the same as the index. At a time when pension fund managers in general were down more than the index, this strategy had the potential to attract a lot of business from all active money managers.

The idea for the American National index fund had come from Rex Sinquefield, a young MBA from the University of Chicago who had been hired by the bank in January 1972. Sinquefield had become interested in finance at St. Louis University but had been turned on to Modern Portfolio Theory at the University of Chicago where his professors included Merton Miller, Eugene Fama, Roger Ibbotson, and Fischer Black, all of them innovative thinkers and later giants in the world of finance. When he graduated from the University of Chicago, Sinquefield wanted to try all the new ideas. He applied to all of the trust banks in Chicago, and, after making it clear in interviews that he wanted to apply the new ideas he had learned at the University of Chicago, he was turned down by all except American National Bank and Trust.

About six months after he started at American National, Sinquefield wrote a memo proposing that the bank start an index fund, which he called an S&P market fund. Although he received no reply to his initial memo, he pursued the issue. A number of objections were raised. At the time, brokerage commissions were fixed, so large trades could be expensive and trading costs were an issue. In addition, there was no Depository Trust Co., so all transactions involved the transfer of paper certificates from one institution to another. But Thomas Ransome, vice president in charge of the investment division of the trust department, favored the index fund idea and pushed it through top management at American National, allowing the conversion of the commingled equity fund, used for accounts that were not large enough to justify the assignment of an individual portfolio manager, to indexing. None of the clients in the commingled fund objected. However, this was just a start. The fund had to be marketed to larger clients, the same problem faced by Wells Fargo.

American National's first index fund client, other than the commingled fund, was the $1 billion New York Telephone fund overseen by Robert (Bob) Shultz. Shultz had been a district manager with the telephone company when, upon the abrupt retirement of the previous supervisor, he was suddenly catapulted into the pension fund world in 1973. The company had recently realized that its pension fund assets had grown to $1 billion and had asked the supervisor, who had been overseeing it for many of his 35-plus years with the company, to begin reporting regularly on its fortunes. The supervisor took the request as a reflection on himself and took retirement with just two weeks' notice. On equally short notice, Larry Smart, the assistant treasurer, called Shultz in to replace the supervisor. Shultz knew nothing about either investing or the company's pension fund, but soon found himself intellectually engaged by the new field and became determined to make a career of it. He discovered that the pension fund had two managers, Manufacturers Hanover Trust Co. and U.S. Trust Co., both of which managed balanced accounts 60% in stocks and 40% in bonds. "The banks moved maybe 5% around those figures," said Shultz, "so it was really not balanced management. It was just a 60–40 equity-debt split." Shultz became intrigued by Modern Portfolio Theory, and he began to examine the index fund idea. After long interviews with and repeated visits to American National, Shultz recommended the concept to the New York Telephone investment committee. The members of the board committee, unfamiliar with the concept, looked to the legendary Gus Levy, senior partner of Goldman, Sachs & Co., for guidance. After pondering for a few minutes while puffing on his ever-present cigar, Levy nodded his assent. The rest of the committee fell into line and agreed, and some of Manufacturers Hanover's account was transferred in kind to American National to start the index fund. Two years later the New York Telephone fund bought a $15 million index fund from Studebaker Worthington Corp.'s pension fund.

Andy Yost, Studebaker Worthington's pension executive, another pioneer, had started indexing in 1974 with the blessing of John Casey, the fund's consultant, and again, that of Gus Levy of Goldman Sachs, who was also a trustee of the Studebaker Worthington fund. Two years later the company's chief executive officer, Derald Ruttenberg, vetoed the concept, saying it was "un-American" because it settled for the average return and the fund could do better than simply earn the index return. Yost had to get rid of the index fund. Upon meeting Shultz at an *Institutional Investor* conference in New York and hearing that New York Telephone was putting $50 million a month into an index fund, Yost suggested that New York Telephone buy Studebaker Worthington's index fund, and Shultz agreed. This sale of a complete portfolio from one pension fund to another was probably the first ever program trade. Such trades became more common in the 1980s and 1990s.

Batterymarch Financial Management in Boston had introduced its own indexed product about a year after Wells introduced its Stagecoach fund and by November 1973 still had found no customers. However, rather than abandoning the concept, Batterymarch lowered the fee for the fund to $25,000 from $100,000 for a $100 million account. The Batterymarch approach was simpler than those of Wells Fargo and American National. Batterymarch simply bought the 250 largest stocks in the Standard & Poor's 500 in the same weighting they were in the index, giving the fund a beta of very close to 1.0. Dean LeBaron's idea was that the largest 250 stocks accounted for more than 90% of the value of the stocks in the S&P 500, and so more than 90% of the movement of the index. Buying only the 250 largest and most liquid stocks would keep transactions costs down. There was no commingled fund. Each of Batterymarch's indexed clients would have its own separate index fund because Batterymarch could not legally pool its clients' assets. However, Batterymarch was not to get its first client for its index fund for another year. It might have had it sooner had it not been for Dean LeBaron's sense of humor. While he was seeking an index fund manager for the New York Telephone fund, Shultz attended an *Institutional Investor* conference in New York, and, by chance, he spied a person he thought was Dean LeBaron. Wishing to speak to LeBaron about Batterymarch's index fund, Shultz approached LeBaron and began to introduce himself. LeBaron, kidding, responded, "Oh, I'm not Dean LeBaron, this is Dean LeBaron," pointed to the person standing next to him, and walked off. When Shultz started speaking to the person, he said: "Well, I'm not really Dean LeBaron. That was Dean LeBaron." Soon after an embarrassed Shultz gave the index fund account to American National Bank and Trust in Chicago.

In March of 1974 American Express Asset Management Co. joined American National, Wells Fargo, and Batterymarch in starting an index fund. By mid-1975 American National had declared indexing to be its primary approach to investing. Henceforth, only about 10% of a typical account would seek to beat the market, while 90% of the account's assets would earn at least the market return.[14]

The index fund concept was initially received with derision, and even hostility, by active managers, brokerage firms, and even many pension executives and the occasional academic. Critics accused those pension executives who invested money in index funds of "settling for mediocrity." Of course, it was possible for active managers to outperform the market, active managers declared. The validity of the index fund concept versus active investment management was a topic of hot discussion at many pension fund conferences. At one such conference, Steve Leuthold, head of a prominent Minneapolis-based investment research boutique, produced a poster of Uncle Sam with the admonition: "Help stamp out index funds."

The debate raged in the pages of *Pensions & Investments* during 1976, with respected academic and practitioner Roger Murray, a professor of finance at Columbia University's Graduate School of Business, writing that index funds were an idea whose time had passed.[15] Murray provided five reasons why index funds were not a good way to manage assets, the key one being that it involved "looking ahead through the rear-view mirror." In the same issue, Townsend Brown, a vice president and director at Wood, Struthers & Winthrop Inc., New York, argued that indexing was a "cop-out," that it would be too expensive, and that these "trendy" funds would go the way of the Edsel. Rex Sinquefield and Bill Fouse each responded, noting that numerous studies had shown professional money managers as a group unable to equal, let alone outperform, the market consistently. Sinquefield argued that the index fund should be the foundation of equity management because it allowed diversification and flexibility. He also proposed that the index fund could be a repository for the stocks active managers did not want to hold and a source for those they wanted to buy.[16]

Over the next few years the index funds beat more than half of the active managers consistently, except for the late 1970s, when small-capitalization stocks were outperforming all others. Small-cap stocks are underweighted in the Standard & Poor's Index, so when they provide higher returns than large-capitalization stocks, managers who have some small-cap stocks in their portfolios will generally beat the index. However, several additional studies in the 1970s supported Sinquefield's position that active managers could not "consistently" beat the index. The key word was *consistently*. Individual managers could beat the index for a few years, but very few could beat it consistently over a long period. As a result, many funds, especially large funds, began to consider index funds for at least part of their assets. Despite the protests of Murray, Brown, and scores, if not hundreds, of active money managers, the growth of index funds could not be stopped.

Bankers Trust Co., the second largest manager of pension assets, became a convert when it announced in September 1976 that it was starting an index fund and would offer it to pension clients, though it intended to continue to offer active management also. At the time, Bankers Trust managed $15 billion of pension assets. And by the end of 1976 the five largest trust banks in Chicago all offered index funds, though, other than American National, they did not regard them as their primary investment approach. By the end of 1976, the index fund managers were reporting a total of $1.7 billion in indexed assets, remarkable growth in less than three years. The great bulk of these assets was in the hands of American National and Wells Fargo, each of which managed $500 million, and Batterymarch, which managed $375 million.[17] As the year ended, United Airlines, General Motors, Shell Oil, and the New York City employees' pension funds had indexed parts of their pension funds.

In part, the initial skepticism over index funds particularly among money managers, and not a few pension executives, was the result of skepticism about Modern Portfolio Theory, the Efficient Market Hypothesis, the Capital Asset Pricing Model, and beta. But in early 1974 a new prophet appeared whose work and words and consulting firm helped convert many skeptics. The new prophet was Barr Rosenberg, a young, softspoken finance professor at the University of California at Berkeley. Rosenberg had graduated from University of California at Berkeley in

1963, then attended the London School of Economics as a Marshall Scholar earning a master's degree in economics and econometrics, and returned to the United States to complete his Ph.D. at Harvard in 1967. He then returned to Berkeley with a National Science Foundation grant to build databases to which he could apply the econometric analytical techniques he had developed while completing his Ph.D. He took on a consulting assignment with Wells Fargo, which introduced him to beta and got him thinking even more about the capital markets. He realized that while beta measured how a stock moved relative to the market as a whole, there must be underlying reasons for that movement. There must be fundamental reasons, related to the financial characteristics of the companies, that explained why one stock moved more than the market and one moved less, and why many stocks moved together more or less independently of the market. For example, during a period when the market as a whole is going nowhere, some groups of stocks will be rising and other groups falling, and sometimes there is no obvious similarity between stocks moving in the same direction. This was Rosenberg's concept of "extra-market covariance"—a movement not explained by the market's movements.

In 1974, with the help of a consulting contract from American National Bank & Trust in Chicago, Rosenberg established a consulting firm called Barr Rosenberg Associates, BARRA as it quickly became known. The assignment at American National was nothing less than the automation of portfolio management, from forecasting security returns to estimating the risks of each security and developing efficient portfolios. During this work, he and his staff developed a program for predicting betas. Until this point, betas had been based on observation of how stocks had moved relative to the market in the past. They were historic betas. Rosenberg's work looked at dozens of financial variables of companies—size, financial condition, and so on—to determine which, if any, explained beta. He found multiple factors contributing to beta and was able to use those factors to accurately predict betas. "Barr's better betas," or "bionic betas" as Rosenberg's estimated or predicted betas became known, provided an intellectual explanation for beta as a measure of a stock's volatility.

The fact that betas could be explained by the kinds of fundamental financial data security analysts generated and were not simply the product of some pointy-headed academic's imagination made them more acceptable to Wall Street. Whereas many in the first half of the 1970s had resisted discussing with clients the betas of their portfolios, or the stocks they bought, Barr's better betas made it more and more acceptable to do so in the second half of the decade; indeed, more pension executives expected and even demanded it. The credibility of beta lent credibility to index funds, which were designed to have a beta of 1.0, the beta of the market as a whole. Rosenberg and BARRA went on to launch a fundamental risk management service based on his betas, and then they developed a product called MULMAN. This product allowed pension executives to combine a portfolio of managers with diverse risk levels into an efficient portfolio of managers, much as stocks with different risk levels could be combined into efficient portfolios. Since then BARRA has continued to develop leading-edge quantitative analytical and risk management tools for pension funds and money managers and today is one of the most influential quantitative investment consulting firms. Rosenberg himself left BARRA in 1985 to set up Rosenberg Institutional Equity Management, which manages assets using the tools and insights developed at BARRA. Hal Arbit, later the founder of Concord Capital Management but then a vice president at American National Bank, deserves some credit for the success of BARRA. When a contract dispute at the bank delayed payment of the second installment of the research contract that was the beginning of BARRA, Arbit mortgaged his house and sent the proceeds to Rosenberg to cover the firm's bills.

Options and Ideas

Besides the beginning of a bear market and the start of index funds, the year 1973 was also notable for another financial model that would have an enormous impact on investing in the years ahead. This was the Black-Scholes options pricing model which in 1996 would win Myron Scholes a share of the Nobel Prize for Economics. His co-developer, Fischer Black, had died before the prize was awarded and thus did not share in it. However, Robert C. Merton, who extended the model, did share the prize with Scholes. In 1965 Fischer Black was a young mathematician who had graduated from Harvard University with a degree in physics and then gained his Ph.D. from Harvard in applied mathematics. He joined the consulting firm of Arthur D. Little and there met Jack Treynor who introduced him to the Capital Asset Pricing Model (CAPM).

Black, intrigued by the CAPM and the financial markets, set out to apply the model to other securities, particularly bonds and warrants. At about the same time, Myron Scholes, who had a Ph.D. from the University of Chicago Graduate School of Business and was teaching at the Massachusetts Institute of Technology, was working on the same problem. When they became aware of the fact, they joined forces. By 1970 they had developed their options pricing model, with the help of a comment from Merton, but it was not published until May of 1973, though a report of their real-life results of applying their model appeared in 1972. The Black-Scholes model gave investors a formula for valuing put and call options, a seemingly narrow segment of the investment world. But it did much more because many financial transactions have implied options embedded within them. For example, a home mortgage contains a put option for the home owner. If interest rates decline so that they are below the owner's current mortgage rate, the home owner has the option of putting the mortgage back to his bank by refinancing. Mortgage-backed securities are, therefore, priced using the Black-Scholes model, or a variation of it. In addition, there are many similar embedded options in corporate finance. The greatest impact of the Black-Scholes model, however, would be felt in the late 1980s and early- to mid-1990s when it led some investors into dangerous waters.

Bear Trap

By mid-1974 the money management community was thoroughly traumatized by the bear market, which for small- and mid-cap stocks was almost four years old and for most large caps, except for the Nifty Fifty, was 18 months old. Even for the Nifty Fifty, the bear market was a year old and had been extremely painful. Numerous trust banks had begun to build cash reserves, trying to catch up to the investment counseling firms and the sentiments of their pension clients. They were late to make their move, however, and as a result, the tide continued to flow against the bank trust departments. For example, Pacific Telephone & Telegraph selected FMR Investment Services, Boston, and Rosenberg Capital Management, San Francisco, to join its management roster, leaving competing banks out in the cold. It was just one of many companies that had lost patience with the trust banks and were looking for new investment talent. Many of the banks moved at exactly the wrong time, building cash just as the market was about to rebound. Hence, they were building cash while investment counseling firms such as Jennison Associates had begun to put their cash back into the market. Some of the trust banks were thus whipsawed, underperforming when the market was declining, and again when the market was rising.

Reform Passes

Meanwhile, in late February 1974 the House of Representatives passed its version of the pension reform bill. One House Ways and Means Committee member was quoted as saying: "This bill will do something to someone, but we aren't sure what and to whom."[18] However, a quick passage through the conference committee was not anticipated. For example, Michael Gordon, minority counsel for the Senate Labor Committee's pension study group, told *Pensions & Investments* at the time: "The difficulties I find with the (House) bill are just too numerous to mention. Let me just say there are problems with every title of the bill."[19] Despite the House action, reform efforts continued in several states, even though the federal legislation threatened to preempt state legislation. Early in March state Senator George Deukmejian introduced a reform bill in the California legislature which would have required 30% vesting after three years, full vesting after 10 years, and portability of benefits from job to job. However, Congress was feeling pressure to move on pension reform quickly. The Watergate scandal had broken, and there was talk that impeachment hearings against President Richard M. Nixon might be necessary later in the year. If pension reform was not finalized soon, it might get buried in those hearings. By July 15 the only issue still unresolved was the effective dates of the various requirements of the legislation. The issue of jurisdiction had been solved by giving it to both the Treasury Department and the Labor Department. The IRS would have final jurisdiction over vesting, funding, and participation regulations. The Labor Department would have full jurisdiction over fiduciary standards. The bill also established a Pension Benefit Guaranty Corp. within the Labor Department, which would be a second line of defense for employees of companies that failed with underfunded pension plans, like that of Studebaker.

On September 4, 1974, a brilliant sunny Labor Day, President Gerald R. Ford signed the Employee Retirement Income Security Act, the nation's first comprehensive pension legislation, in a two-hour ceremony in the White House rose garden. Private noninsured pension plans, those most affected by ERISA, as the law came to be known, had assets of $115 billion.[20] Government experts predicted those assets would grow to about $250 billion by the early 1980s. In fact, by 1980 they were $470 billion, largely because of ERISAs funding requirements, which companies rushed to meet. Besides the funding requirements, the 500-page ERISA established procedures for winning tax qualification for new plans (so the plan did not have to pay taxes on the contributions from the sponsor or on the income from its investments) with the Treasury and Labor departments. It established stringent standards for fiduciaries and prohibited specific transactions. It set participation and vesting standards whereby employees must be covered and when they earned a legal right to their pensions after a specific number of years of coverage by the plan. It required disclosure of plan details to the employees, including all of the employees' rights. It set standards for reporting plan operations to the IRS and the Labor Department at least annually, or when specific plan developments occurred. Finally, it established the Pension Benefit Guarantee Corp. Because of its complexity, the law was nicknamed the Lawyers and Actuaries Full Employment Act of 1974; some said ERISA stood for Every Rotten Idea Since Adam.

Fiduciary Standards

The key provisions affecting pension fund investing were the funding and fiduciary responsibility standards. The funding standards accelerated the flood of money into pension funds beyond even what had occurred after the Inland Steel decision. Companies sponsoring pension plans were required to fund their normal costs (that is, the cost of providing pension coverage for each employee for one year, as calculated by an actuary) annually, as well as to fund their unfunded past-service liabilities (those costs arising for service with a company before a plan started, or which were not funded in the past for some reason) over 30 years. Any additional costs arising because of unsatisfactory investment returns or other experience losses (for example, more employees staying long enough to vest than expected or retirees living longer than expected) had to be funded over 15 years. For jointly trusteed (union–management) plans, the amortization periods were 40 years and 20 years, respectively. Before ERISA some companies had not been funding their plans on a regular basis at all. Others had been funding over 60 years or 100 years, far longer than most companies even survived. So when the funding rules went into effect, many companies had to make large contributions. In addition, even companies that had been funding regularly had unfunded liabilities because of the bear market and had to step up to fund them. Between the end of 1972 and the end of 1974, the assets of private noninsured pension plans declined by $40.5 billion—from $156 billion to $115.5 billion. This was a large hole to fill.[21]

The fiduciary standards set new rules for the behavior of anyone having "any discretionary authority or control respecting management or disposition of a plan's assets, or renders investment advice for a fee or other compensation, direct or indirect, with respect to monies or other property of such plan." Anyone having discretionary administrative authority or responsibility for a plan was also a fiduciary. But the key new rule was a revision of the Prudent Man Rule, the rule that had previously set the standard for investment behavior. The new Prudent Man Rule, which some called a "prudent expert rule," declared: "Fiduciaries are required to discharge their duties with respect to the fund solely in the interests of the participants and their beneficiaries, and with the care, skill, prudence and diligence under the circumstances then prevailing that a prudent man, acting in a like capacity and familiar with such matters, would use in the conduct of an enterprise of like character and with like aims." The new standard rested on a phrase not found in the earlier "Prudent Man Rule." This is the phrase: *"and familiar with such matters."* The fiduciary was not to be held to the standard of how a common layperson acting as a trustee might act, but how an investment professional might act, a far higher standard. In addition, the law seemed to say that the risk level of an investment did not alone make it *per se* prudent or *per se* imprudent. It all depended on how that investment, its risk level and its expected return, fitted within the overall portfolio in meeting the objectives of the plan.

In addition, fiduciaries were specifically directed to diversify the investments (except in the case of employer securities purchased for a profit-sharing plan, stock bonus plan, or thrift and savings plan) "so as to minimize the risk of large losses, unless under the circumstances it was prudent not to do so." The fiduciaries had to make their decisions and act "solely in the interest of the participants and beneficiaries," which, in effect, told fiduciaries to avoid conflicts of interest. They could not serve two masters. The law also contained a list of actions, called *prohibited transactions*, which fiduciaries were forbidden to do. For example, fiduciaries could not use plan assets for their own purposes. They could not transfer plan assets to a party-in-interest (for example, the employer). To back up the rules and prohibitions, fiduciaries were made personally liable for any losses the plan suffered for any breach they were involved in, or which they should have known about. However, plan trustees were specifically authorized to delegate their responsibilities, but they had to monitor the actions of those to whom they delegated.

According to Michael Gordon, the minority counsel on the Senate Labor Committee, it became clear during the drafting of ERISA, with inflation rising, that the common law trust principles of fiduciary investing were not well suited for dealing with employee pension funds, the benefits of which were constantly being improved. What was required was a more flexible, and yet a more demanding system. That is what the New Prudent Man standard was designed to be. "The legislative history, and everything else that the courts have adopted, make it clear that the duties of prudence, the prudent investor standards, are to be considered in the light of the special needs and circumstances of private employee benefit plans."

According to Gordon, the banks and other institutional investors made it clear to Congress during hearings on the bill that if they were to be judged on the basis of each individual security in a portfolio they would be paralyzed. Although Modern Portfolio Theory (MPT) was just becoming widely known and accepted, the investment management community pushed for an MPT interpretation of prudence—that the fiduciary be judged on the results of the whole portfolio, not on the results of each individual investment in a portfolio. This built on the work of Markowitz and Sharpe which maintained that risky investments could be combined in such a way as to to produce a low-risk portfolio. This was not, however, clearly stated in ERISA, and not until the Labor Department issued an interpretive bulletin in 1989 clearly laying out this interpretation did pension funds and their managers feel comfortable with higher-risk investments such as venture capital.

Another important aspect of ERISA was the rule allowing fiduciaries to delegate fiduciary responsibility. As long as the fiduciaries delegated to professional investment managers registered with the Securities & Exchange Commission (SEC), they were largely off the hook, though they did have to monitor the actions of those to whom they delegated. This section of ERISA encouraged the hiring of investment management firms and discouraged internal investment management. However, a few large funds, such as U.S. Steel and General Electric, which had built up and could afford to maintain professional internal staffs, continued to manage their assets internally. It caused heartburn for many money management firms which had resisted registering with the SEC. Before ERISA, they did not have to register as long as they managed 15 or fewer clients. After ERISA, if they wanted to keep any pension fund clients they had, they were required to register. Bob Evans, assistant treasurer at J. P. Penney, called Jay Sherrerd, principal at Miller, Anderson and Sherrerd, one of Penney's money managers, and asked him facetiously how he was going to make a living now. "What do you mean?" Sherrerd asked. "Well, since you're not registered we're going to have to fire you," Evans replied, pointing out ERISA's requirement. Miller, Anderson and Sherrerd, like most such managers, quickly registered with the SEC. ERISA also required all pension funds to develop and maintain an investment policy statement. According to Gordon, the main purpose of this written investment policy was to get the fiduciaries to think about what they were doing. It had the secondary effect of encouraging the corporate pension executives to seek the assistance of consultants and money managers to draw up and execute these policy statements.

Over the next two years, as ERISA's provisions were phased in, pension executives hired investment management consultants not only to help draw up the required investment policy, but also to help them review the performance of their current managers and select new or additional money managers. After all, they were now personally liable if the fund was improperly managed, so if a manager was underperforming, it had to be replaced. Even if the current managers were performing adequately, ERISA required diversification, and that seemed to mean diversification by asset class (stocks, bonds, and perhaps real estate) and investment management style (growth, value, large-cap, mid-cap, or small-cap). A raft of consultant and new manager hirings followed. Hiring additional managers often caused no disruption to good-performing existing managers because companies stepped up their funding contributions, meaning the new managers could be given the new assets to manage. Although investment management consulting firms such as the Frank Russell Co., Evaluation Associates, and Callan Associates may have defined the investment management styles of managers, ERISA imprinted them on the U.S. investment management scene. But ERISA greatly increased pension costs in several ways. First, it required funding of pension liabilities over 30 years. Some companies had not been funding or had been doing so over 100 years. This change alone greatly increased costs for many companies. Second, companies had to pay an insurance premium of $1.50 per year per employee to the Pension Benefit Guaranty Corp. Third, costs for fund monitoring by consultants and actuaries increased. Fourth, ERISA called for more detailed (and hence more expensive) reporting by companies about their funds to the Labor Department and the IRS. Finally, ERISA made fiduciaries personally liable if something went wrong in the fund.

As 1975 began, the bear market was over, but few recognized the fact and the axe continued to fall ever more rapidly on poorly performing managers, especially banks. Atlantic Richfield hired seven new managers for its $650 million fund, including five investment counseling firms, while dropping Chase Manhattan and Scudder, Stevens & Clark.[22] P&I's survey of the investment performance of 33 of the top banks in 1974 did not help matters as the equity fund of the best performing bank in the survey, Chemical Bank, New York, was down 20.6% for the year, and the worst performer, U. S. Trust Co., New York, was down 34.2%, while the S&P 500 Index was down 26.5%.[23] At the same time, the impact of the bear market on the companies sponsoring the plans became more evident as Pensions & Investments reported the company contributions to the plans at the end of 1973 were $5.6 billion, up 6% from 1972, as companies began to make good some of the market's impact on asset values.[24] The contributions would have been even larger had not actuarial consultants helped reduce the impact of the bear market by smoothing and by raising the actuarial earnings assumptions. This latter move had the effect of reducing the size of the unfunded pension liabilities.

The first half of the 1970s was traumatic for pension fund executives and their fund's money managers. It was a period of volatile stock and bond markets, which threw old ways of investing into question. It was a period also of rapid change and much innovation, and a time when many of the tools and techniques such as performance measurement, manager style classification, index funds, and use of beta as a risk measure, that shape investing today by institutions and individuals, were either developed or widely adopted. And, too, it was the period of ERISA, which introduced a concept of prudence that has been adopted not only by pension funds but by most other kinds of institutional investors as well. The foundations of the investment world as we know it today were laid in this period.

Chapter 7

Realty Revolution

ERISA was another stage in the revolution, and while pension fund executives were digesting it and trying to come to terms with its implications, they were also still trying to adjust to the bear market which had severely damaged their pension funds. Noninsured pension assets had dropped to $115.5 billion at the end of 1974 from $156 billion at the end of 1972. The value of the funds' common stocks had dropped to $62.3 billion from $115.2 billion in the same period.[1] As a result, pension executives were looking for alternative investments. Bonds were no solution. Bond prices also had been hit as interest rates continued to climb, driven by rising inflation. When interest rates rise, bond prices fall, often enough to offset the interest payments, so that the total return, the interest payment plus or minus the change in bond value, can be negative. In 1973, for example, the total return on long-term government bonds was –1.1%, and in 1974 it was only 4.4%. Long-term corporate bond returns in 1973 and 1974 were 1.1% and –3.1%, respectively—a lot better than stocks but not really satisfactory.[2] As a result, pension executives were looking for alternatives, investments that would be more stable than stocks and bonds or at least would not be affected by the same economic forces at the same time. They didn't know it at the time, but by the time President Gerald Ford signed ERISA the bear market in stocks was almost over. Only a few investment executives recognized the fact. One of them, Robert G. Wade, executive vice president of Drexel Burnham & Co. who would later head Chancellor Capital Management, the successful investment management subsidiary of Citibank, declared in a speech in July that the bear market was at a bottom and that it was time to buy stocks again.[3] The bear market was just beginning for bonds, however.

Real Estate

One place the funds were looking for relief from the bear market was real estate. A few funds had invested in real estate before the bear market, those of U.S. Steel and General Electric being leaders. By late 1974, General Electric had 14 years of experience investing in real estate, mostly through purchasing office buildings, warehouses, and manufacturing facilities, and leasing them back to the sellers, and it had about $480 million so invested. Too often, however, plan sponsors' investment in real estate involved the pension fund buying corporate property, and often the deal benefited the employer as much as, or sometimes more than, the pension fund. For example, in 1963 Genesco Inc. had sold to the Genesco Retirement Trust for $47 million 347 retail properties that it had acquired when it bought the S.S. Kress chain of department stores. By 1973, however, one-third of the stores were unprofitable, and Genesco announced it would close them. Because the stores were in declining neighborhoods, the properties had declined in value, and the pension fund was faced with a heavy loss. Given the hearings about pension abuses that had been held in Congress leading up to the passage of ERISA, there was little surprise when Genesco announced it would buy back from the pension trust the stores it was closing at no loss to the fund.[4] It also planned to sell the remaining, profitable, S.S. Kress stores as going concerns, and it would protect the pension fund against losses on those sales also. The entire Genesco deal would have been prohibited had ERISA been in effect. But such investment of pension fund assets in corporate real estate, though not common, was not unheard of either. More broadly diversified real estate investing was rare before 1973.

Now, however, because of the advent of PRISA and the missionary work of Meyer Melnikoff and his colleagues, real estate had become an alternative that many funds were considering. By July 1974, 34 of the 100 largest corporate plans were investing in real estate, excluding mortgage investing. Of the 34, 19 were clients of PRISA or its clones offered by Equitable Life, the First National Bank of Chicago, or Wachovia Bank & Trust, or owned shares in real estate investment trusts (REITS). Other funds were actively seeking to invest in real estate. For example, in July 1974 the Nevada State Public Employees Retirement System announced that it would seek legislative approval in 1975 to invest part of its $250 million in assets in real estate.[5] The executive officer of the fund, Vernon Bennett, said at the time that the trustees needed legislative approval and hoped to invest 5% to 10% of the assets in real estate.

By July 1974, PRISA had assets of $450 million from 85 clients, each of which pumped at least $100,000 into the fund each quarter and paid a quarterly management fee of one-fourth of 1%. For the 12-month period ended March 31, 1974, PRISA returned 9.6% compared with a loss of 12% of the S&P 500 Index and a loss of 2.5% of the Salomon Brothers bond index. During 1973 alone, PRISA's acquisitions included 69 industrial properties in the Chicago area, a 15-storey office building in San Francisco, two medical buildings in Atlanta, a shopping center in Kansas City, an industrial complex in Dallas, and an industrial development in Seattle.[6]

But PRISA no longer had the field to itself by 1973. At least four major insurance companies and several banks had established real estate separate accounts or commingled funds. Equitable Life Assurance Society of the U.S., which took in its first client in August 1973, had about $30 million under management by July 1974. Metropolitan Life started its account in 1972 but was not marketing it aggressively and had assets of only $2.5 million by July 1974. Met Life officials were concerned about property prices being too high. New England Mutual Life Insurance Co. of Boston also started its separate account in 1972 but had only about $4.5 million in assets. New England's approach was to invest only 20% of the equity directly in real property, the remainder going into mortgages. John Hancock Mutual Life, on the other hand, had $70 million in its separate account but likewise was putting only a small account into direct real estate investments.[7] Banks also were getting into the real estate investment business.

After Wachovia, the first bank to start a real estate fund was First National Bank of Chicago which established its fund, called Fund F because it was the sixth of the banks' commingled trust funds, in 1972. In 1970, the bank had bought a real estate consulting firm called Real Estate Research Corp. (RERC) because it was available and the price seemed right, not for any specific purpose. In the next two years, however, it noticed that RERC was putting a number of the bank's trust clients into real estate. Clearly, a demand had arisen for real estate investment expertise from pension funds, and there was no reason it should go to other institutions, so the bank started its real estate fund. It made its first investment, in a multitenant housing project in suburban Cincinnati, in September 1973; by July 1974 it had gained 32 pension and profit-sharing fund clients, and had about $65 million invested.[8]

In the southeast, Wachovia found itself in a battle with arch-rival North Carolina National Bank, and Citizens & Southern National Bank in Atlanta. Wachovia had a head start and by 1974 had $12 million in its commingled real estate fund, invested in such assets as industrial properties in Chicago and Phoenix, an office in Garden Grove, California, and a manufacturing facility in Melbourne, Florida.[9] Although most pension funds preferred the commingled or pooled approach, where they owned parts of a number of properties along with other pension funds and therefore had more diversification than they could achieve alone, some banks persisted investing their clients in real estate individually. And some did it at the behest of the clients. Wachovia, besides its commingled fund, managed a separate real estate account for Southern Bell Telephone Co.'s $550 million pension fund. By mid-1975, this account had assets of $30 million in 10 properties, including a $7.5 million half-million square-foot 51-store shopping mall in Atlanta and a $12 million 26-acre industrial and office park also in Atlanta.[10] U.S. Trust in New York had put $25 million of clients' assets into individual real estate deals by 1974, and the First National Bank of Dallas also pursued the individual direct approach.

Some pension funds preferred the direct approach. Besides the U.S. Steel and General Electric funds, the FMC Corp. pension fund, then with $300 million in assets, was among the first to invest directly in real estate when it bought a 2,800-acre ranch in south central Texas, near Austin. FMC's intent was to hold the land for future development and in the meantime lease it for cattle grazing to pay the taxes.[11] Even British pension funds were getting into U.S. real estate in 1974 as in September, Atlanta's Citizens & Southern National Bank won the assignment to invest $12 million in properties in the southeast for five U.K. funds, including the British Post Office Pension Fund, the British Railways Pension Fund, and the British Steel Corp. Pension Fund,[12] and in mid-1975 the British Post Office fund also hired Heitman Group of Chicago to find U.S. properties for it.

Just a few months later, Travelers Insurance Co. announced that it had established a new real estate separate account.[13] And in San Francisco, Claude Rosenberg, senior partner of the successful Rosenberg Capital Management, announced that his firm was starting a real estate investment arm to invest only in established properties.[14] Rosenberg had hired a three-man staff, headed by Paul Sack, a real estate veteran, and within a year it had two clients, a longshoremen's union fund and the pension fund of Pacific Telephone & Telegraph, totaling $16 million. Soon after it had grown to almost $30 million, and by mid-1975 it was at $50 million. Meanwhile, New York Telephone's Shultz had put $2 million of the fund's $1.2 billion assets into agricultural land.[15]

Prudential's PRISA, however, was turning down some accounts by mid-1975 because it could not find a sufficient number of good properties. Meyer Melnikoff blamed a decline in short-term interest rates which, he said, encouraged people to hold on to buildings they otherwise would have had to put on the market. First Chicago's Fund F also was having the same difficulty finding quality properties.[16] It had grown to $80 million by midyear and had begun to slow the rate at which it accepted new clients. By mid-1975 most of the 100 largest corporate pension funds had either made initial commitments to real estate or were studying the asset. It would be tough going for the next several years because there was relatively little nonresidential construction in the mid-1970s because of high interest rates, high inflation, and weak economic conditions. Corporations were not expanding their manufacturing or office facilities. In fact, rents for office and warehouse space were down in major cities. At the same time, pension funds were trying to pour significant amounts into the asset through a number of real estate managers such as PRISA and Fund F; as a result, yields on the investments were declining. PRISA had assets of $857 million by early 1977 but had found it increasingly difficult to find worthwhile investments and so had taken on no new clients since September 1975. Other funds were also restricting their intake of new clients.[17]

The acceptance of real estate as an appropriate asset class was accelerated by the missionary work of the investment consultants, especially the Frank Russell Co. As early as 1970, George Russell had urged pension funds to invest in real estate in a speech to the Treasurer's Club of New York and had hired his first real estate consultant, Blake Eagle, in 1971. Eagle, in the early 1980s, enlisted the help of 14 investment management firms to help create indexes to measure the performance of real estate investments and real estate managers. The founding members of the National Council of Real Estate Investment Fiduciaries, as the group became known, were asked to submit property performance data from December 31, 1977 forward. The initial index contained data on 233 properties valued at $581 million. By 1998 the index tracked 1,622 properties valued at $21.9 billion.[18]

Seeking Guarantees

Not content with one alternative to equities and bonds, by late 1974 pension funds also were seriously considering another alternative, the guaranteed interest contract (GIC) offered by insurance companies. The GIC, a variation on the insurance industry's annuity contracts, promised the investor a guaranteed interest rate on the money invested for a number of years, often three or five, but occasionally 10, and return of principle at the end of the period. In this respect it was like a bond. But the GIC was essentially a private bond issued by the insurance company to the investor, backed by the general account assets of the insurance company. It had no market value and thus suffered no market value fluctuations when general interest rates changed. It never showed a loss of value; it always showed a gain equal to the guaranteed rate. This made it a popular investment for thrift or savings plans, as plan sponsors did not like their employees to experience negative returns on the thrift plan assets. Of course, the guarantee of the interest and principal was only as strong as the insurance company underwriting it, something plan sponsors and individuals lost sight of over the years, a development that 15 years down the road would impose a cost. Toward the end of 1974 some plan sponsors were investing in GICs not only for their thrift plans, but also for their defined benefit plans.

In September 1974, Leo M. Walsh Jr., vice president of pensions at Equitable Life, could report to *Pensions & Investments* that the insurance company had sold some $50 million of GICs to defined benefit plans and $100 million to thrift plans.[19] Most GIC contracts, he said, were of the 5- or 10-year variety. In the first half of 1975, as the extent of the market debacle of 1974 became clear, almost half of the pension business picked up by six of the major insurance companies was for GICs. Metropolitan Life reported gaining 85 new clients and $143 million in assets, of which $59 million—41%—was for GICs carrying rates between 8.5% and 9%. Such a rate was very appealing to pension fund executives who had seen the market decline by 14.7% in 1973 and 26.5% in 1974. At the same time, Travelers Corp. reported $250 million of new pension business in the first six months of 1975, $140 million of it for GICs. Similarly, John Hancock Mutual Life reported $250 million in new pension business, with at least $150 million of it for GICs.[20] By the end of 1975, Equitable's Walsh was reporting that the insurance company had gained $1 billion in new pension business for the year, about 45% of it being in GICs; most of it was from profit-sharing or thrift plans, though about $100 million was from defined benefit plans.[21]

In March 1976, Crown Zellerbach Corp., the San Francisco-based forest products company, shook the pension world when it announced it was moving two-thirds of its $225 million in pension assets into guaranteed investment contracts with Travelers Insurance, the Prudential and Mutual Life Insurance Co. of New York.[22] The GICs offered rates between 8.75% and 9.5% for periods up to 10 years. At the same time, the company dropped Batterymarch Financial Management, BEA Associates, Fayez Sarofim & Associates, and Rosenberg Capital Management. Crown Zellerbach said that it would hire two new equity managers for the remaining equity assets and that a bond portfolio would remain with Bankers Trust Co. The move was prompted by concerns about ERISA's prudence and fiduciary liability standards. Crown Zellerbach had named its board of directors as the "named fiduciary" required under ERISA. Members of the board therefore were concerned about fiduciary liability. Under ERISA, as mentioned earlier, fiduciaries could be sued personally to make up any losses that might occur because ERISA's standards were breached. No wonder the board members wanted to invest conservatively.

Opportunities Overseas

One other investment a few pension funds and money managers began considering in the middle of the bear market was non-U.S. securities, particularly stocks. Though some markets had followed the U.S. market down, especially in the immediate aftermath of the 1973–1974 oil crisis, not all did, and even among those that did, not all were hit as hard as the United States, and some recovered more quickly. Moreover, some investors had noted that certain quality companies outside the United States were highly competitive with U.S. companies. The U.S. Steel & Carnegie and the General Electric pension funds in the 1960s invested in selected non-U.S. stocks. Some money managers were buying stocks of such companies for their clients in the late 1960s. One of them was Capital Guardian Trust, which had hired a young Dutch citizen, Ken Harrison Mathiessen-Gerst. Mathiessen-Gerst had grown up in Indonesia and spoke nine languages. He also had attended the Harvard Business School.

When Mathiessen-Gerst married a Swiss woman and wanted to move to Switzerland, the Capital Group arranged for him to open an office in Geneva in 1963 to research European companies and keep an eye on U.S. companies like General Motors and International Business Machines which were beginning to earn significant parts of their earnings in Europe. Mathiessen-Gerst also hired a young woman, Nilly Sikorsky, and between them they researched and published *Capital International Perspectives*, giving research on all the major companies outside the United States. They also started two unit trusts, one in Italy and one in the United Kingdom. By the early 1970s many Capital Guardian pension clients had non-U.S. stocks in their portfolios, giving the company a head start when pension funds turned their attention to international securities. In 1974 the *Financial Analysts Journal* ran an article by Bruno Solnik, assistant professor of business at Stanford University, which examined the correlations between U.S. stocks and non-U.S. stocks. Solnik found that diversified international stock portfolios were likely to carry less risk than diversified domestic equity portfolios.[23] This paper and others that followed laid the intellectual framework for international diversification by U.S. investors.

Like the Capital Group, Morgan Guaranty had been seeking and buying quality non-U.S. stocks such as Unilever and Deutsche Bank for some of its pension clients on a selective basis since the 1950s, integrating them into the clients' portfolios but usually only for 1 or 2 percent of the assets. This early move into international stocks had been driven by Longstreet Hinton, Morgan's chief investment officer, who had also pushed the bank early into stocks and finally into growth stocks. Hinton had decided that stocks offered investors better prospects in the long run than bonds and so had pushed up the equity allocations of clients' accounts. He then had decided that an investor could afford to pay a premium for companies with a rapidly growing stream of earnings, not only in the United States, but anywhere they could be found. A Morgan portfolio manager could buy any stock he wanted, as long as he could win the approval of Hinton and the investment committee. That meant running the gauntlet of Hinton's sharp mind and acerbic wit. Fear of Hinton's questioning made Morgan's portfolio managers very sure of themselves before they proposed a purchase or sale. Hinton allowed, and even encouraged, Morgan's portfolio managers to consider top-quality growth stocks wherever they could find them— even overseas.

The international investing by Capital Guardian and Morgan was hampered after 1963 by the introduction of the Interest Equalization Tax, designed to help the U.S. balance of payments by reducing the outflow of dollars into foreign investments. This changed when President Richard M. Nixon lifted the tax on January 29, 1974, reopening the doors to international investing. However, the road was still not clear. ERISA seemed to prohibit, or at least make questionable, international investing because it required that "the indicia of ownership" of fund assets remain within the jurisdiction of federal courts. Morgan, Fiduciary Trust, and First National Bank of Chicago, all had international funds up and ready to run, or on the verge of launching, but only Morgan pushed ahead.

Morgan had established an international equities commingled fund "for future use" in late 1973 and by January 1974 had been running it with assets of about $4 million. The fund had been started by Harrison Smith, who was head of Morgan's pension investment department and who had appointed Karl Van Horn as the fund's first portfolio manager. Van Horn was a logical choice in that he had an international background. After getting an engineering degree from Yale, graduating in 1957, he then attended Cambridge University for his master's degree in political philosophy and economics and later took a master's degree at Johns Hopkins University in Baltimore. He joined Morgan in 1961, one of only eight trainees the bank took that year.

Van Horn chose the investment department as the place he wanted to spend his career because Morgan's trust investment department, under Hinton, was at the forefront of investment thinking at the time. Markowitz's paper remained almost unknown, even in academic circles, and Sharpe was just working on his Capital Asset Pricing Model. In 1964 Van Horn was sent to London, and in 1969 to Japan, returning to New York in 1972 to join the pension department.

In the pension department, Van Horn worked under Harrison Smith who believed that international equities offered diversification and risk control—just the point made by the Solnik article—and that all of Morgan's pension clients should be diversified internationally. ERISA was coming, but Smith believed that international investing would help fulfill ERISA's likely mandate that pension funds be diversified. He also believed that ERISA would not prohibit trust banks from investing their clients' assets overseas because most large trust banks had offices in the major countries. Smith decided to be proactive in his belief in international investing. Soon after ERISA was signed, he sent Van Horn and Davis Polk, Morgan's inhouse counsel, to Washington to talk to the Labor Department about whether or not ERISA in fact prohibited international investing. They were told that it did not. As long as the securities were held in the branch offices of the bank overseas, they were within the reach of the U.S. courts, which is what ERISA required. Armed with that opinion, Smith called a meeting of the trust investments committee, presented his idea of investing part of the pension assets of every pension client in the commingled international fund, and asked for opinions. Carl Hathaway, Smith's second in command, declared: "This is a disaster. It's doomed to failure, and I'm not going to have any part of it." Others around the table agreed with Hathaway.

But Smith was not dissuaded. He responded: "Well, gentlemen, in my considered view, it's something we must do. This is as important a juncture as when we went from bonds into stocks in the '50s." Smith had Van Horn draft a letter to all of Morgan's more than 400 clients for whom it had full discretion, saying that if they did not object in writing, Morgan would put 1% of their equity funds' assets into international securities beginning on January 1, 1975. The letter spelled out all of the rationales for international, especially the diversification argument. There was almost no objection from the clients. There were a few phone calls, said Van Horn, but no one withdrew permission in writing, and so the commitment was made.

The first month Van Horn had $100 million to invest. "The whole issue was making country bets," he said. "There were no sector bets. You had to decide whether to be in a market, or out of it, and if you were in, then you bought the liquid stocks. We worked very hard on country and currency. Our view was that Japan would survive and export its way out of the oil crisis." Van Horn called the head of Morgan's Japan office in Tokyo and asked him for a list of the largest exporters in Japan. He then put 60% of the assets of the fund into the stocks of 20 Japanese exporting companies. The first year the fund was up 40% in dollar terms; the next year it was up 70%; and by 1978 it had grown to more than $800 million. Van Horn managed the fund for four years until he moved to London to head J. P. Morgan's international investment operation in 1979.

While Morgan was quietly acting, most trust banks considering moving into international investing were waiting for the Labor Department's approval. First National Bank of Chicago had established its international commingled fund, Fund G., in the Fall of 1974 with a token $1 million, but was awaiting the Labor Department's clearance before actively marketing it. Similarly, Fiduciary Trust Co. of New York, which had gained international investment experience managing the assets of the non-ERISA covered United Nations pension fund, was also holding off marketing its fund, awaiting the Labor Department's ruling, which seemed to be close. They would wait, however, until mid-December 1976, when the Labor Department finally proposed a regulation that allowed the "indicia of ownership"—the stock and bond certificates—to be held by the offshore offices of U.S. trust banks (exactly what Morgan had been told informally). While some pension funds were interested in international investing, others were not rushing in. Gary B. Bland, manager of trust investments at Boeing Corp., told *Pensions & Investments* in October 1975 that: "It's hard enough to know about your own markets; when you start talking about foreign investment, you have to hire somebody who is a specialist." Norman B. Williamson, assistant treasurer at FMC Corp., said: "There are values over there and also here, but you can identify value better here."[24]

Once again, the Frank Russell Co. was a proponent of funds diversifying into international investing. In the same Treasurer's Club speech in which he had advocated real estate investing, George Russell had also urged international investing. He began making inquiries about money managers outside the United States in 1970, and he had Peter Dietz, who was teaching in Belgium in 1971, interview money managers in the United Kingdom and Europe. By 1979 the interest in international investing by U.S. pension funds was serious enough for the Frank Russell Co. to open an office in London, headed by Jan Twardowski. It was Twardowski's job to research European money managers using the same methodology the company used in the United States.

In the meantime, a new consulting firm was established, one that was focused solely on international investing. InterSec Research Corp. was established in September 1975 by Chris Nowakowski to supply research and other services to investors investing internationally. Polish-born, Canadian-bred Nowakowski spent 12 years with the Canadian brokerage firm of Wood, Gundy Inc. before deciding to set up his own firm. Inter-Sec provided guidance on international investing to both pension funds and money managers and proved to be a strong advocate of international investing. In addition, the firm kept track of how much money U.S. pension funds had invested overseas, and which funds had done so, and its reports about how much was being invested overseas helped stir other funds to make the plunge. As many consultants and money managers had found over the years, except for a few pioneering pension fund executives, the first question most fund executives asked when presented with a new idea was: "Who else is doing it?" InterSec was able to answer that question.

Mayday! Mayday!

On May 1, 1975, a seismic event shook the securities world when the New York Stock Exchange abolished fixed commissions. Henceforth, the commission paid by an investor for all transactions carried out by a broker would be negotiated between them. It meant brokers could compete on price. It also threw into doubt the whole world of "soft dollars" which investors had used to pay for research and other services provided by brokers and others. For example, an independent consulting firm might be paid in cash not from the fund that was its client, but from a broker to which the fund had directed additional brokerage transactions from its money managers. That is, the broker got more business from the fund, and it passed on at least part of the payment for that additional business to the consultant.

Soft dollar payment for services had several advantages for the pension executive. First, the executive could buy services for the fund without using corporate money. The executive did not need to ask his or her boss to approve a large expenditure, for example, for consulting help. The fund was generating commissions through its managers' trading activities, and those commissions could be used to pay for the consulting services if the trades were directed to particular brokers. Second, the fund got the advantage of any rebate of commissions from the favored brokers. If the fund did not use those commission refunds (i.e., the soft dollars), the money managers could, and often did, use them to buy research and other services for themselves. One possible disadvantage was that the broker to whom the commissions were directed might not trade as efficiently as the manager's first choice, thus costing the fund money by causing it to pay too much or receive too little for a stock. However, this was a hidden cost, very difficult to measure even today. The "soft dollar" payment was easy to calculate when commissions were fixed, and much more difficult when every trade was negotiated. Moreover, ERISA could be interpreted as saying any trade had to be done at the lowest possible price. Did that leave any room to pass on part of the commission payment to the consultant or other vendor? On February 19 there was a ray of hope that "soft dollars" would survive when Senator Harrison Williams (D-New Jersey), one of the principal drafters of ERISA, submitted an amendment to a securities regulation bill then passing through Congress specifically authorizing pension funds to use soft dollars to pay for research.

At least one leading consulting firm split up over the question of whether soft dollar payments would survive, and if they did, whether a consulting firm could survive in a negotiated commission environment without either its own strong trading execution capabilities or a close affiliation with a firm that had such capabilities. John O'Brien, Gil Beebower, and Richard Ennis left O'Brien Associates to join A. G. Becker & Co., while Dennis and Suzanne Tito, Larry Cuneo, and Wayne Wagner acquired control of the firm, which was soon renamed Wilshire Associates. For a time the O'Brien Associates owners had considered selling the firm to Becker, but Tito and the others became convinced when Senator Williams introduced his amendment that the firm could survive on its own. O'Brien, still concerned, left to join Becker to head its pension consulting unit, started only a year before.

Tito, a quantitative whiz who had designed and programmed the trajectory of the Mariner IV space probe to Mars when he was 23 years old and the Mariner V trajectory at 25, and the holder of a Ph.D. in finance from UCLA, was regarded as the main architect of O'Brien Associates O'Brien 5000 Index and its asset/liability model. O'Brien Associates, renamed Wilshire Associates, went on to become one of the leading quantitatively oriented investment consulting firms serving pension funds and money management organizations. Initially, Wilshire Associates, like O'Brien Associates before it, was mainly selling its beta services to money management firms, offering them online services by which they could analyze portfolios and better understand their sensitivity to market risk and begin to implement portfolio optimization—building portfolios that produced the highest returns for a given level of risk.

The firm also developed a performance attribution model that allowed managers or pension executives to see where a portfolio manager's performance was coming from and to see if he or she was adding value through stock selection. At this time, said Tito, most of the firm's clients were money management organizations trying to better understand what they were doing. The big breakthrough for Wilshire with pension funds was the asset/liability modeling product for which New York Telephone's Shultz was one of the first buyers. The model took all of the demographic and actuarial assumptions about the plan—salary growth, employment growth, employee turnover, mortality, and so on—and used them to project liabilities ahead 20 years, year by year. It then simulated 1,000 different market scenarios to see the impact of different market environments on the plan's funded status, given different investment strategies. The message to pension clients was that the strategic asset allocation decision—how much should be in the various asset classes, stocks, bonds, real estate, and so on, over the long term—was the most important decision for a pension fund's long-term financial health.

Early in 1975 the Frank Russell Co., concerned about the soft dollar issue and ERISA, required all its clients to pay cash for its services, as did Callan Associates. By the time the Williams Amendment became law in mid-1975, however, with the passage of the Securities Acts Amendments of 1975, most money managers and pension funds had decided that because of the huge discounts from previous commissions most brokers were negotiating, there was little chance of them being sued for overpaying in soft dollars for research. In effect, the concern over soft dollars had evaporated. The consulting firms that had mandated cash payments from clients were relaxing their stands and beginning to move back toward soft dollar payment when the client preferred it. The greatest impact of May Day's negotiated commissions was a huge drop in transactions costs for money managers and their clients as discounts as high as 50% from previous levels became common.

Better Numbers

By mid-1975 the stock market was advancing strongly. Some money managers were reporting first-half total returns greater than 30%, and for the year as a whole the market would return 37%, confirming that the bear market was over. It was purely coincidental that Roger Ibbotson, a finance professor at the University of Chicago, and Rex Sinquefield, the index fund pioneer at American National Bank and Trust in Chicago, published their seminal study of the long-term historic returns of stocks, bonds, Treasury bills, and inflation at this time. The Ibbotson and Sinquefield study, as it has become known, examined the returns of the three asset classes from the beginning of 1926 to the end of 1974. They found that over that period, which encompassed the Great Depression as well as the bull market of the 1950s and 1960s, common stock total returns (market gains plus dividends) had averaged 8.5% compounded annually, while bonds had compound annual total returns of 3.6% and Treasury bills had compound annual returns of just 2.2%, equaling the rate of inflation for the period.

The Ibbotson and Sinquefield study updated the earlier Fisher and Lorie study, and differed from it in significant ways. Although the Fisher and Lorie study used as its stock market proxy the equal-weighted New York Stock Exchange Index of all stocks listed on the exchange, the Ibbotson and Sinquefield study constructed an index using the Standard & Poor's 500 Index methodology in which larger stocks carry more weight in the index. This partly explains the difference in equity returns between the two studies. Fisher and Lorie put the long-term return at 10.3% between 1926 and 1965, compared with Ibbotson and Sinquefield's 8.5% for the longer nine-year period 1926–1974. The bear market in the last two years of the Ibbotson and Sinquefield study would also have contributed a little to the lower returns. Ibbotson and Sinquefield used their historic data, efficient market theory, and probability analysis to project returns on the three asset classes out to the year 2000. They projected that equities would remain the best long-term investment, with annual total rates of return of 13.6% compounded. There was a 5% chance, however, that those returns could be as low as 4.9% or as high as 22.9%. Long-term government bonds were expected to return 8.4%, while Treasury bills were expected to give 7.1% compared with an expected inflation rate of 5.9% per year. Although the Ibbotson and Sinquefield projections were criticized at the time, they were not far off the mark through mid-1998.

The Ibbotson and Sinquefield study was timely and significant for two important reasons. It helped reestablish confidence in investing in equities which had been badly shaken by the 1973–1974 bear market. If equities could still show a large long-term edge over bonds after a bear market that cut the value of the Dow Jones Industrial Average and the Standard & Poor's 500 Index in half, then the case for more equity investing was strong. In addition, the study provided academically rigorous data to be used in asset/liability planning models of the kind Wilshire Associates and others were marketing to pension executives.

Pension Benefits Guaranteed

By September 1975 a new fund that was expected to grow rapidly was looking to hire a stock manager and a bond manager, and hundreds of money managers applied for the assignment. The candidates were to be reviewed by Bill Crerend's consulting group at Paine, Webber, Jackson & Curtis, soon to become Evaluation Associates. The new fund was that of the Pension Benefit Guaranty Corp. (PBGC), which was established under ERISA to pay the pensions of employees of companies that went out of business, particularly those that had underfunded pension plans. The assets of the PBGC would consist of the assets of any pension plans of companies that went out of business, as well as any assets the PBGC seized from those companies (it was entitled by law to up to 30% of the net worth of the companies), and the insurance premiums to be paid by all pension plan sponsors, at the initial rate of $1.50 per employee per year. The PBGC was looking for managers capable of managing at least $20 million each, and candidate firms had to have at least $250 million in tax-exempt assets under management as of June 30, 1975.

Steve E. Schanes, a former vice president of Martin E. Segal Co., an actuarial consulting firm, had been named executive director only two months after the passage of ERISA. Schanes had previously served as the director of the New Jersey Division of pensions which oversaw the investment of the assets backing the pensions of New Jersey public employees. He favored an investment approach that was fairly heavy into equities but not 100% in equities. Schanes resigned in February of 1976 "for personal reasons" without settling the question of how the assets would be invested and without hiring the investment managers.[25] He was replaced by Kenneth Houck, a retired Bethlehem Steel executive who had been involved in negotiating that company's first pension plan for hourly workers after the Inland Steel decision. A month later the PBGC announced that Wells Fargo Investment Advisors and Putnam Advisory Co. had been selected as equity managers, and Harris Trust and Savings Bank had been selected as the fixed income manager. State Street Bank & Trust Co., Boston, had been selected as custodian.[26] Interestingly, Wells Fargo was not selected for indexed management but was expected to concentrate on income-producing equities. The outside managers were expected to manage the assets of terminated pension plans which had been taken over by the PBGC, but not the premium income, which, by law, had to be invested in Treasury securities.

Two more years would pass before the selected managers would be free of doubt over their assignments. The Treasury Department challenged the PBGC's right to allow the outside managers to invest even the assets from the terminated plans. The challenge was led by Treasury Secretary William E. Simon, who wrote letters urging Secretary of Commerce Elliot L. Richardson and Labor Secretary William Ussery to join him in preventing the investment of the assets in non-Treasury securities. Simon was concerned about the propriety of a government agency investing in private capital markets. Allowing the PBGC to do so would create a dangerous precedent, he said, and would "inevitably lead to a qualitatively new form of erosion of barriers between public and private sectors."[27] The Labor and Commerce departments shared oversight of the PBGC with the Treasury. However, Labor and Commerce resisted, and in November 1977 the PBGC's board of directors, the secretaries of the three cabinet departments, voted unanimously to allow the assets of terminated plans to be invested in the private capital markets by outside managers.[28] When the dispute was settled, Wells Fargo Investment Advisors and Putnam Advisory Co. each managed about $8.5 million. Harris Trust & Savings Bank was to receive assets to invest in fixed income once the total assets reached $50 million. The board might have voted differently if it had waited five more months to make its decision, as the two equity managers reported relatively poor performance for 1977. Wells Fargo reported that its assets declined 7% for the year, and Putnam's declined 10.1% compared with a decline of 7.3% for the S&P 500 Index.[29] By September 1979 the PBGC was acting like any other pension fund, looking to replace the initial managers because their performance had been disappointing. Wells Fargo had failed to beat its objective, which was to achieve an investment return 10% better than that of the S&P 500, achieving a return "very close to the S&P" according to a PBGC official. Putnam had a target of besting the S&P index by 15% and also failed to achieve it.

At just about the time the outside managers were selected for the PBGC, the full impact of ERISA's stringent funding and reporting rules became clear, and the agency found itself flooded with 5,000 pension plan terminations in the first nine months after ERISA was signed. It was hit with 1,148 terminations in December 1975 alone.[30] A 1972 Treasury Department study had projected a total of only about 1,000 terminations as a result of an ERISA-type pension reform law. Since most companies established pension plans voluntarily (only a minority were the result of labor negotiations), companies were free to terminate them at any time, after setting aside money to meet the vested benefits employees had earned.

Government officials downplayed the effect of ERISA and instead blamed the poor economy of 1973–1974 for the terminations. No doubt the poor economy had some effect, but it seems unlikely that the economy caused plan terminations to be five times the number projected by optimistic Treasury officials. Even surveys of corporate executives on why they terminated their plans were unlikely to reveal the truth because it was easier and safer to blame economic conditions than to tell government officials government regulation was the cause.

By mid-1975, as the stock market was rebounding strongly, the need for an ERISA for public employee pension funds was highlighted as New York City plunged into dire fiscal crisis. Public employee pension plans were not covered by ERISA because of the constitutional doubt about whether the federal government could pass a law regulating them. In addition, politicians at state and local governments didn't want to have to find the money to meet ERISA's funding standards. As it seemed likely that New York City might go bankrupt, the Municipal Assistance Corp., a state agency, was established to help bail the city out of its crisis, and it issued bonds backed by city revenues. The New York City employees pension funds and the New York State employees funds were pressured to buy the bonds, even though the pension funds were tax exempt, as were the bonds, and even though the bonds were below investment grade. The city and state funds, under intense political pressure, agreed to buy $200 million of the bonds between them, though other public pension funds around the country refused to do so, citing the low quality and the tax exemption. When the trustees of the city and state funds balked at buying any more of the bonds, the New York State legislature mandated more purchases, forcing them to buy an additional $725 million of the securities. Arthur Levitt, the state controller, said it was a purchase he would otherwise not have made, but he had to obey the law. Although the state fund was able to resist pressure to buy even more, the city funds eventually purchased $3 billion of the securities.

New York City employees and retirees challenged the purchases in court, claiming they violated provisions in the state constitution guaranteeing safe pensions. However, the New York State Supreme Court rejected the challenge. Another challenge in federal court was also rejected. Although the public pension funds' purchases of MAC bonds would have violated ERISA if the funds were instead corporate funds, no action could be taken against the public funds. And no action could be taken today because the constitutional question, and successful campaigning by states rights advocates, have kept federal lawmakers from attempting a public fund version of ERISA. On the other hand, many states have adopted some of ERISA's standards for their own funds, either formally or informally, and the level of professionalism at state funds has risen close to that of corporate funds.

Market Timers

Mid-1975 saw a surge of manager hirings and firings by pension funds. By midyear most funds had received their performance reports for 1974 from A. G. Becker and the other pension consultants, and for the second year in a row they were not happy. For many, it was the third or fourth year in a row that they were not happy, and the urge to try a different approach was strong. A.S. Hansen & Co., an actuarial and employee benefits consulting firm, released a study that examined investment performance for the 10-year period ended December 31, 1974 and concluded: "Holding common stocks through a declining market in hopes of eventual long-term gains was not a profitable method of operation." The Hansen study also showed there was little consistency of performance by managers from one period to another. That is, the probability of a manager who was in the top 10% of all managers in one period being in the top 10% in the next period was low.[31]

Some pension executives, having looked at the results themselves, decided that the managers who had performed best during the bear market were those who had moved significantly to cash during the period. Those who remained fully invested at all times were asking for trouble. In Greenwich Research Associates' annual survey of the pension funds of the Fortune 1000 companies, pension executives said that the pension fund manager who had stayed fully invested in stocks during the bear market was not doing his job. The funds surveyed had pension assets totaling $105.5 billion and contributions of $10.8 billion. So pension executives began to make changes. Of course, the banks bore the brunt of these changes, but many investment counseling firms were also affected.

Not surprisingly, some money management firms began presenting themselves as "market timers" who would anticipate negative markets and move significantly to invest in short-term instruments, that is, cash equivalents such as Treasury bills, colloquially known as cash. In the first investment manager profile issue of *Pensions & Investments*, published in December 1974, fewer than half of the managers profiled used the words "market timing" or "balanced portfolios" (meaning they could also manage bond portfolios and would switch between stocks and bonds when appropriate) to describe their investment approach. In the second manager profile issue in August 1975, 75% of the managers used one or both of those terms to describe their investment approaches. Others used the word "flexible" as a euphemism for willingness and ability to switch out of equities when appropriate. For example, E. W. Axe & Co., an old-line mutual fund company that had moved into pension management and had $115 million in pension assets under management, declared in its profile that it "adheres to the philosophy that there is a time to own predominantly equities, but, at other times, it is smarter, and even more conservative, to be predominantly in reserves." Bankers Trust Co. said in its profile: "We also feel it is essential to maintain a flexible stance."[32]

The $120 million Kimberly Clark Corp. pension fund typified the reaction of many funds in 1975 when it hired two avowed market-timing managers, Century Capital Associates, New York, and Founders Capital Management, Denver.[33] The new managers were in addition to the existing managers and were funded out of cash flow. A similar approach was taken by Delta Air Lines' Jim Howell, who decided to change the airline fund's investment approach. Previously, the fund had been wedded to a 100% equity investment philosophy; that was changed to 80% equity and 20% fixed income. But Howell, a nonconformist, made an equity-like play with the fixed income portfolio by putting the 20% into triple-B rated bonds yielding between 10% and 11%. These bonds had similar risk and return characteristics to stocks. The lesson Howell took from the 1973–1974 bear market, according to W. Allen Reed, who worked for Howell and later ran the Delta fund, the Hughes Aircraft pension fund, and the General Motors pension funds, was that "buy and hold managers will kill you." In late 1975 Howell hired a "farm team" of 10 market-timing managers, all of whom had survived the bear market by going into cash equivalents, giving each of them $5 million. All of the 10 were small, independent money management firms, which were known at that time as "money management boutiques." They included Forstmann-Leff Associates, Stralem & Co., Atlanta Capital Management Inc., and Wall, Patterson, McGrew & Richards Inc. Howell decided to see if these managers could produce good results over the long run before committing significant amounts of money to them. The real Delta money was divided between nine other firms, including Batterymarch Financial Management, George D. Bjurman & Associates, Los Angeles, Jennison Associates, and Fayez Sarofim & Co. However, pension executives at Kimberly Clark, Delta, and other funds that hired market-timing managers found few of the managers successful over time. Market timing proved to be far more difficult than expected, and many market-timing firms had ceased to exist or had changed their approach 10 years later.

Master Trust

Delta's farm team, which was emulated later by several other large funds, and even the multiple manager structure, would have been almost impossible without the adaptation of a concept that dated back to 1951. This was the *master trust concept*. The master trust, originally called a "general trust," was a way of pooling the assets of several different plans so that each plan had identical performance. It was developed by Bankers Trust Co. to solve a problem for International Harvester Co., now Navistar Inc. Bankers Trust managed the assets of two International Harvester pension plans, a plan for salaried employees, and one for hourly workers. International Harvester was uncomfortable with the fact that the performance of the two funds differed, primarily because of the timing of the contributions to the two plans. This meant they could not always be invested in the same securities at the same prices. The bank developed a unit-value accounting system that solved the problem. In effect, it put the assets of the two plans into an internal mutual fund and divided the value of the assets into units. Then, when the company made contributions to one of the plans it could buy units in the fund without affecting the value of the underlying portfolio. The master trust became the perfect vehicle for the conglomerates of the 1960s, such as ITT and Litton Industries, which, when they acquired companies, also usually acquired pension plans.

The master trust reached its peak of development as a result of the move to multiple managers by pension funds in the 1970s. As companies moved from one bank or insurance company serving as manager for one, two, or three plans to having half-a-dozen or more managers for each plan, driven by ERISA's diversification rules and poor investment performance in the bear market, they were confronted with an explosion of relationships. ERISA required not only diversification, but also disclosure and monitoring. Money managers had to report to the pension executives regularly. The pension executives had to monitor the managers' behavior, and they had to report to the IRS and the Labor Department annually. Pension executives came to expect regular quarterly reporting from the managers. This reporting included not only what returns the managers achieved, but also all period-end holdings and transactions during the period. Thus, the pension executive would receive from each manager, on a quarterly basis, an oral report accompanied by a thick printed report. Each manager presented the information in that report in his own format. It was up to the pension executive to pull the disparate reports from the managers into a single comprehensive and comprehensible report for top management and for the IRS and Labor Department showing the overall status of the fund, the overall performance, the transactions, and the full, end-of-period holdings.

But a master trust could solve this problem. The master trustee could receive the reports from the managers quarterly, and later daily, and pull them together, pre-digesting them, for the pension executive. The big trust banks, such as Bankers Trust, were among the first institutions to invest heavily in computers in order to keep track of their corporate loans and their thousands of trust accounts. So they were far better equipped to receive and massage the reports from the managers into a comprehensive whole. Even so, the concept of the master trust was a tough sell initially, according to Michael L. Costa, principal of the Alliance of Fiduciary Consultants, a pioneer in the development of master trusts and author of *Master Trust—Simplifying Employee Benefits Trust Administration.*[34] In part, this was because when companies dropped a bank as a pension fund manager, they often left it custody of the assets as a "consolation prize." Often these banks were the lenders to the corporation. It was politically difficult to recommend that the corporation now fire its custody banks, which were the corporate lenders, and hire a single master trustee.

The passage of ERISA broke the logjam. ERISA's reporting, disclosure, and monitoring requirements made a master trust virtually irresistible to any fund that had hired multiple managers. The task of reporting and monitoring quickly got out of hand without one. Even for trust banks with their computing power, a master trust was still a difficult chore in the mid-1970s as trading volume picked up. The money managers reported each trade on behalf of every client to the appropriate master trustee (or custodians if there was no master trustee) by phone and confirmed it with a letter. During that decade there were no fax and no computer-to-computer reporting as there are today. The successful master trustee needed a decent computerized accounting system, and it had to be extremely careful about the inputs. "And you were careful about your inputs," said Costa, "by managing the money managers, and insisting they didn't send you garbage. By constantly auditing." Often, Costa said, a money manager would report to the master trustee it had sold 1,000 shares of a stock for a fund when the fund only held 800. The master trustee had to reconcile the discrepancy. Among the first pension funds to avail themselves of the new master trust service for multiple management arrangements were Martin Marietta, Litton Industries, and National Cash Register (later NCR Inc.).

The Martin Marietta fund was overseen by its assistant treasurer, Richard Lohrer, who was an early adopter of multiple nonbank managers. Within six months of joining Martin Marietta in 1971, Lohrer had consolidated the company's three pension plans into a master trust with Bankers Trust. He had also hired the Boston Co. and Loomis Sayles & Co. as investment managers while dropping Chase Manhattan and taking money from Connecticut General Life Insurance. A year later he had added

Alliance Capital Management, the Boston Co., Capital Guardian Trust Co., Jennison Associates, Morgan Guaranty, and State Street Research & Management for the $260 million fund. In 1974, however, Martin Marietta decided to move its headquarters out of New York to Maryland, a location that had no appeal to Lohrer. Instead, he took a job as treasurer of Northrop Corp. in Los Angeles, where he proceeded to shake up that company's $150 million pension fund in a similar manner, dropping a number of banks, including Chase again, and again hiring Bankers Trust as master trustee. The nonbank managers hired included Capital Guardian Trust, Fisher, Francis, Trees & Watts, a fixed income specialist, Putnam Management Co., and Rosenberg Capital Management.

The two pioneers in developing the master trust business were Bankers Trust and Chase Manhattan, both of which began in the 1950s. But it was not long before other large trust banks upgraded their custody services to compete in the master trust business. One of the toughest early competitors was Northern Trust Co., Chicago, which introduced one innovation that Bankers Trust did not have—an automated cash management program. This program automatically swept cash, which could build up in an account from sales of securities or from receipt of dividend payments, into short-term investments earning incremental income for the fund.

Soon after, State Street Bank and Trust Co., Boston, entered the business, building on its expertise in handling accounting and recordkeeping for mutual fund companies. It won credibility by becoming the master trustee for the Pension Benefit Guaranty Corp., which a number of other master trustees, flooded with pension fund business, did not bid on. The PBGC business gave State Street instant credibility with pension funds. Eventually, Citibank, which First National City Bank had become, hired Costa away from Bankers Trust to get it into the master trust business. By the late 1970s, most very large multimanager corporate pension funds had hired a master trust bank, but many midsized pension funds and public employee pension funds were still evolving toward multiple management and toward master trustees.

The development of the master trust made possible another experimental innovation, *the inventory index fund,* a concept that Rex Sinquefield had suggested several years earlier. The idea behind it was to cut transactions costs at large funds by eliminating duplicative trading by the managers. Some large funds had noticed that soon after one manager sold, say $10 million worth of IBM shares, another of the fund's managers might buy a similar amount of IBM. Both managers incurred significant brokerage fees. In addition, each may have adversely affected the price of IBM stock by their trading activities. If, however, there was an inventory fund to which managers could sell stock they no longer wanted, and from which they could buy stock they did want, transactions fees could be saved, and an index fund was the perfect vehicle to house the inventory. The index fund would be rebalanced once a month to bring its holdings and weightings in line with the chosen index. The monthly trading minimized transactions costs. The only danger was that the performance of the fund would differ significantly from that of the index because the weightings would be thrown off by the trading in and out. But that performance difference was as likely to be positive as negative.

Glenn Kent, the creative manager of investments for Honeywell Inc.'s $270 million pension fund, established the first inventory index fund in February 1977. The index fund was run at American National Bank and Trust in Chicago, even though Bankers Trust Co. was the fund's master trustee.[35] The $1.4 billion General Telephone & Electronics pension fund started running an inventory fund in September 1977, using an index fund overseen by its master trustee, Bankers Trust.[36] A year later there were six inventory funds in existence as Illinois Bell, Kraft Inc., Sperry Rand Corp. and United Technologies Inc. had started them. By that time, Honeywell's Kent reported that his inventory fund had saved an estimated $2.3 million in transactions costs. GTE executives estimated that their inventory fund had saved $1 million in transactions costs in its first year of existence and that the fund was able to accommodate 34% of the trading by the pension fund's managers.

By the end of 1978, private pension assets, those in corporate pension plans, had surged to $198.6 billion from the bear-market low of $115.5 billion in 1974. In part, this was due to the recovery of the market in 1975 and 1976 when stocks were up 37.2% and 23.8%, respectively, though 1977 (−7.2%) and 1978 (6.6%) were not as strong.[37] It was also due to the money flooding into the plans from corporate contributions in the wake of the passage of ERISA. Now, funding a plan's obligations over a 30-year period was mandatory. Earlier, funding the obligations at all was optional. And more of that money was flooding into the U.S. equity market, though there was small leakage into foreign stocks, real estate, and guaranteed investment contracts. By 1978 private pension funds had $150.3 billion of their total assets of $326.2 billion in equities, up from $63.3 billion out of total assets of $115.5 billion in 1974. State and local government funds were lagging, with only $33.3 billion out of total assets of $154 billion in equities at the end of 1978.[38] Pension funds were already having an impact on the market. In 1975 they accounted for 69% of the trading on the New York Stock Exchange.[39] They had begun to pioneer international investing, paving the way for individual investors to follow. Moreover, they were pioneering other investment vehicles, such as GICs, which later would be useful for individual investors, and market timing, which proved so difficult to do successfully that individuals could be warned away from it.

Chapter 8

Profit Sharing

Even defined contribution pension plans were affected by the money flood. In particular, the future of profit-sharing plans, a major form of defined contribution plan often used by companies to focus employee attention on the success of the company, was threatened by the 1973–1974 bear market and ERISA. Eventually, a new kind of defined contribution plan would appear which changed the whole structure of pension funds, but not until the mid-1980s. In the meantime, profit-sharing plans were a significant subset of the pension plan universe in the early 1970s. Rather than establish a plan with a guaranteed fixed benefit—a defined benefit plan—some companies established plans into which they promised to contribute based on the companies' profits. They would contribute a lot in good years, but less or even nothing in bad years. Each employee had his or her own account into which the contributions were directed. Although some companies, such as Sears Roebuck and Procter & Gamble, used profit-sharing plans as their primary pension vehicle, many other companies used them to supplement defined benefit plans. Generally, profit-sharing plans were exclusively, or at least heavily, invested in the stock of the sponsoring company. Because they were undiversified, they often suffered heavily in the 1973–1974 bear market. For example, from the beginning of 1973 to the end of 1974, the Sears Roebuck and Co. profit-sharing fund dropped from being the largest employee benefit fund in terms of assets to being the sixth largest. The reason was the decline in the value of Sears stock, which at the end of 1972 was at $116 per share, dropped to $80.25 per share by year-end 1973, and fell further to $48.25 per share by year-end 1974. The profit-sharing plan was Sears' only retirement vehicle for employees, so employees planning to retire at the end of 1974 either had to plan on a reduced lifestyle or delay their retirement. Near the end of 1975 Sears officials took a step toward preventing a similar loss of retirement income in the future. They set up a $75 million actively managed bond fund. In April 1977 Sears announced it would establish a defined benefit pension plan as the primary retirement vehicle for employees.[1] The new plan was to be effective by January 1, 1978 and was to be managed by the investment management subsidiary Sears Investment Management Co. The company had established this subsidiary in October 1976 to manage the profit-sharing plan assets. Sears management said that the new plan was prompted not by the decline in value of Sears shares, but by the general volatility of the stock market which made a profit-sharing plan invested mostly in stock an unsuitable primary retirement plan. The company said that the profit-sharing plan would continue to be invested heavily in Sears stock.

The decision by Sears management to establish a defined benefit plan was apparently made before an employee of Marriott Corp. filed suit in April 1977 against the company charging that failure to diversify in the Marriott profit-sharing plan had caused large losses. The Marriott plan was 50% invested in Marriott stock, and the plaintiff, a retired waitress who had worked for the company from 1954 to 1975, claimed that the value of her profit-sharing account had dropped from $17,764 to $8,638 during the bear market.[2] The plaintiff's attorney said that the complaint was brought not only under ERISA, but also under common law regarding fiduciary responsibility. A month later a $32 million lawsuit was filed against the Tappan Co. on behalf of about 1,000 beneficiaries of the company's $15 million profit-sharing plan. Like the Marriott suit, the complaint charged that the plan had invested too heavily in Tappan stock, causing the value of the assets of the fund to drop to between $5 million and $6 million in the bear market as the value of Tappan stock slipped from a 1973 high of $23 per share to a low of $3 per share.[3] Both the Marriott and Tappan suits lingered in court for many years before being settled. While they were wending their way through the legal system, they worried fiduciaries. ERISA, one must remember, made them personally liable for harm caused by any breach.

Fixed Income

The Sears move to establish a bond fund was paralleled by many other pension plans, both defined benefit and defined contribution. Until the early 1950s, most pension funds were all bonds. Then the trust banks offered "balanced account" management, in which they promised to move between stocks and bonds when appropriate. But as the bull market of the

1950s and 1960s raged, there seemed less and less occasion to carry significant bond positions in the portfolios. The equity-only mantra took over,
and bond management almost disappeared from leading-edge funds and
managers. In the aftermath of the bear market, "equity-only" seemed too
risky, and besides examining alternatives such as real estate and international equities, many funds also looked at specialized fixed income management. Some money management organizations, typically those
managing mutual funds such as Scudder, Stevens & Clark, offered fixed
income management to pension funds. They had fixed income mutual
funds, so they had the fixed income management expertise and records
they could show to pension funds. A few banks, such as Harris Trust in
Chicago, Chemical Bank in New York, and American Fletcher National
Bank in Indianapolis, had stellar fixed income records, which they promoted. Specialized fixed income management firms also were started;
prominent among them were Pacific Investment Management Co. and Fischer, Francis, Trees & Watts. Other equity-oriented firms, such as Jennison
Associates, recognizing the demand, added fixed income management
capabilities, and insurance companies, which should have led the field in
fixed income management, also showcased their wares.

Besides Sears, funds that boosted their fixed income allocations in the
aftermath of the bear market included Shell Oil Co., which moved $40
million, RCA Corp. which began directing 30% of its annual contributions into fixed income, and Mobil Corp., which directed about $130 mil-
lion from equities into fixed income investments between 1972 and 1975.
The move toward fixed income received a boost early in 1976 when the
investment results for the five-year period ended December 31, 1975 were
tallied and reported. They showed that fixed income funds had beaten the
Standard & Poor's 500 Index for the five-year period. The reaction was not
long in coming as Atlantic Richfield Co. pumped $140 million of its $475
million pension assets into fixed income, hiring three managers for their
fixed income expertise: Alliance Capital Management Corp., Brown
Brothers, Harriman & Co., and Trust Company of the West. In addition, it
gave more money to its existing fixed income manager, Fischer, Francis,
Trees & Watts Inc. The reallocation was designed to bring the asset allocation to 40% fixed income, 60% equity from less than 10% fixed income.[4] A
month later, the State of Connecticut hired Harris Trust & Savings and
Scudder, Stevens & Clark to manage part of the $540 million in fixed
income assets that had been managed internally.[5] The bulk of the assets
were to remain internally managed. Harris Trust picked up at least 26 new
fixed income clients in 1976, including IBM, TWA, the Pension Benefit
Guaranty Corp., Phillips Petroleum, and Alcoa. Brown Brothers, Harri-

man gained at least 15 new clients, including Motorola, Atlantic Richfield, Minnesota Mining, and Manufacturing and Motorola. American Fletcher gained at least a dozen, as did several other top fixed income managers.[6] However, the move to increase the fixed income allocation was not well timed. Although long-term bonds gave total returns of 9.2% in 1975 and 16.8% in 1976, they gave negative returns for the next four years, with the worst being a loss of 3.9% in 1980.[7]

The culprit was inflation. In 1972 the inflation rate was 3.4%; it jumped to 8.8% in 1973 and 12.2% in 1974 before settling back to the 7% to 9% range until it exploded to 13.3% in 1979.[8] Much of this increase was caused by the delayed impact of the loose money supply policies used to finance the Vietnam War, worsened by the 1973 Arab oil embargo and its long-term aftermath, and the second Arab oil embargo of 1979. As a result, a few funds looked for ways to take advantage of the high and rising oil and gas prices; others sought ways to earn additional income from their investments; and yet others sought ways to hedge their fixed income investments to protect against rising interest rates. Fixed income futures contracts became available in 1976, and at least one fixed income manager for pension funds, the American Fletcher National Bank in Indianapolis, Indiana, used them on a limited basis to hedge some of its fixed income investments. In 1978 Aetna Life Insurance Co. developed a $100 million "indexed income contract" for the Ford Motor Co. This contract guaranteed Ford a rate of return above the consumer price index, with a minimum return slightly below the then available interest rates and a maximum guaranteed return in the double digits. Most of Ford's $4 billion in assets at the time was in balanced accounts, heavily weighted to equities, managed by 16 firms. Robert C. White, Ford's assistant treasurer, was "looking for a guarantee, but we did not want a guaranteed investment contract." The contract agreed upon provided that if inflation was 6% and the Aetna portfolio earned a 7% return, the Ford fund would receive 6% plus part of the excess return over inflation.[9]

Another Option

On Labor Day, 1976, President Ford signed another bill that was significant to pension funds, though nowhere near as significant as ERISA. The new bill paved the way for pension funds and other tax-exempt investors to use *call options* as a hedging device—a device to reduce the risk of investing in stocks. Options were the first variety of what would become known 15 years later as *derivatives*. Before the passage of the bill, which had been introduced by Representative Dan Rostenkowski (D-Ill.), later to become speaker of the House of Representatives, premium income earned by the tax-exempt funds for writing covered call options could have fallen under the IRS's definitions of unrelated business income and thus been taxable. In addition, too much unrelated business income could have threatened the funds' tax-exempt status. The Rostenkowski bill specifically exempted the premium income from option writing from the unrelated business income tax.

A few pension funds and pension fund managers, undeterred by the tax question, had been experimenting with covered call options since the establishment of the Chicago Board of Options Exchange in the early 1970s. In covered call options, the writer sells to another investor, for a small premium, the right to buy (call) a stock at a set price within a particular time period. The premium the funds earned for selling the option enhanced fund investment returns. The danger was that the price of the stock might rise, making it profitable for the buyer of the option to exercise it and call away the stock. This would limit the fund's share of any gain in the stock's price, which might well be greater than the premium earned. Most of the gain would go to the option buyer. In such options transactions, however, the option seller believes the stock price is unlikely to rise within the allotted time and is willing to take that chance to lock up the sure return of the premium. Among the early pioneers were the Tennessee Consolidated Retirement System and the pension funds of D. H. Baldwin & Co.,[10] Irving Trust Co., Continental Illinois Bank, and Stauffer Chemical Co. Stauffer had an $8 million program with two managers, and between March 1973 and June 1978 it produced a 7% compound annual return, compared with 1.3% for the Standard & Poor's 500 Index, according to Ken Drucker, director of investments at the time.[11]

The Tennessee fund's program was the largest among pension funds at that time and produced about $600,000 of additional income for the $550 million fund, which had $120 million in equities. The fund used the options to provide additional income for some downside protection and some investment return when the market or a particular stock was moving sideways. However, the Tennessee fund had to temporarily halt its options programs during the bear market because of a lack of demand.[12] Few investors wanted to purchase calls when few stocks were likely to move up. It had resumed the program in mid-1974 when demand had picked up, and it had written call options on about 10% of its equity portfolio by the end of 1974.

Many other funds had expressed interest in writing call options on their portfolios as the market recovered, including the City of Memphis,

Tennessee, FMC Corp., American Motors Corp., Dayton Hudson Corp., and Armco Steel, but they were held back by the tax question. Another public pension fund, the Kansas City Employees Retirement System, confident of the passage of the Rostenkowski bill, began a covered call option program in September 1975 with the investment management firm of Research Management Associates, a subsidiary of Waddell & Reed, the Kansas City-based investment banking firm.[13] Nevertheless, interest in options far exceeded actual use of the derivative security early in 1976. One of the first money management firms specializing in covered call option writing, Balch, Hardy Inc., New York, had only $5 million under management at the beginning of 1976.

Passage of the Rostenkowski bill accelerated the use of covered call options, with the $500 million Los Angeles Employees pension fund gaining approval for a covered call option program in December.[14] In April 1977, Grumman Corp.'s $380 million internally managed pension fund hired two outside managers to run a $5 million covered call program,[15] and the Utah State Retirement System started a $40 million program in May.[16] A year later the Stauffer Chemical Co. fund became the first corporate pension fund, and probably the first pension fund, to engage in buying covered call options. That is, the fund bought options that allowed it to call stocks away from the investors selling the calls at a certain price during a certain period. The options buying program was managed by Chase Investors Management Corp., the investment management subsidiary of Chase Manhattan Bank.[17] For the next several years, option writing gained slowly and steadily in acceptance. Options were the first variety of what would become known 15 years later as "derivatives."

Pension Fund Socialism

By the end of 1976 private noninsured pension assets had climbed to $172 billion, of which $110 billion was invested in common stocks and $35 billion in corporate bonds. State and local government pension funds had assets of $121 billion, of which $30 billion was in corporate equities. These figures led highly respected management expert Peter Drucker to write a book: *The Unseen Revolution: How Pension Fund Socialism Came to America*. Drucker argued that, through their pension funds, American employees owned at least 25% of the equity capital of American business and perhaps as much as 35%. According to Drucker, pension funds, acting through their institutional managers, were the actual employers of most workers since the funds owned the controlling interests in most companies.

That is, since the pension funds belonged to the employees, and the funds owned controlling interests in most of the country's leading companies, the employees owned the controlling interests in the companies—hence pension fund socialism. The thesis was not accepted without argument. For example, ERISA seemed to say that the assets belonged neither to the employees nor to the employer, but to the pension trust. In addition, although pension funds owned up to 60% of the stock of some large companies, they owned, on average, only 25% of the stock of New York Stock Exchange companies. Nevertheless, the thesis became a justification for resisting federal government efforts to further restrict private pension funds after ERISA.

Drucker was not the only author noting the burgeoning pension assets. Two years later another book with lasting impact, at least on unions and the trustees of Taft-Hartley pension plans, was published: *The North Will Rise Again: Pensions, Politics and Power in the 1980s*.[18] The authors, Jeremy Rifkin, a Wharton School of Finance graduate and an intellectual gadfly who later turned his attention to environmental concerns, particularly the dangers of genetically engineered food, and Randy Barber, a Dartmouth graduate and antiwar and union activist, extended Drucker's argument and declared that whoever controlled the investment of pension assets could determine the future of the U.S. economy. They called on labor and political leaders in the northern states, which at that time were stagnating and appeared to be heading toward terminal decline, to use the pension assets of the unions and public employee funds to bolster those economies. They urged the union officials and politicians not to give the assets to the financial community to invest in other regions or other countries, but instead to find alternative investments within their home states which would increase employment in those states. Over the next 15 years, a number of unions and states would attempt to implement the Rifkin–Barber strategy, sometimes with modest success, but also sometimes with expensive failures. However, the idea was virtually ignored in the states at which it was aimed, the northern and rust belt states. In those states only tiny amounts of pension assets were set aside for in-state investing and most of that went into mortgages to stimulate housing for lower income workers. Little went to finance industrial rebuilding. The states revived without pension capital being diverted from the markets. Over the coming years activists and economists debated whether in-state investing could be effective or whether the pension fund capital would simply displace other capital, at the same time earning a lower return than it would if allocated simply by the capital markets.

Union Funds

Union funds, led by the Teamsters Central States, Southeast, and South-west Area pension fund, figured in the news in unpleasant ways during the 1970s. The Central States Teamster fund is what is known as a Taft-Hartley or jointly trusteed pension fund. The funds are generally found in industries in which there are many small employers contributing to a multi-employer pension plan. The Taft-Hartley Act of 1947 required that such funds be jointly trusteed; that is, the board of trustees had to have a membership equally divided between management and labor. In time, union trustees came to dominate the operations of such funds. Union trustees were united: They were representing one entity—the union. In contrast, employer trustees were often divided, each trustee representing the interests of one employer; the interests of all employers did not necessarily coincide. The union trustees could usually rely on gaining one employer trustee vote to get their way, if only to secure labor peace. As a result, Taft-Hartley plans were, and are, generally invested more conservatively than corporate plans, and even public employee plans. Generally, the union trustees have been far more conservative in their investments than executives overseeing corporate plans. In part, this is probably because they are less familiar with the capital markets and investment options than corporate financial executives. Since the trustees often serve limited terms and are then replaced by new trustees who have to begin the learning process, the conservatism of uncertainty does not pass quickly. Another possible reason for their conservatism may be that they see no real connection between increased investment return and their benefits. The benefits are negotiated by the union, and there is no apparent connection between what the fund could earn and the level of those negotiated benefits. Any improvement in return serves to cut the required contributions of the many employers and does not directly improve benefits for union members.

Because of the potential to gain control over the investment of millions of dollars, Taft-Hartley plans have attracted the attention of dishonest union members and even the Mafia. The Central States Teamster fund, for example, had been linked to organized crime since the 1950s, when some of its assets helped finance the early hotels and casinos in Las Vegas. The questionable investments to questionable characters continued into the 1970s, especially during the reign of Jimmy Hoffa as Teamster president. After Hoffa was replaced as president by Frank Fitzsimmons, a number of outside investment managers were hired to supplement the inhouse management of the assets: American National

Bank and Trust, Chicago, Continental Illinois Bank and Trust, Chicago, Federated Investors, Pittsburgh, Loomis Sayles & Co., Boston, and T. Rowe Price & Co., Baltimore. In January 1975, however, in an apparent resurgence of Hoffa's influence within the union and the fund, four of the outside managers were fired.[19] Fund officials claimed the trustees had lost faith in the equity markets.

In 1976 a joint Labor Department–Justice Department task force began investigating the fund, and two influential trustees, William Presser and Frank Ranney, resigned after they refused to testify, citing Fifth Amendment rights.[20] In October of the same year, six management and five labor trustees resigned and were replaced by new faces, but government officials regarded the changes as largely window dressing.[21] At the end of 1976, the Teamster fund had entered into negotiations with the IRS and the Labor Department about how the assets of the fund might be managed to stave off the IRS's move to rescind the pension plan's tax-exempt status. Loss of tax-exempt status would expose both the companies contributing to the fund and individual plan members to large tax penalties. This was a potent weapon for the IRS in its efforts to investigate and clean up corruption in the fund. In January 1977 the fund hired additional inhouse staff to help sell enough of its mortgage holdings to get the allocation in mortgages down to 50% of the assets from 80%. The fund imposed a moratorium on new loans, and all of its annual contributions of $173 million a year were earmarked for the securities markets. At the same time, it invested $20 million in GICs with five insurance companies.

Six months later the first real step in cleaning up the Central States fund occurred when trustees appointed the Equitable Life Assurance Co. as "managing fiduciary" of the $1.5 billion in assets.[22] This meant that it had the power to hire and fire other managers, as well as to decide the asset allocation. At the same time, they appointed Equitable as real estate manager for properties east of the Mississippi and Victor Palmieri & Co. of Los Angeles as manager of properties west of the Mississippi. The fund had approximately $1 billion in real estate-related investments and $500 million in securities. At the time, the portfolio which Palmieri & Co. found itself managing for the Teamsters' fund consisted heavily of Las Vegas gambling casinos and hotels as well as southern California resorts such as Rancho LaCosta and Rancho Los Penasquitos.

As the decade ended the fund was in Equitable's good hands, and the financial improprieties that had marred it in the past had ceased. At the end of 1983, Morgan Stanley Inc. replaced Equitable Life as the managing fiduciary for the then $4.7 billion Central States Teamster fund and put the bulk of the fund's equity assets, about $2.5 billion, in its own investment management subsidiary, Morgan Stanley Asset Management.

The Central States Teamsters' fund was not the only one tainted by scandal or mob connections. In 1977, for example, the Labor Department sued the Southern Nevada Culinary and Bartenders Pension Trust to halt a $31 million loan to Morris Shenker, a controversial real estate developer. At about the same time, Al Bramlet, a fund trustee and secretary-treasurer of Culinary and Bartenders Local 226, disappeared. He reportedly had been quarreling with Mafia figures over his cut of the profits to be skimmed from the use of pension assets to set up a clinic-pharmacy to treat union members. His body was found two weeks later, buried in the desert outside Las Vegas.[23] In addition, money management organizations that managed Taft-Hartley fund assets often saw their reputations sullied. In 1979 both Forstmann-Leff Associates and American Management Enterprises, an affiliate of M. D. Sass Investors Services, were named in a series of newspaper articles as being involved in kickback schemes with relatives of union officials and reputed mobsters.[24] The articles alleged that the two firms, in return for being selected to manage Teamster fund assets, directed excessive brokerage to three brokerage firms that employed relatives or friends of reputed organized crime figure and former president of Teamster Local 560 Anthony Provenzano. Provenzano and Anthony Bentro, a director of Chromalloy-American Corp., a New York-based conglomerate, who owned 46% of American Management Enterprises, later were convicted of seeking kickbacks for loans from Teamster pension funds. Although Labor Department and Securities and Exchange Commission investigations of the newspaper allegations cleared the two management firms, their reputations were stained for some time.

ERISA's standards of fiduciary behavior—no self-dealing; personal responsibility for any wrongdoing the trustee should have known about—were largely the result of the problems associated with the Central States Teamster fund and other Taft-Hartley funds. These standards were designed to make fund trustees more resistant to attempts by organized crime and others to gain control of union pension assets for their own purposes. ERISA's provisions were also designed to give the IRS and the Labor Department more weapons with which to attack corrupt trustees. Although ERISA's standards of fiduciary behavior did not legally apply to other investment areas, they have set an informal standard that helps protect other investors.

Prudence Defined

While ERISA clearly spelled out fiduciary behavior, it was not until August 1977 that pension funds were given specific guidelines as to how the Labor Department would interpret ERISA's prudence standards. There should have been no question, given ERISA's definition of prudence as being how a prudent person familiar with such matters would act; moreover, the law clearly stated that investments had to be diversified so as to minimize the chance of large losses. Nonetheless, money managers and pension executives were still uncomfortable. They wanted an unambiguous statement assuring them that prudence would be determined on a total portfolio basis, and not on the basis of each individual investment in a portfolio. In August 1976 James D. Hutchinson, chief administrator of ERISA for the Labor Department, had attempted to clear the air in a speech at the American Bar Association annual meeting in Atlanta. "Advocates of modern portfolio theory reject the view that focuses solely on the risky assets held by a plan and instead realize that each investment should be evaluated in the context of the entire portfolio," he said. "Diversification is the key to this expanded concept of risk. To the extent that a portfolio is structured in a way that variation in the value or return of one security is offset by a variation in another, the riskiness of each individual investment is decreased."[25] He added: "The prudent investment manager, however, must arrive at what would be a suitable degree of risk for the particular plan before a portfolio can be constructed to meet its needs. This is arrived at by an intimate knowledge of such factors as a plan's need for liquidity, and its desired rate of return, because the character and objectives of each plan determine the appropriate amount of risk." In addition, Hutchinson observed that the amount of investment concentration that would violate the diversification requirements of ERISA "cannot be stated as a fixed percentage." It depended, he said, on the purposes of the plan, the amount of plan assets, the financial and industrial conditions of the plan, the type of investment, geographic distribution, and the like. Hutchinson's speech did not have the desired effect of calming pension executive and investment manager fears of violating ERISA's prudence standards. A speech, even one by the top pension regulators, did not carry enough legal weight. And so most pension executives continued to avoid any investment that appeared to be out of the mainstream, and to use even the others conservatively. In addition, in response to critics of ERISA who had charged that ERISA was driving pension funds to invest only in large company stocks, several U.S. senators had proposed bills to amend Section 404 of

ERISA, the prudence section, to specifically allow investment, or even encourage investment, in small companies.

Only weeks after his speech, Hutchinson resigned his post and was replaced, after an interim appointee, by Ian D. Lanoff, who had been pension counsel to the Senate Labor Subcommittee. Lanoff, a graduate of the University of Michigan and Georgetown University law schools, began his career as a labor law attorney with the National Labor Relations Board and then became the general counsel to the United Mine Workers of America Health and Retirement Funds. He moved on to become the employee benefits counsel to the Committee on Labor and Public Welfare on the U.S. Senate. While working on the committee, he had heard no discussion of the basic issue of prudent investment, and when he arrived at the Labor Department the staff had already drawn up a list of priority items for him to rule on—ERISA interpretations, regulations, prohibited transaction exemptions, and so on. Not long afterward, however, he received a phone call from Senator Jacob Javits, one of the fathers of ERISA, who proposed that Lanoff develop a regulation defining how prudent investment under ERISA would be judged. Later, Lanoff heard that Javits had been approached by representatives of the venture capital and real estate communities who were having trouble getting pension executives to invest because of fear of ERISA's prudence standards. Lawyers had apparently warned these pension executives that venture capital and some real estate investing was too risky for pension funds under ERISA, and Hutchinson's speech in 1976 had not been definitive enough. Labor Department officials resisted issuing a ruling both because they felt it was unnecessary and because there were more important issues to address. Therefore, Lanoff was "rebuffed," despite the fact that the idea had come from Javits, a respected and powerful senior senator.

Given the resistance, Lanoff decided to go outside the Labor Department bureaucracy to develop his interpretation. Through his authority to hire consultants, he began to look for someone who could help him develop the idea behind the regulation. A friend who worked for Senator Harrison Williams of New Jersey, another of the fathers of ERISA, mentioned a law professor at New York University who might be able to help. The professor was Robert Pozen who had written a book about all the laws that applied to all the entities that are responsible for investing money: pension funds, mutual funds, banks, insurance companies, and so on. Over the next six months, Pozen, who in 1998 would become president of Fidelity Management & Research Co., the investment adviser to the huge Fidelity family of mutual funds, worked with Lanoff to develop the prudence regulation. "I've always considered it to be Pozen's regulation as well as mine to some extent," Lanoff said.

Lanoff announced the new regulation at a speech at an American Bar Association conference in Chicago in August 1977, the forum Hutchinson had used a year before for his speech. This time, however, the speech was backed up by a forthcoming regulation. Lanoff told the conference: "My position, and the position of the Labor Department is that, under Section 404 of ERISA, the prudence of any investment for a pension plan should be judged in relation to the role the proposed investment is to play in the portfolio." Lanoff specified five considerations that must be examined in order to determine whether a proposed investment was appropriate:

(i) The composition of the whole pension portfolio with regard to diversification of risk

(ii) The volatility of the whole pension portfolio with regard to the general movement of stock prices

(iii) The liquidity of the whole pension portfolio relative to the payment schedule for retirement benefits

(iv) The projected return of the whole pension portfolio relative to the funding objectives of the pension plan

(v) The prevailing and projected economic conditions of the entity in which the plan proposes to invest[26]

The speech was backed up with the issuance of the regulation early in 1979.

Despite some lingering concern over the prudence question, most pension executives and money managers took comfort in Lanoff's interpretive regulation. This comfort was most apparent in the surge of interest over the next two years in so-called special equity funds managed by banks and insurance companies, as well as in money management firms specializing in small-cap stocks, or offering small-cap stock investment options. The regulation was well timed as pension funds had noted the superior performance of small-cap stocks from 1975 on. In 1975, small-cap stocks had a total return of 52.8% compared with 37.2% for large-cap stocks. In 1976 the smaller company stocks were up 57.4% compared with 23.8% for the large company stocks. In 1977 small company stocks were up 25.4%, while large company stocks were down 7.2%. Small company stock outperformance of large company stock continued until 1984.[27] By 1977 money managers who had focused all or large parts of their portfolios on small-cap stocks, were showing superior three-year performance records, and pension funds began to hire them. A classic example was Batterymarch Financial Management, which, besides its index fund, followed a contrarian active investment approach. This approach led it into small-cap stocks in 1971 when they seemed undervalued relative to large-cap stocks, especially the Nifty Fifty. The move paid off handsomely in 1975 when small-cap stocks rebounded and Batterymarch's assets under management ballooned to $1.9 billion at the end of 1978 from $50 million in 1973 and grew by almost $1 billion in 1978 alone.[28] Typically, Batterymarch was already putting more large-cap stocks into its portfolios, believing small-cap stocks were becoming overpriced.

Nothing Ventured

Ironically, the prudence regulation did not immediately help venture capital significantly. Managers and pension executives quickly found another section of ERISA—the definition of what constituted pension plan assets—as a source of ambiguity and concern. If the plan assets definition were interpreted by courts in a particular way, it could be read as virtually prohibiting investment in venture capital, and even some forms of real estate investment. Lanoff therefore had more work ahead of him: he needed to devise an interpretation of the plan assets rule that would satisfy the protective purposes of ERISA while at the same time allowing venture capital and the private partnership form of real estate investing to be used by pension funds. That regulation would take another two years to develop and refine to everyone's satisfaction. A few pension funds had made small commitments to venture capital before the complication of ERISA and were very happy with the results. General Mills, once again pioneering, had committed $3 million to a venture capital partnership sponsored by Donaldson, Lufkin & Jenrette (DLJ) in 1970 and, despite the uncertainty of ERISA, was rolling the commitment into another DLJ partnership as the original one matured. Robert Hoffman, director of benefit finance at General Mills, announced that the original investment had been "very successful" and that a number of companies that the venture capital partnership had bought had gone public or had been sold. Similarly, Stauffer Chemical Co. had invested less than $1 million in a venture capital partnership in 1972 and had seen the returns outpace the S&P 500 Index returns.

Both General Mills and Stauffer Chemical planned to maintain their commitments and took comfort in Lanoff's definition of prudence.[29] By the late 1970s, while Lanoff was wrestling with the prudence regulation, a number of other venture capital firms were turning their attention to pension funds as a source of capital. Among them were Alan Patricof of Alan Patricof & Associates, now Patricof & Co.; Peter Brook at TA Associates;

C.R. (Dick) Kramlick at New Enterprise Associates; Pitch Johnson at Asset Management Inc.; and Reid Dennis at Institutional Venture Partners.

Patricof's story may be typical in that, like many of the others, he got into institutional venture capital through managing assets for wealthy families. Patricof had graduated from Ohio State University and started work with a money management firm in New York while he did his MBA at Columbia University at the same time. He then moved on to Lambert & Co. and Central National Corp., managing money for wealthy families at both firms. Patricof noted that while the wealthy families often employed staffs to actively seek out and manage their stock and bond market investments, any venture capital investments they made floated in over the transom, so to speak, as investment bankers called to see if the families were interested in taking part in various deals. Aware that no one was out seeking deals for the families, Patricof decided to start his own firm to manage private investments for such families. He opened his doors in 1969 with nine wealthy family clients and a pooled fund from 20 individual participants each of whom had put up $100,000.

Although the company's investments were successful overall, by 1980 Patricof began to seek out institutional clients because the wealthy families were too unstable a foundation on which to build a successful business. Some would periodically get scared out of the market, while others could not be reached when a timely decision was critical to winning participation in a deal. Having noted the growth of pension assets, Patricof decided to take his business there. It was a tough sell, he noted, when he told pension executives that out of 20 deals, four or five might go bankrupt, three or four would return up to 20 times the initial investment, and the rest would at least give the money back or perhaps pay market rates of return. Luckily, Lanoff's prudence regulation helped with some pension executives, and Patricof soon had $23 million from the Continental Oil Co., AT&T, New York Telephone, Sherwin Williams Paint, and Grumman Corp. pension funds. Most other pension funds were content to wait until the plan assets question was settled. That came in 1982 when the new plan assets regulation was announced. By 1984 Patricof had closed a $109 million fund, and that was just the beginning. Two years later he was even investing in venture capital in Europe for his growing list of pension fund clients. Other venture capital groups were also prospering under the new regulation, so much so that they attracted new entrants to the field, generally started by young executives who had served an apprenticeship with one of the established firms. By the mid-1980s too much money was chasing too few deals, and both the returns and the quality of the deals were declining.

Ian Lanoff's two great interpretive regulations—one on prudence and the other on plan assets—were critical steps forward in the pension fund investment revolution. They conferred federal blessing on Harry Markowitz's concept of risk and efficient investing. They also allowed the channeling of the pension fund money flood into fertile investment fields where the outcomes were often less certain but where the rewards, if the investments were successful, were great for both the funds and the economy at large. They made possible the funding of the commercial development of innovation at reasonable cost. In addition, even though the regulations in theory only applied to corporate pension funds, they became the standard for most other forms of investing, including mutual funds.

Chapter 9

Inflationary Doldrums

The first few years of the 1980s saw economic events broaden, deepen, and accelerate the pension fund revolution. As the decade began, the U.S. economy was in the doldrums. It was stagnant, verging on recession, with high inflation, giving rise to the term *stagflation*. In 1978 the inflation rate had hit 9%, up from 6.8% the previous year. In 1979 it had climbed to 13%, and for 1980 it would turn out to be 12.4%. As inflation soared, so too did interest rates, knocking the bottom out of the bond market. Bond prices plunged as long-term government interest rates surged above 13%, and corporate rates were even higher. In June 1980, New England Mutual Life Insurance Co. boosted its GIC rates to existing clients to 13.5%.[1] The stagnant, almost recessionary economy, was brought about by Federal Reserve Chairman Paul Volcker stepping hard on the money supply brakes to wring inflation and inflationary expectations out of the economy.

These moves to halt inflation inevitably affected pension fund investing. By the end of 1979 private pension assets had risen to $386 billion, up from $326 billion the previous year, and from $271 billion in 1977. State and local government pension funds had grown more slowly, to $170 billion in 1979 from $133 billion in 1977, reflecting the lower commitment to corporate equities at a time when stocks were performing well.[2] Many investors believed stocks were a good hedge against inflation, and so they seemed to be in 1979 and 1980 while the bond market was collapsing. In 1979 large company stocks gave a total return of 18.4%, while small company stocks returned an extraordinary 43.5%.[3] Though private pension funds (including Taft-Hartley funds) had 45% of their assets in stocks, public employee funds had only 22% of their assets so invested.[4] This clearly hit public fund investment returns in 1979. Another effect of the small-cap stock performance was that more than half of all money managers beat the Standard & Poor's 500 Index because their portfolios generally contained more small-cap stocks than the index did. In 1980 large-cap stocks gave a 32.4% total return, and small-cap stocks did better at 39.9%.[5] Naturally, the high equity returns, poor bond returns, and high inflation affected investment behavior, but in many and often confusing ways. In general, however, they accelerated the revolution in pension fund investing, dragging public employee pension funds more fully into it.

Bond Bind

One of the first effects of the investment environment was that most public employee pension funds found themselves in a bind as 1980 began. Many were trapped in high fixed income allocations by legal restrictions on how much they could invest in equities. As a result, they had suffered substantial losses on their long-term bond portfolios as the bond market virtually collapsed in late 1979. The paper losses on some long-term bond portfolios exceeded 20%. Only the fact that there was no widely reported bond index being broadcast on television every day to point up the losses saved the funds substantial political embarrassment. In addition, many public employee pension funds still carried their bond portfolios at book value (usually the purchase price) rather than market value, thus hiding the impact of the bond price declines. The $18 billion California Public Employees Retirement System and California State Teachers Retirement System had more than $9.2 billion in bonds at the beginning of the year, with only 17% in stocks, and that was up from 12% in the middle of 1979.[6] The funds had a limit of 25% of assets in stocks and filled the remainder of its portfolio with real estate and cash equivalents.

Change was a slow process. For example, the State of Connecticut stepped up its equity buying during 1979 but at the beginning of 1980 was still only 34% in equities compared with 28% in 1978.[7] Even where the legal restrictions allowed a high equity commitment, some pension executives at public funds invested cautiously well below their limits, knowing there would be a political price to pay if they invested too heavily. The Arizona State Retirement System was permitted to invest up to 60% of its assets in stocks but at the beginning of 1980 was only 25% invested in equities.[8] Fund officials knew that they would have many questions to answer if they were ever to invest in equities up to the legal limit and the stock market fell even for a year.

More Equity

The poor performance of bonds and the volatility of bond prices could not be ignored completely, however, and persuaded some public funds that maybe equities weren't so bad after all. The $1 billion Mississippi Public Employee Retirement System won legislative approval to buy common stocks in June 1980, though the limit was set at 20% of the assets. In addition, the legislature restricted the types of stocks that could be bought. They had to be of companies with market values of at least $100 million, investment in any one stock could not exceed 1% of the assets of the fund, and the fund could not own more than 5% of the outstanding shares of any one company.[9] At the same time, the $230 million San Diego County Employees Retirement System won approval of its board to invest up to 25% of its assets in equities. At the time, the fund was 90% in bonds and 10% in cash equivalents.[10] The board also approved the use of real estate as an investment for the first time.

Public pension funds were not the only ones rethinking their fixed income allocations. In February 1980 the $1.6 billion Southern Bell Telephone & Telegraph Co. pension fund decided to boost its equity commitment to between 60% and 65% of the assets, while cutting the fixed income commitment. "We think in the long haul equities will be a better hedge against inflation and better performers," H. Hodson Thomas, district staff manager, explained at the time.[11] Later in the year the $340 million B. F. Goodrich Co. pension fund dropped its two active fixed income managers and reallocated all of its fixed income assets to equities and real estate. The fund would invest 80% of its assets in stocks and real estate, and the remainder in cash equivalents, reported David Hammerstein, manager of Benefit Assets. Of the noncash assets, 95% would be in U.S. stocks, and the remaining 5% would be invested in international equities, real estate, and venture capital. Furthermore, the fund boosted the indexed portion of its equities to 50% from 30%.[12]

Active Batterymarch

B. F. Goodrich was not alone in boosting its indexed assets during this period. By July 1980 total indexed assets had climbed to $9 billion and then continued climbing.[13] However, during this strong period of indexing, the ever contrarian Dean LeBaron told Batterymarch Financial Management clients late in 1981 that his firm would no longer offer index fund management. LeBaron said his firm was abandoning indexing first because it was not being used the way he felt it should be, that is, with 75% to 80% of each fund's assets indexed, and second because the index then in use, the S&P 500 Index, was flawed. Twice in the previous 10 years, he said "half of the index acted like a single stock." The first time was in the early 1970s when high multiple-growth stocks accounted for half the index, and the next time was in the 1979–1980 period when energy stocks made up 40% of the index. "Last year the S&P 500 was up 32% because of energy," he said. "The whole market wasn't up that much."[14] Competitors scoffed that LeBaron had abandoned indexing because his method of investing in only the 250 largest stocks in the index was not working well. His index fund had often failed to track the index closely. In 1975, for example, when the index was up 37.3%, Batterymarch accounts were up only 34.8%, and in 1979 when the S&P 500 was up 18.6%, Batterymarch's index fund clients were up only 16.9%. Although some clients had complained about the tracking error, as the difference in return between the indexed portfolio and the index itself was known, Batterymarch still had indexing clients with assets of $2 billion. It had another $2 billion of clients with actively managed accounts, and LeBaron said the company would emphasize its active management process. After LeBaron's decision, a number of clients moved their index funds to other managers, among them the $387 million index fund of the New York City Teachers Retirement System, which moved it to Wells Fargo Investment Advisers, and Allied Corp., which moved its $75 million index fund to Bankers Trust. The defections did not slow Batterymarch's growth. By September 1983 its assets had grown to more than $10 billion, as had the assets of Jennison Associates and Capital Guardian Trust.[15] Batterymarch's active approach was thematic and tended to be contrarian, being built on out-of-favor stocks, often those of smaller companies. As a result, its performance had lagged behind the market only 3 of the previous 13 years.

Jennison Associates' assets had climbed to $10.6 billion in September 1983 as the firm's growth stock philosophy had paid off. It, too, had provided clients with investment returns greater than the market more years than not. Capital Guardian had $10.1 billion under management by September 1983, up from $8.3 billion a year earlier. Capital Guardian had had some rough times during the later stages of the Nifty Fifty era but had continued to follow its value approach. Clients who stuck with the firm had been rewarded with consistently excellent performance from the end of the 1973–1974 bear market.

Passive Wells

Despite the success of these active managers, in November 1982, Wells Fargo Investment Advisers, another of the indexing pioneers, made exactly the opposite decision from Batterymarch and dropped active management completely. Wells decided to concentrate on offering its clients a range of equity index funds.[16] At the time Wells Fargo had $6.5 billion of assets under management, but only about $800 million was actively managed. Of that, $482 million was converted to indexing, $167 million in small accounts moved to the personal trust division of Wells Fargo Bank where it would still be actively managed, and five clients totaling just under $150 million left Wells Fargo to seek active management elsewhere. This was offset by about $800 million in new index fund clients during the year. Wells executives were convinced that their indexed funds would outperform the median active money manager over any 10-year period. The move to indexing worked brilliantly. As of December 31, 1981, Wells Fargo Investment Advisers ranked twentieth among money managers in terms of pension assets under management with $6.4 billion, according to *Pensions & Investments*.[17] A decade later it ranked second with assets of $96 billion.[18] In fact, Wells's timing was impeccable as this was the beginning of a boom period for indexing, exemplified by the California Public Employees Retirement System hiring Bankers Trust to manage a $1 billion index fund in January 1983[19] and by the Washington State Investment Board hiring Mellon Capital Management to manage a $780 million index fund late in the year.[20] The Washington State Investment Board oversees all of the public employee pension funds in the state.

Mellon Capital Management was a brand-new subsidiary for Mellon Bank, established in August 1983 to accommodate Bill Fouse and three other top Wells Fargo Investment Adviser executives who had resigned from Wells in a philosophical dispute with the new manager of the division, William Joss. It was an ironic return to Mellon for Fouse, who had gone to Wells when Mellon refused to back his index fund ideas just over a decade earlier. Mellon didn't make the same mistake twice, and it backed his new index fund management subsidiary. The move paid off handsomely for the bank. A decade later Mellon Capital Management was managing $33 billion in tax-exempt assets and ranked sixteenth among pension fund money managers.[21] Meanwhile, the departure of Fouse and key members of his team threatened Wells's reputation and client base. The bank's management kept Patricia Dunn, a senior member of Fouse's team, by offering her a substantial bonus, reportedly equal to her salary, and increased responsibilities. It also quickly hired Fred Grauer, a former Columbia University Graduate Business School professor, and later vice president of institutional sales at Merrill Lynch Capital Management Group, San Francisco, as chief investment officer. Grauer, Dunn and Tom Middleton, director of marketing, made a whirlwind tour of the country to reassure Wells's clients that the division would continue running smoothly, and so Wells managed to keep all of the clients. However, Wells was still faced with a strong new competitor headed by a high-profile pioneer in indexing.

More International

Just as the B. F. Goodrich fund's increased indexing mirrored moves being made by others, so, too, its commitments to international equities and real estate also mirrored the decisions of many pension funds faced with the devastation of the bond market and inflation. At the beginning of 1980 U.S. pension assets invested internationally totaled only $1 billion. But right at the beginning of the year the pattern was set as the $2.1 billion General Telephone & Electronics (GTE) pension fund appointed three new international managers, bringing its roster of such managers to 10 and boosting its international allocation to almost $200 million, or 10% of assets.[22] GTE was the first fund to publicly acknowledge such a high international investment target.

In March executives of the $120 million internally managed Cleveland-Cliffs Iron Co. pension fund committed $3 million to investing in stocks of companies in the Far East and the Pacific Basin—emerging markets—because they felt that area offered the best growth prospects. It was also a revolutionary concept at that time among pension fund investors, most of whom still were reluctant to invest even in Europe.[23] However, the tide was turning. At almost the same time, the Board of Pensions of the United Presbyterian Church committed $20 million of their fund's $500 million in assets to the Templeton World Fund, becoming one of very few pension funds to use a mutual fund to invest.[24] In May executives of the $700 million Sun Company Inc. pension fund hired four international managers to invest $35 million. "The rationale behind international diversification," said E. B. Warwick, manager of employee investment funds at Sun, "is an attempt to dampen the fund's volatility. The markets don't all move in unison; they tend to have different cycles."[25]

As the year wore on, many more funds made the plunge into international equities or boosted their existing commitments, including Lockheed Corp., United Technologies Corp., the National Rural Electric Cooperative Association, Standard Oil of Indiana, and McGraw-Hill Inc. By the end of 1980 the assets invested internationally had surged 500% in one year to $5 billion. The momentum continued in 1981 as Xerox Corp. hired four managers to each invest $15 million internationally for the $750 million fund.[26] American Airlines hired three managers and divided $40 million between them, with the prospect of adding another $20 million later.[27] And later in the year Sperry Corp., Warner Lambert, and IBM, which hired nine managers, were among the funds committing to international investing.

As a result of the boom in international investing by U.S. pension funds, not only were U.S. money management firms developing international investment capabilities, but foreign firms, particularly British firms, were invading the U.S. market either alone or in partnership with U.S. firms. Although Morgan Guaranty had been the first U.S. manager overtly to invest significant amounts of U.S. pension assets internationally, it had been quickly followed by Fiduciary Trust Co., Brown Brothers, Harriman, Citibank (formerly First National City Bank), Capital Guardian Trust, and a few others. Among the first non-U.S. money management firms offering their international capabilities to U.S. pension funds were S. G. Warburg & Co., London, Lombard Odier & Cie., Geneva and London, Morgan Grenfell & Co., London, Ivory & Sime, Edinburgh, Baring Brothers, London, and ABD International, a joint venture between Dresdner Bank and Hypo Bank, Frankfurt, all of which had gained some business in the United States by 1980. Other foreign firms pursuing business at the end of 1980 included Julius Baer Securities Inc. of Zurich, Martin Currie Inc., Edinburgh, Pierson, Heldring & Pierson, B.V., Netherlands, and Schroder, Munchmeyer Hengst Management, Frankfurt. Only the British firms had much success, and most of the European firms retreated to their home markets within a few years.

Weddings and Divorces

Joint ventures also sprang up. In 1979 T. Rowe Price Associates had set up a joint venture with Robert Fleming & Co. of London called Rowe Price-Fleming International, which was to become the most successful and long-lasting of the joint ventures, partnerships, or alliances. By the end of 1980 it already managed $78 million; others wanted to emulate its success, though few did. Generally, firms went into joint ventures to acquire skills they did not have more quickly and at less expense than was possible by building them internally. Usually, the U.S. partner wanted the international research and management expertise of the non-

U.S. firm, and the non-U.S. firm wanted the marketing experience and the pension fund contacts of the U.S. firm. In 1980 S. G. Warburg & Co. announced a joint venture with Aetna Life & Casualty to create Aetna Warburg Investment Management Ltd., even though Warburg already had an international operation in the United States through its own subsidiary, Warburg Investment Management International. The partnership lasted just over two years before breaking up as the partners could not see eye to eye. Over the next three years a number of firms formed joint ventures, including IDS Advisory Ltd., Minneapolis, which formed a joint venture with Gartmore International Inc. of London called IDS-Gartmore; Mellon Bank, Pittsburgh, which joined forces with Pictet & Cie of Geneva, Switzerland; and Kemper Financial Services Inc., Chicago, which formed a partnership with Murray Johnstone Ltd. of Glasgow, Scotland, called Kemper Murray Johnstone. Few of these partnerships stood the test of time, even though the flow of pension fund dollars into international investing continued steadily. InterSec Research's Chris Nowakowski noted that the partners in joint ventures almost expect a divorce as soon as each partner learns the other's skills. Therefore, they're often suspicious of one another's motives from the outset. Still the money flowed. For example, late in 1982 AT&T gave $50 million to Brown Brothers, Harriman & Co., while aiming for a target of 5% of assets.[28] Similarly, LTV Corp. set its international target at 5% of fund assets as did many others. As a result, by late 1983, assets invested internationally by U.S. pension funds totaled close to $11 billion.[29]

Global Custody

The flood of money into non-U.S. securities, particularly equities, gave the major trust banks the opportunity to develop and offer a new service to pension funds—the global custody account. A global custody account was, in effect, an extension of the master trust idea to include the additional services international investors needed. These services included the safekeeping of the assets invested overseas, the tracking and reporting of foreign purchases or sales, the capture and crediting of dividend payments, and the conversion of the currency involved in the transactions. It also included the payment of any taxes, particularly transactions taxes, due to the foreign countries; the recapture of those taxes when allowed for tax-exempt investors such as pension funds; and the monitoring of the investment manager's activities in the foreign markets. The first global custodians were the major master trust banks—Bankers Trust, Chase Manhattan, Northern

Trust, Citibank, and State Street Bank and Trust—but many others joined the field, including the investment banking firms of Brown Brothers, Harriman and Morgan Stanley. However, the global custody business proved just as competitive as, and even more capital intensive than, the master trust business. The computer systems needed were larger, more complex, and more expensive because they had to deal not only with multiple managers but with multiple currencies and even different reporting conventions and often different languages. The global custody banks also had to build, maintain, and monitor networks of subcustodian banks around the world, wherever pension fund managers wanted to invest, from Latin America, to Europe, Asia, and Africa. This usually involved putting their own employees into the offices of the subcustodian banks to ensure quality control, and that too was expensive. Initially, global custody fees were higher than master trust fees, but like master trust fees, competition soon brought them down. Over the ensuing years the combination of competition driving fees down and the increasingly complex world driving technology costs up led to a shake-out of global custodian banks. The technology the global custodians developed for pension fund clients later benefited individual investors who ventured overseas through international mutual funds.

Real Estate Too

The story in real estate as the 1970s ended was similar to that in international investing. The economic conditions, particularly the high inflation, turned the attention of pension fund executives toward real estate because it was often presented as an asset class that would provide inflation protection through price increases. In addition, the cash return from rents could equal or better the cash return on bonds. As a result, many pension funds either started real estate investing or added to their real estate commitments. The Standard Oil of California pension fund, for example, boosted its real estate commitment to 4% from 1% of its $800 million in assets during 1979 and then raised the target to 10% by "early in the decade." R. L. Norman, manager of financial analysis for the fund, said Standard Oil officials were seeking real returns between 1% and 5% from the real estate holdings. "Real estate is particularly attractive given the uncertainties with respect to inflation," Neil Darling, another fund executive, told *Pensions & Investments* at the time.[30] Such was the rush into real estate that the assets of Prudential Insurance Co.'s PRISA fund jumped by $500 million just between the end of 1979 and June 30, 1980.[31] At the same time, Owens-Illinois Inc. decided to double its commitment to 10% of the $500 million fund's assets, with the money being split between its managers, Rosenberg Real Estate Equity Funds and the Boston Co. Real Estate Counsel.[32] The $2.8 billion Los Angeles County Retirement Association decided to invest $250 million of its assets in real estate over the next five years using Thomas L. Karsten & Associates as investment adviser.[33]

Pension executives were beginning to look beyond the open-ended funds such as Prudential's PRISA and were willing to tie their assets up for eight to 10 years.[34] The Rosenberg Real Estate Equity Funds were the largest of the closed-end funds with assets of $600 million in five funds by June 30, 1980, followed by Coldwell Banker Capital Management Services with total assets of $225 million in four funds.[35] By the end of 1980 pension funds assets in real estate had doubled since the end of 1979 to $6.1 billion.

At that time PRISA was the largest of the real estate investment vehicles with assets of $2.5 billion, up from $1.5 billion a year earlier, followed by Equitable Life Assurance Society's Separate Account No. 8 with $1.4 billion, up from $903 million a year earlier.[36] A few funds were willing to invest directly. In 1981 the $5 billion Pennsylvania State Teachers Fund committed to financing three proposed office buildings, one in Chicago, another in Cambridge, Massachusetts, and a third in lower Manhattan which would become the home of Goldman, Sachs & Co.[37] In October, the Bell System Trust committed to investing more than $300 million in three projects in the Loop area of downtown Chicago.[38] However, late in the year there was a hint of trouble on the horizon. Prudential had announced in August that it would take in $1 billion in new commitments for its PRISA I and PRISA II accounts by the end of the quarter. However, it fell more than $200 million short of its ambitious target. In October the real estate consulting and management company of Julian Studley & Co. warned that the office market boom had peaked.[39]

Indigestion

Real estate investing developed indigestion in 1982. Although some funds, particularly AT&T and a number of public employee pension funds continued to commit money to real estate in 1982, other corporate funds were pulling back on their commitments, particularly to open-ended funds such as PRISA. Some wanted out of PRISA so that they could invest directly. A few wanted to step back and see which way real estate investing was likely to move: pooled funds? open ended or closed ended? direct deals? In addition, new real estate investment organizations were started—for example,

Trust Company of the West's real estate investment group headed by real estate veteran Vince Martin, formerly executive vice president and general manager of Coldwell Banker Capital Management Services, and Sol Rabin, formerly head of research at Coldwell Banker. All of these entities had marketing executives out in the field offering something supposedly better than PRISA. As a result, PRISA, which by this time had $4.2 billion in assets, suffered a rash of withdrawal requests in the first quarter of 1982.[40] Contractually, PRISA was not obligated to honor withdrawal requests until the quarter after the request was made. Previously, so much money had been flowing into PRISA that it had been able to honor the infrequent withdrawal requests almost immediately from cash flow. Now, however, the withdrawal requests exceeded cash flow, and PRISA had to ask funds to wait for their money.

A Prudential executive noted that PRISA had about 60 competitors, and the competition had slowed the flow of funds into PRISA. In addition, many funds had reached their target level for commitment to real estate and were not making additional commitments to PRISA. At the end of March the withdrawal requests totaled $150 million from 19 clients. By the end of June that total had risen to $259 million from 26 clients.[41] As of June 30, 1982, pension funds, endowments, and foundations had $18.9 billion invested in real estate, the great bulk of it from pension funds.[42] PRISA was helped in June 1983 when the IBM fund, under the direction of fund director William (Bill) Hoyt, put up almost $540 million to buy the PRISA shares of all the funds seeking to withdraw, thus clearing the withdrawal glut. The flows into real estate continued, capped in November by 13 funds, including those of the State of Washington and Pacific Gas & Electric Co., contributing $479 million to three new funds managed by Rosenberg Real Estate Equity Funds.[43]

The flow of pension fund money into real estate provided crucial support not only to the real estate industry but to the construction industry and its suppliers, for example, the steel and concrete industries. In addition, it allowed many corporations to sell real estate they no longer wanted to own—unneeded land, factories, warehouses, even their own headquarters buildings (which they often then leased back). This in turn provided them with low-cost capital as they struggled to become more competitive.

Oil and Gas

Oil and gas deals provided another investment avenue that attracted some pension fund attention for its apparent ability to provide protection from the ravages of inflation. These deals came in three key varieties: oil well development, oil well completion, and royalty participation. Although they were too exotic ever to attract the attention of many funds, a few of the larger funds began to invest. One of the first deals involved providing capital to Standard Oil of Indiana (now Amoco) to explore its leases in the Williston Basin in North and South Dakota, Montana, Manitoba, and Saskatchewan. The General Electric and Hughes Aircraft Co. pension funds, together with a consortium of insurance companies and other institutions, agreed to put up $150 million in capital to finance the exploration. Gary Helms, director of investments at Hughes Aircraft Co., reported that oil well investment "uniquely has the ability to keep up with inflation."[44]

Soon after, the pension funds of E. I. DuPont, General Electric Co., Firestone Tire & Rubber Co., and the Teachers Insurance & Annuity Association agreed to provide $60.5 million to help finance a deep gas drilling project in the Anadarko Basin in Oklahoma, sponsored by Amerex Inc. The funds were to be used for well completion and could not be drawn on until the project was proven. For their capital, the funds received a 10% net profit royalty interest.[45] However, as oil prices began to slide from their 1979–1980 peak, pension fund interest in oil and gas ventures waned. Most of the deals pension funds participated in were relatively small, and the same half a dozen or so funds, including IBM, GE, Hughes Aircraft, DuPont, AT&T, General Motors, and Ford Motor Co., were participants in various combinations.

Dedication and Immunization

To offset the volatility of the bond market, some funds, both public and private, adopted a new investment approach called *bond immunization*. Immunization was a way of structuring a bond portfolio so that a target return would be achieved, no matter which way interest rates moved. One of the first funds to commit to an immunized bond portfolio was the White Motor Co., a truck-building company, which put $60 million of its pension assets into it.[46] By the end of 1979 Manufacturers Hanover reported it had $200 million in immunized bond portfolios, including assets from New York State Electric & Gas Co. and the Bakery and Confectionary Workers International Union.[47] Early in 1980, the Central States Teamsters committed $120 million to an immunized bond fund, putting to work the money recaptured as it reduced its real estate holdings.[48] A year later, Chrysler Corp., which was in deep financial trouble and facing bankruptcy as a result of poor car sales and high interest rates, established a $150 million immunized bond portfolio with Manufacturers Hanover Trust for its $500 million salaried employees pension plan.[49]

This was the fund's entire bond portfolio, and it locked in a 13% rate of return, which was enough to pay the benefits to Chrysler's retired salaried employees. Because the immunized rate was far higher than the company's actuarially assumed rate of return on investments, it saved the company about $7.5 million in annual contributions. This was a very important factor, given Chrysler's precarious financial position at the time. Chrysler was just the first large immunization of 1981. Later in the year the Central States Teamsters fund increased the size of its immunized portfolio by $275 million, taking it to $405 million.[50] By the end of 1982 the Teamsters had more than $700 million in its immunized bond fund. A year earlier, Santa Fe Industries immunized 65% of its pension fund assets so as to lock in the very high interest rates available.[51]

In October 1981 American Airlines established a different kind of protective, locked-in portfolio called a *dedicated portfolio*.[52] This was a portfolio structured so that the cash flows would exactly match the payment needs of the fund. That is, if a company needed $100,000 per month cash flow to pay $1,000 per month to 100 retired employees, the portfolio was structured to generate that cash flow from interest payments and maturing bonds. American Airlines' $200 million dedicated bond portfolio allowed American to substantially increase its interest rate assumption (i.e., the expected rate of return on part of its assets) and to cut its pension contribution. This was a vital saving as the nation's airlines struggled with fewer passengers because of the recession and higher fuel costs because of oil price increases imposed by the Organization of Petroleum Exporting Countries (OPEC). In November Pan American World Airways Inc., afflicted by the same passenger and oil price woes, established a $140 million dedicated portfolio with Mellon Bank to cover its retired lives liabilities.[53]

The dedication and immunization trend continued through 1982 and into 1983 while interest rates were high. Yet dedicated bond funds were established more often than immunized funds because they were simpler to implement and required less maintenance. International Harvester Corp., struggling with poor sales of farm equipment in the 1981–1982 recession, sold stocks from its $1.3 billion pension fund and set up a $300 million dedicated bond portfolio in May 1982.[54] In September, B. F. Goodrich Co. reversed its 1980 decision to purge its long-term bonds and invest 95% of its $450 million fund in equities. Instead it put 85% of its portfolio into a $380 million dedicated bond portfolio managed by Wells Fargo Investment Advisers.[55] Other large dedications were Niagara Mohawk Power Corp.,

$120 million, Reynold Metals Corp., $375 million, and Republic Steel Corp., $100 million.

The Kansas City Public School Employees Retirement System was one of the earliest public employee funds to establish a dedicated bond fund when it selected Scudder, Stevens & Clark to set up a $28 million portfolio in March 1982.[56] However, public funds were far slower to adopt dedicated and immunized portfolios than corporate funds, and far fewer eventually did so. This was probably because the funds were often internally managed and had employees managing the bond investments. Dedication or immunization would have left those employees underemployed. In addition, public funds had a more secure source of funding than corporations—tax revenues—so there was less pressure to cut pension costs.

Gold in Alaska

Meanwhile, the State of Alaska Retirement System took an unusual approach to combating inflation: It bought gold. Peter Bushre, deputy treasurer, waged a 16-month campaign to win legislative approval for the $700 million fund to invest in gold, foreign securities, real estate, and the use of financial futures for hedging purposes. The legislation gave the fund permission to invest up to 10% of its assets in gold bullion, and within a few months Bushre had bought a ton of gold at $651 per ounce.[57] By the end of 1980 the fund had bought a second ton of gold for $575 per ounce. Bushre said the gold was bought because "the record for gold is enviable in preserving real dollar value in times of inflation."[58] No other pension fund made a significant commitment to gold following Alaska's lead. A year later the gold move appeared ill-timed as the gold price had dropped to $470 an ounce. The Alaska Public Employees Retirement Fund sold its ton of gold in March 1983 at $414.25 an ounce, or $16.6 million, representing a loss of almost $9 million. The Alaska Teachers Retirement Fund held on to its ton longer before it, too, sold at a loss.

Bell Rings

In August 1980 the Bell System shook the pension world when it announced it was merging the 33 separate pension plans of its subsidiaries into just two—one for salaried employees and one for hourly employees—and merging all of its matching pension funds into two, with total combined assets of $28 billion.[59] The two new plans had different benefit structures, with salaried employee pensions being based on the career average salary rather than the average salary of the final five years of employment. The object of the exercise was to save money. The new benefit formula and the savings possible on the investment management side could amount to $400 million a year. The subsidiaries employed, at substantial cost, a total of 117 investment management organizations, 70 trustee banks, 11 investment management consultants, and seven master trustees. In addition, 225 Bell System employees were employed to oversee the funds throughout the company. The subsidiaries spent $35 million in management fees and $16 million in brokerage fees each year. The $28 billion of the two new funds made it the largest centrally controlled pool of assets in the country, ahead of Equitable Life, the largest manager of pension assets at that time with $21.9 billion.

The consolidation was spurred by a new contract with the Communications Workers of America, which required that assets backing the pension benefits of hourly workers be split from those backing the benefits of salaried workers. Money managers working for the Bell System braced themselves for fallout as they expected the company to significantly reduce the number of managers it employed. For example, all three major index fund managers—Wells Fargo Investment Advisers, American National Bank and Trust, and Batterymarch Financial Management Inc.—managed index funds for Bell subsidiaries. In addition, AT&T ran an inhouse index fund. Four index funds were not needed. The move to centralize reversed a process of decentralization which began in 1959 when the Bell System's assets, all managed by Bankers Trust, were gradually taken under control by the subsidiaries. By the end of 1980 the combined assets had grown to $30 billion, but David P. Feldman, assistant treasurer, and John English, director of pension fund administration, had made no dramatic moves to whittle down the number of managers or to reallocate the assets.

The managers need not have worried. Less than 18 months later AT&T entered into a consent decree with the Justice Department agreeing to break itself up so that it could pursue opportunities in the new world of telecommunications and computers. At first the details of how this agreement would affect the nation's largest pension fund were skimpy. The company had to submit a plan to the Justice Department on how the 22 operating companies should be grouped regionally. The pension fund issue was not at the top of anyone's agenda in drafting that plan, even though the assets had now grown to more than $35 billion. Eventually, the company and the Justice Department agreed to break the Bell System up into seven regional operating companies, known as regional Bell operating companies, or RBOCs. As a result, the energies of David Feldman, assistant treasurer overseeing the pension fund, Robert Angelica, his deputy, and the staff were focused on breaking up the fund rather than whittling down the number of managers. In fact, Feldman was involved in determining how much of the assets each of the funds of the new operating companies would receive, how the managers and trustees should be allocated, and how illiquid assets such as real estate and oil and gas investments could be handled.

In its divestiture plan, released December 6, 1982, AT&T announced that it would divide the money management organizations handling the $36.5 billion assets among the seven new regional operating companies, as far as possible, on the basis of the relationships that had existed at the time the funds were consolidated in 1980.[60] The plan also called for the seven regional operating companies to get their shares of the assets in two stages. Those with well-developed pension staffs could get 60% of their assets within a few months of the divestiture's effective date. The remainder of the assets would follow within 12 to 18 months when actuarial calculations were completed. Subsidiaries that did not have well-developed pension staffs by 1984 could leave their assets with AT&T until 1987. The fund's $3.1 billion in real estate investments were to be handled through real estate group trusts, which AT&T was establishing to house the assets and in which each regional operating company could participate. Each regional company could then withdraw its share of the assets invested in real estate as it desired, subject to the availability of funds. In June 1983, four regions declared they would be ready to accept their assets on the January 1, 1984 effective date.[61]

Russell Trust

In October 1980 the Frank Russell Co., the most influential of the nation's pension consultants, shook up the pension management world by putting itself into competition with the money management community by launching the Russell Trust Co.[62] The company, in effect, was putting its ability to select the best investment managers on the line. It offered four commingled funds, each managed by several of the best investment managers the Frank Russell Co. consultants could identify. If those funds failed to provide superior performance, and performance was not ahead of the relevant index over a long period, Russell's consulting reputation, based on its supposed expertise in selecting the best money management firms for its clients, would suffer.

The four commingled funds offered were an equity fund, a fixed income fund, an international fund, and a short-term investment fund. The equity commingled fund had eight managers in four styles: growth, broadly diversified, rotating, and defensive yield. The fixed income fund had four managers, and the international fund three. The short-term fund was to be managed internally. But this could be a mixed blessing for the chosen firms. Being hired by the Russell funds enhanced their reputations and brought them additional assets to manage and so additional revenues. If they performed poorly, however, they would surely be quickly replaced, and the firing would be a public confirmation of failure, which might hurt future efforts to gain clients. In addition, Russell negotiated a lower management fee for the assets it delivered to the managers—in effect, a volume discount. In this way it could add its own fee on top and still give the clients total fees competitive with other managers. The managers selected for the Trust accepted the lower fees because of the additional volume and because they had zero marketing costs for the assets Russell brought them. Russell was doing the marketing. For the clients, the Trust offered the promise of access to the best performing managers the best investment management consulting talent could identify. Often the funds were too small to hire those managers directly because many of the managers had minimum account sizes of $20 million or greater.

In starting the Russell Trust Co., George Russell was in part responding to the demand for his firm's services. When he started the consulting operation, he promised his first clients he would never take on more than 40 consulting clients. After those first 40 clients were onboard, however, and as the firm gained in stature, more and more pension funds sought its help, especially small and medium-sized funds. Even if he had been able to take on more clients, the Russell approach was impractical for many funds because a fund needed at least $2 billion in assets to be able to employ the number of managers with different styles required by the approach. At a meeting with Burlington Industries in 1979, Russell was challenged by Burlington executives. The company had just bought a subsidiary with a $35 million pension fund which they could not for some reason include in the parent's master trust. "What are you going to do for the subsidiary's fund?" the executives asked Russell. Thinking quickly, he responded that he would set up some commingled funds using multiple managers in which their small fund could invest. The Russell Trust Co. was established after George Russell had cleared the concept with his 39 primary clients. (He had dropped one that was too difficult to deal with.)

One year later Russell started the Frank Russell Investment Management Co., which manages mutual funds on the same multiple-manager basis as the trust company manages commingled funds. IBM was one of the first clients, hiring the firm to manage assets used to fund its retiree medical insurance program. Needless to say, the Frank Russell Trust Co. and the Frank Russell Investment Management Co. were not greeted with enthusiasm by the money management community. Most viewed them as direct competition. Even those who had been recommended to pension funds by the Frank Russell Co. feared the company would recommend the trust company to its clients in the future rather than them. Many felt it was a conflict of interest for Russell to be both consulting and managing money. Nevertheless, the growth of the Frank Russell Trust Co. in particular was rapid. A decade later it offered 15 commingled funds and managed $9.3 billion through the managers it selected. The performance of the funds appeared to validate the Russell approach to manager selection.

The Frank Russell Co.'s move into money management was soon followed by several other leading consulting firms, among them Rogers, Casey & Barksdale Inc. and Evaluation Associates Inc. In November 1983 Wilshire Associates joined the money management bandwagon when the Minnesota State Board of Investment hired it to manage $1 billion in an index fund that would track the Wilshire 5000 Index.[63] According to Jeff Bailey, the assistant director of the $7 billion system, the fund chose the Wilshire 5000 to capture the entire equity market. Trust banks that bought Wilshire's index fund tracking software and consulting services were not pleased that a supplier had suddenly become a competitor. All the consultants had realized that consulting was a low-margin business because it was difficult to leverage the consultant's expertise. Each consultant could service only so many clients, and the clients would pay only so much.

At the same time, the pension investment world was becoming more complex, requiring more research into such topics as active management styles in stocks and bonds, not only for U.S. securities, but also international securities; expertise in real estate and oil and gas deals; knowledge of options strategies; and, just on the horizon, fixed income and stock index futures. New investment vehicles were constantly being created, and new investment firms were being formed. With more personnel needed to stay on top of all of these developments, costs went up at least as fast as revenues. Asset management, on the other hand, particularly active equity management, was a high-margin business in which additional clients did not necessarily add to costs because of economies of scale. One portfolio manager using computers could just as easily manage a dozen $20 million accounts as one $10 million account if they followed the same basic investment style. The multi-manager approach pioneered by Russell, while it offered lower fees to both manager and consultant, offered more assets.

They more than made up in volume the revenues they lost through the lower fees.

CAPM Attacked

The Frank Russell Trust Co. was not the only controversy of 1980. Another erupted when a UCLA finance professor challenged the alphas apparently being produced by many money managers and indirectly questioned the Capital Asset Pricing Model. Professor Richard Roll had noticed that many managers in the late 1970s appeared to be producing positive alphas. That is, they were producing returns above those that would be expected from the level of risk (as measured by beta) they were taking. According to the Capital Asset Pricing Model, that extra return, known as *alpha*, was the result of taking risk specific to each stock and reflected the manager's ability to select stocks that outperformed the market. That is, it was a measure of a manager's stock-picking skill. Roll argued that in most cases, this alpha was a result of using the wrong benchmark to reflect the market. An example of this was when the Standard & Poor's 500 Index was used as a benchmark for the calculation of beta and the performance of money managers. The S&P 500 is not truly representative of the whole market and is an inefficient portfolio. Therefore, as Roll observed, it would give a false impression of the risk being taken by money managers. Roll argued that the positive alphas of many managers in the late 1970s was the result of their overweighting small-cap stocks when those stocks, which are underweighted in the S&P 500, were doing well. That is, the managers were taking advantage of a weakness in the index. Measured against an efficient portfolio (i.e., a better index), their stock-picking ability might well disappear.[64]

In contrast, other finance professors defended the utility of the Capital Asset Pricing Model and beta. Burton Malkiel, a professor at Princeton University, said that while beta's measurement of the risk of individual stocks was not very accurate, the beta of a large and diverse portfolio was accurate. Barr Rosenberg, still a professor at the University of California at Berkeley and president of the consulting firm BARRA, said CAPM made unrealistic assumptions about the world but nevertheless remained a useful theory. Other defenders of CAPM acknowledged that no one believed beta was a perfect measure of risk, but it was the best available measure at the time and would not be abandoned until a better one was developed.[65] Beta remained the most common measure of portfolio risk even at the end of the 1990s. However, Roll's criticism of CAPM and beta had the effect of prompting consultants and pension executives to look more skeptically at managers' alpha. It made them more aware of the fact that the S&P was not a very good replica of the market, and it accelerated the search for better indexes.

The Wilshire 5000 Index became more widely used, and in the mid-1980s the Frank Russell Co. developed the Russell 1000, 2000, and 3000 indexes. Another professor, Stephen Ross of Yale University, developed a possible replacement for the Capital Asset Pricing Model, the Arbitrage Pricing Theory (APT). However, APT was never as widely accepted or adopted as CAPM, though Ross and Roll founded an investment management firm called Roll and Ross Asset Management Corp. to manage money using the insights of the Arbitrage Pricing Theory.

Benchmark Portfolios

Another solution to the problems arising from using the S&P 500 Index as the common benchmark for all equity managers was to develop benchmarks specific to each manager. This was a more complex task than it might seem. Indeed, it was a task beyond the ken of most pension fund internal management teams, even if they had the resources, and it was not something mainline consulting firms, with the possible exceptions of BARRA and Wilshire Associates, were interested in providing. This provided a business opportunity for two veteran pension executives, Tom Richards and Dave Tierney, both of whom had strong mathematical backgrounds—a vital requirement. On April Fool's Day 1984, they opened the doors of Richards & Tierney, a boutique consulting firm specializing in developing "normal" or benchmark portfolios against which money managers could be measured while preventing the gaming of the benchmark.

Tom Richards was a mathematics major from Bucknell University and had started his working career at Corning Glass. After an MBA at Penn State and several years with the Allis Chalmers pension fund, he joined Harris Trust and Savings Bank in Chicago to help develop quantitative analytical services for Harris's master trust department. While Richards and his staff built a solid book of business with clients like Owens Illinois, Collage Co., Mannville Corp., and Delta Airlines, it was not as successful as Harris expected. Richards found some funds interested in the analytical services but not in the master trust services. Others were interested in the master trust services but not in the analytical services. So by the end of 1983 he was seeking something with more future. Dave Tierney gave it to him on a golf course. Why not develop benchmarks that would show whether or not managers were adding value within their proclaimed area of expertise? If a manager claimed to be able to select growth stocks that would outperform, Tierney suggested he be measured against an index of growth stocks.

Tierney, like Richards, was mathematically oriented. He had a Ph.D. in mathematics from the University of Wisconsin and had joined Amoco in 1970, soon moving into the treasury department. Eventually, by doing statistical asset and liability simulations for the pension fund, he entered into the pension area. When Tierney joined the pension fund staff, he found the fund managed by several balanced managers as the first step away from insurance company annuity contracts. Tierney worked with Phillip Binzel, the fund director, to restructure the management of the fund. It became a pioneer in venture capital, international investing, and in the early 1980s, leveraged buyouts. Its participation in the Forstman Little leveraged buyout which took Dr. Pepper private earned the fund a 40% annualized return.

Once the Amoco fund was restructured and was investing in a broad array of investment options, Tierney was ready to do something entrepreneurial. He had been wrestling with the problem of determining precisely what value managers were adding, and to do so thought of using benchmark portfolios. Tierney's idea was first to get each manager to specify his or her investment style and then to identify the universe of stocks that were appropriate for that manager to buy using that style. From that universe, he would construct a benchmark portfolio that would provide an appropriate benchmark return against which the manager's efforts could be measured, for good or ill. That is, the manager would be expected to beat the investment return of the passive benchmark portfolio. This was the product Richards and Tierney began offering in April 1984, and its first clients were Owens Illinois and Air Products & Chemicals. Over the course of the next few years, the company broadened its product line—for example, developing a market completion fund for the IBM pension fund. A market completion fund is a portfolio designed to fill in the gaps left after the fund's other active managers buy their portfolios. Richards and Tierney also analyzed the efforts of money managers for pension fund clients to determine where the managers gained their positive returns versus the benchmarks, or lost value when they underperformed. In 1998 they had 23 pension fund clients. Today pension funds and mutual funds are often measured not only againt a market index and peer groups, but also against benchmark portfolios.

Chapter 10

Social Investing

Because of the 1981 and 1982 recession, and a weak economy for several years afterward, tax revenues trailed the rate of spending growth at both the federal and state levels, increasing deficits and threatening future spending. Politicians and social activists therefore turned once again to pension funds, especially public and union funds, as possible sources of funds to finance what they viewed as necessary expenditures. This built on the ideas in Rifkin and Barber's book *The North Shall Rise Again*. The interest in such spending was not limited to the Northeast; actually, interest spread across the country as the 1981–1982 recession bit. Use of the investing power of pension funds took on several different forms, all of which came to be loosely called *social investing* for a time.

The first form of social investing involved using the threat of institutional sales of a company's stock, with its impact on the stock price, or the power of the pension funds' proxy votes, to change corporate behavior. This eventually became known as *social responsibility investing* or *corporate governance*. The second form involved the use of pension assets to stimulate economic activity in a particular region, as Rifkin and Barber had proposed. This was known as *targeted* or *in-state* investing. The third form was akin to the second, but involved making investments in troubled areas at concessionary rates—that is, at below-market rates. This became generally known as *social investing*. That is, social investing came to mean giving up returns to achieve a social good, and the Department of Labor ruled that violated ERISA, because the assets were not being invested solely in the interests of the beneficiaries. They were being invested to meet others' needs or concerns also. Targeted investing did not violate it if the investment promised market rates of return on a risk-adjusted basis. Of course, public funds were those most under pressure to engage in social investing, and they were not covered by ERISA.

The social responsibility or corporate governance form was the first form of social investing to gain momentum, driven by opposition to the apartheid regime in South Africa. Many public employee and Taft-Hartley pension funds urged or ordered their money managers to divest their portfolios of the stocks of companies doing business in South Africa and to boycott the stocks of those companies in the future. The hope was that by reducing demand for the stocks their prices would be affected, encouraging other shareholders to pressure corporate managements to withdraw from South Africa. For example, the San Francisco Board of Supervisors passed a resolution late in 1973 urging the San Francisco City Employees Retirement System to divest itself of South Africa-related stocks.[1] The fund resisted because as many as 400 stocks would therefore become off-limits. Needless to say, an institution sprang up to provide research identifying the companies doing business in South Africa; those producing defense equipment, cigarettes, and alcoholic beverages; those accused of violating the Occupational Health and Safety Act; and those considered anti-union or discriminatory in some other way. This institution was the Investor Responsibility Research Center, formed in 1972 with the backing of Harvard University and the Carnegie Foundation. The initial corporate responsibility moves were not limited to public or union-related funds. In 1974 the $10 million Phillips–Van Heusen pension fund took a substantial loss when it sold its holdings of International Telephone & Telegraph Corp.'s stock because of its "irresponsible behavior concerning political contributions and intervention in political process, both domestically and internationally."[2] ITT had been accused of involvement in the overthrow of the president of Chile, Salvador Allende. At about the same time, the Annuity Board of the Southern Baptist Convention sold its $350 million retirement fund's $450,000 holding of Braniff International stock because the airline offered alcoholic beverages on its flights.[3] In 1979 Control Data Corp. issued social investment criteria which its pension fund managers were to consider in buying common stock. To the usual social criteria it added a ban on companies initiating unfriendly takeovers.[4]

For the next 15 years, however, the dominant issue in corporate social responsibility was doing business in South Africa, and many large public funds sold their holdings of the stocks of companies doing business in or with that country. Some were ordered to do so by their legislatures. One of these was the New Jersey Division of Investment, which managed $11.4 billion in assets for New Jersey public funds, and the staff of which was unenthusiastic about the law. It meant the fund would have to sell the stock of any company doing business in or with South Africa. The staff of the New Jersey fund believed, as did many others, that selling all South Africa-connected stocks would adversely affect the performance of the fund because many of the leading U.S. companies had operations in South Africa, or their products were sold there.[5] By August 1983 24 states had introduced legislation calling for public employee pension funds to sell their holdings of the stocks of companies doing business in South Africa.[6] A study by SEI Funds Evaluation Services, a consulting firm, concluded in 1986 that divestiture of South Africa-related holdings would cost the Wisconsin state pension funds $131 million over six years.[7] The New Jersey Division of Investment found that in the first 10 months it sold stocks of targeted companies worth $721 million. Roland Machold, the director of the investment division, said the law had reduced the quality of the available investment universe. The transactions costs, he reported, were $8.3 million in the first 10 months and were estimated to be $50 million by the end of the program.[8] By the end of the 1980s, most state funds and many large city and county funds had divested. However, with a few exceptions, corporate pension funds did not join in the divestiture movement. Most pension executives were reluctant to tie the hands of their money managers by restricting the stocks they could buy, and most believed the stock boycott would have little effect on corporate behavior. One study showed that boycotting stocks considered socially undesirable would have cut investment performance by more than 25% in the five years ended July 1979. Nevertheless, by 1986, public employee funds with assets of more than $220 billion had divested their portfolios of stocks of companies doing business in or with South Africa.

In the 1980–1987 period the targeted investment movement—that is, investing to benefit the economy of the state or locality where they originated, or directing the assets into investments that would help meet social needs—accelerated. This concept was not a new one, even when Rifkin and Barber wrote their book. In 1974 the National Association of Home Builders was looking for a sponsor on Capitol Hill for a bill that would direct up to 25% of pension assets into residential mortgages to stimulate home building. This was during the 1973–1974 recession when home-building activity had all but dried up. Vice President designate Nelson Rockefeller, the former governor of New York, had testified before the Senate at the time that he believed there should be some "more effective" means of channeling savings into the capital-starved housing construction market. He noted pension funds had been investing heavily in the stock market. "I think they have found out that was a mistake," he said. However, pension executives reacted negatively to the proposal, the stock market recovered strongly, and it was never acted on.

Nevertheless, many states and municipalities began investing part of their assets in in-state mortgages to help lower mortgage rates and stimulate housing construction. Among the first were Hawaii and the Virgin Islands, and Alabama soon followed suit.[9] The action picked up as the 1981–1982 recession began. In Illinois, a civic organization attempted to have Illinois state and city pension funds redirect a portion of their $9 billion in assets into financing local businesses through Small Business Administration loans and direct loans.[10] At the same time, efforts were made to divert significant amounts of the $12 billion assets of the New York State Common Retirement Fund into mortgages and targeted mortgage-backed securities. In Florida, the president of the International Union of Operating Engineers Union Local 675 began a program of making below-market-rate mortgage loans to union members from the union pension fund's $25 million in assets.[11] In California, a state task force appointed by Governor Jerry Brown proposed redirecting part of the $60 billion in assets held by public and private pension funds within the state into mortgages and small and medium-sized firms in the state.[12] The $1.5 billion Connecticut State Trust Fund announced in early 1981 that it would invest $450 million over five years in home mortgage loans within the state. The initial $40 million pool sold mortgages at a 13.75% rate, even though the market rate at the time was 15.75%.[13] The New York City Funds, on the other hand, invested in targeted Government National Mortgage Association mortgage pools at the market rate. The proceeds were to be reinvested by Ginnie Mae back into the New York City region.[14] In the 1982 election season, the question of in-state investing by pension funds became an issue in state gubernatorial races from Pennsylvania to Illinois to California. In-state investing was not always limited to housing. The $3.2 billion Alabama Retirement System pension fund provided $75 million of the $495 million financing for a new steel plant in Fairfield, Alabama, for the U.S. Steel Co.[15]

David Bronner, the chief executive of the Alabama Retirement System, was not reticent about using the pension fund's assets to help build up the state economically. He probably did more in this area than any other state fund executive over the next two decades. Bronner gained a bachelor's degree and a master's in finance from Mankato State University, Minnesota, and then followed his mentor to the University of Alabama to take his Ph.D. in administration and higher education. At the same time, he attended law school and gained his J.D., becoming assistant dean of the law school. However, five or six months later, in 1973, the dean of the business school, Paul Garner, recommended Bronner for the soon to be vacant position of secretary treasurer of the retirement system.

When Bronner joined the retirement system in April 1973, he found a woefully underfunded system with $500 million in assets and $1.5 billion in unfunded liabilities. He also found the system invested about 7% in cash, 5% in stocks, and the remainder in the fixed income area, with 15% of that in municipal bonds. The last-named were unsuitable for tax-exempt pension funds because, since the interest was tax exempt, they paid less interest than federal or corporate bonds. Often these bonds had been bought as a favor to a well-connected broker. Bronner halted the practice and sold the bonds, raising the ire of the brokers who realized it meant no more sales of municipal bonds to the Alabama Retirement System. One of the brokers made an effort to have Bronner ousted, but it failed. Bronner also found a poorly administered system. He discovered, for example, $7 million or $8 million in checks sitting in the drawers of the office at any one time. Processing the checks so slowly cost the fund interest income that could be earned if they were deposited quickly. Bronner took immediate steps to protect and process the checks and have them deposited the day they arrived so that they could begin earning interest. He also discovered one of his office workers carrying several million dollars worth of bearer bonds—unregistered bonds that anyone could sell easily—across the city unescorted, and unaware of what she was carrying. Checking further, he found another $80 million of bearer bonds sitting in an unlocked safe in the fund's offices. He quickly had the bearer bonds locked in bank vaults and then registered so that they could not be misappropriated.

Bronner realized that the Alabama Retirement Systems would never be fiscally healthy unless the state's economy could be improved. The state, he said, had first-rate benefits financed by an economy that was ranked near the bottom of all the states. "If we have a poor state, and we have huge pension benefits compared with every other place in this country, then my philosophy needs to be the stronger economically I can make Alabama, the stronger the pension fund will be because the pension fund is dependent on the economy of the state. I cannot survive without a growing economy," Bronner said. Before he committed the money for the U.S. Steel plant, Bronner had begun a targeted Ginnie Mae program designed to funnel pension fund money into mortgages for Alabama workers. Soon after, he began building office buildings in Montgomery for state workers. The first one housed the offices of the Alabama Retirement Systems, but others became home to other state employees as they were completed. They also housed commercial enterprises. The buildings made Bronner unpopular with the politically connected local real estate interests who lost the state departments as high-paying tenants in their buildings. But the state government became more efficient because workers in the same department were not scattered in small buildings across the city.

By the beginning of 1983 Bronner had invested $540 million of the system's $3 billion in private placements designed to bring companies to or keep companies in Alabama. Among these were a medical center and loans to such foreign companies as Dynamite Nobel, Ciba Geigy, and MacMillan-Bloedel Ltd. In later years, Bronner would invest $120 million of the retirement systems' assets in building an archipelago of championship public golf courses designed by famed golf course designer Robert Trent Jones. This project was intended not only as an investment that would earn a return for the funds, but one that would encourage tourism and retirement in Alabama. In this way, it would improve quality of life and help to attract more industry, thereby creating jobs and increasing the tax base. Bronner argued that the investments earned competitive returns, but it was not clear that they did so on a risk-adjusted basis. That is, even if the returns appeared competitive with market returns, there was no measurement of the relative riskiness of the investments. In addition, there was no accounting for all the costs—for example, for the land and infrastructure of the golf courses, much of which was donated by local governments, who thereby incurred costs. These were typical of the problems associated with measuring the true risk-adjusted returns of social investments. Most of Bronner's investments were not directed into the state, though often they were far from conventional. In the early 1980s, as interest rates on bonds began to decline, he invested in equipment trust certificates, which are basically private placement fixed income investments secured by specific pieces of equipment, such as aircraft or rail cars. Bronner invested in both for the Alabama Retirement Systems, financing Boeing 737 and 757 aircraft for Delta Airlines, American Airlines, and U.S. Air, and railcars for a number of railroads. Because they are private placements and relatively illiquid, they pay higher interest returns than other fixed income investments with similar maturities.

Bronner's program of in-state investing was by far the most aggressive and creative in the nation. In most other states the programs were far smaller and far more conservative. According to a survey conducted by the Municipal Finance Officers Association, by the end of 1982 public pension funds had $3.5 billion, or 2% of their assets, invested in job-creating or housing-related investments. However, of the $3.5 billion, almost $1.1 billion was accounted for by the New York City retirement funds' targeted Ginnie Mae program.[16]

In-firm Investing

The recession of 1981–1982 took its toll not only on tax revenues, but also on corporate profits. Some companies now found themselves strapped for cash just at the time they were expected to accelerate the funding of their pension plans to meet the requirements of ERISA. They adopted their own form of in-state investing. Although ERISA prohibited the companies from directly using pension fund assets to buy real estate or plant and equipment for them without an exemption from the Labor Department, which was not easily obtained, it did not clearly prevent them from contributing other than cash to their funds. They could contribute stock to the funds rather than cash as long as the funds did not then have more than 10% of their assets in the sponsoring companies' stocks. One of the first of the noncash contributions was a 3.35 million share contribution of convertible preferred stock by cash-strapped U.S. Steel Corp. to the $5.6 billion U.S. Steel and Carnegie pension fund. The company valued the contribution at $335 million.[17] The fund was already the largest single holder of U.S. Steel Corp. stock, with holdings valued at $297 million. The year before, U.S. Steel had contributed $255 million in cash to the fund. The convertible preferred was the company's first, so the contribution raised questions about the value of the preferred stock, especially as the issue was not registered and therefore could not be easily sold by the fund. However, the issue was valued by Morgan Stanley Inc. Both the Internal Revenue Service and the Department of Labor examined the contribution but took no action. Just before the end of the year, the pension fund was able to register and sell part of the issue to institutional investors through a syndicate led by Morgan Stanley for $107 a share, a profit of $7 per share.

The U.S. Steel contribution seemed to open the floodgates to noncash contributions. Within a month both Reynolds Metals Co. and Wheeling-Pittsburgh Steel Corp. had contributed newly issued stock to their funds. Reynolds Metals contributed 600,000 of convertible preferred shares valued at $30 million to its $610 million fund, and Wheeling-Pittsburgh contributed 753,000 shares of cumulative nonconvertible preferred stock valued at $26.3 million to its $260 million fund. The Reynolds contribution was half of its $60 million annual contribution; the remainder was made in cash. Wheeling-Pittsburgh would not reveal its total annual contribution.[18] On September 30, 1982, Eastman Kodak Co. issued 3 million shares of common stock, valued by Goldman Sachs & Co. at $80.25 per share, or $240.8 million, to its $2.5 billion pension fund. Three weeks later, the fund sold the stock for $94.28 per share to a syndicate of investment banking firms, giving the fund a tidy profit as the price of the stock rose while it was holding it. The syndicate fared less well, for a few days after the deal Kodak's share price fell back to $88 a share.[19] The Kodak deal had investment bankers and others wondering because the company, unlike U.S. Steel and Reynolds Metals, was not short of cash. At the time of the contribution, the company had more than $500 million in cash. However, this total was down from $1.3 billion a year earlier, and the company may not have wanted cash reserves to fall any lower. It may also have feared that going directly to the market with the shares itself to raise the cash, and then contributing the cash to the fund, might negatively affect the company's share price. At the time of the contribution, the executives of the Kodak fund had reaffirmed the long-standing policy that the fund would not hold a large amount of company stock.

LTV Corp. contributed its own bonds rather than stock to its $1.2 billion pension fund. The placement of the debt into the pension fund was piggybacked on to a $150 million bond offering the company made in November 1982. Of the $150 million issue, $25 million par value was placed with the pension fund. However, since the bonds sold at a discount, the market value of the block contributed was only $22.1 million. LTV's annual contribution to the fund was about $200 million.[20] In December, Boise Cascade Corp., the paper company, contributed timber tracts worth $15.6 million to its $437 million pension fund, realizing a profit on property that had been held on the company's books at a very low value. It then leased the property back so that it could continue to harvest the timber.[21] Also in December, Martin Marietta contributed convertible exchangeable preferred stock worth $25 million to its $1 billion pension fund. In January 1983 Martin Marietta, American Airlines, and Republic Steel Corp. all contributed stock to their pension funds. American Airlines and Republic Steel made the contributions as parts of larger public share offerings. Martin Marietta's common shares in its second contribution apparently were acquired by the company as it successfully fought off a takeover attempt by Bendix Corp.[22] While the American Airlines' fund was free to sell its shares, Republic Steel's fund could not sell its shares until April 16 unless the price of the stock rose or unless holding them violated fiduciary standards. Martin Marietta's fund could not sell its shares because the board of directors of the company retained investment authority over the shares.

As the year progressed, the pace of noncash contributions quickened. American Motors Corp. contributed $17.6 million of stock to its $300 million fund.[23] Lear Seigler contributed a Hawaiian leasehold worth $5.6 million to its $161 million fund to cover its $6 million contribution.[24] Diamond Shamrock Corp. contributed an $18 million oil and gas royalty interest to its $145 million pension fund.[25] Burroughs Corp. sold four light manufacturing plants worth $30 million to its $470 million pension fund.[26] Exxon Corp. contributed a 15.1-acre office and retail development in Houston's North Belt area near Houston's Intercontinental Airport to its $3.5 billion fund.[27] The property was valued at $54 million. Armco Steel contributed $50 million of cumulative convertible preferred stock to its $1.1 billion fund in June of 1983,[28] and U.S. Steel and LTV Corp. both made second noncash contributions in August. This time the LTV contribution was 2 million cumulative preferred shares worth $50 million.[29] The U.S. Steel contribution was $250 million of exchangeable preferred stock.[30] However, as the economy continued to recover in 1984, the pace of noncash contributions declined, no doubt because contributions of stock reduced the value of outstanding shares (by increasing the supply). Contributions of other assets reduced shareholder equity, which also did not please shareholders if taken too far.

Pensions as Defense

Contributing the company's stock to the pension fund to save cash was one thing; getting the pension fund to buy stock to help prevent an unwelcome takeover was quite another, at least according to the Department of Labor. In October 1981 Grumman Corp.'s $650 million pension fund bought $40 million of Grumman stock to help block an unwelcome takeover bid by LTV Corp.[31] LTV had offered $45 a share for 70% of the outstanding stock and convertible shares of Grumman. Before the takeover bid, the Grumman pension fund owned 525,000 Grumman shares and had not bought any in the previous 10 years. The fund bought the stock at an average price of $38.61 a share, compared with the share price of $22 a share before LTV made its bid. The Grumman trustees naturally said they had bought the stock because it was a good investment, and not specifically to block LTV's takeover attempt. The Labor Department did not buy that explanation and charged the trustees with breach of fiduciary duty and not acting solely in the interests of the employees. "This case presents a classic example of plan fiduciaries whose dual loyalties have prevented them from acting exclusively in the plan's interest," said the government's complaint. In December, U.S. District Court Judge Jacob Mishler found the trustees had acted imprudently.[32] Judge Mishler said the trustees had made their decisions without "sufficient inquiry into the facts upon which they based their decisions." He added: "We find their conduct was solely motivated by their all-consuming desire to defeat the tender offer." He noted that the LTV takeover, with its consequent runup in prices, represented an opportunity for the trustees to see how the plan might be served by tendering the stock. In May 1982 a U.S. Court of Appeals upheld Judge Mishler's finding that the trustees had been imprudent. In March 1983, with the LTV takeover defeated and the Grumman stock selling for just over $49 a share, the Grumman trustees sold the stock with a nice gain for the fund.[33]

Other companies found other ways to turn the pension fund assets to their advantage. Late in 1981 the Great Atlantic and Pacific Tea Co. (A&P) terminated its $550 million pension plan to take back $200 million in assets.[34] The plan was to use the recovered assets to help restructure the company, which a short time before had been acquired by the Tengelmann Group, a family-controlled West German retailer. At the time, the present value of accumulated vested plan benefits was $179 million, and the present value of nonvested benefits was about $9 million. The company was able to buy annuities with interest rates of 15% to pay these benefits, leaving about $200 million in surplus assets. A&P had closed 1,624 unprofitable stores between 1975 and 1981, and for the second quarter of 1981 had reported a loss of $11.4 million. Employees and former employees of A&P filed suit to block the termination, and in April 1982 the company and the plaintiffs settled out of court after A&P agreed to spend an extra $50 million to increase their benefits.[35] A court fight promised to be a messy one because the trustees of the A&P plan had specifically changed the rules of the plan to allow the company to recover the surplus. Until only months before the termination, the plan documents had specified that any surplus assets belonged to the employees.

Also late in 1981, executives of Harper & Row, Publishers, Inc. terminated the company's defined benefit pension plan and used $9.6 million in surplus assets (after buying annuities to pay accrued vested benefits) and $1.5 million of profit-sharing plan assets to buy for $20 each more than one million of the company's shares that had been held by the *Minneapolis Star & Tribune*.[36] To replace the pension plan, the executives set up an employee stock ownership plan (ESOP) to hold most of the acquired shares, though the profit-sharing plan also received some shares. The executives acted when the *Minneapolis Star & Tribune* decided to sell its 33% holding in Harper & Row. The executives did not want the block to fall into other hands and felt the ownership of the stock by the employee stock ownership plan and the profit-sharing plan would discourage any unwanted takeover attempt. As in the Grumman case, the executives portrayed a decision made solely for the benefit of the company as being in the best interests of the employees. But the employees had clearly lost the security of a diversified, well-funded defined benefit plan and had seen it replaced by an ESOP invested solely in company stock. Not only were the employees' jobs now dependent on the future success of Harper & Row, but so, too, were their retirement incomes. If Harper & Row should fail, both would be lost. A few years later Harper & Row was bought by News Corp. which bought all the employees' stock and replaced the ESOP with another retirement plan.

Terminations

As the recession continued in 1982, more companies found themselves unable to continue to carry the burdens of their defined benefit pension plans. Braniff International Corp., the parent of Braniff Airlines, terminated its four pension plans in August 1982, dropping a $37 million unfunded liability on to the Pension Benefit Guaranty Corp.[37] A few months later two more plan terminations, by Rath Packing Co. and White Farm Equipment Co., added at least another $83 million to the PBGC's burden, which was already over $300 million.[38] The PBGC appealed to Congress for a premium increase to $6 per plan participant from $1.50, but Congress was slow to act. As concerned as it was about the termination of underfunded plans and the plight of the PBGC, Congress was even more concerned about the growing incidence of companies terminating over-funded plans to recapture the excess assets, like A&P, or to use the assets for corporate purposes, as Harper & Row had done.

The termination rush continued in 1983. The high interest rates meant the present value of future liabilities was low, so the value of the assets was greater than the value of the liabilities. The plans were over-funded. If terminated, there would be surplus assets for the company to recapture. Companies were able to buy annuities carrying interest rates of between 14% and 15% from insurance companies to pay future benefits to employees. Since in most cases they had assumed future growth of only 9% or 10% for the assets, buying such annuities gave them immediate gains. Early in 1983, financially troubled Western Airlines terminated one of its two pension plans for its pilots, which had assets of $129 million.[39] The termination resulted in $23 million in excess assets reverting to the company to help it overcome its financial difficulties. In May 1983 Occidental Petroleum Corp. terminated its four defined benefit pension plans to use an estimated $250 million in surplus assets to pay down its debt.[40] The debt had been incurred when Occidental bought Cities Service Co. a year earlier for $4 billion. The fact that $160 million of the surplus came from the termination of one Cities Service plan raised suspicions that the plan's overfunding had helped make the company attractive to Occidental. By the time the company completed its plan terminations, the total surplus had grown to almost $400 million because of the strong market gains. At almost the same time, AM International, formerly Addressograph Multi-graph, which was operating under Chapter 11 of the bankruptcy laws, filed to terminate its pension plan to recapture as much as $65 million from its $145 million plan. The fund had been 65% in equities when the market took off in August 1982, boosting the value of the assets.[41] The defined benefit plan was to be replaced by a combined profit-sharing and employee stock ownership plan (ESOP), with contributions based on the company's net income. Half of the contribution was to go into the profit-sharing plan, and half was to buy stock for the ESOP.

In midyear, AMAX Inc. devised a new approach to recapture the excess assets in its pension fund.[42] It proposed to split its plan for salaried workers into two separate plans: one for active workers and one for retired employees. The company would then fully fund the plan for active employees and move the remaining assets into the plan for retired employees. After buying annuities to pay the benefits for the retired workers, the company would terminate that plan and keep the excess assets, estimated at between $100 million and $130 million. The approach became known as a *spinoff termination*. The Internal Revenue Service, in a private letter ruling, approved the approach, but the PBGC opposed it, fearing the remaining plan could become underfunded in the near future if economic conditions worsened. However, the PBGC was between a rock and a hard place because if it opposed AMAX's proposal too strongly the company might terminate both plans. While one plan was operational, AMAX was at least paying the PBGC premium. If it ter-minated both, it would pay nothing to the PBGC and probably still would recover the surplus assets. Between the beginning of 1980 and the beginning of 1983, PBGC figures showed, 104 companies had terminated 114 pension plans and recovered $443 million.[43]

The number of plan terminations and the amounts recaptured enraged some members of Congress. "The proliferation of these self-interested employer activities is spreading unchecked, like some insidious disease," said Representative Edward R. Roybal (D-Calif.), chairman of the House Select Committee on Aging. The committee held hearings on the issue at which members were highly critical of the IRS, the Labor Department, and the PBGC for not doing more to prevent terminations with surplus asset recapture, especially spinoff terminations. The IRS promised to reexamine its position, which had previously held that spinoff terminations were legal. While the IRS, the Department of Labor, and PBGC were trying to decide what action they could take, other companies hurried to terminate. In October 1983 Celanese Corp. announced that it would do a spinoff termination to recapture $300 million of its $700 million fund.[44] At the same time, Reynolds Metals Co. announced it would terminate its pension plan for salaried employees, which had assets of $470 million, to recapture $130 million of excess assets.[45] However, Reynolds said it would start a new defined benefit plan for salaried employees offering higher benefits. Stroh Brewing Co., reacting to the PBGC's delay in approving spinoff terminations, announced in October that it would terminate its entire $138.6 million pension plan to recapture $81 million. Stroh had previously announced that it would do a spinoff termination. By November the IRS was considering a 50% excise tax on recaptured surplus assets. However, as one IRS official told *Pensions & Investments* that month: "It's a lousy situation. It's a private system. You don't want to discourage funding." The official also correctly warned that the problem would not be solved quickly and that the issue of surplus recapture would remain a hot issue for several more years.

Golden Age

The 1979–1984 period marked a second golden period for the birth of new money management organizations. Corporations, at least those that were financially stable, were pouring money into their pension funds to meet ERISA's funding requirements. Corporate pension assets increased at an 18% compound annual rate during the period, and their equity holdings climbed at a 16% compound annual rate.[46] Since the stock market provided a 15.4% compound annual return at this time, it was clear that corporate asset growth was not just from market returns. Even many public officials were becoming serious about funding their pension plans. Their assets grew at a 16% compound annual rate, and their equity holdings increased at a 21% compound annual rate.[46] The recovery from the 1973–1974 bear market left many funds with larger pools of assets to manage. Such was the growth of pension assets that some executives were concerned there was not enough investment capacity to handle the growth in the existing institutional firms. This was because some of the firms that started in the late 1960s didn't want to grow much more. Many wanted to remain a certain size because that's what they had committed to their clients and because, before the era of the inexpensive personal computer, managing individual portfolios was more manpower-intensive and expensive than it is today. In addition, many of the boutique money management firms used investment approaches in which the universe of suitable stocks was relatively small. John Casey of the consulting firm Rogers, Casey & Barksdale spent 15 months traveling the country with a research associate identifying and analyzing small money management firms not yet used by pension funds, where there might be hidden talent. They visited 184 managers in 76 cities and 34 states and produced written reports on 95 of them. The problem was on the verge of being solved as there was a surge of new money management firm startups. Many portfolio managers at large institutions decided they could do what they were doing just as well in their own firms. The cost of entry was low. All they needed was an office, a telephone, perhaps one of the new personal computers, a small administrative staff, and a marketing person. The potential rewards were great; if successful they could soon double or triple their incomes.

Batterymarch Financial Management, one of the success stories of the first golden era, was the source of two startups in this period. The first was Grantham, Mayo, Van Otterloo, which started just ahead of the boom in 1977 when two of the principals, Grantham and Mayo, had a falling out with Dean LeBaron, whom they had helped start Batterymarch. The second startup was Pacific Financial Research, established by James Gipson, a portfolio manager at Batterymarch. Grantham and Mayo felt, with some justification, that they were providing more than their share of Batterymarch's good investment ideas but were getting less than their share of the credit and the profits of the company. To many institutional investors, LeBaron was Batterymarch and vice versa. When they realized the situation would not change, Grantham and Mayo joined with financier Eick Van Otterloo to start a new firm bearing their names. Their results were impressive from the start, and by 1980 Grantham, Mayo already had $240 million under management, showing other would-be entrepreneurs what was possible.

Other firms started in this period were Gray, Seifert & Co. Inc., which five months after opening its doors had $120 million under management; Delafield Asset Management, which soon had $85 million under management; and Lynch & Mayer Inc., which registered with the SEC in February 1979 and by mid-1980 had six tax-exempt clients and $50 million under management. This was only the tip of the iceberg, with growth surging in 1981 and 1982. By late 1983 a number of successful firms, even some new ones, closed their doors, at least partially, to new clients. Grantham Mayo Van Otterloo had closed its doors to domestic equity clients, keeping a promise to clients to close when they reached $250 million, though they remained open to international clients. Lincoln Capital Management, Chicago, closed to equities but would still take fixed income clients. First

Pacific Advisors, Strong/Corneliuson Capital Management, and Neuberger & Berman Pension Management all closed their doors, at least partway. All eventually reopened after they had time to digest the assets and staff up to manage more money.

Perhaps the most interesting startup of 1980 was a firm called United Asset Management, founded by Norton Reamer, a former chief executive officer of Putnam Management Co. Although Reamer had been a successful portfolio manager, he did not intend for his firm to directly manage stocks. He would manage a portfolio of money management firms, and his firm would be a holding company owning those firms. The idea had been tried previously, in the early 1970s, when the Boston Co. put together a constellation of money management firms around the country, some acquired and others started from scratch with local talent. They were firms such as the Boston Co. of Louisville, the Boston Co. of the Southeast, and Kennedy Boston Associates. But the Boston Co. constellation fell apart between 1977 and 1980 as it tried to exert too much control over the firms, alienating the entrepreneurs who had started them. As a result, most of the firms bought themselves back from the Boston Co. and went on to be very successful.

Reamer graduated from Harvard Business School in 1960, and by 1977 he was chief executive officer of Putnam Management Co. Reamer wanted to do something entrepreneurial, and he saw tremendous growth in the pension and institutional investment management business in the 1980s. He decided that growth would make money management firms more valuable and that the rising values would disrupt the natural way of transferring ownership from one generation to another. The younger generation would not be able to afford to buy out the older generation, and psychologically they would be unwilling to pay the high prices because they had helped build the firm. The only way for the founders to realize their capital investment in 1980 was to sell out to giant corporations such as American Express, Prudential Insurance, Chemical Bank, Merrill Lynch, or Marsh & Mclennan Inc. That solution was unsatisfactory for most entrepreneurs because of cultural differences and because they disdained the prospect of being just faceless senior executives running a division among legions of senior executives.

Reamer's idea was to start a holding company, United Asset Management (UAM), which would buy the money management firms, allowing the senior management to turn its ownership into cash or easily marketable shares for future retirement and estate purposes. However, key personnel would be tied to their firms by long-term contracts, an attractive revenue-sharing arrangement, shares of UAM stock, and other financial incentives.

At the same time, these executives would be left to manage their firms as they saw fit, without interference. Each firm was encouraged to continue managing and investing in its own time-proven fashion. The former owners could continue to increase their own earnings and wealth by continuing to grow the revenues and earnings of their firms. They shared in the earnings, and growing earnings would lift the value of UAM stock. In this way, Reamer believed he could avoid the problems the Boston Co. had encountered. The Boston Co. had tried to realize economies of scale by producing all the investment research for its firms and charging them for it. But none of the firms wanted the research because they could get it for soft dollars—essentially for free—from other firms. Furthermore, the Boston Co. tried to impose its investment philosophy and strategy on all the firms. This infuriated all the founders of the firms. In addition, the strategy proved to be wrong for the times, so all the firms were wrong at once. The result was an explosion that ended the Boston Co.'s grand experiment in the late 1970s.

Reamer made his first acquisition in August 1983, and by the time United Asset Management went public in August 1986, it had acquired 11 firms with $13.6 billion under management. A decade later the company had 49 investment management subsidiaries in the United States, Canada, and Europe, and Reamer seemed to have solved the problems that perplexed the Boston Co. However, he faced other problems as the investment management world changed. One key change was the slowing growth of defined benefit pension plans and the rapid growth of the defined contribution pension plans. A handful of mutual fund companies quickly began to dominate the defined contribution plan business, and few of them were for sale. All the firms UAM acquired were in the defined benefit market. A second key change was more competition to purchase the best firms from companies similar to his own and from money management organizations trying to grow through acquisitions. This second change drove up the prices of the successful defined benefit money management firms.

Another unusual firm started at this time was Dimensional Fund Advisors. It was begun in 1981 by Rex Sinquefield, who had left his position as head of the trust department of American National Bank in Chicago, and David Booth, who had left A. G. Becker Funds Evaluation. Sinquefield had kept up with the academic literature while at American National and had noted the research that seemed to show that over the long term small-cap stocks outperformed large-cap stocks. This made sense intellectually as smaller companies were, on average, intrinsically riskier than larger companies because they had fewer resources to draw upon. If investing in smaller companies was riskier, then it had to offer higher returns in the long run than investing in large companies, or no one would do it. Although small company stocks had outperformed large company stocks from the mid-1970s into the early 1980s, the research suggested this was not just a cyclical event. Even before the research was available, Sinquefield and his colleagues at American National had developed the Market Expansion Fund, an index fund that invested in stocks that were not in the S&P 500 universe.

Sinquefield and Booth, who had known each other at the University of Chicago, decided to start a firm that would invest in small-cap stocks in a passive, or at least a semipassive, way. They decided to develop an indexed approach that would invest in the smallest stocks. Initially, they used the stocks in the bottom two quintiles of the New York Stock Exchange in terms of capitalization, buying 300 stocks in the fund, which was registered as a private mutual fund. Now the fund has about 2,000 stocks in it, the smallest stocks on the New York Stock Exchange, American, and Nasdaq exchanges. "We had the misfortune of starting at the worst nine-year period ever for small stocks in terms of performance relative to the S&P 500," said Booth. "We underperformed the first nine years by about 750 basis points (7.5%) a year; ouch! But we were nevertheless able to grow the business because the story was so solid. People believed in it." By the end of 1982 the company had $234 million under management. Just a year later the total was $800 million, and it reached $1 billion by March of 1984. The $10 billion level was reached in 1994, and by 1998 it had climbed to $27 billion. In the meantime Booth and Sinquefield introduced new products, including the 6–10 fund which buys the stocks in the sixth through tenth deciles of the market. Dimensional Fund Advisors was the quintessential quantitatively driven money management organization.

Women and Minorities Last

Women and non-Caucasian men were distinct minorities in the pension management business in the late 1970s, but by 1983 a few women-owned money management firms had gained a foothold in the business. Possibly the first to do so was MEG Asset Management, a fixed income firm headed by Madeline Einhorn Glick. Glick had been a fixed income manager at BEA Associates in 1980, during the startup boom, and within three years had $200 million under management. About the same time, Joan Payden and Sandra Rygel left the Los Angeles office of Scudder, Stevens & Clark Inc. to start Payden & Rygel as a fixed income manager concentrating on short-term investment. Within two years they were managing about $500 million. Susan Byrne left GAF Corp., where she had been an assistant treasurer running the pension fund, to start Westwood Management Corp. Byrne had started her career as an analyst at William D. Witter Inc., then moved on to Bankers Trust Co. managing money, and moved over to GAF to oversee the pension fund and manage money as well. A year after she established Westwood, she had $50 million under management. Unlike Glick and Payden & Rygel, Byrne managed equities.

Although most of these women said they had experienced no discrimination in their careers, Kathryn Magrath had a different experience. In January 1982, Magrath, former director of equity investments at the Ford Foundation, established ValueQuest in partnership with her husband Terry and two others. Magrath had begun her career at the St. Louis Union Trust Co., St. Louis, in 1963 as a junior analyst trainee, over the opposition of the head of personnel who felt women were unsuitable as analysts and only wanted such jobs to find husbands. She then became an oil analyst, studying with some of the best analysts in the business, but by 1966–1967 she wanted to manage money. However, the head of personnel resisted her promotion to portfolio manager, maintaining that women were too emotional to manage money. Magrath thereupon took a job which doubled her salary with Waddell & Reed, the Kansas City investment banking and brokerage firm, from which came so many top investment managers, including those at Jennison Associates. In 1969 Magrath moved on to Keystone Custodian Funds, Boston, where she managed the $500 million Keystone K-2 fund with good results. However, in October 1974, with mutual funds experiencing massive redemptions near the end of the bear market, Magrath, the only woman among 13 fund managers, was let go. "I was told I was female, I was married, and I had a husband who had a good job at Fidelity, and it was not right to fire the men because they had families to support," Magrath said. "My performance was the best on an absolute and relative basis, and I was running the second biggest fund." Magrath filed suit against Keystone in 1975, and it was settled in her favor in 1976. As a result of the suit, no one in the Boston financial community would hire her, but she was hired by United Brands, New York, to oversee its $110 million pension fund. Four years later she was hired as director of equity investments at the Ford Foundation. Two years after that, with venture capital backing, she launched ValueQuest as a value-oriented money management firm. It was a struggle. The first pension fund client, Baker International, did not come for almost 18 months, and that was followed after an interval by Washington University, Boeing Aircraft, and the New York City Teachers Retirement fund. But it was 10 years before the firm's assets climbed to $500 million in tax-exempt assets, but then in just two years more it hit $1 billion under management. By early 1998 ValueQuest had $1.5 billion under management, making it one of the largest women-owned money management firms in the United States.

Another firm started in this period grew to be the largest minority-owned money management organization in the country by 1998. This was Sit Investment Associates, founded in 1983 by Eugene Sit, who was born in China in 1938 and came to the United States at the age of nine. His grandfather and grandmother had come to the United States in the 1860s to help build the western railroads. They saved much of the $1 a day the grandfather earned and eventually returned to China with their children and bought property. Sit's father, an American citizen by birth, came to the United States in 1938 to start an import-export business, planning to send for his family later. First Japan's invasion of China and then World War II, however, postponed his reuniting with his family until after the war.

Gene Sit attended DePaul University, majoring in accounting, and after graduation he joined Commonwealth Edison in Chicago. Soon, however, he was involved in running the company's pension fund. Discovering he liked the investment field, by 1968 he joined IDS Advisory Services in Minneapolis as a fund manager. In 1977 he became chairman and president of IDS Advisory Services, building it from $500 million under management to $3 billion by 1981, and he also became chairman of IDS Trust Co. In 1981 Sit founded his own firm. Because of his excellent record and reputation at IDS, and because pension funds were looking for new money management firms, his firm grew quickly. By 1998 it was managing $6.2 billion, with $3 billion in domestic equities, $700 million in international equities, and $2.5 billion in fixed income portfolios.

Many of the money management firms started in this second golden age, including Grantham Mayo, Pacific Financial, Payden & Rygel, and Sit Investment Associates, eventually offered their own mutual funds or managed funds offered by other mutual fund companies. They thus broadened the range of investment expertise available not only to pension funds but also to individual investors.

Leveraging Up

In September 1981 three names that were to become familiar to pension funds and other institutional investors and, the public at large, appeared in *Pensions & Investments* for the first time: Kohlberg, Kravis, Roberts & Co. The firm was offering a new form of investing—the leveraged buyout, or LBO. *P&I* reported that the $2.6 billion Oregon Public Employees Retirement System would invest at least $100 million in the leveraged buyout of Fred Meyer Inc., the Portland-based merchandising company. In an LBO, a group puts up some cash and borrows a lot of money to buy up all the stock of a public company, or a division of a company, often an underperforming or undervalued company or division. The purpose is to take steps to realize the hidden value of the company or to improve its performance in ways that are difficult for public companies to do. The group hopes it can manage the company more efficiently or reorganize it so that the market will eventually recognize the true value of the company. At some point the company or division that has been privatized is taken public again, and the investors in the buyout group share in the gains. The LBOs were put together by groups such as Kohlberg, Kravis, Roberts & Co. (KKR) and Forstmann, Little & Co., which sought out groups of investors to put up the money and then found the underperforming companies to buy.

In the case of Fred Meyer Inc., the fortunes of the merchandising operations obscured the value of real estate the company owned. KKR split the company into two, one containing the real estate and the other the merchandising operations. When KKR took Fred Meyer public again in 1983 after the restructuring, returns to investors of up to 400% were produced.[47] Although a few corporate pension funds, such as Textron Inc., had been quietly involved in LBO investing before, the Oregon investment was the first to come to light.

In 1982 the State of Michigan Retirement System had followed Oregon's lead and committed $15 million to a KKR LBO fund. It also allocated $3 million to a venture capital fund that would invest primarily in Michigan. William A. Ammerman, director of investments for the Michigan fund, said the LBO investment was attractive to the fund because of the potential for superior returns.[48] In October 1983, nine pension funds committed $250 million to an LBO partnership managed by Forstmann Little & Co. They were a virtual roll-call of innovative pension funds: Standard Oil of Indiana, Texas Instruments Inc., Honeywell Inc., Minnesota Mining & Manufacturing Co., GTE Corp., General Electric Co., Phillips Petroleum Co., Boeing Co., and Boise Cascade Corp. Each committed between $10 million and $90 million. "We were looking for an opportunity for diversification," said Jan Yoemans, manager of 3M's $1.2 billion pension fund. The LBO investment should produce "roughly double the short-term rate," said Standard Oil's Philipp Binzel. "We see it as a substitute for fixed income." Jerry Barnett, director of pension investments at Phillips Petroleum, said: "We went into it as an intermediate fixed-income investment with an equity kicker."[49] Before the end of 1983, the Oregon Public Employees Retirement System and the Washington State Investment

Board had each contributed $100 million to KKR's newest LBO fund, for which KKR aimed to raise $1 billion. The pace of LBO investing would pick up in the years ahead, and so would the controversy. Yet, over time, it would become clear that LBO investing, while it imposed costs on some workers (those who lost their jobs as the companies cut costs and operations to become more efficient), played a vital role in making U.S. companies more efficient in their use of shareholder assets. The LBO movement would not have been possible without the participation of pension funds. It was a small but powerful tributary of the money flood, sweeping away much deadwood.

Chapter 11

Consolidation

The mid-1980s in pension investment was a time of consolidation of the revolutionary developments of the 1970s and early 1980s. The assets of both private and public pension funds grew phenomenally under the impact of both increased funding by the sponsors and the improved capital markets, particularly the equity markets. At the end of 1983, private pension assets, excluding those with insurance companies, totaled $811 billion; a year later they were $880 billion; and by the end of 1985 they were over $1 trillion. Public fund assets grew from $311 billion at the end of 1983 to $404 billion by the end of 1985. In addition, at the end of 1985 pension assets in insurance company accounts—annuities, GICs, and so on—totaled an additional $400 billion.[1] Thus, total pension assets were approaching $2 trillion, and they were having an enormous, growing, but largely invisible impact on the economy through the capital markets. Pension funds owned more than 25% of the stocks in the equity markets, and they accounted for more than 60% of trading on the New York Stock Exchange. As a result, their investment decisions, or the decisions of their agents, the money managers, moved the markets.

Pension Fund Power

Pension funds owned billions of dollars of real estate—hotels, office buildings, factories, and warehouses—and there were signs that their financing of these was causing an oversupply. Their common stock investments set the cost of equity capital for corporations, in effect channeling capital first to those companies that were most likely to use it most efficiently. Through their investments in fixed income securities, the pension funds were financing the government and the growth of companies, large and small; also, through their purchases of Ginnie Mae securities, they were helping to finance housing. Through their investment in venture capital, they were financing the next wave of American corporations. Although the institutions of government were largely unaware at the time, the power of this pension capital was beginning to intrude on the powers of government. Of course, government still held the power of life and death over pension funds, but the time was quickly coming when government would have to consider the possible impact of its policies on pension funds more carefully than it had in the past. Pension fund capital would soon influence the direction and implementation of government policies, at first only in the United States but ultimately in the rest of the world as well. Initially, this pension fund power was felt in the bond market.

As the budget deficits ballooned during the Reagan administration—the result of tax cuts and a large increase in government spending—the federal government had to borrow more in the bond market to finance the growing debt. Bond investors, particularly professional bond investors managing money for pension funds, had only recently emerged from a period of high inflation which had destroyed the value of their long-term bond portfolios. Not about to stand idly by and let that happen again, they continued to demand high real rates of return from government (and corporate) bond issuers, even as inflation steadily declined. At the slightest hint that government policies might lead to renewed inflation, they fled the bond market, driving interest rates even higher and bond prices down. These bond investors became known as the "bond vigilantes" and became a disciplinary body on the Federal Reserve and the U.S. Treasury.

Gross Power

One of those vigilantes, though he would have rejected the title, was William Gross, chief investment officer of Pacific Investment Management Co. (PIMCO), the investment management subsidiary of Pacific Mutual Insurance Co. During the late 1970s and early 1980s, PIMCO built an enviable record in fixed income management, largely through the efforts of Gross and the team he built, and soon it surpassed other fixed income managers in assets under management. In 1975 PIMCO had only $22 million of pension assets under management. By 1980 that total had climbed to $2.2 billion, and by the beginning of 1985 it was $7.9 billion, 65% of it in fixed income securities.[2] Gross grew up in Middletown, Ohio, and Los Altos, California, and graduated from Duke University with a major in psychology. Also at Duke he spent four months teaching himself how to count cards, and upon graduation in 1969 he went to Las Vegas with $200 and turned it into $10,000 at the Black Jack tables. Then the Navy beckoned. Gross initially wanted to be a pilot, but he quickly found pilots had to be detail oriented "and that wasn't me. I was and am a conceptual person, and conceptual pilots are dead pilots, basically." Instead, he found himself appointed chief engineer of a destroyer, and while there he decided the stock market offered a field where he could use his mathematical ability. After completing his Navy service in 1971, he completed an MBA at UCLA and took a job as a private placement analyst in the bond department at Pacific Mutual Life Insurance Co. "I took the job knowing I wanted to jump over into the stock department a few years later when I got the experience. But, as fate would have it, I had found my niche."

After a year at Pacific Mutual, Gross wanted to try actively managing $10 million of the insurance company's bonds. At the time, like most insurance companies, Pacific Mutual bought bonds with the idea of holding them to maturity. But on the East Coast, fixed income managers were beginning to follow Andy Carter's ideas to actively manage bond portfolios. Gross took the concept to Pacific Mutual's investment committee which accepted the idea in early 1973 and gave him $10 million from the general account to manage actively.

Gross was so successful that he was soon moved over to PIMCO, the investment management subsidiary that was managing a small equity mutual fund for the insurance company's salesmen to sell. There he was joined by Jim Muzzy, who was managing the preferred stock in the mutual fund but was assigned to market Gross's active bond management track record. PIMCO's first bond client was the Southern California Edison pension fund, which gave Gross a $50 million account to manage. "We had to sell it to their investment committee, but it was really a matter of cross relationships with board members," said Gross. PIMCO's first nonrelated account was $50 million from the AT&T fund in 1976. "Once they hired us it was easy to open doors," he said. The State of Hawaii, R. J. Reynolds, and Bechtel Corp. all followed in the next six months. Gross admits the approaches used in the late 1970s were relatively unsophisticated. They were more "touchy-feely," he said. "There was maturity management and sector management," but without the mathematical basis.

As inflation and interest rates accelerated in the late 1970s and early 1980s, new insights and tools for bond management were developed or rediscovered. These concepts included *duration*—a concept for measuring the volatility or risk of a bond or a bond portfolio which had been developed in the late 1930s and had been used by insurance companies, but was now adopted by active bond managers such as Gross. Bond management became a computer-driven, mathematical market. "We realized we had to compete in this new world," said Gross. He and Muzzey brought in graduates from the top business schools, such as the University of Chicago and Stanford, to keep their team on top of the latest techniques. Gross broadened not only the techniques, but also the kinds of fixed income securities he would buy for pension portfolios. He moved into lower-grade bonds, mortgages, mortgage-backed securities, and non-U.S. bonds. By the end of 1998, PIMCO managed $157 billion of assets, $130 billion of it for pension funds and other tax-exempt investors such as college endowment funds and charitable foundations, and much of the remainder for fixed income mutual funds.[3] The sheer size of these assets meant that any debt issuer in the U.S. market of significant size, whether government or corporate, had to consider how Bill Gross of PIMCO and his colleagues and competitors would view the terms of any issue before it was brought to market. If Gross and his peers did not like the terms of an offering, its price would be battered; it might even fail and be left in the underwriter's hands. Such was the power of the pension funds and their money managers.

Termination Concerns

Although government officials were largely oblivious to the power pension funds and their money managers were gaining through their fixed income portfolios, they remained very concerned about the trend of pension fund terminations. The PBGC estimated that by the end of 1983 companies had terminated 138 pension funds and recaptured $517 million during the previous three years.[4] At the time it reported 25 pending terminations that would return an additional $676 million to the plan sponsors. The terminations, most of them aimed at recapturing surplus pension assets, continued at a high pace in 1984. In January, Interstate Bakeries Corp. filed to terminate its fund and recapture $35 million to help reduce its debt load. In May 1984 J. P. Stevens & Co. announced it would terminate its plan and recapture $50 million from its $189 million fund. A few months later, Firestone Tire & Rubber Co. announced it would terminate its pension plan for salaried employees and recapture between $250 million and $300 million of its $609 million in assets.[5] The Reagan administration, in an effort to slow outright plan termination, had accepted spinoff terminations, calculating that employees were better off if the existing plan continued than if it were terminated and a new plan established.

In the Congress, however, concern about terminations was growing, with Senator Howard Metzenbaum (D-, Ohio) and Representative Edward Roybal (D-, Calif.) calling for curbs on the ability of companies to terminate plans to recapture assets.[6] According to Representative Roybal's calculations, in the previous five years 261 overfunded plans had been terminated, returning almost $3 billion to the employers. He offered a draft bill to curb the practice, writing in the introduction: "Unless Congress acts swiftly to curb such practices, many of America's pension funds will quickly and silently be bled dry, robbing workers of their future retirement security." Representative Roybal's bill would have ended the Reagan policy on spinoff terminations; it banned companies from starting a comparable plan for five years; it required employers to provide cost-of-living adjustments to the employees before the plan was terminated and to give employees within five years of retirement benefits to cover their expected future accruals; and it imposed a 10% excise tax on surplus assets recaptured by employers.

Representative Roybal and his like-minded colleagues argued that the employees lost benefits even when another plan was immediately started to replace the terminated plan. That is because, even if it were a defined benefit plan, the employees had to begin accumulating service credits again, and benefits in most cases were in part based on years in the plan. All too often, the terminated defined benefit plan was replaced by a defined contribution plan that offered employees far less retirement security. Needless to say, employers opposed any curb on their ability to recapture surplus assets. They argued that they had voluntarily started the pension plan and that the surplus assets were there only because, acting conservatively, they had contributed more than was necessary to fund the plan. They also took the investment risk, particularly the risk of investing in equities, and they would have had to make up the difference if the equity investments had failed. If they had to pay the price of any losses, it was only reasonable that they should not be prevented from taking part of the rewards of successful equity investing. They also maintained that the employees were better off with the company taking the surplus assets and ensuring its continuity than not taking the assets and going out of business. Roybal's bill went nowhere for the time being, and many more efforts would be made over the next several years to end plan termination.

Takeover Targets

Unfortunately, the pension surpluses made some companies takeover targets. A study by analysts at Oppenheimer & Co. in 1984 found a high correlation between the degree of overfunding of a company's pension fund and the number of 13D filings on the company at the Securities & Exchange Commission.[7] Investors must file 13D reports whenever they acquire 5% or more of a company's stock, and such filings are often the first sign that someone is planning an attempted takeover. The ability of companies to recapture surplus pension assets meant that they could borrow large sums to take over another company, terminate the acquired company's overfunded pension plan, and use the surplus assets to pay down the debt issued to finance the acquisition. Thus, corporate executives had an incentive to take the surpluses themselves and use them in their companies to help maintain their companies' independence and help them grow. However, a number of companies developed a new technique they hoped would deter takeover attempts. They amended their pension plans in ways that allocated the surpluses to the employees. Union Carbide, for example, amended its plan to provide that in the event of an unfriendly "change in control" surplus assets held in the plan would be used to increase benefits.[8] The company retained the right to terminate the plan and use the surplus for corporate purposes. The technique was known as establishing a "pension parachute," and among the other companies establishing them were Sun Co. and American Hospital Supply Corp. However, the pension parachutes were never tested, and there was doubt they would work because a similar device had failed when A&P was taken over by the Tengelmann Group of Germany.

Congressional talk about curbs on plan terminations seemed to spur more plan sponsors into action, as the pace of terminations quickened in the second half of 1984 and into 1985. Among the companies that filed to terminate their plans in 1984 and 1985 were giant insurance broker Frank B. Hall & Co.,[9] to recapture $20 million, Harcourt Brace Jovanovich Inc., to recapture $50 million,[10] AMF Inc., to recapture $100 million, and Getty Oil Co., $250 million. (Getty had been acquired by Texaco Inc., and Texaco was terminating the plan to pay down debt used in the acquisition.)[11] By March 31, 1985, according to the PBGC, corporations had recaptured $6.1 billion from terminated defined benefit pension plans, and another $1.5 billion in excess assets was at stake in 93 pending terminations.[12] Late in the year, the House of Representatives and the Senate passed compromise legislation that made it more difficult for companies to terminate plans, whether underfunded or overfunded. However, it was attached to a budget reconcilliation bill the Reagan administration would not accept, and it, too, died.

The threat of congressional action did not fade, however, but continued into 1986. So, too, did terminations, as the continued strong stock and bond markets boosted the funding level of the plans. Meanwhile, falling oil prices were putting pressure on oil company profits, and as a result oil companies looked to their pension plans for cash infusions. In June Exxon Corp. announced a spinoff termination of its $5.2 billion defined benefit pension plan to recapture $1 billion in excess assets.[13] Phillips Petroleum announced it would recapture $400 million in surplus assets through a termination,[14] and Ashland Oil Corp. aimed to recapture between $200 million and $300 million.[15] The multiplying oil company terminations recapturing such large amounts led to an immediate reaction in Congress. By August 1986 the Congress had passed legislation imposing a 10% excise tax on surplus assets recaptured.[16] This excise tax was in addition to the regular income taxes due on the assets. Terminations slowed under the impact of this excise tax and lower interest rates, which were reducing the size of many surpluses and lessening the temptation to recover them. Surplus recapture did not end, however.

A New Plan

In the meantime, a new form of employee benefit plan had appeared on the scene that would not only change the face of retirement planning in the future, but further complicate the lives of politicians and economic policy makers. This was the 401(k) plan, named after Section 401(k) of the Internal Revenue Code. The first 401(k) plan was established by the Johnson Companies, an employee benefit consulting firm in Newton, Pennsylvania. It was based on a design by Theodore (Ted) Benna, one of its benefit consultants, and it was literally the answer to a prayer. Benna is a scholarly, religious man. As he tells the story, he was working at home on a Saturday afternoon in 1979 trying to devise a new plan for a bank client who wanted to convert a cash bonus plan to a deferred profit-sharing plan. This was not an easy task because many lower-salary employees were reluctant to give up the immediate cash bonus for about the same money they could receive as, in effect, an improved retirement benefit in the future, even if the deferral did save them a few dollars in taxes. Benna was aware of another bank that had made such a conversion, with negative effects on employee morale. After a prayer for inspiration, he thought about Section 401(k) of the Internal Revenue Code which had been added only in 1978. Benna's solution was for the company to convert its cash bonus plan into a deferred compensation plan under the regulations of Section 401(k). Under this plan, the employees would defer part of their wages into the bonus or deferred compensation plan, and then the employer would match, to some degree, the employee's deferral. In effect, the employer's match became the bonus. The employee could only get it by deferring. The tax advantages of deferring salary, and the nontaxed employer's matching contribution, Benna thought, might be enough to encourage employees to participate in the plan and offset the loss of the cash bonus.

The (k) section Benna relied on was added to the Internal Revenue Code as a result of the efforts of Representative Barber Conable (R – New York) to solve a problem for companies, and employees of companies, such as Xerox Corp. and Kodak Corp. and some large banks that had generous profit-sharing plans. If the employees received payouts from the plans in cash, they would owe income tax on them. If the company required that they be deferred into the plan, the employees would not owe taxes. The cash or deferred compensation plans had grown up without formal legislation authorizing them, and the Treasury Department had begun expressing doubts about them. It was concerned that because higher-paid employees were deferring and gaining the tax benefits of deferral, and lower paid employees were not deferring but taking the money and paying the taxes, this was somehow unfair to the lower-paid employees. To end the disparity, it also began planning "nondiscrimination" regulations. However, when ERISA was passed in 1974, Congress made it clear that Congress, not the Treasury, would set any nondiscrimination regulations. Congress did not get around to defining the regulations until 1978, however, and it did so almost as an afterthought—and only because of Representative Conable. Congress was, in fact, debating adding Section 457 to the Revenue Code which would allow deferred compensation plans for public employees. Representative Conable, responding to Kodak and Xerox and others, piggybacked the Section 401(k) provisions on to the Section 457 amendment. The new section provided the legal framework for the existing cash or deferred compensation plans and inadvertently for Benna's creation of new deferred-only plans which became known as 401(k) plans. The new legislation allowed a discrepancy in deferral rates between low-paid and highly paid employees, as long as it was within certain limits.

Benna's design was greeted with skepticism, even by his superiors at the Johnson Cos., who doubted the IRS would accept it. Ironically, the bank for which Benna designed the plan rejected it when attorneys at its law firm said the idea would not fly with the IRS. But the Johnson Cos. ultimately backed Benna and started a 401(k) plan. Then Benna began a two-year effort to convince the IRS and get it to issue interpretations and regulations. Luckily, President Ronald Reagan had been elected in 1980 and was interested in boosting American savings, especially through expanded IRAs. Benna told Treasury officials that in Section 401(k) they had a better vehicle to stimulate savings than by trying to expand IRAs, and they eventually agreed. The IRS issued its regulations, formally recognizing the 401(k) plan in November 1981.

The IRS interpretation allowed employees to defer taxes on salary contributed to a qualified plan set up under Section 401(k), much as they could defer taxes on Individual Retirement Accounts (IRAs). Depending on the plan, an employee could contribute up to 15% of salary up to $30,000 a year to the 401(k), and that part contributed was not taxed until it was later taken out of the plan. The employer could match the employee's contribution in whole or in part, if it wished. In effect, the 401(k) was like a giant, company-sponsored group IRA, and its limits were far more generous than the IRA limits. There were complications, the most important of which were the strict nondiscrimination rules designed to ensure that highly paid executives did not reap a disproportionate share of the benefits.

The complications did not stop companies from originating 401(k) plans. Among the first after the Johnson Cos. were Quaker Oats Co., Honeywell Inc., Girard Bank, Johnson & Johnson Cos., and Continental Grain Co., all of which had plans in operation, or were in the process of establishing them, by mid-1982.[17] Most had converted an existing thrift or savings plan, or a profit-sharing plan, into a 401(k). Quaker Oats, for example, converted an existing profit-sharing plan because it wanted to add an element of employee contribution to the plan. Employee contributions might have affected the tax-exempt status of the profit-sharing plan. In Quaker's 401(k) plan, employees could contribute up to an additional 5% of pay to the plan on top of the bonus. The employees were given three investment options: Quaker Oats stock, a diversified stock portfolio managed by Institutional Capital Corp., Chicago, and a guaranteed interest contract run by several insurance companies.[18]

Honeywell Inc., on the other hand, started its 401(k) plan from scratch, because it did not have a plan it could convert. It was interested in adding a thrift element to its retirement plan, and the advent of the 401(k) provided a perfect vehicle. It set up a 401(k) that allowed individual contributions up to 4% of salary each year. Honeywell also offered three investment choices: a GIC from Travelers Insurance Co., a 100% equity fund, and a 50% equity-50% bond fund, the latter two managed by Chase Manhattan Bank.[19]

Such was the interest in 401(k) plans that the first conference on the plans, sponsored in June 1982 by the Employers Council on Flexible Compensation, attracted a standing-room-only crowd of several hundred employer representatives. A Greenwich Research Associates survey of

1,000 large pension plans found that 19% had started a 401(k) plan or had converted a plan to a 401(k) during 1982, despite the uncertainty about the final regulations.[20] Another survey, by Hay/Huggins, a Philadelphia-based employee benefit consulting firm, found that 31% of 869 companies surveyed offered a 401(k) plan, up from only 13% the year before.[21] Among the other large companies that had done so were Ford Motor Co. and Ciba-Geigy. The trend toward 401(k) continued growing in subsequent years, during which time major companies such as Burroughs Corp., Litton Industries, Shell Oil Co., and American Airlines joined in. A few companies that had terminated their defined benefit plans to recapture surplus assets had replaced them with 401(k) plans, a trend that would accelerate in future years. In addition, 401(k) plans proved immensely popular with employees, and many companies reported high voluntary participation rates. Employees often saw the benefit of saving on a tax-deferred basis, especially when the company promoted it. In addition, employees could see their 401(k) accounts growing year by year, and they knew they could take their own contributions, as well as the vested part of the employer's contribution, with them when they changed jobs. They could not do so with a defined benefit plan. The Brown-Foreman Corp., the Louisville, Kentucky, distilling company, reported that 93% of its employees signed up when it started its 401(k) plan.[22] State and local governments were also starting 401(k) plans. By April 1985 Tennessee and North Carolina already offered plans to their employees, while Mississippi, South Carolina, Texas, and Utah had received IRS approval for their plans.[23]

The 401(k) plans were becoming so popular that the Treasury Department, the Internal Revenue Service, and the Congress became concerned about the "revenue leakage" they caused—that is, the revenue they kept out of the government's hands. By the end of 1984 the IRS was looking for ways to make 401(k) plans less attractive to employees, initially by tightening the hardship withdrawal regulations.[24] A few weeks later the Treasury Department proposed repealing Section 401(k), thus killing the plans, noting that they were likely to deprive the Treasury of $4.6 billion in revenue between 1986 and 1989. The public rationale for considering repeal, however, was that higher paid employees took more advantage of the plans and that the law discriminated against employees whose employers did not offer the plans. The outcry from employers and their trade groups was so strong, however, that by April 1985 the Treasury was backing away from its elimination proposal. Instead, trial balloons were floated suggesting the maximum contribution might be cut from $30,000 a year to as low as $2,000 a year. Cuts in the maximum contribution were clearly coming, but the new level would not be set until after significant haggling.[25]

Initially, insurance companies gained most of the 401(k) plan assets as employees invested conservatively and were attracted by the "guarantee" in guaranteed interest contracts. Among the biggest were Equitable Life Assurance Society, the Travelers Insurance Co., CIGNA Corp., Aetna Life & Casualty, and Metropolitan Life Insurance Co. Strong mutual fund firms such as Fidelity Management & Research and Vanguard Group soon also gained business. Because of their recordkeeping systems for their mutual fund clients, they were well positioned to service the 401(k) participant. In addition, they had recognizable brand names, and they had many different fund options from which employers could choose to offer employees.

The growth of the 401(k) plans revitalized the mutual fund industry which had been struggling since the early 1970s. Although the industry had gained assets through the invention of the money market fund, this was a low-fee, low-profitability business. Through the late 1970s and early 1980s, the public showed little interest in equity mutual funds, and mutual fund companies largely missed out on the initial flood of pension money. There were several reasons for this. First, as George Russell had discovered, most large corporations did not want their pension assets managed on a pooled basis; rather, they wanted the attention of an individual portfolio manager. Second, smaller companies might have been more amenable to the use of mutual funds except for a provision in ERISA which stated that a mutual fund did not become a fiduciary to a pension fund when a pension fund invested in it. In other words, a pension fund's trustees did not reduce their fiduciary responsibility when they invested in a mutual fund's shares. They retained all the responsibility. When they hired a money management firm, the money management firm picked up a share of the fiduciary responsibility. Because pension fund trustees liked reducing their fiduciary exposure by sharing it with the money managers, even trustees of small funds were reluctant to use mutual funds. Ironically, the mutual fund companies had sought the provision in ERISA to protect themselves from pension fund liability. Instead, it simply protected them from defined benefit pension fund business. In addition, mutual fund loads and management fees made them more expensive than most money management firms or banks.

Although many mutual fund companies, including Fidelity, Vanguard, T. Rowe Price Associates, and Putnam Management Co., established pension fund management arms, they had only modest success in winning defined benefit fund business. This was undoubtedly because they were not single-minded about seeking the business. For most of them the mutual fund business was the dog, and the pension fund business was the tail, and the tail couldn't wag the dog. As of January 1, 1982, Fidelity Management

Trust Co., the pension arm of Fidelity Management and Research, reported assets of only $65 million, a drop of $1 billion from the previous year.[26] Pension funds had pulled their assets largely because they were getting poor performance, and some believed the best portfolio managers at Fidelity were set to manage the mutual funds while pension funds got the less experienced or talented managers. In *Pensions & Investments'* annual ranking of pension fund managers that year, the largest mutual fund company was T. Rowe Price, which ranked twenty-first with $6.3 billion in pension fund assets. Scudder, Stevens and Clark was ranked twenty-fourth, and Putnam Advisory, the pension arm of Putnam Management Co., ranked twenty-ninth.[27]

The advent of the 401(k) plan changed that. Now the companies were passing the investment decision, the investment return, and the investment risk on to the employees, and the mutual fund was the perfect vehicle for the employees' investments. Its shares were valued daily, and they could be bought and sold daily. In addition, the companies were educating the employees about investing and about mutual funds. Since in most cases the employees were paying the mutual funds' management fees, the employers didn't care too much about the higher costs. The flow of money into pension funds, including the new 401(k) plans, helped lift the stock market in the 1980s, and that helped lure 401(k) plan participants into investing more and more of their assets in stock mutual funds, reviving the mutual fund business. Corporate pension assets more than doubled between 1980 and 1985, from $469 billion to $1,038 billion. Similarly, the amount invested in common stocks increased to $462 million from $223 million. Public employee pension funds also swelled to $404 billion from $198 billion, and public fund equity holdings increased from $44 billion to $120 billion.[28]

Fidelity and Vanguard, the two most successful mutual fund companies in gaining 401(k) business, were headed by polar opposites. At the helm of Fidelity was quiet, publicity-shy Edward Crosbie (Ned) Johnson III whose family owned Fidelity Management and Research. Johnson's father, Edward Johnson, was a Boston lawyer who became involved in the infant mutual fund business in the 1930s and in 1946 started Fidelity Management and Research, which became the investment adviser and distributor of the Fidelity Fund which he had bought in 1943. Ned Johnson was born in 1930 and attended Harvard, majoring in psychology and social relations, joining Fidelity Management in 1957 as a security analyst.

For a time Johnson worked with Gerald Tsai, one of the very successful portfolio managers who helped put mutual funds in general, and Fidelity in particular, on the map. In 1961 Ned Johnson was given his own mutual fund to manage, the Fidelity Trend Fund, and in the next five years the fund outperformed all rival growth funds. Johnson senior turned the company over to Johnson junior in 1972, by which time Fidelity managed more than a dozen funds with total assets of about $4 billion. When in 1973 Dreyfus Corp. introduced the first money market fund, Ned Johnson responded quickly with an innovation of his own—a checking account tied to a money market fund. That is, investors could withdraw funds from their money market funds simply by writing checks. The money market funds became as convenient as bank checking accounts, and since they were not hampered by Regulation Q, which limited the amount of interest banks could pay, investors began to move money out of banks into money market funds. At the end of 1974 money market funds totaled only $1.7 billion; by the end of 1975 the total was $3.7 billion.[29] The money market fund helped spur the growth not only of Fidelity but also that of many other mutual fund companies. They helped them survive when investors bailed out of equity funds during and immediately after the 1973–1974 bear market.

Vanguard was headed by John Clifton (Jack) Bogle, an outgoing and outspoken self-made man. Bogle, born in 1928, attended Princeton where in 1951 he wrote his thesis on the mutual fund industry which at the time had only $2 billion in assets. Largely because of the thesis, Bogle was hired by Walter Morgan, founder and chairman of Wellington Management Co., which managed the Wellington Fund, then the fourth largest mutual fund in America. In 1958, at Bogle's urging, Wellington Management started the Wellington Equity Fund, later called the Windsor Fund. Bogle had perceived the imminent passing of the balanced fund, such as the Wellington Fund, and was certain that pure equity funds would become more popular. By 1965 Bogle was executive vice president of Wellington Management and oversaw a merger between Wellington Management and Thorndike Doran Paine & Lewis, a Boston firm managing the Ivest Fund. By 1970, however, friction had developed between Bogle, who was then president of the combined firm, and the four Boston partners who managed to have him fired by the board of the combined company.

Bogle may have been fired as president of Thorndike Doran Paine & Lewis/Wellington Management Co., but he remained president of the 11 individual funds managed by Wellington, each of which had a separate board of directors and was able to fight back. Supported by the boards of each of the funds, he started the Vanguard Group Inc., jointly owned by the original 11 funds, to provide administrative services to the funds. Over the next few years, Bogle had Vanguard appointed as manager to many of the 11 funds and other funds which the company started. Most important, in 1975 he started the first Standard & Poor's 500 Index mutual fund offered to individual investors and by 1998 the world's second largest mutual fund (after Fidelity's Magellan Fund), as well as one of the first money market funds. In addition, Bogle made Vanguard a no-load mutual fund company, meaning investors did not pay an initial sales charge when they bought their shares. Up to that time, most mutual fund companies charged investors a 7% front-end load; that is, out of every $100 invested in the fund, $7 went immediately to the mutual fund company to reimburse the salesperson and to cover other marketing expenses, and only $93 was invested for the investor. Because of its pioneering money market and index funds, as well as other active stock and bond funds, and because of its low management and administrative costs, Vanguard was well placed to prosper when the 401(k) market surged in the mid- to late 1980s. By 1998 Vanguard's index fund was capturing more 401(k) dollars than any other single mutual fund, and Vanguard was the second largest mutual fund company after Fidelity.

The most successful bank in the 401(k) business was Bankers Trust, which was among the first to recognize the growing trend based on a survey it conducted among employee benefits managers every two years. Bankers also was well positioned to handle 401(k) assets because it had a full range of pooled funds, especially an index fund, and it was a powerhouse in the master trust field which required strong recordkeeping systems. It aggressively marketed its services to its clients and others establishing 401(k) plans, and it became one of the top-five 401(k) providers by the mid-1980s. Most trust banks, even those with master trust capabilities, failed to recognize the advent of the 401(k) market until mutual fund companies and the insurance companies were well entrenched.

By early 1985 the average 401(k) participant had 38% of his or her assets in GICs, 19% employer company stock, 19% equity mutual funds, 10% bond mutual funds, 9% short-term funds, 4% balanced funds, and 1% life insurance, according to a Hewitt Associates survey.[30] The GIC would remain the most popular option for many years. While the Congress and the IRS would change the rules for 401(k) plans in ways designed to make the plans less attractive to employers and employees, the Congress would also take other actions against defined benefit plans that had the unintended effect of making the 401(k) more attractive. As 401(k) plans grew more popular, employers gave employees more investment choice and more investment education to handle their investment options. As more employees gained more assets and more investment freedom, it became more difficult for Congress to kill 401(k) plans. Congress could, however, impose new limits on the plans designed to make them less attractive. In

October 1986 the Congress passed legislation that reduced the maximum annual salary deferral to $7,000 a year from $30,000, and imposed new nondiscrimination tests on companies to ensure 401(k) plan benefits did not flow mostly to higher paid employees. The $7,000 cap meant an executive earning $200,000 a year could defer only 3.5% of salary before running into the limit. The legislation also made it more difficult for employees to withdraw assets from 401(k)s before age 59$^1/_2$, limiting withdrawals to the employee's own contributions and imposing a 10% excise tax on the amount withdrawn. The legislation also included additional restrictions designed to make 401(k)s less useful to higher paid employees. For example, it limited to $112,500 per year any tax-free distributions from a 401(k) plan, imposing a 15% excise tax on any additional amounts in addition to ordinary income taxes. Some pension experts correctly predicted the restrictions would reduce senior management's interest in retirement plans for rank-and-file employees and would take care of themselves with nonqualified pension plans, that is, plans that were not tax-exempt and were therefore unaffected by the rules.

Real Estate Redux

Meanwhile, defined benefit funds continued to pour money into real estate and international investing. Early in 1984 the Florida State Board of Administration, which oversees the Florida retirement systems, entered the real estate investment field for the second time. In late 1982 it had divided $300 million between Equitable Life, LaSalle Partners, and First Capital Financial Corp. for direct investment.[31] A year later it fired all three, deciding that direct investing was too risky for the fund. Instead, it decided to go the open-ended pooled fund route. It hired five new managers, including PRISA, Aetna Life & Casualty, and John Hancock Mutual Life Insurance, and it rehired Equitable to invest $265 million through their open-ended funds.[32] In midyear, 15 institutions, including at least five major pension funds, AT&T, ITT, and Bechtel Power among them, committed $150 million to Corporate Property Investors (CPI), a private real estate investment trust more than half owned by institutions. CPI specialized in shopping malls, but also invested in office buildings.[33]

Late in the year, the pension fund of US WEST, one of the new regional operating companies spun off from AT&T, hired TCW Realty Advisors and Jones Lang Wooten Realty Advisors and gave them each $100 million for direct separately managed investments.[34] In addition, the California Public Employee Retirement System and the California State Teachers Retirement System joined together to buy a $315 million portfolio of 97 commercial properties in the Pacific Northwest, particularly in Seattle and Portland.[35] A number of funds, including those of GTE, Hallmark Cards Inc., Eastern Air Lines, and the Southern Co., also were investing in timberland through pooled vehicles offered by Travelers Insurance Co., John Hancock, the First National Bank of Atlanta, and Wagner Southern Forest Investments Inc.[36] However, timberland would remain very much a minor investment vehicle for pension funds, as would agricultural land. Despite the continued interest in real estate, PRISA was still experiencing high withdrawals as some pension executives moved to direct investing from pooled investing. Nevertheless, Prudential Insurance remained the largest manager of pension investments in real estate, and at the end of 1985 pension funds had more than $30 billion invested in real estate.

Late in 1985 commingled fund returns fell, and declining interest rates meant quality properties became scarce. Some sponsors of open-end funds closed them and sold off some of their properties. Goldman, Sachs & Co. announced it would close its fund, send $100 million in contributions back to the clients, and concentrate only on megadeals for separate accounts. Bank of America also announced it was closing its $80 million open-end fund and selling off the properties, as did Crocker Real Estate Investment Group.[37] At the same time, other open-end funds continued to suffer from withdrawals as a result of terminations, the weak market in real estate, and a shift to closed-end funds and direct investing. During the year ending June 30, 1986, pension funds invested $12.3 billion in real estate and $5.6 billion, or 45%, in direct, noncommingled accounts.[38] Although other funds were cutting back on real estate, the new Bell operating companies were bucking the trend. Between mid-1984 and mid-1986, they hired a total of 23 real estate managers so that they could control their own destinies in real estate investing. At the same time, they were preparing to withdraw from the Telephone Real Estate Equity Trust, the $4 billion private REIT established by AT&T before the breakup.[39]

International Interest

International investing also remained an area of great interest for pension funds in 1984, 1985, and 1986 as AT&T, Kodak, GTE, Delta Airlines, Pacific Telesis Group (which was spun off from AT&T), Motorola Inc., and the State of Delaware hired international managers. Twelve more large funds hired international managers in the first quarter of 1985,[40] and by the end of the quarter the 25 largest international managers had $15.9 billion invested overseas for U.S. pension funds.[41] Ten more large funds hired for international investment in the second quarter, including US WEST, Sperry Corp., ITT, and Coca-Cola.[42] By the end of the year, the total was close to $26 billion as funds took note of the strong investment returns being turned in by the international managers. The pace of international hiring picked up in 1986 as more pension executives noticed the strong returns. They saw that the Europe Australia and Far East Index (EAFE) was up 86% for the 12 months ended March 3, 1986,[43] and by midyear assets invested internationally had climbed to $32.6 billion.[44]

Some money managers, together with their pension fund clients, began to look beyond the major markets, such as the United Kingdom, Germany, and Japan, and began to invest in emerging markets. Emerging markets were located in rapidly developing countries that were just beginning to start stock exchanges as growing companies looked beyond bank financing to fund their future growth. Initially, the interest was limited to places such at Hong Kong, Singapore, and Malaysia which had legal and financial systems based on the British systems. This gave investors confidence. The money flows from the pension funds through their money managers into stocks listed on these new but growing exchanges helped finance the growth of companies in these markets. It also helped push up stock prices. The money flowing into these markets also attracted the world's leading investment banking firms seeking to finance companies by selling their shares to the public. The flows of pension monies into both the developed and emerging markets contributed to the extraordinary returns many of these markets produced. The emerging markets, in particular, often had relatively few listed companies compared with the U.S. or European developed markets and relatively few shares of each stock traded each day. As a result, any significant flow of funds into or out of such markets dramatically affected price stock prices.

New Index Fund

Two other trends continued strongly in the 1984–1987 period—indexing and immunization and dedication. Early in 1984 the Minnesota State Board of Investment indexed $1.3 billion.[45] The transaction to construct the index fund was carried out by Wilshire Associates, which was to manage the fund indexed to the Wilshire 5000 Index. Only 1,000 stocks were to be bought, but the portfolio was to be constructed in such a way that it mirrored the movements of the whole index. The fund had to sell $1 billion in securities to establish the portfolio, and that was handled in an unusual way. Since the State Board had been criticized a year earlier for liquidating a $500 million portfolio in a way that drove market prices down significantly the day of the trading, it turned to Wayne Wagner, Wilshire's expert on stock market trading, to structure the bigger transaction. Wagner developed a trading strategy designed to eliminate leaks of information that might allow traders or other investors to take advantage of the Minnesota fund by buying or selling ahead of it.

First, the stocks to be sold or bought were divided into two categories: those that could be transacted with minor market impact, and those where market impact would be a problem. In the case of the stocks to be sold, this was a function not only of the liquidity of the stocks, but also the size of the holdings. Standard practice in a large trade was to tell the brokerage firms a day in advance what stocks were to be bought or sold. The brokers in return agreed not to buy or sell the stocks for their own accounts for two hours before the transaction. There was still the chance, however, that information on the planned transaction might leak out. Wagner, therefore, got the brokerage firms to bid on packages of the most liquid stocks without knowing exactly what stocks were in the packages. The packages contained randomly assembled shares of stock, and the brokers were told how many shares and how many companies were represented in each package. They were also told the average trading volume for each stock represented in each package, and each package had a balance of stocks to be sold and stocks to be bought. The names of the securities in each package were not identified, but the brokers had to bid for and guarantee the transactions costs for each package. The brokers were told the names of the stocks in the packages only minutes before the New York Stock Exchange closed and the transactions had to be completed. For the more thinly traded issues, Minnesota became a buyer or seller of opportunity, moving only when it was unlikely to significantly affect the price. This trading technique was adapted and used by many institutions making strategic portfolio switches in the years ahead.

Almost a year later, Morgan Stanley Asset Management engineered a $1.55 billion switch to indexing for the Central States Teamster fund, hiring both Bankers Trust Co. and Mellon Capital Management.[46] Bankers Trust got $750 million and Mellon Capital $800 million, with the money coming mainly from terminated active managers. The move, which would save the plan more than $4 million a year in active management fees, followed a refusal by the Department of Labor to allow Morgan Stanley to manage all the fund's equity assets in its own subsidiary. The Labor Department ruled that that idea produced a potential conflict of interest. By the end of 1985 total indexed assets had leaped 70% to $81 billion, with $70 billion of that in equity index funds and $11 billion in the newer bond index funds.[47] Early in 1986 IBM announced it was moving 75% of its fund to passive management.[48] It was already almost 50% passively managed. In mid-1986 the Illinois State Universities Retirement System more than doubled its passive investments to $1.1 billion of its $2.3 billion assets.[49] All was handled by Wells Fargo—$657 million in a stock index fund, $246 million tracking a bond index, and $118 million in an international index fund. Two months later the $2.7 billion Mississippi Public Employee Retirement System increased its passive investments to 50% from 20%.[50] The System used Bankers Trust as its indexed equity manager, and Wells Fargo and Lehman Brothers as passive fixed income managers.

Although there was a boom in demand for index funds, the fees the index fund managers could charge for running indexed portfolios were dropping because there were now many index fund managers. Besides Wells Fargo, Bankers Trust, and American National Bank and Trust of Chicago, Mellon Capital Management, State Street Bank and Trust, Boston, Alliance Capital Management, and Wilshire Associates were all strong competitors for the business. In addition, there were a dozen other smaller index fund managers. As a result, the profitability of managing index funds had virtually disappeared. Index fund managers looked for ways to restore some profitability to index fund management. One way was to offer so-called enhanced index funds. These were funds structured to provide the same risk as the market as a whole, that is, to have a beta of 1.0, but structured also to provide slightly more return than the market. Usually this was done by overweighting some sector of the index fund that research suggested was likely to outperform the whole index over time, while underweighting some other sector and keeping the beta at 1.0. Perhaps the first attempt was a "yield tilt" fund started by Wells Fargo in 1976. The yield tilt fund took an index fund and overweighted stocks with high dividends while keeping the beta at 1.0. This was based on some research that suggested high-dividend stocks outperformed in certain periods. However, enhanced indexed management did not begin to grow significantly until the middle of the 1980s. By 1998, however, enhanced index funds accounted for almost 25% of all domestic equity index funds.

Dedicated Moves

As indexing continued to boom, so, too, did bond portfolio dedication and immunization as funds tried to lock up the high interest rates. Early in 1984 Signal Cos. dedicated a $1 billion portfolio, taking all the assets from

11 of its money managers.[51] The move, like so many others, was spurred by the high real interest rates available, and it was only the first of many mega dedications. On July 19 Chrysler Corp. was blamed for triggering a nine-point decline in the Dow Jones Industrial Average as it sold $450 million in stocks to set up a $1.1 billion dedicated bond portfolio with a locked-in interest rate of 14%.[52] That rate allowed Chrysler, which appeared to be on the mend, to halve its unfunded pension liability, said Fred Zuckerman, vice president and treasurer. "We saw an opportunity to take advantage of the unusually high yields in the bond market," he told *Pensions & Investments*. Besides the $450 million in stocks, the company also used $200 million in fund cash and a $456 million cash contribution to the fund to execute the transaction. The slide in the Dow was likely a coincidence as the transactions to establish the dedicated bond fund were executed by Salomon Brothers, using every available technique to cover its tracks.

The largest single dedication up to that time was undertaken in December 1984 by American Information Technologies Corp. (Ameritech), the Chicago-based spinoff from AT&T. The objective in establishing a $2.4 billion dedicated bond fund, according to Donald W. Phillips, was to allow the $6.4 billion fund to pursue an aggressive investment course with the remainder of the assets. He planned to invest half of the remaining $4 billion in domestic equities and half in venture capital, real estate, and international equities "which are the most inefficient investments and the ones that will give us the greatest return," he said.[53] Goldman, Sachs & Co. executed the bond trades in markets in the United States and London. The dedication yielded 11.5% and enabled Ameritech to raise its assumed rate of interest and cut its annual contribution from $200 million to $140 million. The dedicated portfolio was structured to closely match the monthly cash flow needed to pay benefits to the company's 43,000 retirees. The dedication was financed by $1.4 billion of the $2.1 billion in bonds inherited from AT&T when the former parent's pension fund was split up, and with cash. Some of the inherited bonds were transferred to the dedicated portfolio. However, falling interest rates reduced the attraction of dedicated and immunized portfolios during 1986. As a result, some companies began to look at unwinding their dedicated portfolios to lock up the huge gains in value the portfolios had.

More Venturesome

More corporate and public employee pension funds also turned to investing in venture capital as the shake-out in venture capital firms neared completion and the excess of money chasing too few deals was absorbed and returns again looked promising. In addition, as the growth of Silicon Valley accelerated, many more venture capital opportunities became available. Thus, only two months after inheriting $2.3 billion from AT&T in February 1984, US WEST, one of the regional Bell operating companies that split off from the telephone giant, hired Citibank as a venture capital adviser and gave it $15 million.[54] Three months later, the Washington State Investment Board hired four venture capital advisers and split $41 million among them.[55] A month later, Pacific Lighting Corp. hired three venture capital managers and planned to invest up to 3% of its $400 million pension assets in the asset class.[56] New Enterprise Associates, a venture capital partnership, picked up commitments of $125 million from 16 institutions, including the General Electric, Oregon Public Employees, and IBM pension funds.[57] Although venture capital remained of interest to only a minority of funds in the mid-1980s, interest and the flow of pension money grew steadily through the period.

At the same time, public funds continued to lead the way into investing in leveraged buyouts of corporations. Another early LBO deal was the May 1984 $2.4 billion buyout of Esmark Inc. by a $1 billion fund also put together by Kohlberg, Kravis, Roberts (KKR), financed in part by investments by the Washington State Investment Board, the Oregon Public Employees Retirement System, the Michigan State Employees Retirement System, and the Minnesota State Board of Investments.[58] The State of Washington had earlier participated in a KKR buyout of the Dillingham Corp., a Hawaiian food conglomerate. KKR broke up Dillingham and sold off the parts for returns which John Hitchman, executive director of the Washington State Investment Board, characterized as "superior to the market return."

The pace of LBO activity quickened late in 1984 as the Washington and Oregon funds again participated with KKR in the purchase of the Red Lion Hotel chain. This deal caused some ill feeling between the two funds as the Washington State Investment Board tried to "squeeze" the Oregon Retirement System out of it. According to Washington's Hitchman, this was because Oregon's deliberations about such deals had to be conducted in public, and this action could alert competitive bidders for the deal. However, Oregon participated.[59] The same month, at least six other pension funds, including those of GE, GTE, Hughes Aircraft, Minnesota Mining and Manufacturing, and Texas Instruments Inc., joined in the first LBO fund established by Forstmann Little & Co.[60] Before the end of 1985, the Washington, Oregon, and Minnesota funds committed large amounts to KKR's $2 billion fifth LBO fund,[61] and *Pensions & Investments* estimated that at that time more than $12 billion of pension fund assets had been invested in LBO pools.[62] The trend would continue to grow during 1986 and into 1987.

New Standards

Late in 1985 the Financial Accounting Standards Board released new accounting standards to be followed by companies reporting their pension obligations in their financial statements. The hotly disputed standards required companies to use only one actuarial cost method for calculating their pension expense for disclosure purposes. They also required companies to disclose any unfunded pension liabilities in their financial statements. The companies also had to disclose more information about the components of their liabilities and pension costs, including the accrued benefit obligation, the projected benefit obligation, the net annual pension cost, and the interest and salary assumptions. Pension executives and money managers feared the standards would affect pension investment strategies. They were concerned that companies would become far more conservative in their pension fund investing to reduce the chance of becoming underfunded because of a stock market decline and having to disclose the unfunded liability. Initially, some companies did adopt approaches similar to dedicated or immunized bond portfolios. Salomon Brothers, the Wall Street investment banking firm that specialized in bonds, offered an approach developed by bond whiz Martin (Marty) Liebowitz, called *surplus protection*, which structured assets in such a way that the movements of the stock and bond markets could not erode a pension fund's surplus. Over time, however, fears about the impact of the new pension accounting standards on investment strategies evaporated as the continuing bull market reduced concerns that the funds would become underfunded. In addition, companies with overfunded plans found they could record earnings gains by adopting the new standards. In April 1986 IBM was able to boost its reported earnings by $100 million,[63] and a week later AT&T reported it had a $200 million gain.

Incentive Fees

Meanwhile, money managers, especially those managing venture capital, real estate, and LBOs, as well as some pension executives were lobbying the Labor Department to allow the use of incentive or performance-based fees. Hedge funds, which were not then used by pension funds, as well as venture capital and some real estate managers, used performance fees for their individual clients and wanted to be able to do so for their pension clients. The pension funds sought a better way to pay all managers. The traditional way was a flat percentage of assets managed. The average active equity manager charged 0.75% of assets for the first dollar managed, and after, say $20 million, this declined to perhaps 0.65% and declined further as the assets in the account grew. This was, in effect, something of a performance fee in that if the manager succeeded in making the assets grow, the manager's income fee would grow. However, in a bull market the manager was getting paid more just because the market, over which he had no control, was rising, and in a bear market his fee income was cut just because the market declined. Pension executives wanted to pay managers only for their real contribution to the growth of the assets under their control, that is, only for their investment expertise. If the managers subtracted value, then the pension executives wanted to reduce the fees commensurately.

A Greenwich Associates survey of almost 1,500 pension executives found that 43% said they would want all of their funds' managers to be on performance-based incentive fees, and 54% wanted only some of their managers on incentive fees.[64] Dennis Kass, assistant secretary of labor for pensions, gave a conditional nod of approval to performance fees in 1986 as long as they met several requirements: First, the returns must be based on both realized and unrealized gains or losses. Second, they must be based on an annual measurement of the returns. Third, the fees must be fulcrum fees, that is, the manager must lose fee income for underperforming, not just earn extra income for above-benchmark performance.[65] Although no corporate funds would adopt performance fees until they received formal approval from the Labor Department, several public pension funds, which did not require Labor Department approval, quickly moved to use them. The Minnesota State Board of Investment put 10 of its 11 active equity managers on performance-based fees effective July 1, 1986. The 10 invested about $1 billion of the fund's $8 billion in assets. The Pension Reserve Investment Trust, Boston, put two of its seven active managers on to incentive fees.[66] However, the Labor Department finally approved incentive fees in September 1986, freeing corporate funds to use them. Despite the interest, there was no great rush. The first two corporate funds to use incentive fees were GTE Corp. and Allied Signal Corp., both of which acted before the end of 1987.

Gee, GTE

One of those wrestling with the problem of paying managers was John Carroll, president of GTE Investment Management Corp., which oversaw the pension assets of GTE Corp. Carroll proved to be one of the most innovative of pension fund executives. He was unusual in that he had experience in all three major parts of the pension management industry: as a trust officer and marketing executive at Chemical Bank; as a pension fund consultant at Chemical Bank and at Evaluation Associates Inc.; and lastly as a pension executive at GTE.

Carroll started out wanting to be a teacher, but in 1958 he took a temporary job at Chemical Bank while waiting to go back to college to get his teaching credits. He never went into teaching; instead he moved up through the ranks of the pension department at Chemical Bank servicing such corporate pension funds as General Tire & Rubber Co., Uniroyal Tire Co., and Eli Lilly Corp. as the bank managed balanced pension accounts for them. Carroll became a vice president in the early 1970s and found himself more and more responsible for marketing and sales, with little control over how portfolios were constructed.

Carroll accidentally discovered the consulting business when, soon after ERISA was passed, one client, Phillip Morris Co.'s board, asked how much it could be insulated from the investment decision-making responsibility and thus have its fiduciary liability reduced. Carroll suggested that the board give Chemical Bank the responsibility for hiring and firing managers. "That would move the board a step or two from direct liability," said Carroll. "They bought it, to our surprise." One of Chemical Bank's first actions as fiduciary was to fire three competitor banks—Chase Manhattan, Citibank, and Bankers Trust—and hire investment counseling firms. A few months later Carroll added another consulting client, the City of Baltimore, and soon after several more came onboard. But in 1981, uncomfortable with the internal politics at the bank, Carroll left to join Bill Crerend and his group at Evaluation Associates, one of the pioneer consulting firms. Then, in 1984, he was approached about the job of overseeing the GTE pension fund. Carroll decided that being the consultant to one fund would be just as satisfying as being a consultant to a dozen funds and would involve less pressure, so he accepted and joined GTE Corp.

At GTE Carroll found a $3 billion fund with about 50 managers. When he examined the characteristics of the total portfolio, he found the fund had a very high-risk, high price/earning, high price-to-book value, small-capitalization portfolio. That is, it was taking inadvertent bets on one particular style. Carroll and his team started managing the equity portfolio in terms of its aggregate characteristics, actively choosing what they wanted the bias relative to the market to be, rather than letting that just be an accident of the managers who had been hired. Carroll gradually whittled down the number of equity managers and increased the fund's commitment to international equities. At the time he joined the fund, GTE's commitment to international equities was nominally 6% of its equity assets. But since all the managers had global mandates and the global benchmark was 50% weighted to U.S. equities, all the managers had 50% of their assets in U.S. securities, giving GTE only a 3% commitment to non-U.S. equities. Carroll changed the benchmark to a non-U.S. benchmark. Although the managers still had the freedom to invest in U.S. equities, the U.S. stocks virtually disappeared from the portfolio, giving GTE a true 6% international exposure. Then over three years he increased the fund's international equity exposure to 20% of the equity allocation, which was about 75% of the fund's total assets. Eventually, the international equity allocation went to 30% of equities. At the same time he was increasing the international exposure to a true 6%, he committed $100 million to timberland investing, making GTE one of the first pension funds to make a significant commitment to that asset class.

In 1987 Carroll also pioneered performance-based fees. In December he issued an edict to all 24 of GTE's domestic equity managers announcing that if they did not achieve their benchmarks their fees would be cut. The GTE performance-based fees pay managers based on the number of basis points a manager returns over a hypothetical passively managed portfolio that reflects the manager's style of investing. The passive portfolio is known as the normal portfolio or benchmark. Managers generally had to achieve returns 200 basis points greater than the normal portfolio to earn their normal fees. If a manager beat the normal portfolio by a significant amount he or she could earn up to twice the stated fee. On the other hand, underperformance could reduce the normal fee by up to 75%. The performance is measured over a three-year period, with the managers receiving a minimal fee quarterly, and adjustments are made at the end of the year, plus or minus, to reflect performance. "There were times when managers owed us money and we terminated them," said Carroll, "and those were kind of difficult." One of GTE's first money managers to have a specific performance target relative to a benchmark was Rosenberg Institutional Equity Management Inc., the money management firm started by Barr Rosenberg, the former UC Berkeley business professor and founder of BARRA. Rosenberg promised GTE that his firm would beat the S&P 500 Index by 400 basis points a year using his computer-driven approach based on the work he did in developing his beta measure. As a result, GTE became Rosenberg Institutional's first significant client, giving it $100 million.

Another pioneer of performance-based fees for corporate pension funds was Edward T. Tokar Jr., vice president for investments at Allied-Signal Corp. Tokar began a pilot program for a number of the $4 billion fund's equity managers with smaller accounts in 1986 and then extended it to other managers in 1987. Tokar reported resistance to the performance fees from some of his fund's 35 managers. His approach differed from Carroll's in that he used the S&P 500 Index as a benchmark for all of his managers. Few corporate pension funds hurried to follow the examples of Carroll and Tokar, though many eventually adopted performance-based fees for at least some of their managers, often those such as venture capital or LBO managers where performance fees were normal. Enough public and private funds eventually adopted performance-based fees for at least some of their managers to provide a nice boost to the business of Richards & Tierney Inc. which developed benchmark portfolios that fairly reflected each manager's investment style. The performance-based management fee has also been adopted by some mutual fund managers.

Corporate Governance

In July 1984 California State Treasurer Jesse Unruh asked the nation's public employee pension funds to support a new shareholder organization to review and possibly fight corporate management decisions that would financially hurt the funds. On July 7 the seven largest California funds, which had about $50 billion of assets, met and agreed to support such an organization, and Unruh quickly gained the support of other major public funds. At the first meeting of the public fund executives to discuss forming an organization, they agreed it would focus on financial, not social, issues. This was the birth of the Council of Institutional Investors. Its formation was prompted by greenmail activities—corporate raiders buying up large amounts of a target company's stock and threatening a takeover attempt unless they were paid a premium by the company for their stock. The payment of such a premium to make the raider go away alienated the other shareholders, who realized corporate assets were being used to pay off the raiders at the expense of the other shareholders. The formation of the Council was also sparked by attempts by some managements to entrench themselves by using "poison pill" defenses to fight off legitimate takeover bids that would be good for the shareholders. The poison pills usually involved changing company bylaws so that the company disbursed critical assets or took on massive debts in the event of a hostile takeover attempt, leaving the acquirer with less than he had counted on. It was rather like the scorched-earth strategy that enabled the Russians to defeat both Napoleon and Hitler. The Council members also opposed managements awarding themselves "golden parachutes"—large amounts of money in the event they were forced out as a result of a successful takeover. The group hoped to marshall the voices of the fund executives to protest actions that were inimical to institutional shareholder interests, and even to vote their proxies against management proposals.

Robert A. G. Monks, the U.S. pension administrator, supported the formation of the group, even though ERISA did not cover the public funds heading its formation. Monks had argued before that pension funds should use their proxy voting power to improve corporate management's performance. The Council was officially formed in January 1985, with 22 public and union pension fund members controlling $100 billion in assets. A month later it scheduled a meeting with executives of Phillips Petroleum Co. and corporate raider T. Boone Pickens to hear each side in Pickens' battle for control of the oil company. The Council members agreed to treat the meeting as an educational one, after which each fund would make its own decision as to how to vote its proxies. In July the Council gained its first corporate member, US WEST Inc.,[67] and in October the Council decided to address deeper corporate management issues such as corporate compensation, election of corporate boards, and use of pension assets in takeover battles. By September the Council had grown to 30 members with the addition of the five New York City funds. Its list of critical issues was growing as it turned its attention to leveraged buyouts and the question of whether or not they served shareholder interests. In April the Council endorsed a shareholders' bill of rights, the key points of which were opposition to shares carrying fewer voting rights, a demand that corporations seek shareholder approval before paying greenmail or establishment of "poison pills" or "golden parachutes," and a call for a majority of outside directors' approval of any extraordinary bonuses or other payments to corporate executives.[68] As part of their increased shareholder activism, some public funds began to hire outside firms to analyze corporate proxy statements and advise them how to vote on the issues.

Robert Monks resigned as head of the Labor Department's pension department in December 1984 in order to establish a consulting firm, Institutional Shareholder Services, to advise on corporate governance issues.[69] In the coming decade pension funds, led by the Council of Institutional Investors (CII), would use their proxy voting power to influence, and even topple corporate managements, in the interests of better use of shareholder assets. Generally targeted were those companies that were underperforming their peers and competitors in the marketplace, and those firms where the pension executives felt management was not working in the shareholders' long-term interests. The CII campaigns quickly gained the attention of corporate America and were another way in which pension funds improved U.S. economic performance. Eventually, other institutional money managers such as mutual fund executives lent their votes to corporate governance campaigns, which improved corporate performance for all investors.

Chapter 12

Portfolio Insurance

In 1981, John O'Brien, formerly of O'Brien Associates, left A. G. Becker Funds Evaluation to join two academics at the University of California at Berkeley in a new firm, Leland O'Brien Rubinstein, which quickly became known as LOR. The firm offered a revolutionary new idea to pension funds and other institutional clients: portfolio insurance. The name was catchy, and the product was designed to protect equity portfolios against more than minimal losses, no matter what the market did. The new idea had been developed by Hayne Leland and Mark Rubinstein, both of whom were finance professors at Berkeley. The concept was deceptively simple. Leland and Rubinstein had developed a computer program that would tell a pension fund, or the fund's money manager, to sell stocks and increase cash in a carefully measured way as stock prices fell. By the time the stock prices had declined the maximum amount the pension fund could tolerate, the fund would be all cash. For example, if the fund was willing to accept a 5% loss of capital on its equity portfolio, the program would begin to sell stocks as prices began to decline, and the portfolio would be all cash by the time its value had declined by 5%. As stock prices began to recover, the program would control the purchase of stocks until the portfolio was again fully invested. In effect, the program was replicating a put option but doing it through programmed, dynamic hedging. The price of the option, in this case, was the slight underperformance the portfolio would suffer because its actions on both the upside and the downside would lag the market. In addition, there were the transactions costs of selling and later buying the stocks. The more volatile the market, the greater would be the underperformance and hence the cost of the insurance.

Leland tested the program for a year with his own money and had great success. Then, after a year of trying to market the product themselves to a skeptical pension fund universe, Leland and Rubinstein joined forces with O'Brien, who was well known and respected in pension fund circles. Soon after, O'Brien signed the first client of portfolio insurance—the A. G. Becker profit-sharing plan—for $500,000. Six months later three bigger clients came in on one day, bringing a total of $50 million: the pension funds of Honeywell Corp., Gates Rubber Corp., and the Auto Club of South Carolina.[1]

The Honeywell fund presented a significant challenge. It used seven equity managers, and changing the stock–cash mix for the fund meant working with each of those managers. At first, LOR encountered some resistance, but Trust Co. of the West volunteered to try it with its Honeywell portfolio. When Trust Co. found the program was successful and did not unduly interfere with its investment process, the other managers agreed to try it. Soon after, LOR was running a $200 million dynamic hedging program for Honeywell. Nevertheless, the concept was a hard sell. Managers resisted having parts of their portfolios taken away and replaced with cash. However, a solution was at hand. Instead of selling the stocks in the portfolio as the market declined, LOR could sell S&P 500 futures contracts and leave the underlying stocks untouched. "Fortunately," said John O'Brien, "the S&P 500 futures market began to develop in 1982 and mature in 1983. It became a non-invasive procedure." After mid-1984 all portfolio insurance involved the use of futures.

The first client for which the futures-based version was used was the Manville Corp. LOR got the bulk of the business but not all of it because J. P. Morgan objected. Morgan had been the banker for Manville since the beginning of the firm, so it had clout. It told Manville's finance committee it could also run a dynamic hedging program. As a result, LOR got 80% of the $350 million pension fund, and Morgan got 20%. Soon after, portfolio insurance become fully accepted as BEA Associates, Wells Fargo Investment Advisors, and Aetna Capital Management licensed the technology. The number of funds covered by portfolio insurance, and the amount of assets protected, began to grow. Among the funds adopting it were Texas Instruments, Deere & Co., and Hughes Aircraft Co. Many pension executives signing up for portfolio insurance had become concerned about the level of the stock market as the Dow Jones Industrial Average climbed through 1,500 and continued on toward 2000.

One of those concerned executives was Allen Reed, now president of General Motors Investment Management Co., but in 1987 he was president of Hughes Investment Management Co., overseeing the $3.2 billion Hughes Aircraft pension fund and the $1.1 billion 401(K) plan. "In 1987, like a lot of other pension plans, we got concerned about the market valuations and signed up for three portfolio insurance programs," he said. "The three managers were LOR, BEA and J.P. Morgan." Meanwhile, pension executives who had portfolio insurance in place in 1986, when the market was more volatile than usual, found the program more expensive than expected. Although portfolio insurance proponents had projected normal costs of 200 to 300 basis points a year, the actual costs in 1986 were 50 to 100 basis points higher. The extra cost led Manville Corp. to modify its program, which had aimed at a minimum return of 0% over a three-year time horizon, to accept a loss of 5% as the minimum three-year return.[2]

By the beginning of 1987, 18 of the top 200 pension funds, as well as a large number of smaller funds, used portfolio insurance to protect their assets.[3] Still, great skepticism remained that portfolio insurance would work as promised. One who issued early warnings about portfolio insurance was Bruce Jacobs, a finance professor who later formed his own money management firm, Jacobs, Levy Asset Management. Jacobs warned that the strategy was unstable and not equivalent to a true insurance policy, and that it could destabilize the market. Another skeptic was Robert D. Arnott, then president and chief investment officer of TSA Capital Management, who with Richard Boling, a managing director of the firm, wrote in *Pensions & Investments:*

> Let us assume that by 1988 pension assets subject to portfolio insurance total $50 billion. What happens if at this point the market drops 5% during the course of several days? Managers of most insured portfolios would seek to reduce stock market exposure by perhaps 20%. Given this scenario, some $10 billion of sell orders would hit the S&P 500 futures pit in just a few days. ... The S&P contract would be forced to trade far away from fair value. The initial decline might fuel still further declines as arbitragers bought favorably mispriced S&P 500 futures and simultaneously sold an index portfolio. ... The decline would continue, feeding on itself.[4]

One of the most prescient of the pension executives was John Steinbach, assistant treasurer of K mart Corp., who reached a similar conclusion. "I don't have any way to substantiate this," he said, "but when the market starts to decline, I can't help but believe when these programs kick in, the selling of one program will make it so another program has to sell. Logically, it seems you're going to have more volatility."[5]

All three—Jacobs, Arnott, and Steinbach—would be proven right. Steinbach was concerned enough to take action. During the summer he reduced the K mart pension fund's equity exposure to 58% of assets from 70%, dropping its aggressive equity account with T. Rowe Price Associates and cutting its $175 million growth stock portfolio with Alliance Capital Management by $40 million.[6] Steinbach was not the only pension executive concerned about the high level of stock prices as pension funds liquidated a record $16.7 billion of U.S. stocks in the first quarter of 1987, moving half of that into cash, with the remainder going into bonds, real estate, or international investments. In September the Maryland State Retirement and Pension System sold $2.3 billion of stocks and set up a $4 billion dedicated bond portfolio,[7] and for the year bond managers reported that their assets from new clients increased by 31% over the previous year.[8] Equity managers also began building their cash reserves during the third quarter. INDATA, a Southport, Connecticat, investment analysis service, reported the average cash position of managers had increased to 7.4% from 7.1% in the third quarter, but many managers surveyed by *Pensions & Investments* reported more substantial increases in cash holdings. Clearly, investors were getting nervous.[9]

Portfolio insurance received a test on September 11, 1986, when the Dow Jones Industrial Average dropped 86.6 points, its largest one-day point drop ever. The Standard & Poor's 500 Index dropped 11.88 points. The product passed its test, but not without some difficulty, and critics said the cost of the insurance was increasing.[10] The pricing of stock index futures changed throughout the day, and when they were severely underpriced, Advanced Investment Management Inc., Pittsburgh, sold stocks in the cash market rather than sell the futures at too low a price. "The liquidity wasn't there," said William M. Morris, senior investment consultant at William M. Mercer-Meidinger Asset Planning Inc., "and the futures contract was so undervalued that anybody who would have executed it was crazy." LOR chose not to trade on September 11 because of the market conditions. Despite the questions raised by the test, interest in portfolio insurance continued to increase as the stock market continued to climb after the mild correction. Some companies began to apply portfolio insurance to their defined contribution plans, among them the plans of Trans World Airlines Inc. and Burlington Industries Inc. By the end of 1986 Wells Fargo reported gaining $7.5 billion in portfolio insurance business for the year, followed by Bankers Trust Co., $2.1 billion.[11] By October 1987 the total amount of assets so protected was $68 billion.[12]

Crash Test

The ultimate test for portfolio insurance occurred on October 19, 1987, when the market dropped more than 500 points in one day. It failed the test. In fact, many analysts blamed portfolio insurance for deepening what would have been a normal market correction. The causes of what became known as the crash of 1987 were many: stock prices had run well ahead of fundamentals so that many investors expected a correction (hence the demand for portfolio insurance); interest rates were rising, as were concerns about the federal budget and trade deficits; and a decline in the dollar had reduced foreign demand for U.S. securities. The immediate triggers were a threat of a trade war between the United States and West Germany, poorer than expected trade deficit figures, and a House Ways and Means Committee proposal to limit the tax deductibility of interest payments on money borrowed to finance takeovers or stock buybacks.

The market had fallen by 250 points on the Dow the week before, with almost half of that occurring on Friday, October 16. Over the weekend more sell orders built up, and by noon on Monday the Dow had dropped 100 points. It dropped another 200 points in the next two hours and more than 200 points in the final hour, for a total decline of 508 points, or 22.61%. Portfolio insurance firms struggled to keep their promises. They found they could not carry out their stock index futures sales at any reasonable price because there were few buyers. Allen Reed reported that the performance of Hughes Aircraft's three portfolio insurance managers was dramatically different. Leland O'Brien Rubinstein could not trade and shut down its efforts. BEA Associates had moved the Hughes account 100% to listed put options before the crash, so the portfolio was protected. J. P. Morgan had moved to a mix of options and futures, and had told Reed they were continuing to try to trade. In the end, what Reed thought was the equivalent of a 5% deductible insurance policy turned out to be a 60% deductible. That is, the Hughes protected portfolios were down about 60% as much as the market. "We were better off to have had it than not, but obviously things didn't turn out the way we thought," said Reed.

As Peter L. Bernstein elegantly explained in his book *Capital Ideas*,[13] the problem was there was a significant difference between an insurance policy and the synthetic insurance policy represented by portfolio insurance. In a true insurance policy, the insurance company is contractually bound to make good in the event of a claim of loss, and that promise is backed by the insurance company's assets. Similarly, in the case of the put options BEA bought for the Hughes fund, the seller of the option has to post cash collateral to guarantee the buyer is protected. In the case of portfolio insurance, however, no one was contractually bound to take the other side of the trade when portfolio insurance managers wanted to sell stock index futures, and there was no collateral to draw on. Leland and Rubinstein had assumed stock index arbitrageurs—investors who bought stock index futures and sold stocks when the futures were cheaper than the stocks, and vice versa when the stock were cheaper—would always be ready to trade. At the opening on Monday, according to John O'Brien, LOR and the other portfolio insurance managers were offering a lot of futures contracts for sale because of the decline in the market the previous Friday. The prices of the futures were therefore quickly driven below the prices of the actual stocks. That should have prompted the arbitrageurs to buy the futures and sell the stocks, pushing the futures prices up and stock prices down until they were in line again. At first, the arbitrageurs bought the futures, as expected, but they had trouble selling the stocks on the New York Stock Exchange since buyers of stock were scarce. As a result, the prices of the stocks were quickly driven below the prices of the futures again. Now the arbitrageurs wanted to sell the futures and buy the under-priced stocks, causing a spiraling down of both futures and stocks. Portfolio insurance caused exactly the market effects that Jacobs, Arnott and Boling, and Steinbach had feared.

When the market started down dramatically, the arbitrageurs either got out of the way of the falling elevator or were overwhelmed by it as those selling stocks kept stock prices falling as rapidly as the futures prices. The arbitrageurs were aware that at least $68 billion of portfolio insurance-programmed futures selling was lined up to be executed if the market should continue to fall. Unable to cope with that or to sell stocks at any reasonable price, most stopped buying. With few buyers, the futures markets virtually ceased to operate at times on Monday. Although many portfolio insurance managers did get some trades off, the prices were far lower than anticipated. Leland and Rubinstein had overestimated the depth and liquidity of the futures market. Like the Hughes fund, most of those funds covered by portfolio insurance suffered less in the market plunge than those not covered. But there were two problems with portfolio insurance. First, it did not perform as advertised. Most pension executives who bought it expected either no losses or minimal losses. Actually, they suffered losses of 10% of the value of their equities or more, but less than the 21% the average equity portfolio suffered. Second, portfolio insurance was blamed for deepening the crash. The critics blamed the futures selling for helping to trigger more sales of stock and setting off a vicious circle as stocks and futures followed each other downward. Using portfolio insurance in a pension fund became politically incorrect. As John O'Brien said, however, dynamic hedging did not disappear after the crash, although the term "portfolio insurance" almost disappeared. Allen Reed acknowledged that the Hughes Aircraft fund continued to use dynamic hedging with BEA Associates, though it modified the program to make it more "catastrophe insurance." In a survey of portfolio insurance managers in mid-December 1987, *Pensions & Investments* found that the amount of assets covered by the program had dropped by almost 66% in the month after the crash.[14]

The crash of October 19, 1987, had no lasting impact on the size of pension fund assets; most funds were taken back only to where they had been the previous April and returned to pre-October 19 levels in less than two years. All the same, it had an important result. The crash showed the size and power of pension funds and their managers. Pension fund equity managers liquidated only a fraction of their stock holdings—probably less than 15% overall—yet both the cash and futures markets were overwhelmed, and the Standard & Poor's 500 Index plunged more than 20%. Up to this time, some experts had argued that the institutionalization of the market—that is, the fact that more and more stocks were owned by institutions such as pension funds—would make it less volatile then when individual investors dominated. Surely professional managers would take a calmer, longer-term view of stocks and the markets. The experts had overlooked the pressures the pension fund managers felt to deliver short-term performance. Most managers believed they were being judged on their performance quarterly, in part because they had to report their activities and performance to the pension executive on a quarterly basis. Most pension executives professed to be unconcerned with short-term performance and to measure manager performance over a minimum of three years. Money managers did not believe them. In addition, the crash showed the potentially negative impact on the capital markets when pension fund money managers objected strongly to some threatened government action—the proposed taxes on money borrowed to finance takeovers—or were made uncertain by a proposed policy change. Either reaction caused money managers to sell some of their stocks or bonds. Even if only 5% of 10% of their holdings were sold, the impact could be enormous. The government's task in manipulating the economy was becoming more and more difficult.

Some pension funds and money managers took advantage of the crash to pick up stocks at what they regarded as bargain-basement prices. The California Public Employees Retirement System committed part of its $3 billion cash reserves to buying stocks selectively on October 19 and October 20, said Greta Marshall, chief investment officer. Peter Anderson, senior vice president of investments at IDS Financial Services, Minneapolis, said his company had bought "hundreds of millions of dollars in stocks, mostly great big blue-chip companies—the ones that got the hell beat out of them." Similarly, Independence Investment Associates, which earlier in the year had raised its cash level to 20% of assets, committed a good part of that to the market on October 19 and the days immediately following.[15]

One of the mysteries in the immediate wake of the crash was: Who sold? *Pensions & Investments* surveyed the 100 largest money management organizations after the crash, and 48 responded. Of those 48, only three said they had been selling during the market drop. Of the remainder, seven said they were buying.[16] Although most sat on their hands on October 19, many more said they were in the market buying on the days following. Of course, the nonresponse of 52 of the managers might indicate guilty consciences. Surveys of mutual fund companies by the Securities Industry Association also found most such companies denying they sold on October 19. Another *P&I* survey conducted two months later revealed that about 10% of pension fund executives had reacted to the crash by lowering their funds' long-term equity commitments by an average of eight percentage points—enough to take $10.4 billion out of the equity market permanently. Another 10% of respondents were considering reducing their funds' long-term allocations to equities.[17]

The market crash seemed to validate a new approach that had appeared in the mid-1980s—*tactical asset allocation* (TAA). This approach, pioneered by Bill Fouse at Wells Fargo, had been around since 1972–1973. The initial Wells Fargo product was a relative value-based product switching between stocks and bonds, and it produced excellent results. The valuation model, based simply on a comparison between the expected rate of return on stocks as calculated by a dividend discount model and the yield on bonds, got Wells's tactical asset allocation clients out of the stock market in early 1974 and back in time for the market rally in 1975.

The Boston Co. and Citibank in New York began working with multivariate tactical asset allocation programs in late 1981, the Boston Co. under Rob Arnott, later of TSA and First Quadrant Inc., and Citibank under Chuck DuBois. By sheer chance, both adopted similar approaches, adding macroeconomic and monetary factors to the relative valuation factors. Using these multifactor computer models, they determined when the relative values of various asset classes were out of line and when to switch from one asset class into another. For example, if a model told a manager that U.S. equities were overvalued relative to U.S. bonds and that U.S. bonds were overvalued relative to international equities, the manager would reduce his exposure to U.S. equities and increase it in international equities, and possibly U.S. bonds also. Or the manager might determine that all three asset classes were overvalued and move much of the money to cash equivalents. When moves were made between U.S. stocks and bonds, the shifts in weighting were often made using stock index and bond futures. The results of TAA managers during the 1987 crash were positive. The Common Fund, for example, which manages assets for university and college endowments, reported the $900 million it had invested in a TAA program with TSA Capital Management had been fully protected and actually had positive results during the crash.[18] Most TAA models had signaled the managers to significantly reduce their holdings of U.S. equities well before the market peaked. For example, TSA Capital Management had its clients' portfolios 60% to 65% in bonds just before the crash. Similarly, First Chicago Investment Advisors had its clients 17% in stocks, versus a normal position of 65%, 35% bonds versus 30%, and 48% cash equivalents versus 5%. As a result, TAA managers gained clients rapidly in 1988.

By September 1988 the 15 key TAA managers reported they had $38.3 billion under management, up 41% over the previous year. Wells Fargo Investment Advisors reported the largest TAA client base, $9.1 billion. This was just the beginning of the growth of tactical asset allocation managers.[19] One of the most interesting TAA clients was Bechtel Power Corp. Whereas most early TAA clients opted for simple U.S. stocks, U.S. bonds, and a cash equivalent strategy, Bechtel chose a global TAA strategy for part of its $1.2 billion pension fund. The Bechtel strategy, implemented by the San Mateo-based Bailard Biehl & Kaiser Inc. and Wells Fargo Investment Advisors, used domestic equities, bonds, and cash as well as international stocks and bonds, an index of gold stocks, and real estate investment trusts.[20] The experience of First Quadrant, a new TAA manager started in 1988, showed the attractiveness of the product. The firm began operations in April and by the end of the year had more than $1 billion under management. By the middle of 1998 it had $26 billion under management.[21] However, even TAA was not a magic bullet. Many pension executives expected TAA managers to provide positive results relative to the broad U.S. market every year and were disappointed when they could not do so. Although most of the major TAA firms produced positive results over three- to five-year periods, even they, with their quantitative models, could not do so every year. The investment world was far too complex. Many pension funds who could not accept this reality dropped tactical asset allocation as a strategy over the next few years. Nevertheless, the strategy remained popular and is even offered by a number of mutual funds to individual investors.

GM Versus Perot

The crash of 1987 was not the only dramatic event of the year for pension funds. The year had opened with the sudden departure of H. Ross Perot from the board of directors of General Motors Corp. Perot had been appointed to the board by virtue of his holdings of GM stock, which he acquired when GM bought his company, Electronic Data Systems (EDS) Corp. However, Perot had angered Roger B. Smith, chairman of GM, with his constant criticisms of GM management's actions and policies. Smith denied Perot's criticism of management had led to Perot's departure; instead, he claimed it was Perot's refusal to allow GM to audit EDS's books. Whatever the reason (and most people believed it *was* Perot's constant sniping), Smith got the GM board to buy Perot's shares back for $742 million, a substantial premium over the market value of the shares, and remove him from the board. Institutional investors, who owned large amounts of GM stock, reacted strongly, knocking GM's common stock price down to $66 a share from $73 a share in a matter of days, though it recovered in about a month. The institutional investor reaction was based on several factors. First, many agreed with Perot's criticisms of GM management and thought he served a useful purpose on the board of directors by preventing it from being complacent. Second, they felt the price GM paid for Perot's stock was outrageous and a waste of corporate assets. The Council of Institutional Investors invited Smith and Perot each to give their sides of the dispute to members, and while Perot attended, Smith did not.[22] As a result, the State of Wisconsin Investment Board introduced a shareholders' resolution for the Council to submit to be voted on at the GM annual meeting. It protested the Perot buyout and sought to amend company bylaws to prohibit similar transactions in the future. Smith, realizing he had made a tactical error, later met with officials of some of the leading public pension funds, after which Wisconsin withdrew its support of the resolution, though others continued to support it.[23] The Council of Institutional Investors did not ultimately affect the outcome of the dispute between GM and Perot, but it had flexed its muscle and even caused the chairman of one of the nation's largest corporations to pay attention to it. The GM dispute validated the potential power of the proxy votes that could be wielded by institutional investors and gave new impetus to the corporate governance movement.

Corporate Reaction

Two months later corporate chief executives began to react to the Council of Institutional Investors by lobbying money managers for support of poison pill, antitakeover provisions in proxy proposals. The chief executives of Rockwell International Corp. and GTE Corp. wrote letters to their Fortune 500 counterparts asking them to lobby their pension executives and pension fund money managers to vote in favor of antitakeover proposals being put before shareholders during the 1987 proxy season.[24] GTE and Rockwell shareholders approved the antitakeover measures soon after the letters went out. The letters were followed by a memorandum from Martin Lipton of the corporate law firm of Wachtell, Lipton, Rosen & Katz, urging its clients to follow the examples of GTE and Rockwell and lobby their pension executives and money managers. "It has become clear that institutional investors are supporting corporate raiders for the purpose of continuing the junk-bond bust-up takeover frenzy," Lipton said in his memo. In fact, institutional investors had reacted differently to different takeover bids by corporate raiders and LBO groups. Some had supported takeovers by selling their stock to the acquirer when they felt the company's performance was poor and unlikely to improve in the foreseeable future under current management. They had supported managements in other cases. And some funds had remained aloof from the fights.

The letters were interpreted as inappropriate pressure by some institutional investors and as appropriate management communication with shareholders by others. The SEC considered the letters to be appropriate management–shareholder communication, but Dennis Kass, assistant secretary of labor overseeing pension law, was not so sure, saying the letters were "troubling." He noted that the money manager retained the fiduciary responsibility of voting the proxies responsibly and solely in the interests of the plan beneficiaries. Robert E. Mercer, chairman and chief executive officer of College Retirement Equity Fund which owned 2.5 million shares of GTE and 1.3 million shares of Rockwell, was concerned about the letters: "As holders of shares we would be very concerned about any pressure on a fiduciary to violate their fiduciary responsibilities under ERISA. These letters represent unfair and inappropriate pressure," he said. "It's really asking managers of those funds to violate their responsibilities."[25]

The criticism did not deter other chief executives from joining the letter-writing campaign. The CEOs of International Paper, NCR Corp., Anheuser-Busch, American Airlines, and Colgate Palmolive all sent similar letters in the next month.[26] But some proxy experts thought they were already losing their effectiveness. Others thought the whole proxy voting system was malfunctioning. The Investor Responsibility Research Center commented in a study that "institutional investors, a potential check on corporate management, face serious conflicts of interest in voting, and many institutions have succumbed to management pressures to support voting proposals that are not in the shareholders' interests." On the other side, corporate management believed that institutional money managers were too focused on short-term investment performance and therefore too willing to take the quick gain offered by corporate raiders when they made a hostile takeover bid. This also inclined institutional shareholders to vote against poison pill provisions designed to make it difficult for hostile takeover bids to succeed. In March 1987, Hicks B. Waldron, chairman of Avon Corp., told his company's pension managers that they would be evaluated only every three years, rather then quarterly. He asked them to keep a company's long-term prospects in mind when voting a proxy, and he began reviewing managers' votes on such proxies.[27]

In April 1987, in the middle of the proxy season, several representatives of the Business Roundtable, a top management group, attended the annual meeting of the Council of Institutional Investors to defend poison pills, saying they gave boards time to consider the long-term implications of takeover bids without undue pressure. A few weeks later, Jesse Unruh, founder of the Council of Institutional Investors, died of cancer, having lived to see the organization develop real influence. A year later the Council recorded its first proxy vote victories when shareholders voted to eliminate the Santa Fe Southern Pacific Corp.'s poison pill and approved an anti-greenmail proposal at Gillette Co.[28] At the beginning of the proxy season the Labor Department had written a letter to Helmuth Fandl, chairman of Avon's retirement board, reminding the board of the role of fiduciaries in proxy voting and making it clear corporate executives could not pressure fiduciaries into voting management's way on issues. Many observers saw the letter as a timely warning to all chief executives in reaction to the letter writing of a year earlier.[29]

At the end of the season, as if to bolster the warning, the Labor Department sent letters to dozens of money managers requesting their proxy voting records concerning as many as 20 companies.[30] Over the next two years the poison pill battle remained a hot issue, and it was joined by the battle to get corporations to end their operations in and involvement with South Africa because of apartheid, which moved into the proxy arena. More large institutional shareholders accepted the view long espoused by Ned Regan, New York State controller, that putting resolutions on corporate annual meeting agendas, and then exercising shareholder voting rights in favor of the resolutions, would be far more effective in changing corporate behavior than selling the shares. This was the policy he followed with the funds of the New York State Retirement System, of which he was the sole trustee. Once the shares were sold, Regan argued, the institutions had no further influence over the company. Institutional investors had discovered proxy voting rights were a valuable asset in efforts to improve corporate management and social performance, and they would grow more sophisticated in its use in future years.

More Taxes

For the second year in a row, Congress clobbered pension funds when the 1987 budget bill was passed in December. The law increased the insurance premium for the Pension Benefit Guaranty Corp. to between $16 and $50 per employee per year, from $8.50, depending on the funding situation of the plan, and reduced the period over which some past-service liabilities had to be funded to 18 years from 30. Employers could no longer make tax-deductible contributions to their plans when the plans were 150% funded on a termination basis. Previously, the limit was based on the projected liability, including the expected future service of current employees, a far more generous limit. In addition, companies had to pay their pension contributions to their plans quarterly, whereas earlier they could make them up to almost nine months after the end of the plan year. The ability to terminate an underfunded plan was severely restricted.[31] The result of these changes was to make defined benefit plans far more expensive to corporations. In addition, it was clear that Congress was not finished with defined benefit plans. Senator Metzenbaum was still running his campaign against reversions of surplus assets and was determined to make it virtually impossible for companies to recapture surplus assets from their pension funds. If companies put too much into the pension funds, either because they were conservative and wanted to make sure the benefits were fully funded, or because the investment returns were far greater than had been anticipated, too bad, Metzenbaum said. The only way to get that money back was to cut the annual contributions in future years, even if the company desperately needed the money now. As of the end of 1987, according to the Pension Benefit Guaranty Corp., 1,634 companies had terminated pension plans and recaptured $17.9 billion.[32]

Although Congress was oblivious of the fact, it was greatly weakening corporate support for defined benefit plans and ironically increasing the attractiveness of defined contribution plans, something they did not wish to do. The Democratic Party, in particular, believed that defined benefit plans were far better for employees than defined contribution plans because the employees were protected from market risk. The pension was guaranteed by the fund assets, by the corporation's assets, and by the Pension Benefit Guaranty Corp. Initially, corporate support for defined benefit plans had been harmed by the costs, liabilities, and bureaucracy imposed by ERISA. It had been further weakened by the Financial Accounting Standards Board's rules for accounting for pension costs, which required pension liabilities to be reported in the company's financial statements. These costs and burdens were bearable as long as top management had something to gain from the defined benefit plan. But the 1986 law restricting how much of senior management's pension could be funded on a tax-exempt basis, and the additional costs imposed by the 1987 law, further seriously eroded top management support for defined benefit pension plans. Top management gradually realized it could cut the cost of providing pensions for the rank-and-file employee by shifting over to a defined contribution plan such as a 401(k) plan. Then the company's contribution could be limited to matching the employee's contribution, most of the expenses could be shifted to the employee, and there would much less reporting to government, no PBGC premium, no actuarial expense, and no liability to report on the company's financial statements. Top management lost little in the switch because it was now getting most of its retirement income from non-qualified plans. These plans were funded by the corporation but were not tax-favored and therefore were subject to only minimal IRS or Department of Labor regulation.

Not that all, or even most, companies terminated their defined benefit plans, though some did. More companies simply stopped allowing new employees into the defined benefit plan. This tactic guaranteed that the plan would shrink and die as current employees retired or moved to new companies. New employees were given only the defined contribution plan, whereas others stopped improving the benefits of the defined benefit plan. These companies started 401(k) plans alongside their defined benefit plans. Some large companies, however, maintained both kinds of plans and continued to wrestle with the problems of managing the huge pools of defined benefit assets. GTE's Carroll, besides switching to performance-based fees, gradually cut back the number of managers his fund used, especially domestic equity managers. He was not the only pension executive who was reducing the number of managers used for pension fund management. Several had decided their manager rosters had become unwieldy and had already begun to cut back. At RJR-Nabisco, Bob Shultz, formerly of New York Telephone who had moved there after a stint at the IBM fund, cut the 31 managers he inherited back to 19. Those 31 managers resulted largely from the merger in 1985 of R.J. Reynolds and Nabisco Brands Inc. Similarly, General Dynamics Inc. cut its roster to 13 equity managers from 25, and three fixed income managers from five two years before.[33] This would become a continuing trend in pension fund management over the next several years as companies made greater use of indexing, became comfortable with giving large managers more assets, and sought to reduce the amount they paid in management fees.

KKR+RJR = LBO

Meanwhile, RJR-Nabisco Inc. was in the news in 1988 for a different reason: It was the target of a takeover bid by Kohlberg Kravis Roberts, for which pension funds provided a significant part of the financing. KKR offered $20.3 billion for RJR-Nabisco after chief executive officer H. Ross Johnson tried to do a management buyout of the company for $75 a share, believing the stock price did not correctly reflect the value of the company. The board of directors agreed the stock price was too low, but they also thought Johnson's $75 a share was too low and called in the investment bankers to seek higher bids. This put the company "into play," and so a bidding war ensued, which eventually involved not only KKR but also Forstmann Little & Co., Shearson Lehman Hutton, and Salomon Brothers Inc. KKR ultimately won the battle at $120 per share, a rich premium for the shareholders, but the leveraged buyout raised important issues for the pension funds, which found themselves involved as participants in most of the LBO pools. First, were they helping to reduce the number of stocks on the stock exchange by financing the LBOs that took companies private? If so, was this a serious concern?

Jim George, investment manager of the $8.8 billion Oregon Public Employees Retirement System, a pioneer in LBO investing, thought not. "Why would anyone be concerned?" he said. "It means that equity prices will go higher. It seems they would welcome equity prices moving higher. In this wonderful economic system there has never been a shortage of stocks or bonds."[34] The Oregon fund had about $600 million invested with KKR. Second, corporate pension executives had a different concern. The RJR-Nabisco LBO showed that no company was safe. Corporate pension executives who had money in LBO funds with KKR, Forstmann Little, or any of the other major pools could find one day that their pension assets were financing the takeover of their own company.

This concern explained in part why corporate funds were generally slower to embrace LBO investing than public employee funds. Another concern expressed by some pension executives was that the huge RJR-Nabisco deal represented the highwater mark of LBOs as an investment. They believed that the price KKR paid for RJR-Nabisco was too high and that if other deals were made at similar prices returns would be affected. "I don't think the days of 40% annualized returns in the U.S. domestic market will be seen again," said Paul Quirk, executive director of the Massachusetts Pension Reserve Investment Management Board. A final concern was the fees the investment bankers behind such deals collected before the investors saw any investment return. In the case of RJR-Nabisco, the investment bankers collected more than $200 million in fees when the deal was completed, in addition to any share of the ultimate investment return, if and when the company was broken up and sold, or taken public again.

Although KKR paid a high price for RJR-Nabisco and it took many years for the investors in the deal to earn a solid return, some large pension funds profited handsomely immediately from the deal. These were the funds whose managers held large amounts of the stock. Institutional shareholders held about 95 million shares of RJR common when KKR made its bid, and at the time of the bid the stock was selling at $55 a share. The successful KKR bid gave the institutional holders of the stock profits of at least $5.1 billion.[35] However, the LBO cost one top pension executive his job: Shultz. As part of the post-LBO downsizing to get costs down, he was ordered to cut the RJR pension staff to a level he believed "irresponsible," and he objected. He was asked to resign and was replaced by a more accommodating pension executive.

Manager Troubles

Meanwhile, two large trust banks with long histories in pension fund management abandoned the business in May 1988. Citicorp, once known as First National City Bank, sold its investment management subsidiary, Citicorp Investment Management, to an insurance company, Baltimore-based USF&G Corp., for $102.5 million.[36] Citicorp Investment Management had $17.5 billion under management at the time of the sale, but it was struggling to maintain its market share. In addition, Citicorp needed the money as it dealt with bad loans in Latin America. Citicorp Investment Management eventually became Chancellor Capital Management, and its executives bought it from USF&G in a leveraged buyout. It is now part of INVESCO.

A month after Citicorp sold its investment management arm, Chemical Bank closed its investment management subsidiary, Favia Hill & Associates.[37] Favia Hill had been spun off from the bank in 1983 with $9 billion of institutional assets as the bank attempted to overcome the image of stodgy investment methods and performance clients associated with banks. However, the investment management subsidiary continued to produce lacklustre investment performance.

The banks were not alone in experiencing trouble retaining pension clients and assets. The once high-flying Batterymarch Financial management saw its assets peak at $12.1 billion in 1984, and by May 1987 they had fallen to $7.7 billion, most of that loss occurring between the beginning of 1986 and May 1987 as 42 clients pulled out almost $4 billion.[38] The falloff was caused by three years of performance below the S&P 500 Index and the defection of several top professionals from the firm to start their own firm, Martingale Asset Management Inc. Batterymarch's contrarian, value-oriented investment approach led it to small-cap issues, and during the bull market that began in 1982 small-cap stocks underperformed the S&P 500. Between 1981 and 1987 small-cap stocks underperformed large-cap stocks by 3 percentage points a year. Batterymarch's troubles were just beginning. Perhaps because of the loss of key professionals who were not easily replaced, Batterymarch's performance continued to lag even when small-cap stocks outperformed in the early 1990s, and the firm's assets dropped to just over $3 billion by 1998.[39] By then it was a subsidiary of a brokerage firm, with LeBaron having sold out in 1996.

At about the same time that Citicorp was sold and Favia Hill folded, General Electric Co.'s pension fund management group GE Investment Management Inc. registered with the SEC as an investment adviser, thus becoming eligible to sell its services to outside organizations.[40] It was not the first pension fund to do so. Owens-Illinois Inc.'s investment management subsidiary, Harbor Capital Advisors, began offering five mutual funds to outside clients, mostly defined contribution plans, in December 1987, and American Airlines' AMR Investment Services, which oversaw the airline's pension assets, also offered mutual funds to outside clients. Both Harbor Capital and AMR Investment Services used the manager-of-manager approach pioneered by the Frank Russell Trust Co. They did not build up internal investment staffs to select stocks or bonds; rather, they used their skills at selecting investment management firms to put together teams of outside managers to invest the assets. GE Investment Management was far larger than the others, managing $30 billion in company assets, including $20 billion in pension assets. In addition, GE Investment Management was not offering U.S. equity management. Instead it was offering international equity, real estate, and equity-linked private placement expertise. All of GE's own pension assets were managed internally by a staff of 15 portfolio managers, and GE Investment Management was marketing the skills of these executives.

More Terminations

Some companies were still reacting to FASB 87 and to Senator Metzenbaum's threat to halt pension fund reversions by terminating their pension plans. But now a new, even more worrisome trend emerged. More companies were terminating their plans and were not starting any kind of replacement plan. In 1985, according to the Pension Benefit Guaranty Corp., 18.5% of companies that terminated plans did not replace them. By 1987 that figure had jumped to 25.7%, and in the first quarter of 1988 it was 29.4% of the total.[41] Most of these terminations were by smaller companies which found the FASB rules and the new PBGC premiums and funding restrictions too onerous to bother with. Some of these companies apparently later joined the trend toward starting 401(k) plans, but for a time their employees were without any form of retirement plan. Terminations in the first half of 1988 were up 70% over the same period the year before. Among them was Occidental Petroleum's thirteenth plan termination. The oil company terminated the $382 million plan of one of its subsidiaries, Midcon Corp., and recaptured $95.2 million.[42] Overall, Occidental had recaptured $624 million from its 13 terminated plans. Another was Goodyear Tire & Rubber Co's. termination of a $929 million plan for salaried employees, which returned $400 million in surplus assets to the company.[43] Goodyear officials said that the company had acted when it did in response to the threat of congressional action to make terminations and reversions more difficult and to finance a corporate restructuring.

Index Issues

During the early months of 1988, research seemed to show that stocks included in the Standard & Poor's 500 Index outperformed similar stocks not included in the index.[44] The research, carried out by William Jacques, chief investment officer at Martingale Asset Management and the consultants at BARRA, the consulting firm, showed that for the eight years ended December 31, 1987, stocks included in the S&P Index outperformed similar stocks not included by 400 basis points. In 1987 alone the S&P stocks outperformed by 600 basis points. That is, a portfolio manager selecting stocks similar to those in the index, but not including in his portfolio the actual stocks in the index, had no chance of beating or even equaling the index funds.

The experts attributed the outperformance in part to the growth of U.S. stock index funds, which by mid-1988 had $120.9 billion in assets. These funds increased the demand for stocks in the index, while at the same time depressing the demand for similar stocks not in the index. This was dubbed the "membership anomaly." Another factor was the increased use of stock index futures for investing. The stock index futures were based on the S&P 500 Index. A third factor was believed to be the tendency for foreign investors to invest in the best-known stocks, and the stocks that were included in the index were better known than their peers simply because they were in the index.

Research by Salomon Brothers, the investment banking company, showed that when a stock was added to the S&P 500 Index, its price immediately rose by an average of 3.11% on the day it was added. Over the following 20 days its price rose an average of 5.92%. Some investors expressed concern about the S&P effect as a distortion of the capital-raising function of the market. It implied that companies in the index could raise capital more cheaply than other companies simply by virtue of their inclusion in the index. However, others were not worried. They suspected that once the anomaly was pointed out, the market would sooner or later arbitrage it away by anticipating which companies might be included in the index and buying them when a change was expected. And so it proved to be. Within three years the anomaly was no longer detectable.

Both the anomaly and its elimination were further demonstrations of the influence of institutional investors. As the end of the 1980s approached, the power of pension funds and their effect on investing and the economy were undeniable. Pension assets from defined benefit plans were flowing into venture capital and leveraged buyout funds and were helping to power the restructuring of the economy, though the effect was as yet barely discernible. Pension funds had contributed to a real estate boom but had begun to pull back as the market became overheated owing mainly to Savings and Loan Associations pouring money into ill-advised projects, many of which would eventually collapse. Pension funds had also shown their power in the 1987 market crash where sales of only a tiny fraction of their assets had caused a severe market plunge. Because it was short-lived, it had no significant impact on the economy. All the same, it was a warning signal to government officials.

Pension funds had also fired shots across the bows of corporate executives through the corporate governance movement, warning them that their management performance was being watched by long-term investors who would tolerate no performance less than excellent. But change was in the wind as the steps Congress had taken to stanch the flow of tax revenues they saw escaping into pension funds began to fatally weaken defined benefit plans. Defined benefit plans were steadily being replaced by defined contribution plans where workers had the investment control (and risk). The movement was about to change Americans into a nation of investors.

Chapter 13

Metzenbaum Wins

In November 1990, after more than five years of battling, Senator Howard Metzenbaum of Ohio won his fight to make plan terminations for the seizure of surplus pension assets almost impossible, and locked in the change in direction of the pension fund revolution.[1] The fiscal 1991 budget passed by Congress imposed a 50% excise tax on surplus assets that reverted to the employer after a termination. In addition, the employer was required to immediately vest all employees in their accrued pension benefits. However, the excise tax dropped to 20% if an employer either started a new plan that covered at least 95% of active employees covered by the previous plan and transferred 25% of the surplus assets to the new plan or used at least 20% of the surplus to increase the benefits of all plan participants and retirees. One pension expert commented that Senator Metzenbaum had halted the termination of overfunded plans because employers now would make sure their plans did not become overfunded since they could never get the assets back. In addition, the budget law increased the annual PBGC insurance premium to $19 per employee for fully funded plans and to as much as $72 per participant for underfunded plans.

These provisions made defined benefit plans even less attractive than they had been and spurred the further growth of 401(k) plans. Ironically, Senator Metzenbaum had driven the final nail into the coffin of defined benefit plans, the plans that he and his Democratic Party colleagues in Congress had professed to prefer over defined contribution plans because they provided more certain pensions. By the end of 1989, 38 million employees were covered by 599,245 defined contribution plans, compared with 40 million covered by 132,000 defined benefit plans. But because of 401(k) plans, defined contribution plans were growing rapidly. Although the number of defined contribution plans increased between the end of

1989 and the end of 1990, the number of defined benefit plans plunged to 113,000.[2] Only in assets did defined benefit plans lead, but here again, defined contribution plans were gaining rapidly. After the passage of the fiscal 1991 budget, the number of defined benefit plans declined further as plan terminations, underfunded or just fully funded, continued and few new plans were started. The first budget of the Clinton Administration further weakened senior corporate management interest in defined benefit plans and even reduced it for 401(k) plans, when it reduced the maximum salary on which a tax-exempt pension benefit could be based to $150,000 from $235,800 per year. The effect of this change on defined benefit plans was immediate as more of them disappeared. The effect on 401(k) plans was less obvious and less immediate. But over the rest of the decade senior management shifted more of the costs of 401(k) plans on to the beneficiaries, while many also ended the company match of employee contributions.

So strong was the growth of 401(k) plans in the late 1980s and early 1990s that money management firms reported that the assets they managed for defined contribution plans grew by 31.5% in 1992 alone.[3] Although mutual fund companies and GIC providers dominated the business, others were attempting to break in, among them benefits consulting firms and banks. Benefits consulting firms, such as Hewitt Associates and Hazlehurst & Associates, put together "alliances" of money management firms, an investment consulting firm, an administration firm, and themselves to provide all of the services defined contribution plans required. The benefits consulting firm provided the investment education and communication services required; the administrative firm provided the recordkeeping; the investment management consultant helped select and monitor the managers; and the managers actually made the investment decisions. In this way managers who did not have a full range of mutual fund products could enter the booming 401(k) market. The benefits consulting firms, which had started as actuarial consulting firms but were losing that business as defined benefit plans declined, kept their feet in the corporate doors. The alliances allowed companies to avoid what many saw as the "cookie cutter" approach offered by the mutual fund companies. However, brand-name mutual funds were a strong attraction for both companies offering plans and for the employees, and the success of the alliances was limited.

For much of the period from 1981 to the early 1990s, guaranteed investment contracts (GICs) were the preferred investment for most employees. This growth in the number and assets of 401(k)s attracted competition for both GIC providers and mutual fund companies. In 1987 banks had begun offering bank investment contracts (BICs), their own version of guaranteed interest contracts, which had been so successful for insurance companies. The bank version was guaranteed up to $100,000 per participant by the Federal Deposit Insurance Corp. By September 1989 banks had gained 10% of the GIC market. However, the more than 20% annual growth in demand for guaranteed products over the next two years, driven by the continued double-digit growth of 401(k) plans, provided more than enough demand to satisfy both banks and insurance companies. Eventually, BICs were provided through managed bond portfolios, around which the bank wrapped an insurance policy bought from an insurance company. Later still, fixed income managers developed synthetic GICs using fixed income futures contracts to provide the guarantees.

In addition, a group of GIC managers emerged to help 401(k) plan sponsors select the best guaranteed contracts and to construct efficient, diversified portfolios of them. These GIC portfolio managers included such major institutions as Bankers Trust Co., Fidelity Investments, T. Rowe Price Associates, and Vanguard Group. It also included companies for which GIC portfolio management was the primary business. One pioneer in this area was Peter W. Bowles, who began to manage GIC portfolios at Citytrust, a small Bridgeport, Connecticut, trust bank in 1977. At about the same time John Appleton, a vice president at giant State Street Bank and Trust in Boston, began to do the same. They believed that a carefully selected, diversified portfolio of GICs made as much sense as a carefully selected diversified portfolio of stocks or bonds in that it could minimize risk without reducing expected return. Within a few years, Bowles and Appleton had been joined by firms such as PRIMCO Capital Management, Certus Asset Advisors, and Morley Capital Management specializing in GIC management, as well as the banks and mutual fund companies offering it as a product. Bowles eventually started his own firm, Fiduciary Capital Management. Over time, employees put smaller and smaller percentages of their 401(k) assets into GICs, but the growth of 401(k) plans was so vigorous that the flow of dollars into stable-value investments remained strong.

Guaranteed Disaster

In January 1990, Drexel Burnham Lambert, the investment banking firm that had virtually created the junk bond market, collapsed, and in April the junk bond messiah, Michael Milken, pleaded guilty to six felony charges of breaking federal securities law. Without Milken and Drexel to support it, the junk bond market weakened and junk bond prices fell. The situation worsened when Congress ordered the savings and loan industry to rid its portfolios of junk bonds. The S&Ls had invested heavily in high-interest junk bonds in an effort to compete with money market mutual funds, which were paying higher interest than they could. In addition, the S&Ls had demanded and won the right to invest in more than home mortgages. Besides junk bonds, some invested in real estate development projects, at least a few of which were fraudulent. The S&Ls were able to trumpet that the interest they paid on accounts was almost as good as that of the money market funds. In addition, each account was insured by the Federal Savings and Loan Insurance Corp. for up to $100,000. But the fall of Milken and the virtual collapse of large sections of the real estate industry in 1990 caused Congress to order the S&Ls to dump their junk bonds. The sudden dumping of the junk bond holdings of the S&Ls on to the already weak market knocked junk bond prices down further, in many cases below 40% of their face value (and, in the process, causing many otherwise secure S&Ls to become insolvent).

Although at first these events caused barely a ripple in the GIC market, their impact would soon be felt in many pension funds. The GIC industry initially was complacent because the average portfolio backing GICs had only small holdings of junk bonds. However, one insurance company, Executive Life, a subsidiary of First Executive Corp., had a substantial amount of its $3 billion in GICs backed by junk bonds. In addition, Executive Life had sold annuities to companies terminating their defined benefit plans. These annuities guaranteed future benefit payments to employees and retirees, and they too were heavily backed by junk bonds. Within a year of the collapse of the junk bond market, Executive Life was in deep financial trouble as the value of its junk bond holdings collapsed, wiping out much of its capital. Insurance regulators had to step in to prevent the collapse of the company, and they froze annuity payments and GIC contracts.

Pension plan sponsors, including Honeywell Inc., Unisys Corp., and the State of Alaska followed suit, freezing payouts from their employee benefit funds that held Executive Life GICs or annuities.[4] Honeywell acknowledged that $72 million of its $450 million fixed income assets for its savings plan was in GICs with Executive Life. The company announced that it would make payouts to employees from the GIC account only as payments were received from Executive Life. Unisys Corp. reported $134 million in Executive Life GICs. The Alaska fund had $132 million in Executive Life GICs. The first lawsuit against Executive Life was filed by retirees of Pacific Lumber Corp. which had been acquired by Maxxam, Inc. in 1989. Maxxam partly financed the acquisition by selling junk bonds to Executive Life. It then terminated the Pacific Lumber Corp. pension fund, recaptured surplus assets, and bought annuities for the retirees from Executive Life. Now the retirees' benefit payments were frozen.

Only months after the Executive Life collapse, more suits were filed, this time by employees of Honeywell Inc. and Unisys Corp. seeking to recover losses on GIC contracts.[5] In the Unisys suit the employees charged Unisys breached its fiduciary duty by failing to recognize how much of its assets Executive Life had in junk bonds, and therefore how vulnerable it was to economic forces. The inclusion of the Executive Life GICs as an option was therefore imprudent, the employees charged. However, Executive Life had been rated highly by the insurance industry's primary rating agencies and had been cleared by Unisys's pension consultant. The company was thus exonerated by a federal district court in 1997.[6] Executive Life was not the only insurance company brought down by the junk bond and GIC crisis. Five months after Executive Life failed, Mutual Benefit Life Insurance Co., an old-line New Jersey-based insurance company, was seized by New Jersey insurance officials after client withdrawals threatened its viability.[7] The Executive Life crisis apparently prompted thousands of participants in 403(b) plans, plans similar to 401(k)s offered to the public and nonprofit sectors, to begin withdrawing their assets from GICs and annuities. These withdrawals were made easier at Mutual Benefit than at most insurance companies because it had lower withdrawal penalties than most companies; moreover, many of the clients were long-time clients, and withdrawal penalties usually decline with the length of the relationship. Mutual Benefit was vulnerable because its policies were backed by relatively undiversified and illiquid real estate and mortgage portfolios, and it was relatively thinly capitalized.

At least 25 large corporations, including AT&T, Allied-Signal Corp., Bell Atlantic Corp., General Mills Inc., and Grumman Corp., had multimillion-dollar GICs with Mutual Benefit. However, the New Jersey Department of Insurance developed a plan to stabilize Mutual Benefit and to allow the orderly payment of withdrawals. Eventually, Mutual Benefit's GIC customers had a tough choice to make: They could settle for receiving 55% of their principal back virtually immediately, or they could wait as long as 17 years to receive 100%. Ironically, in December 1991, the pioneer of GICs, Equitable Life Assurance Society of the U.S., announced that it was leaving the GIC business.[8] After a tumultuous period in the mid-1980s, when interest rates plunged and it lost $1 billion on high-interest-rate GIC contracts issued years earlier, Equitable had gradually reduced its GIC business from a high of $2 billion a year to about $500 million a year. Equitable finally decided that its capital could be allocated to higher-return businesses.

In the wake of the Executive Life collapse, a number of companies reported that they were deemphasizing GICs in their 401(k) plans and were stepping up efforts to educate employees about the investment markets, about long-term returns of various assets, and about the relationship between risk and return. One company quick to make the change was Avon Products Inc. An Avon official said the company was not giving investment advice to employees, but "we're showing them the possible alternatives to GICs, to think about it and evaluate it, and to consider where they want to end up and how to get there. GICs are not the only way to get there."[9] Many more 401(k) plan sponsors adopted this approach in the next few years. As companies stepped up their investment education programs for employees, the average allocation to GICs dropped to about 30% of assets by 1997 from 70%, while the allocation to common stock investments through mutual funds increased strongly. Nevertheless, demand for guaranteed interest contracts continued to grow because of the sheer volume of money flowing into 401(k) plans. However, pension executives generally renamed GICs "stable value investments" in their pension literature, removing the concept of "guarantee" that had proved irresistible (and misleading) to many individuals.

In many cases, this was in reaction to the Department of Labor's publication in late 1992 of Section 404(c) regulations. These regulations, published after almost 10 years of haggling between the Labor Department and the industry, spelled out what investment choices employers had to offer employees to enter a "safe harbor" from fiduciary liability. The regulations required the employers to give employees the opportunity to choose from at least three investment options, each with different risk and return characteristics; to change their investments as often as appropriate given the market volatility of the investment; and to make informed investment decisions based on the information made available to them. Employers did not have to comply with the regulations, but many did. Even though employers and employees began to shy away from GICs, by 1994 they still accounted for more than 35% of the asset mix of the average 401(k) plan participant when more bad news hit. Confederation Life Insurance Co., a major Canadian insurer that had substantial operations in the United States, and that was a major factor in the GIC and pension annuity market, was seized by Canadian regulators when its financial condition became critical.[10] Many GIC and annuity holders were faced with the probability that they would receive less than 100% of their investment back.

Other employers not only stepped up employee investment education, but offered programs designed to make the investment decisions easier for the employees. The programs offered the employees pre-mixed packages of mutual funds of various risk levels designed to be appropriate to groups of employees at different stages in their working careers. The package for younger employees typically invested more in equity mutual funds and less in fixed income and money market funds than the package for midcareer employees, whereas the one for employees nearing retirement was more conservative than the packages for young or midcareer employees. These packages were known as life-cycle funds. One of the first companies to offer such an option was GTE Corp.[11] GTE offered four life-cycle funds to participants in its $3.6 billion defined contribution plans after focus groups revealed many employees did not feel comfortable making investment decisions and didn't know how to go about diversifying their investments. For those comfortable with making their own investment choices, GTE offered five Fidelity mutual funds and a company stock option. Honeywell Inc. offered employees two customized balanced portfolios among its 14 options. The balanced options allowed employees to choose investments diversified across domestic and international stocks, bonds, and cash. Other employers simply offered employees a wider choice of investment options, most of them from mutual fund companies.

Real Problems

GICs were not the only problem investment for pension funds as the 1990s began. Real estate, too, was a disappointment, especially as the skies had seemed to be brightening as the 1980s ended. The real estate returns for the 1980s were about equal to the returns on bonds. Although the Shearson Lehman bond index returned 11.27% for the 10 years ended June 30, 1989, the median open-end real estate fund returned 11.8% before fees, and the median closed-end fund returned 11.6%.[12] Over the last five years of the decade the results were even worse as annual real estate returns were only 8.7% compared with 13.2% for bonds and 20.3% for stocks. That is not what real estate managers had promised pension funds. They had promised equity-like returns with lower risk. They justified the higher return as an offset for lack of liquidity. When the returns trailed those of equities, many pension funds were disappointed. However, as the decade ended, the situation seemed to be improving. For example PRISA's assets were rising in value after four years of decline because of increased new client contributions, reduced client withdrawals, and better investment returns.[13] Houston's property market, one of the nation's weakest in the mid-1980s because of overbuilding during the oil boom of the late 1970s followed by declining oil prices, appeared to be rebounding, and office vacancies around the nation had begun to drop. In addition, commitments to real estate jumped 20% in 1989, taking total real estate investments to $113 billion and making pension funds major owners of office buildings, shopping centers, and industrial properties.[14]

But the light at the end of the tunnel proved to be the proverbial express train going in the opposite direction, in large part because of the savings and loan crisis which dumped billions of dollars of real estate onto the market at distressed prices. The S&Ls had been major sources of financing for developers in the 1980s, but while they were now out of the market, the Resolution Trust Corp. was trying to market many of the buildings they financed at a time when office supply equaled 20 years of demand in many markets and 100 years of demand in others.[15] In addition, the bankruptcy of Federated Stores Inc. suddenly threw into question the value of the shopping malls pension funds owned through pooled funds. Looking at the S&L situation, the office supply vacancy figures, the probable drop in mall values as overextended retailers went bankrupt, and the economic outlook, many pension funds decided to cut their real estate commitments. Withdrawals hit one of the oldest of the real estate open-end funds, First Wachovia's. Early in 1990 its clients filed to withdraw 37% of its $385 million in assets.[16] Travelers Insurance Co. decided to liquidate Separate Account R, its real estate fund, sparking threats of lawsuits over how the assets would be allocated among the participant funds.[17] First National Bank of Chicago's Fund F was also sued by pension funds seeking the return of their assets.[18] By midyear the rush to exit real estate pooled funds was on in earnest as pension funds had filed to pull $1.9 billion from open-end funds.[19] This forced some funds to sell properties to meet the redemptions, further weakening the real estate market. Although some of the money withdrawn was earmarked for direct investing, it would not flow rapidly back into real estate as the investors looked for bargains.

The problems continued into 1991. More pension funds cut their allocations to real estate, and the $22 billion IBM pension fund froze its allocation at 10% of assets.[20] Fund officials said that even if the allocation dropped below 10% because of the growth of the fund or a decline in property values, they would not buy more. The decline in interest in real estate affected the professionals of the management organizations. Prudential Insurance, the largest manager of real estate investments for pension funds with about $5 billion in assets, laid off 10% of its 1,100 real estate staff. Soon afterward, Equitable Life Assurance, the second largest manager with $3.7 billion in assets, laid off 90 real estate employees.

When the real estate investment returns were in for 1991, they were horrendous. The median fund had a return of –8.6%.[21] The previous low

median total return was 2.2% in 1990. The value of the assets in the JMB
Institutional Realty Corp. Fund IV dropped 25.2% in 1991 alone. Income
of 4.6% helped bring the total return to –20.6%. The LaSalle Street Fund
of LaSalle Advisors Ltd. lost 18.3% of its property value, but income of
5.9% improved total return to a loss of 12.4%. The terrible results were the
result of writing down the values of buildings in the funds. In some cases,
the buildings were written off. GE Investments Inc., the investment arm
for General Electric Co.'s pension fund, placed two buildings in which it
had the majority equity interest into bankruptcy when the values fell
below the mortgage, which was held by Metropolitan Life Insurance Co.[22]
Because of the declines in the market values of the properties, the total
value of real estate owned by pension funds declined to $94.9 billion in
1992 from $101 billion a year before.[23] At the end of 1992, the $19.7 billion Minnesota State Board of Investments cut its real estate target from
10% of assets to 6% while boosting its target for venture capital to 7.5% of
assets, and following that up with a $65 million commitment to three ven-
ture capital partnerships.[24] Some fund executives were beginning to wonder if it was not time to buy, and at the end of 1992 the Virginia
Retirement System committed $420 million to real estate investing, on top
of the $700 million it already had invested in property.[25]

The move was early, however, as companies, in an effort to become
more competitive in the global economy, began massive efforts to reduce
their employee headcounts, bringing about huge layoffs and greatly cutting
the need for office and industrial space. Some funds began to recognize their
real estate losses. In mid-1993 the $16 billion Washington State Investment
Board wrote down a $450 million real estate portfolio to $250 million, and
it and the $24 billion Ohio State Teachers Retirement System sued the
New England Mutual Life Insurance Co. and its real estate subsidiary Copley Real Estate Advisors Inc. over investments Copley had made for them.[26]
Late in the year PRISA, the grandfather of all open-end real estate funds,
received a black eye when Mark Jorgensen, the $2.3 billion fund's portfolio
manager, charged that the appraisal of two of its properties had been
inflated to protect the fund's performance record.[27] Jorgensen had apparently been demoted and reassigned after expressing his unhappiness with
the appraisals to his superior, and he filed suit to regain his former position.
Prudential then dismissed him. During an investigation into Jorgensen's
charges, an outside appraisal firm found 17 of the properties in PRISA I and
PRISA II overvalued by more than 10%. As a result, Prudential settled Jorgensen's suit out of court and asked his boss to resign.

Meanwhile, there was one bright spot in the real estate investment
picture: timberland. Though still very much a minor asset class, some pen-

sion funds found it attractive. As GTE's John Carroll noted, even when the value of the property did not change, the trees on the property still grew at least 4% a year, faster in some parts of the country. Hancock Timber Resources Group reported in September 1993 that it had $2 billion of pension and other tax-exempt assets invested in timberland, up from $1.3 billion the year before.[28] Much of that gain was the result of appreciation in the value of the property because of a rise in timber prices. Hancock announced nine new clients for the fund a month later, including the Michigan Municipal Employees Retirement System, the Hoechst Celanese Corp. pension fund, and the Colorado Fire & Police Pension Association.[29] By mid-1994, however, pension funds appeared to be increasing their commitments to real estate again, driven by disappointing returns in the stock market in 1992 and 1993, when equities returned 7.7% and 10.0%, respectively, and by a growing feeling that the real estate market had bottomed. Real estate managers reported that their assets under management in June 1994 were 2.8% greater than a year earlier when adjusted for 4% investment returns.[30] By then the nation's pension funds had about $120.4 billion invested in real estate.

By June 30, 1995, the value of real estate managed for pension funds had climbed to $136.8 billion,[31] though not every fund liked real estate's prospects. Digital Equipment Corp. executives announced late in the year that they were gradually selling all the pension fund's real estate investments because they believed stocks and bonds would outperform property over the long run.[32] But many pension funds again moved their assets into real estate investing during the next three years, though many changed their approach. Some spurned the open- and closed-end commingled real estate funds in favor of direct investing with one or two other pension funds, or they went to the opposite extreme and invested through real estate investment trusts, which are, in effect, open-end real estate mutual funds. The pension funds hoped the public nature of REITs would give them almost the liquidity of common stocks with returns better than those of fixed income investments. Although total pension fund commitments continued to grow, reaching $145 billion by mid-1997, the mid-1990s saw consolidation among real estate investment management companies: Firms such as Copley Real Estate Advisors and AEW Capital Management merged, Lend Lease Corp. acquired Equitable Real Estate Investment Management, the real estate management subsidiary of Equitable Life, and Heitman Financial Corp. acquired JMB Realty Corp., the real estate investment pioneer. The ups and downs of real estate taught many pension executives valuable lessons: Don't get carried away by rising prices, and don't pour too much money into an apparently hot asset class. Also, take the long view. If an asset class truly makes sense, don't panic at temporary market declines.

International Commitments

Meanwhile, as pension funds were pulling back from estate investing in the late 1980s, they were stepping up their international investing. Commitments to international investment grew 43% in 1989 as public employee pension funds[33] joined corporate funds in venturing overseas. Following on the heels of the Colorado Public Employees Retirement System, the Los Angeles County Retirement System and several others that had made international commitments in 1988, the California State Teachers Retirement System committed $2.5 billion to international investments,[34] and the Massachusetts, New Jersey, Idaho, and Oregon public employee funds all entered the arena in 1990 and 1991. As a result, pension assets invested internationally surged another 22% in 1990. The rise in interest followed strong investment returns in the 1980s when the international markets returned a healthy 17.5% compounded annually.[35] Some of the pioneering funds and managers were beginning to invest outside of the major European markets and Japan into some of the emerging markets. One of the first was ITT Corp., which allocated $30 million of its $1.6 billion pension assets to them in October 1989.[36] One survey found that 35% of the international management assignments in 1990 were for investment in emerging markets.[37]

Among the emerging markets being explored in 1990 and 1991 were the former Communist-bloc economies which were freed when the Berlin Wall crumbled in 1989. George Russell of the Frank Russell Co. put together a group of 20 large pension funds and 20 large investment management organizations to explore investment in emerging markets. The so-called 20-20 Group made its first overseas foray in June 1991 to the newly free countries in Eastern Europe. It later made exploratory educational trips to Japan, China, and emerging markets in Southeast Asia. Russell firmly believed U.S. pension funds could earn higher investment returns in such markets, in the long run, than in the United States.

Two other organizations became involved in educating pension executives to the investment opportunities overseas, particularly public pension fund executives. These were the Institute for Fiduciary Education and Pensions 2000. Both groups arranged for money management firms to pick up most of the costs for pension executives traveling on these educational and "kick the tires" expeditions to Eastern Europe, Latin America, Japan,

China, and Southeast Asia. Partly as a result of these efforts, but even more because of the strong investment results, international investment by pension funds, especially public pension funds, increased dramatically during the early part of the decade. Between March 1993 and March 1994 alone, the assets invested internationally for U.S. tax-exempt institutions, mainly U.S. pension funds, increased by 52%, with market appreciation accounting for less than half of that gain. Despite the poor international market results in 1994, funds continued to pour assets into foreign markets in 1995. Typical was the $26 billion Minnesota State Board of Investment which increased its long-term allocation to international investing to 15% of assets from 10%, a boost equal to $1 billion. Some of this increased allocation by the pension funds went to emerging markets, and the emerging markets trend would continue to gather steam during the 1990s. The money flows from U.S. pension funds helped further the development of the capital and stock markets in the emerging countries in Asia and South America. The funds were attracted to the apparently high growth rates of these countries, for example, Thailand, Taiwan, Singapore, Malaysia, Argentina, Brazil, and Chile.

The money provided by the pension funds help the economies grow by financing investment not only in plant and equipment, but also in infrastructure, such as toll highways and bridges, and in power stations. Two U.S. pension funds, those of US WEST and Hughes Aircraft Inc., even joined with the Rockefeller Foundation and Bridgewater Associates to finance a new merchant bank in China. The new bank was to offer a full range of investment banking and merger and acquisition services, as well as mutual funds for investors seeking opportunities in China. The only cloud on the international investment horizon was the plunge in the Japanese market beginning in 1990. However, many funds had underweighted Japan simply because they had feared it was overvalued: The Nikkei Index had surged above 40,000, and the price-earnings ratio on the average Japanese large company stock climbed to 40, compared with a U.S. average price-earnings ratio of 16 at the time. While some experts had argued that the 40 p/e was acceptable because "Japan is different," most international managers were cautious. Therefore, the plunge did not initially hurt or concern them.

Indeed, U.S. pension funds continued to add to their international investment portfolios during 1996 and 1997. As of March 31, 1997, they had more than $455 billion invested overseas, up 27.5% from the previous year.[38] Unfortunately, in mid-1997 disaster struck as first Thailand and then Indonesia, Korea, Malaysia, and most of the developing Asian markets fell into crisis as speculative excesses, some of them financed indirectly by the flood of U.S. pension fund money, finally were recognized. As the economies stumbled and their currencies were attacked by currency speculators and plunged, pension fund money managers began to cut back their investments in the markets. As they had contributed to the rise, so they contributed to the fall. The money managers felt they could not ride the markets down and wait for them to recover because they had to report their performance quarterly to pension fund trustees who had the reputation, sometimes deserved, of being notoriously impatient. Some of the stock markets plunged 50% or more by the end of the year, and some of the economies declined into near depression. Because emerging markets investments were only a small part of the international portfolios of U.S. pension funds, the damage to their asset bases was minimal. Most funds maintained their commitments to emerging markets, and others, perceiving a buying opportunity, hired their first emerging-market managers.

Manager Moves

Meanwhile, at the other end of the manager spectrum, there were significant developments among large money management organizations. The 1990s became a decade of mergers and acquisitions, often across borders, as money management organizations positioned themselves to manage the pension assets of global corporations and the assets of individuals worldwide. They sought size and a full range of products for both defined benefit and defined contribution pension plans, and for individuals. They also sought investment insight and talent.

A key development was the acquisition of U.S. money management organizations, or parts of them, by non-U.S. institutions. This began in the 1980s with, among others, the purchase of a part-interest in Wells Fargo Investment Advisors by Nikko, the Japanese brokerage firm, and the acquisition of Boston's Gardner and Preston Moss Inc., Denver's Financial Programs Inc., and Atlanta's INVESCO Capital Management Inc. by Britannia Arrow Holdings, a British financial services company. In April 1990, Hill Samuel Investment Management Group Ltd., London, bought Atlanta Capital Management, which had $1.7 billion under management. A month later, Nationale-Nederladen US Holdings Inc., the U.S. subsidiary of a Dutch insurance company, bought 22% of AIM Management Group, the Houston-based mutual fund company with $13 billion under management. In late June, Credit Suisse, Zurich, a Swiss institution, bought 80% of BEA Associates, one of the most respected pension management organizations with $10 billion under management.[39] In 1991

Union Bank of Switzerland bought Chase Investors Management Corp., the investment management subsidiary of Chase Manhattan Bank and one of the most successful bank investment subsidiaries, and renamed it UBS Asset Management.

Often these early acquisitions were driven by two primary motives. One was to gain access to the burgeoning U.S. pension market. The other, as in the Wells Fargo Nikko deal, was to gain insight into American investment management techniques, which appeared to work better than many others. Later, the issues of global reach and a full range of products became paramount. Often, after the takeover, the American investment team came to dominate. Such was the case with the Britannia–INVESCO deal. INVESCO was headed by Charles (Charlie) Brady, a courtly Atlantan who had begun his career in the investment business out of Georgia Tech by joining a local brokerage firm, Goodybody & Co. in 1957 after two years in the Navy. In 1963 he joined Citizens & Southern Bank as an investment officer, and in 1971 he was tapped by Mills Lane, the visionary president of the bank, to start the first investment management subsidiary of a bank, INVESCO. Lane, aware that much of Atlanta's wealth, including that of the region's pension funds, was being invested by northern firms, wanted to bring it home. He believed he could set up a free-standing investment management subsidiary and attract much of that money. INVESCO was registered with the Securities and Exchange Commission in late 1971 and started business on January 1, 1972.

By 1978 Citizens & Southern Bank was reeling from losses on real estate deals it had financed and it needed capital. Brady and eight partners bought INVESCO, and they ran it as a successful independent counseling firm until 1980 when Britannia Arrow bought a 45% interest in INVESCO's income stream. It was an arrangement that was designed to help both firms. INVESCO hoped to get access to an international investment capability, something the partners felt would be essential if the firm was to compete successfully for U.S. pension business in the future. Britannia Arrow hoped to get access to the American market and American methods for its Montague Investment Management (MIM) subsidiary. However, in 1992 the senior British executives were implicated in a financial scandal involving British financier Robert Maxwell, who had drowned after falling off his yacht. Maxwell was found to have unlawfully looted the pension funds of some of his companies, and a number of senior MIM investment executives had failed to stop him. On top of that, MIM's investment performance had been poor. As a result, Brady and his American executives stepped in and took control of the firm. Now called simply INVESCO, the firm continued to expand its global reach and product line through acquisitions. In 1997 it bought the AIM Management Group, which managed $60 billion in the AIM funds, giving INVESCO an excellent family of mutual funds to use in pursuing the 401(k) market. In early 1998, INVESCO, renamed yet again and now called AMVESCAP, bought Chancellor-LGT from Liechtenstein Global Trust, which had acquired it only in 1996. By the end of 1998, AMVESCAP managed more than $200 billion, $90 billion of which was for U.S. pension funds. It was well positioned in most parts of the market, but it was late to the 401(k) party as most such funds of any size had already selected their managers.

Another example of the dominance of the U.S. investment methods was the acquisition of Brinson Partners by SBC Corp. (the Swiss banking company) for $705 million in 1994. Brinson Partners Inc., founded in 1989, was headed by Gary P. Brinson who was regarded as one of the brightest money managers in the pension investment business. His firm was a management buyout of First Chicago Investment Advisors, the investment management subsidiary of the First National Bank of Chicago. Brinson began his career with Travelers Insurance Co. in 1970 and, after integrating Modern Portfolio Theory techniques into its investment process, was named president of Travelers Investment Management Co. early in 1979. In July that year he was lured away to First National of Chicago to head its $3.7 billion trust department, and in 10 years he built the assets under management to more than $10 billion, based on a top-notch investment performance. In 1988, however, when the bank needed capital, Brinson and other senior executives of the subsidiary bought it with the help of the San Francisco-based investment banking boutique Hellman & Friedman. The bank retained a 10% ownership position in the new firm, a position that paid off handsomely five years later when SBC bought it. At the time, Brinson Partners had $33 billion under management and a stellar investment performance. Within four years Gary Brinson assumed control of the worldwide investment management operations of Swiss Bank Corp.

Less than a year later, Wells Fargo Nikko Investment Advisors was sold to Barclays PLC, the British bank, creating one of the biggest investment management organizations in the world with $205 billion under management.[40] The price was $440 million in cash, lower than the price for Brinson because although most of Brinson's assets were high-fee, actively managed assets, Wells Fargo's were lower-fee passively managed (indexed) assets. Barclays combined Wells Fargo with its own investment management subsidiary, BZW Investment Management. The merger gave Barclays access to the U.S. market and to Wells's indexing and enhanced indexing techniques, while giving the Wells Fargo team an opening to other markets for its products. In 1995 Kemper Corp., the $62.3 billion Illinois-based insurance and asset management firm, was acquired by Zurich Insurance Group, and late in the year Dresdner Bank AG acquired RCM Capital Management, giving Dresdner a window on the techniques of one of the most successful boutiques started in the early 1970s golden age. More and more money management firms, U.S.-based and non-U.S.-based, were beginning to operate globally, seeking clients, as well as investment opportunities, in other parts of the world. They were not only reacting to the increasing globalization of the world's economies and capital markets, but were also helping to drive the process.

There were purely domestic mergers also, driven in large part by the 401(k) boom, as money managers sought mutual funds to offer in that market. A classic example was the acquisition of the Boston Co. by Mellon Bank Corp. in 1992 for $1.45 billion.[41] The deal gave Mellon the Boston Co.'s mutual fund and pension fund management business, as well as its master trust and global custody business in the Boston Safe Deposit and Trust Co. to add to its own substantial master trust and global custody business. A year later, Mellon bought the Dreyfus Corp., a pioneering mutual fund company, as it continued to seek mass and mutual funds to speed its entry into the defined contribution market. In 1993 alone 53 mergers or acquisitions involving firms managing more than $270 billion and valued in excess of $4 billion were announced.[42] More than half of these involved the search by one or both partners for mutual fund products to fill gaps in their product lines. Later, in mid-1994, the Twentieth Century Funds, Kansas City, merged with the Benham Group of Mountain View, California, to form a more broadly based $30 billion firm.[43] This merger was designed to fill gaps in product lines as Twentieth Century offered mostly equity mutual funds while Benham Group offered mostly fixed income funds.

Even investment banking firms acquired investment management firms for the same reasons. Morgan Stanley Asset Management added to its product line in 1995 by acquiring Miller Anderson & Sherrerd, another of the boutiques started in the early 1970s golden age,[44] and then in the first half of 1996 it added Van Kampen American Capital Management, a manager of $57 billion in mutual funds.[45] The merger and acquisition pace continued to accelerate as more and more companies decided they could not succeed in the long run without critical mass and without a full range of investment management products, domestic and international, aimed at both the defined benefit and defined contribution markets.

Late in 1995, Goldman, Sachs & Co. released a study by its investment banks and analysts which argued that the investment management business would become only a two-tier business. The very large money man-agement firms would get larger, and the small, one-product boutiques with something unique to offer would survive, though their margins would be squeezed. Midsized, multiproduct firms would have a difficult time surviv-ing, the report said. The report also predicted that over the succeeding five years, some firms would grow their assets under management by as much as five times. It predicted that just 20 to 25 firms would dominate the invest-ment management market by the year 2000. In the U.S. tax-exempt market (pension funds, foundations, and endowments), it said, 10 to 12 companies would account for 50% of the market by the year 2000.

Whether or not the Goldman, Sachs report, which confirmed the feel-ing of many in the industry that size was vital to survival, sparked action, the biggest mergers were yet to come, and they came in 1997. The first was the merger of Travelers Corp. and Salomon Brothers Inc., which brought together eight money management organizations, including Travelers Insurance, Travelers Investment Management Co., Smith Barney Capital Management, and Salomon Asset Management Co., overseeing $150 bil-lion, of which only about $32 billion was for pension and other tax-exempt funds, and $80 billion was for mutual funds.[46] The remainder were insur-ance assets and the assets managed for individuals. In November, Merrill Lynch & Co. announced it was buying Britain's most successful money management firm, Mercury Asset Management, gaining Mercury's institu-tional and high-net-worth individual assets.[47] The deal gave Merrill access to Mercury's strong international investment products for U.S. defined benefit and defined contribution pension funds. It also positioned the com-bined firm to compete strongly for defined contribution business around the world. Merrill had total assets under management of $272 billion, while Mercury's assets under management totaled $177 billion, giving the combined firms $449 billion.

Two weeks later, the two giant Swiss banks, Union Bank of Switzer-land and Swiss Bank Corp., merged to form United Bank of Switzerland, or UBS. This created a $340 billion institutional investment operation headed by Gary Brinson, as Union Bank's UBS Asset Management and PDFM Ltd., which managed $197 billion, combined with SBC Brinson, which managed $143 billion.[48] The mergers were confirming evidence of several trends in pension management: the trend toward globalization of the business; the trend toward huge, multi-asset firms; and the trend of companies seeking distribution, particularly mutual funds they could sell into the defined contribution market, which was developing not only in the United States, but also the United Kingdom, Australia, South Africa, Chile, Mexico, Argentina, and a number of other countries. Defined contribution plans seemed to be the favored pension structure around the world. In April 1998, Travelers Group Inc. agreed to merge with Citicorp, adding the $99 billion of assets managed by Citibank Global Asset Management to the $150 billion resulting from the Travelers-Salomon Brothers merger.[49] However, the new merger added only $6 billion to pension assets. The new firm therefore remained a relatively minor player in the defined benefit pension area, but a potentially strong challenger in the 401(k) pension field with a wide range of mutual funds and other pooled products to offer.

The money manager merger activity of the 1990s, especially the international mergers and acquisitions, meant that the individual investors, whether within pension funds or outside them, whether in the United States, the United Kingdom, Europe, or Asia, were being offered a wide range of investment vehicles by large, well-financed money management firms. In some countries these firms were helping to create real capital markets, replacing crony capital markets where the average investor was often viewed as a sheep to be fleeced rather than a customer or client to be served. These new mega-firms certainly were not perfect. Some offered products that underperformed, and some charged fees that were too high. But they generally tried to do an honest job of investing the assets to the best of their abilities. That was a major improvement for millions of investors. But for the growth of U.S. pension funds, however, such development would have been long delayed.

Chapter 14

Pension Exports

Money management firms weren't the only institutions globalizing their operations. Some companies with worldwide operations were attempting to harmonize as far as possible the pension fund investing in the many countries within which they operated. Because of differences in pension and investment laws, companies could not simply run their pension operations from the United States, but there could be much more coordination. The pension funds in different countries could use many of the same managers; they could all use the same global custodian bank; they could use the same investment management consultant; and they could follow basically the same investment approach and use the same techniques. Exxon Corp. may have been the first as it established two indexed equity pooled funds in 1986, one for all its U.S. pension assets and one for all non-U.S. plans, both managed by Wells Fargo Nikko Investment Advisors (later renamed Barclays Global Investors). Another pioneer in coordinating its worldwide pension operations was Ford Motor Co., which had about $30 billion in pension assets around the world, of which $23.4 billion was in the United States. Ford wanted to ensure, in particular, that common standards were being used in evaluating money managers. DuPont, which had about $17 billion in defined benefit assets worldwide, also began a program in 1995 to more closely coordinate the pension operations around the world, especially in investment management policies and actuarial practices. In early 1996 Eli Lilly began to attempt to manage all its worldwide pension funds as if they were one large pool of assets, Frederick Ruebeck, director of investments, told *Pensions & Investments*. For example, Brinson Partners, which was first hired to run part of Lilly's British pension fund, was also hired to run part of its Australian fund as well as part of the U.S. fund. Xerox, also seeking more coordination between its pension funds around the world, put Bob Evans in charge of the coordination effort. Through the acquisitions of U.S. money management firms by foreign firms, through the exporting of U.S. pension fund investment standards and techniques by multinational corporations to their foreign subsidiaries, and through the missionary world of U.S. pension consultants, U.S. investment management techniques spread throughout the world markets. Most developed markets have begun classifying their stocks as value or growth, and as large, mid-, and small-cap. Many have developed local index funds.

Corporate Heads Roll

Meanwhile, although the number of U.S. defined benefit pension plans was declining, the assets continued to grow, largely because of the growth of the stock market, and pension funds, particularly public pension funds, continued to flex their muscles to improve the performance of corporate management. The pension funds in the Council of Institutional Investors believed that much of the malaise in U.S. industry in the 1980s, when American companies were uncompetitive in world markets, was caused by mismanagement and short-sightedness at the top. The CII pension funds stepped up their campaign to hold chief executives responsible, and put pressure on boards of directors to act against CEOs whose companies were underperforming. One of the first victims of this increased pressure from institutional investors was Robert Stempel, chairman of General Motors who had replaced Roger B. Smith upon Smith's retirement. When Stempel failed to take swift, decisive action to improve GM's performance, investors called on the Board of Directors to do something. It did so in April 1992, replacing Stempel with John G. Smale, former chairman and CEO of Procter & Gamble and a member of the board.[1]

In the mid-1990s the activists also turned their attention to executive pay, arguing that many chief executives were overpaid, especially in relation to their performance, and demanding that corporate pay be more closely tied to performance. In the 1998 proxy season 71 shareholder resolutions dealing with executive compensation were filed by institutional investors.[2] By the mid-1990s too, the Council of Institutional Investors had taken the corporate governance movement overseas, first to Japan and then to Europe. Funds in the CII attempted to vote their proxies in Japan, Europe, and Australia in much the same way they did in the United States to influence corporate behavior. However, the institutions quickly encountered procedural difficulties, especially in Japan where all annual shareholder meetings are held on the same day. Nevertheless, led by the CII,

CalPERS, and the New York City Employee funds, U.S. pension funds and their managers stimulated corporate governance movements in the United Kingdom, Europe, and Australia.

Active Managers

Money managers took a leaf from the Council's book when, less than a year after Stempel's ouster, they caused the American Express Co. board to reverse itself and replace James D. Robinson III as chairman and chief executive officer.[3] The board had at first decided to retain Robinson as chairman, despite American Express's poor performance for much of the 1980s and the early 1990s. Immediately after the announcement of Robinson's reappointment, the stock price fell 9.3% as some large institutions decided to dump it. A dozen large institutional shareholders, in a meeting with Robinson and Harvey Golub, the newly appointed chief executive officer, sharply questioned Golub's ability to manage the company freely with Robinson in the picture. At the same time there were reports that other large institutional holders were preparing to slowly sell off their American Express holdings if Robinson remained. Recognizing the power of the institutions—the dozen at the meeting with Robinson and Golub between them owned 20% of all outstanding Amex stock—the board capitulated and fired Robinson, replacing him as chairman with Richard Furland, an outside director. At least seven shareholder proposals backed by activist institutional investors won majority support in 1993, confirming it as the year the corporate governance movement reached maturity.[4]

Having established that they could discipline corporate managements, the institutional investors next focused on the performance of boards of directors, many of which they believed to be dominated by do-nothing friends of the chairman or CEO who appointed them. Part of the program to discipline the directors and corporate management included the publication by the Council of Institutional Investors of a list of the 50 worst-performing companies. In addition, the Council decided to withhold proxy support from directors at nonperforming or nonresponsive companies—that is, companies that refused to make changes that received majority support from shareholders.[5] In March 1995, the institutional shareholders forced another CEO out of office when, as a result of their pressure, Joseph Antonini was ousted at K mart.[6] Immediately afterward, the directors of the company, recognizing the importance of institutional shareholders, met with a group of them, including the California Public Employee Retirement System and the State of Wisconsin Investment Board, and the money management firms of Hotchkis & Wiley, INVESCO, and Wellington Management to discuss the future of the company.

Relationship Investing

Meanwhile, some institutions had taken to heart the criticism by corporate management that investors, particularly pension fund money managers, were often part of the problem, that they were short-term investors seeking immediate investment returns, and that this often drove corporate management to seek quick fixes and boosts to return rather than managing for the long term. These institutions set about establishing what they called strategic long-term relationships with a small number of companies whereby they would invest in the companies to provide capital and provide management expertise, insights, and feedback when needed, perhaps even serving on the boards of directors. Dillon, Read & Co., a Wall Street investment banking firm, began marketing its Allied Investment Partners L.P. in late 1991. It was followed soon after by Lazard Freres, another investment banking firm, which set out to raise $1.65 billion to provide cash infusions for companies with sound management that needed long-term patient capital.

Robert A. G. Monks, the former chairman of the Boston Co. and the former head of the Labor Department's Pension and Welfare Benefits Administration, established the Lens Fund to take substantial minority share holdings in a few underperforming companies and to provide guidance and patient capital to them. While he was with the Labor Department, Monks was an early proponent of corporate governance activities by pension funds through their shareholder proxies. He was also an early proponent of investing for the long term, not just a short-term gain. CalPERS invested $200 million in Relational Investors L.P., another relationship fund that was started by Batchelder & Partners. In late 1997, CalPERS committed $200 million to another activist corporate governance fund, Active Value Fund Managers. Even the General Motors pension fund made a commitment to Corporate Partners L.P., another of the relationship investment funds. Some U.S. pension funds, including the State of Wisconsin, Howard Hughes Medical Center, and GE Investment Management, invested $200 million in closed-end funds managed by Arlington Capital Management, a London-based firm that invested in smaller companies with unrealized potential in Europe, and provided them with additional management expertise and guidance to help them become more successful. Arlington, which kept a low profile, was headed by Karl Van Horn, the international pioneer of the mid-1970s while at Morgan Guaranty.

Other Enhancements

Pension funds continued to seek ways of enhancing their long-term investment results through means other than corporate governance activities. Private investing continued to burgeon, and in 1993 a new burst of venture capital activity became evident as a result of a surge in high-tech, internet, and biotech startups. In 1993, 105 private equity funds closed after raising $12.7 billion, up from 82 funds raising $10.7 billion in 1992.[7] Some funds had become so comfortable with private investments that they had begun to invest directly, shunning the funds offered by KKR, Forstmann Little and Castle Harlan, and others. Among those choosing the direct route were the California Public Employees Retirement System, the Pennsylvania Public School Retirement System, and the Wisconsin Investment Board.

Commodity Futures

A few funds, including those of Eastman Kodak and the Virginia Retirement Systems, diversified into commodity futures through managed futures programs. In these, a money management firm selected a diversified group of commodity futures specialists and allocated money to them for investment in commodity futures. The Eastman Kodak fund became one of the first funds to invest in this asset class when Russell L. (Rusty) Olson, director, pension investments, began its program in 1987 with Mount Lucas Management. At about the same time the Virginia Retirement System (VRS) also began its program, which eventually grew to an investment of more than $500 million. Ironically, both funds ended their programs as a result of changes at the top. The VRS dropped its program in August 1994 after changes in its nine-person board of trustees. An internal review of the program showed a compound annual return of 6%. However, because of a lack of a suitable benchmark, the fund officials were unable to determine if this was a respectable risk-adjusted return for the program, which was a factor in ending it. Eastman Kodak ended its program in 1995 because of a change in top corporate management, after what Olson felt were nine successful years.

Managed futures programs might have been more widely adopted if inflation had been the problem in the 1990s that it was in the 1970s and early 1980s. But for most of the period during which managed futures programs were run by Kodak, Virginia's inflation rate was declining. Nevertheless, at about the time the Virginia fund dropped its managed futures program, Consolidated Rail Corp. began a $50 million managed futures program, using five commodity trading advisers (CTAs). Echlin Inc., Branford, Connecticut, and the Wayne County Retirement System, Detroit, both made their first commitments to managed futures in mid-1997, while the San Diego County Retirement System, which had made its first commitment several years before, increased its participation.[8]

Other funds experimented on a small scale with market-neutral managers and hedge funds. Market-neutral managers generally attempt to take all or most of the risk out of investing in stocks and still beat the return on short-term fixed income securities by a significant margin. They do so by matching long and short positions in a mix of equities and other asset classes, often globally. At a time when the stock market was producing compound annual returns of more than 15%, the single-digit returns of market-neutral managers were relatively unexciting. As a result, by the end of 1997 they managed only $55 billion of pension and other tax-exempt assets. However, some funds used market-neutral managers to manage their cash reserves because such managers generally produced better returns than short-term fixed income investments. Among the largest market-neutral managers were J.P. Morgan, First Quadrant Corp., and Numeric Investors L.P.[9]

Hedging on Hedge Funds

Although the mid-1990s saw the emergence of a number of high-profile hedge funds, only a few pension funds entered the hedge fund world. Hedge funds, like market-neutral managers, ostensibly offset risks in one part of their portfolios with counterbalancing investments, or hedging programs, elsewhere, while seeking to exploit apparent discrepancies in the prices of similar assets in different markets. Hedge fund managers, however, often borrow money to increase the amount of money they have to invest, and hence increase their profits. The leverage usually more than offsets any hedge. Most hedge fund managers are very secretive about their investment methodologies and their leverage as they seek to exploit what they perceived to be inefficiencies in the market prices in the securities or markets in which they trade. As a result, pension funds, particularly corporate funds constrained by ERISA, have been reluctant to make virtually blind bets. Nevertheless, a few pension funds got burned when Askin Capital Management, a hedge fund that invested in complex securities based on home mortgages and leveraged three or four to one, collapsed in 1994. Virtually all of the $600 million provided by equity investors was wiped out as the markets moved against Askin's positions. Pension funds reportedly had only about $100 million invested in the fund, all of it through pooled funds, so that no one fund suffered a significant loss.[10] Despite the Askin disaster, the $2.6 billion RJR-Nabisco pension fund hired six hedge fund managers in September 1994 and gave each $30 million.[11] All of the managers ran manager-of-manager programs, investing in a portfolio of other hedge funds. RJR's move was typical of the small-scale, conservative investments in hedge funds by pension funds.

Derivative Disasters

The Askin disaster, besides increasing pension fund awareness of hedge funds, also increased their wariness of derivatives, particularly exotic derivatives. Derivatives are defined as securities whose prices are based on the value or price of other securities, such as options and stock and bond futures. Pension funds had been using derivatives since the mid-1970s, though they rarely thought about it. Options were the first derivatives used by pension funds. Then came fixed income futures, stock index futures, Ginnie Maes, private mortgage-backed securities, and eventually swaps and swaptions and other more exotic instruments. At first derivatives were looked upon with favor as hedging devices to help control risk or to enhance portfolio liquidity and facilitate portfolio moves without disturbing the underlying prices. But derivatives often carried hidden flaws. The key one was that derivatives were often far less liquid than the investor expected when he or she wanted to sell or needed to sell.

The first example of this hidden flaw was the failure of portfolio insurance in 1987 when the futures markets proved less liquid in a time of stress than many had expected and prices moved far out of the historic bounds. It was reinforced during the Askin debacle when the spreads widened rather than narrowing. Then came what became known as the Orange County derivatives disaster.[12] The county treasurer, Robert L. Citron, who was managing a multibillion dollar pooled short-term investment fund for the cash reserves of the county and a number of public employee pension funds, used a leveraged derivative strategy to enhance returns, and interest rates moved against him. The fund suffered losses of more than $1.5 billion, and the Orange County Employees Retirement System was among the losers. It had $59 million of its cash reserves with Citron's fund. In addition, it had another $65 million from the sale of pension obligation bonds parked in the fund until it could be invested long-term. By the end of 1994, losses by investment managers, corporations, local governments, and insurance companies on derivatives programs totaled $9.6 billion. Although pension funds suffered only tiny losses, pension executives became even more wary of the use of derivatives.

This was unfortunate for Bankers Trust Co. (BT) because in late 1993 it had decided to lean more heavily on derivatives in most aspects of its business, especially in pension fund management. Early in 1994 the senior executives of BT's successful investment management operation were pushed aside and replaced by Ivan Wheen, an Australian-born currency trader who had built a successful record in both Hong Kong and London. Although Bankers Trust was the second largest manager of tax-exempt assets in the United States, with $130 billion under management at the end of 1993 and $180 billion worldwide, much of that was relatively low-fee low-risk indexed assets. Only $16 billion was actively managed equity assets. The aim of the restructuring was to make Bankers a more significant factor in the higher-fee active equity management arena and to make greater use of derivatives in doing so. The bank also intended to offer derivative-based fixed income products. BT was considered a leader in the use of derivative securities, particularly interest rate swaps, in the corporate finance arena and hoped to leverage off that reputation in the investment management arena.

The Askin and Orange County disasters, as well as the derivatives disasters on the corporate finance front, made the new approach a much tougher sell. It got even tougher early in 1995 when another derivatives disaster involving futures caused the collapse of the historic British investment bank, Barings PLC. Within two years, Bankers Trust had largely abandoned its aggressive efforts to get pension funds to adopt a more derivatives-driven approach and returned its attention to its index fund and enhanced-index fund approaches. Ivan Wheen relinquished his chief investment post and transferred to the Singapore office. Bankers' inattention to the index fund business for those two years allowed State Street Bank and Trust to gain ground on it in indexing. While Bankers Trusts' domestic equity indexed assets doubled in the period, State Street's more than trebled.

Risk Management

Following the Barings collapse, a number of pension funds began to take a fresh look at the risk controls within their funds and within the money management firms they hired. Several large pension funds, among them those of GTE, IBM, and General Motors, established the new staff position of risk control officer. The task of the risk control officer was to examine the risk inherent in the fund's investments in various asset classes and various investment management approaches, as well as the overall risk position of the total fund. Previously, the risk of each investment within a portfolio had been considered in relation to the overall riskiness of that portfolio, as was required by ERISA, but too often, each portfolio was considered in isolation from others. There was too little consideration of how a single event could cause the individual risks in each portfolio to compound on the total fund. The task of the new risk control officers was to identify all the risks the funds were taking and to consider how they might interact to damage the fund and to design protection schemes. "There has been an assumption in our business that the risk controls and procedures present at many of the organizations that we work with are sufficient, and I think now there is some question as to whether they are," GTE's Carroll said after instituting the risk control position. "We are trying to get a better handle on how to look at the risk exposure for our portfolio in total. That goes beyond the obvious derivatives exposure."[13] Other pension fund executives began looking for risk control computer software that would alert them to dangerous situations.

Ironically, the pioneering software in the risk control area was RAROC 2020, developed and marketed by none other than Bankers Trust to help its corporate finance clients. One of the first pension funds to use the software was the $12.5 billion Chrysler Corp. fund in 1995. According to Russell Flynn, pension director at Chrysler, the software helped the fund identify the risks it was taking, breaking it down into such categories as interest rate risk, currency risk, and equity risk, and allowed the fund to quantify the risks in dollar terms. A group of pension executives also banded together with endowment and foundation fund executives to develop risk control guidelines for their own benefit and that of other pension executives. In 1996 the group produced a report with 33 risk standards designed to guide fund executives in their risk control efforts. "The tools designed for risk management have really come out of the dealer world," said Michael deMarco, director of risk management for GTE Investment Management and a member of the working group.[14] He noted that the dealer world usually dealt with the risks of the trading desk, which were of a shorter-term nature than pension fund risks. General Motors' pension fund executives improved their risk control practices by focusing on 10 risks: compliance, corporate financial risk, credit or counterpart risk, fiduciary risk, liquidity risk, market risk, modeling risk, monitoring risk, operational risk, and systems risk. They also improved the flow of information among fund executives. Desmond MacIntyre, director of risk management for General Motors Investment Management Co., which oversees the pension fund, said the biggest day-to-day risk for the fund was probably that portfolio managers might take unintended bets or inadvertently violate guidelines.[15]

Global Balance

The ever innovative GTE pension staff introduced a new approach early in 1995 when it hired four large multiline money management firms, gave each $1 billion (20% of the total fund), and told them they had full discretion to invest it in any marketable securities anywhere in the world. The four were J.P. Morgan & Co., Morgan Stanley Asset Management, Goldman Sachs & Co., and Grantham, Mayo, Van Otterloo. The concept was developed by Britton Harris, John Carroll's second in command at the fund who in 1998, upon Carroll's retirement would replace Carroll as president of GTE Investment Management.

Harris's innovative approach, giving each manager $1 billion to invest without restriction, was called global multi-asset management, or global balanced management. It returned the global asset allocation decision to those best equipped to handle it—the large money management organizations with large research staffs scattered throughout the world. It also reduced the number of managers GTE had to monitor. Three years after the program was instituted, each of the managers was more than 200 basis points ahead of the assigned benchmark. GTE still managed part of its $20 billion in pension assets internally and used more than 20 outside managers as well.

Although the executives at GTE did not know it, the staff at the $1 billion Times Mirror Co. pension fund had developed a smaller version of GTE's global multi-asset approach in 1993 as a way of coping with a shortage of inhouse staff.[16] Mark Schwanbeck, assistant treasurer at Times Mirror, tapped existing managers at J.P. Morgan and Capital Guardian Trust as the fund's multi-asset managers and entrusted 40% of the fund's assets to them. After GTE instituted its program, many more large funds examined the concept, but none admitted to adopting it as extensively or on as large a scale as GTE, possibly because they or their companies were uncomfortable with giving up the control to the managers.

At the same time, many funds were cutting back the number of investment management firms they used to manage their defined benefit pension assets. Many, without adopting the global multi-asset manager concept, nevertheless hired some money management firms for more than one asset class. This development was driven by pressures to reduce costs. In many companies, the size of the staff overseeing the pension fund had been cut back as companies became leaner and more efficient. Pension executives therefore had less manpower to oversee their stables of money managers.

The most obvious solution was to reduce the number of managers to a manageable number. This had an important side benefit in that each remaining manager received a larger slice of the assets to manage, and that lowered the average fee per dollar invested which the fund paid since managers offer ever larger discounts from their starting fee as assets grow. As a result, money management firms that offered a variety of investment styles or products gained market share at the expense of single-product firms. Greenwich Associates reported in 1996 that despite the rapid growth of assets among the 2,165 pension funds it surveyed, the average number of investment managers used had remained stable at 9 between 1993 and 1995.[17] This may have marked the end of the "golden era" for money management firms.

Greenwich reported, however, that large funds had reduced the number of managers they used, while small funds had added managers. The trend continued in 1996, 1997, and 1998. This development led some to believe that large multiproduct money management firms that could offer pension funds one-stop shopping would come to dominate the business, that middle-bracket firms with only one or two products would suffer, and that small boutiques with unique approaches or strong records would survive. This was the thesis of a Goldman, Sachs report on the trends in the industry. Certainly, the money manager merger and acquisition activity indicated that many in the money management industry bought this scenario. By mid-1998, however, there was little indication that the midsized firms were suffering.

There was one other development that suggested the midsized firms could run into difficulties in the future—*total fund outsourcing*. Some small and midsized companies, those whose defined benefit pension funds had assets between $100 million and $1.5 billion and who wanted to keep the defined benefit plan, began asking themselves if the time and resources they spent running a pension fund might not be better spent focused on the company's primary business. A $250 million pension fund generally required one treasury executive to spend at least half of his or her time on it, hiring, monitoring, and firing managers, meeting with possible new managers, and dealing with an actuary, an investment management consultant, and the fund's master trustee or custodian. Some companies decided that they would be better rewarded to turn over complete administration of the pension fund investment program to an outside firm and use those staff resources on the company's main business. A number of firms, the Frank Russell Trust Co., SEI Corp. (which in the mid-1980s had acquired the A. G. Becker performance measurement and consulting services), and State Street Bank and Trust of Boston were among those prepared to accept the fiduciary responsibility of hiring and firing managers.[18]

Often the outsourcing led to a replacement of the managers the fund had been using by the pooled funds of the firm to whom the fund was outsourced. In the case of Russell and SEI, these pools are managed by groups of selected managers. Since the midsized pension fund was the natural territory for midsized money managers, outsourcing often represented a loss of business for such firms. One example of outsourcing was that of General Signal Corp. which in late 1997 handed the management of its $930 million defined benefit and 401(k) assets to Rogers Casey & Associates, the Darien, Connecticut, investment management consulting firm. It then let go its two pension executives as part of a one-third reduction in its administrative staff. Rogers Casey,[19] unlike Russell, SEI, or State Street, was not expected to replace all of the managers. While Rogers Casey was a relatively new entrant in the total outsourcing business, Russell, SEI, and State Street Bank all reported billions under management in total outsourcing arrangements at the end of 1997.

By the end of 1999 most major pension funds backing defined benefit pension plans used almost the full array of investment vehicles in the search for additional returns. Although the academic evidence suggested it was difficult for any money manager to achieve an investment return on its equity portfolio greater than the market as a whole, as well as on the fixed income portfolio, pension executives nevertheless persisted in the belief that they could identify managers who could, over the long term, achieve risk-adjusted returns superior to an index fund. The executives believed they could build teams of such managers which, on the whole, could achieve higher returns for the funds than could be achieved by investing the funds solely in index funds.

Canadian pension consultant Keith Ambachtsheer of K.P.A. Advisory Services conducted an annual study of cost effectiveness to determine how well the funds achieved this goal. His conclusion was that on average, the return achieved by the funds' manager teams, adjusted for operating costs (that is management fees, oversight cost, etc.) and for the level of risk taken was below that which could be achieved with passive portfolios. However, his research also showed that those funds with the best internal management structures, those most focused on a goal and organized toward achieving that goal, had the highest probabilities of achieving a positive risk-adjusted investment return in excess of that achievable by passive portfolios. That is, positive risk-adjusted returns in excess of the funds' benchmarks were not impossible to achieve, just very difficult.

Lifting the Market

Defined contribution plan assets continued to grow, rising to $1 trillion by the beginning of 1996, with 47% of that being in 401(k) plans. As participants in 401(k) and other defined contribution plans continued to increase their allocations to common stocks, usually at the expense of guaranteed investment contracts and money market funds, the flood of contributions helped equity mutual funds boom. By September 1998 the average 401(k) participant among the largest companies had boosted his or her equity position to 64% of assets.[20] This money flow helped lift the stock market, helping to preserve one of the longest bull markets in U.S. history, which some experts dated from the end of 1974, when companies began to step up the funding of their pension funds with the passage of ERISA. Others said that it started after the short, sharp market plunge of October 1987. The rapid rebound after the 1987 plunge convinced many 401(k) investors that the stock market might be volatile, but being out of it was also risky.

By 1997 most major companies had adopted a 401(k) plan, either as a replacement for a defined benefit plan or as a supplement to it or to an existing defined contribution plan. A few, however, were still making the transition. Wal-Mart Stores Inc., for example, started its 401(k) plan only in 1997.[21] Previously, Wal-Mart relied on a generous profit-sharing plan as its sole retirement plan for employees. On the other hand, many large companies were into their second iterations of their 401(k) plans. Eastman Kodak, for example, revised its 401(k) plan in 1996[22] to give the employees more investment options in three tiers. The first tier offered three time-horizon funds—funds with preset asset allocations suitable to investors with different time horizons. The second tier offered six core commingled funds managed by Boston's State Street Global Advisors, including a bond index fund, an S&P 500 Index fund, and Kodak stock. The third tier offered the employees the choice of 27 mutual funds, including domestic, international, and emerging market equity funds. Similarly, E. I. DuPont de Nemours & Co. revamped its 401(k) plan in mid-1997 to provide the employees with three prepackaged asset allocation funds: conservative, moderate, and aggressive.[23] The conservative fund, for example, is 70% stable value, 20% S&P 500 Index fund, and 10% other index funds. The aggressive portfolio is 20% stable value, 40% S&P 500 Index fund, 20% small-cap index fund, and the balance from other index funds. The options were provided by Merrill Lynch Group Employee Services. DuPont already offered employees eight other options.

The flood of 401(k) money caused indigestion at some of the large mutual fund companies. At Fidelity Research & Management, the rapid growth of its flagship Magellan Fund to more than $50 billion, largely from 401(k) assets, was followed by a period of underperformance and turnover in portfolio managers. After averaging 50%-plus a year between 1993 and 1995, Magellan's growth rate dropped to only 4% in 1996. Eventually, Fidelity closed the Magellan Fund to new clients, though it continued to take contributions from existing clients.[24] Pension executives began to wonder if other large mutual funds such as Putnam Management's $18 billion Voyager Fund and its $15.4 billion New Opportunities Fund should not also be closed, noting that performance often declined as the funds grew. Capacity constraints caught up with the Vanguard Group in August 1997, and it was forced to refuse any new full-service 401(k) business for the rest of the year. Vanguard's administrative systems were unable to handle the flood of new business won in the first half of the year. The company continued, however, to accept investment-only business from 401(k) plans.

Some pension executives were becoming wary of not only the size of some of the public mutual funds, but also the fees charged to participants by some of the mutual fund companies for full-service 401(k) plan accounts. They looked for less expensive alternatives, and many turned to the investment managers they used for their other pension plans. At Xerox Corp., for example, Myra Drucker, assistant treasurer, established a unitized structure that allowed 401(k) plan participants to buy "shares" in the investment vehicles being used for the company's defined benefit plan. The options were managed by the investment managers handling the defined benefit plan assets. Other companies, including Novartis Corp. and General Motors Corp., adopted similar approaches. Indeed, in early 1999 General Motors began offering its investment expertise to other 401(k) plans, offering, in effect, private mutual funds run by GM's money managers.

During the 1990s, as noted earlier, large and midsized companies devoted time and money to educating their employees about how to invest their 401(k) plan assets. Virtually all companies provided their employees with booklets outlining the basics of investing: the power of compounding; the long-term return histories of stocks, bonds, and cash; how risk and return are related; how diversification can reduce risk without harming long-term return; how each employee should determine his or her own risk tolerance and build a portfolio appropriate for that risk tolerance; and so on. The companies also generally held group investment education sessions that were taught by employees of the mutual fund providers and company staff. They used videos and computer-based tools to get across the investment education lessons. IBM went even further and subsidized employees who wanted the advice of an outside financial planner. Companies such as Investment Technologies Inc., 401(k) Forum, and Financial Engines sprang up to deliver computer-based programs that helped employees make the correct investment decisions. Although many employees still did not understand the difference between a stock and a bond, many others had learned that key distinction for the first time as a result of these educational efforts and were making better investment decisions. For those who were still uncomfortable after the educational efforts, companies introduced the life-cycle funds—prepackaged mixes of mutual funds suitable for employees with different levels of risk tolerance or at different stages in their working lives.

The flood of assets into 401(k) plans, together with the investment education companies provided to their employees, changed the course of the debate about "fixing" Social Security. Concern about the Social Security program had been building during the 1990s when it became apparent that the system would go into a negative cash-flow situation by about 2013 and would run out of money by 2029 if changes were not made. President Clinton's Advisory Council on Social Security, appointed in 1993 to examine possible solutions, reported in the Spring of 1996 with three proposals, none of which was supported by all commission members. All three called for some part of employee and employer Social Security contributions to be invested in market-related investments with the aim of earning a greater return than paid on the Treasury securities the money currently is invested in. Two of them called for employees to control the investment of that part invested in marketable securities in accounts in their own name. The fact that such proposals were being considered seriously in the Social Security reform debate was a testament to the success of 401(k) plans. The reformers recognized that millions of American workers had become comfortable with and at least somewhat familiar with investing in the stock and bond markets through their participation in 401(k) and other defined contribution plans. The 401(k) plan had thus provided one possible solution for the Social Security crisis. In addition, other countries, led by Chile and Australia, had adopted the 401(k)-type defined contribution plan as the solution to the crises in their own social security systems, and others were considering following suit.

Era of Giants

By the fiftieth anniversary of the NLRB decision, the results of the investment revolution it sparked were impressive. For a start, many of the
nation's pension funds had grown to enormous size. The largest fund was
that of the California Public Employees Retirement System, known generally as CalPERS. On September 30, 1998, it had assets of $133.5 billion, all
but $75 million of which was in a defined benefit plan. The fund execu-
tives managed $84.9 billion internally, $50.3 billion of it in equity assets,
and most of that in an index fund. The giant fund used dozens of outside
money managers. It used, for example, 14 active domestic equity managers,
eight international equity managers, four international fixed income managers, and 22 real estate managers. In addition, it invested in more than 50
limited partnerships investing in venture capital and leveraged buyouts.
Overall, 45.3% of its assets were in U.S. stocks, 16.4% in foreign stocks,
25.2% in domestic fixed income investments, and 4.1% in foreign fixed
income. It had 4.6%, or $6.1 billion, in real estate, and $4.1 billion in
alternative investments such as venture capital and leverage buyouts.[25]
The huge fund used its clout by voting its proxies at shareholder meetings
to try to change the behavior of corporate management when it believed
that behavior was inimical to the long-term interests of the shareholders.

Although CalPERS was more than $30 billion bigger than the next
largest fund, the New York State Common Retirement Fund, the $99.7 bil-
lion fund backing the pensions of most New York State employees, its
investment practices were similar to those of most large, sophisticated pension funds. The differences were largely only in scale and the details. The
largest corporate fund, for example, that of General Motors with $67 bil-
lion in defined benefit assets, also invested across a wide spectrum of
investments not significantly different from CalPERS and New York State
Common, using at least 50 investment management firms.[26] The two key
differences were that GM had an additional $20 billion of assets in a
defined contribution plan (compared with $75 million for CalPERS), and,
though like CalPERS it was a member of the Council of Institutional
Investors, it was not as aggressive or as public in using its proxies to change
corporate behavior.

Even smaller pension funds used, on a smaller scale, an investment
management structure similar to CalPERS or General Motors to manage
their assets. Typically, they hired a number of managers using different
investment styles to manage up to 60% of the fund's assets in stocks,
including non-U.S. stocks. Often, as much as one-third of the equity assets
was invested through an index fund manager. (In the case of CalPERS it

was almost 70%.) Typically, the larger the fund, the greater the percentage invested through index funds. They hired one or two fixed income managers, again using different investment styles, to invest 25% to 30% of the assets in bonds and other fixed income instruments. They invested up to 10% in real estate and smaller percentages in venture capital and leveraged buyout funds.

So large had the pools of pension assets grown in the 50 years from the NLRB decision that the 100th largest fund, that of the Kansas Public Employees Retirement System, had assets of $8.3 billion,[27] while the 200th largest fund had assets of just more than $4 billion.[28] Even the 1,000th largest fund had combined assets of more than half a billion dollars, and the 1,000 largest funds had assets totaling $4.4 trillion.[29] The 200 largest funds alone had more than $80 billion invested in real estate in the form of office buildings, hotels, shopping malls, warehouses, and so on. They had $253 billion invested in the stocks of non-U.S. companies, including $27 billion in companies in emerging markets. They admitted to having more than $54 billion invested in venture capital, leveraged buyouts, and other private equity investments. The correct figure was probably double that, all of which helped the development of a more advanced and efficient economy.[30]

The institutions managing the nation's pension assets for the likes of CalPERS and General Motors also had grown to enormous size. At the end of 1998 the largest was State Street Global Advisors, the investment management arm of State Street Bank and Trust, which had $334.4 billion under management, virtually all of it for pension funds. The second largest was Barclays Global Investors, which was the former Wells Fargo Investment Advisors renamed by the British bank that bought it, which had $330 billion. The top five was rounded out by Fidelity Investments, the mutual fund giant, with $250 billion, Bankers Trust Co., $218 billion, and TIAA-CREF, the institution established by Andrew Carnegie to back pensions for teachers in institutions of higher education, which had assets of $213 billion. The 100th largest money manager, Panagora Asset Management, had $11.8 billion under management, while the 200th largest had $4.1 billion under management.[31] Managing the nation's pension assets had become a significant, highly profitable industry, generating revenues of at least $30 billion.

Pension funds and their managers had pioneered new, more sophisticated ways of investing, and most of the methods, techniques, and products they pioneered have been offered to individual investors by banks, insurance companies, and mutual funds. Through their pioneering activities in all aspects of the capital markets, these institutions changed investing for all investors.

The capital markets were dominated by these huge institutions and the assets they controlled. The pension fund flows, whether from defined benefit plans or defined contribution plans, supported the stock and bond markets. Defined benefit plan assets also supported the real estate, options, futures, private equity (venture capital, LBO, etc.), and debt markets. Indeed, the growth of the assets had lifted the stock market to record heights, helped drive interest rates down, boosted real estate development of every type, sometimes to extreme levels, and stimulated the growth of the derivatives markets to unforeseen levels. Companies attempting to raise capital could not succeed if these institutions were not willing to buy the stock or bond issue. The investment of the nation's pension assets made the capital markets more efficient and helped make the U.S. economy more efficient, flexible, and resilient. Even government's attempts to borrow by issuing bonds were at the mercy of the institutional investors. The institutions set the prices and the terms. The pension fund assets also boosted venture capital investing and hence the start of thousands of small companies, which, particularly in the high-tech area, put the United States ahead of the rest of the world. Abundant capital is the fuel of economic growth; venture capital is the highest octane fuel.

Chapter 15

Trouble Ahead

By the fiftieth anniversary of the NLRB decision, the money flood had changed course, and the revolution it powered had been pushed in new directions that held serious implications for the economy and the nation's workers and retirees. Politicians such as Senator Howard Metzenbaum and Representative Edward Roybal, in their attempts to stem the money flood, had damaged the long-term economic well-being of the nation. Although they didn't realize it, through their efforts to limit the leakage from the federal budget by cutting benefits for top executives, and their efforts to prevent companies from recapturing surplus pension assets, they had directed the financial revolution into less productive directions that might ultimately reduce the competitiveness of the U.S. economy. In addition, although again they didn't realize it, they had also made the pensions of millions of employees less secure.

The Flood Tide Turns

By 2000 it was clear that the highwater mark of the money flood in the United States was in sight. The crest of the wave created by the growth of assets backing defined benefit plans had long passed. At the end of 1998, the nation's pension plans had total assets of $8.7 trillion, of which $4.3 trillion was in corporate pension funds—defined benefit and defined contribution—and $2.4 trillion was in public employee pension plans. An additional $2 trillion was in annuity contracts at insurance companies. This looked exceedingly healthy. By the end of 1998, however, the number of corporate defined benefit funds had declined to 46,000 from 116,000 in 1985.[1] Their assets continued to rise, climbing to $2.1 trillion, lifted by the bull market in both stocks and bonds, and by continuing contributions from the still underfunded public employee pension plans. Except for the continuing bull market, and the continued flow of contributions into public employee defined benefit plans, defined benefit assets would have begun to decline.

The companies sponsoring the 100 largest corporate pension funds poured $4 billion into defined benefit funds between September 30, 1997 and September 30, 1998. But those funds paid out eight times as much, $33.5 billion, in benefit payments in the same period.[2] In part, the discrepancy between contributions and benefit payments arose because many corporate funds are so overfunded that the companies did not need to make annual contributions, and in many cases they were prohibited by tax law from doing so. Still, in the absence of drastic changes in pension legislation to encourage the rebirth of defined benefit plans, it is clear that their days are numbered—at least for corporate plans. Even among the largest companies, the growth of defined benefit assets has slowed and in some cases has gone into reverse.

Too Expensive

The government, through legislation and regulation, had made defined benefit plans too expensive, too inflexible, and of little use to senior management. Perhaps the first government official to recognize, or at least the first to acknowledge the fact, was David Strauss, executive director of the Pension Benefit Guaranty Corp. Strauss had a vested interest in defined benefit plans. As their numbers declined, so too did the insurance premiums his agency relied upon to pay pensions to employees whose pension plans were terminated with insufficient assets to meet those benefit liabilities. When companies abandon defined benefit plans, they are free of any obligation to the PBGC if their plans have sufficient assets to pay their liabilities. Then they cease paying the huge PBGC insurance premiums—at least $19 per employee per year, and up to $70 per employee per year for some underfunded plans. The PBGC depends on the premiums from healthy plans to help it make pension payments to retirees from underfunded plans that have been terminated. As more and more defined benefit plans are abandoned, that stream of premium payments becomes thinner and thinner.

The abandonment of defined benefit plans therefore threatened the future of Strauss's agency. Therefore, late in 1998 and again early in 1999 he proposed easing some of the restrictions that had caused companies to abandon defined benefit plans. Strauss proposed simpler forms of defined benefit plans which would be cheaper to administer. He also proposed reducing the PBGC insurance premium for smaller pension plans. Others proposed raising the maximum annual salary on which employers could base pensions to as much as $1 million from the 1998 limit of $160,000, hoping to encourage more employers to continue, revive, or start defined benefit plans. It had been reduced to $150,000 by the first Clinton budget in 1993, after being set at $235,000 by Congress in 1987. The maximum annual pension that could be paid from a tax-qualified defined benefit plan was only $130,000 a year, and that was up from $120,000 in 1996, a pittance for senior executives. These cutbacks had virtually eliminated top and upper-middle-management interest in defined benefit plans, since they had nothing to gain from them. Few experts believed a new $1 million limit would be passed, though there was a chance the limit would be raised above $160,000. But even if passed, a $1 million limit might not be enough to revive defined benefit plans. Employers have found 401(k) plans simpler, cheaper, and more appreciated by employees than defined benefit plans, and top executives have provided for their own rich pensions through nonqualified plans not affected by ERISA or IRS tax rules, so why bother with defined benefit plans?

The defined benefit tributary of the money flood thus appears to have almost run its course. The money flow will not dry up completely because some companies will cling to such plans as long as solid stock and bond market returns pay most of the bill, and union and public sector employees continue to demand defined benefit plans. Many public employee-defined benefit plans are still growing. Many are still underfunded, and so they still receive billions of dollars of employer contributions each year. According to *Pensions & Investments*,[3] the 78 state and local governments with the largest defined benefit plans for public employees poured $32 billion into their funds from September 30, 1997 to September 30, 1998. But they paid out $56 billion in benefits to retirees. The strong stock and bond markets kept the assets growing.

In addition, by 1998 some companies were replacing their defined benefit plans not with 401(k) plans, but rather with a hybrid, the *cash balance plan*. In a cash balance plan, the employer establishes a hypothetical account in each employee's name and credits each account each year with a percentage of pay, say 3%. Each account then is credited with "interest" each year, perhaps 5%. The employee receives, on retirement, the amount in the account. In the meantime, the employer retains control of the investment of the assets and pockets any difference between the interest credited to each account and the rate of return actually earned on the underlying assets. If cash balance plans grew significantly, it would slow the leakage of assets from such investments as venture capital and leveraged buyouts because employers, seeking to maximize their investment return, would continue to use those vehicles. However, cash balance plans became controversial late in 1997 when older employees at Onan Corp., a unit of Cummins Engine Co., sued the company, claiming the cash balance plan it introduced discriminated against older employees. Younger employees would likely have better retirement benefits under the new plan; older employees would have far lower benefits than if the old plan had remained in force. Their future was thrown into even more doubt in 1999 when IBM employees protested against the company's plan to install such a plan which disadvantaged long-term employees in their forties. The future of cash balance plans likely will be affected by the outcome of any congressional interest in the issue. But cash balance plans will only slow the erosion of defined benefit plans. Virtually no cash balance plans are being started from the ground up. They generally are conversions of existing defined benefit plans. The 401(k) plan, in which the employees contribute most of the money and the employer does not contribute unless the employee does so, is still by far the least expensive kind of pension plan for an employer to offer.

The Other Stream

While employer contributions to defined benefit plans were drying up, the pension flood as a whole, though diminished, still had power at the end of 1998 because defined contribution plan assets were still growing strongly. At the end of 1998 they were $2.2 trillion and continuing to grow at about 6% per year from employee and employer contributions alone. Although the rate of new 401(k) plan formation had slowed, new plans were still being started by small and midsized companies, and by mid-1998 there were an estimated 200,000 401(k) plans. The constant flow of contributions, month after month, from employees into their defined contribution plans, and from there into mutual funds of various types, especially equity funds, was clearly a factor contributing to the continuation of the bull market of the 1990s, which from the end of 1994 through 1998 produced four consecutive years of 20+% returns.

Individuals in 401(k) and other defined contribution plans have been taught that, in the long run, the stock market gives higher investment returns than the bond market, and so they have put more and more of their assets into stocks. Not everyone thinks this is good for the market or the economy in the long run, especially as, despite the investment education efforts, individuals can hardly be considered expert investors. "In the past five years, the public has taken the place of the investment professionals and other sophisticated investors as the most powerful stock market factor," wrote market commentator Steve Leuthold in his monthly research publication *Perception for the Professional* in July 1999. "The stock market keeps going up because, in the aggregate, the now dominant public knows little (or nothing) about investing. What represents a value? What doesn't? P/e ratios, cash flow, balance sheets are typically some foreign language".[4] Given that new 401(k) plans are still being formed at small and startup companies, given that entrepreneurial companies are still hiring employees (the unemployment rate dropped throughout 1998 to a little over 4%), and given that the percentage of employees participating in defined contribution plans is still rising and the average contribution is increasing, the money flood from 401(k) plans is expected to continue to lift the market for several more years.

Even for defined contribution plans, however, the highwater mark can be foreseen. It is likely to occur soon after 2010 when the first of the baby boom generation reaches normal retirement age. The great surge of the flood will then recede to become a steadily flowing river. And the receding of the flood will have significant implications for the U.S. and other economies, both in the short term and in the longer term. In the immediate future, the drying up of defined benefit asset flows and their replacement with defined contribution flows is likely to mean less money for investment in venture capital, less money for investment in leveraged buyout and other private equity investment pools, less money for real estate investing, less money for junk bond investments, and less money for international investing. This is because most companies offering defined contribution plans to their employees give their employees a choice of investments in the form of mutual funds. Most commonly, they offer the employees a choice of equity, bond, balanced (a mix of stock and bond), and money market funds, and a stable-value fund. Very few offer the employees an international fund. Virtually none offers a real estate fund or a venture capital or junk bond fund. And none has reported offering an LBO fund. Although international mutual funds and real estate investment trusts (REITs) can be used in 401(k) plans, there are no suitable pooled vehicles through which the small investor might invest in venture capital or leveraged buyouts.

Even if such vehicles are developed, most employers are unlikely to offer more complex and risky investment choices because most employees, even after investment education efforts by their employers, still have only a rudimentary understanding of investing and remain relatively unsophisticated in their investment strategies. As a result, the flow of money into venture capital and other forms of private investing, and even into real estate equity investments, is likely to decline as the number of defined benefit plans continues to fall. That means less money will be available for startup companies that need additional capital to grow, or for leveraged buyouts of companies that need to be restructured. A decline in the amount of money available for such investments means increased competition for what money is available. That suggests the investments must ultimately deliver higher long-term risk-adjusted returns than they currently deliver. What money is available for venture capital will thus be more expensive, and fewer companies will be able to find financing. Fewer potential startups will get off the ground.

401(k) Implications

Most 401(k) money now is flowing, and likely will continue to flow, into market-traded stocks. At the end of 1998 about 60% of 401(k) assets was invested in common stock. In addition, when offered the opportunity, employees in 401(k) plans invest up to 30% of their 401(k) assets in the stock of the companies that employ them. These assets are locked within those companies, whether or not they are the most efficient users of that capital. Often the employees invest in the stock of the companies that employ them because of a sense of loyalty to the employer, or because they know and feel comfortable with the company and its industry, or because it has been successful in the past. At other times it is because the employer's matching contribution to the 401(k) plan is made in company stock, and often restrictions are imposed on employees as to when and how they can dispose of that stock. The money will not flow through the capital markets to help set the price of capital. The situation will be analogous to that of Japan and Germany, where pension money is often trapped in companies that use capital inefficiently. However, the scale of the problem will be smaller because much of the money committed to equities in the plans of companies with a company stock contribution still flows into diversified, externally managed portfolios. Nevertheless, this "trapped" capital, along with the reduced cash flow into venture capital and leveraged buyouts, will increase the cost of capital and reduce the number of startup companies getting off the ground, or reduce the number of companies made more efficient through restructuring. Ultimately you have an economy in danger of arteriosclerosis.

This change in the source of the money flowing into pensions also has significant implications for the money management industry. By the end of 1998, the competition for the business of defined benefit pension funds was virtually a zero sum game. The pie was growing only slowly—by the market returns plus net contributions from public employee plans, minus the benefit payments from corporate plans. A money manager now, in general, can win significant new business only by taking it from another money manager. The best way to be assured of being able to win new business from others is to have a menu of investment products. The more investment styles or vehicles a money management firm has, the more likely that at least one of those products will have above-average performance and therefore be able to attract new business, even as other products are losing business. The pressure to round out the product line, and the difficulty of growing by gaining new business, continues to drive mergers and acquisitions of money management organizations.

Growing assets and product line offerings by acquisition or merger is the quickest way to achieve the size many believe will be critical to survival, let alone future success. In particular, money management firms with mutual fund arms have been highly sought after because of the demand for mutual funds by 401(k) plans. By the beginning of 2000, however, most significant mutual fund companies were either large enough to remain independent—for example, Fidelity, Vanguard, or T. Rowe Price—or had been acquired by a money management firm or insurance company. The 401(k) market was dominated by about a dozen major mutual fund companies, with little evidence others would be able to break into the charmed group.

Even success in the 401(k) market will not ensure the long-term growth of money management firms, particularly firms offering actively managed equity portfolios and mutual funds, because, as already noted, beginning soon after 2010, as the baby boom generation begins to retire, the 401(k) flow will also begin to decline. At first the baby boomers may merely switch an increasing amount from stock funds to bond funds and then live off the interest. Eventually, however, they will most likely have to eat into their accumulated balances. So at first the withdrawals should have a negligible effect on the capital markets and money management firms. As more and more baby boomers retire the effect will become more pronounced. Unless there is some new source of demand for stocks, bonds, and real estate investment trusts, the prices of these investments must be negatively affected. That is, stock prices must fall, or at least not rise as fast as in the past four decades, as demand for investments declines. Some experts believe the baby boomer withdrawals will be offset by the money the boomers are likely to inherit from their parents, much of which is currently tied up in housing but which would presumably be liquidated and moved into the stock and bond markets. Others, however, believe that the medical expenses the parents are likely to incur in the last years of their lives, even allowing for Medicare, will reduce the value of their estates to almost negligible levels for most.

Stocks likely will be the first affected as many retirees will move some or all of their 401(k) balances into fixed income investments or annuities when they retire to ensure a stable monthly income. Ultimately, however, all asset classes used by 401(k) plan investors must be affected. This will negatively affect the health and growth rate of the U.S. economy by making investment in plant and equipment more expensive and ultimately less rewarding. If companies find the cost of capital increasing, many will decide they can't earn a reasonable return on investment from new plant and equipment and therefore will cut back their investments in such improvements. The demand for capital goods will decline, unemployment may rise, and the growth, efficiency, and competitiveness of the U.S. economy will suffer. In addition, the declining flow of new business must affect the profitability of money management firms and lead to a shake-out. More firms will merge, others will shut their doors, and many will continue to plod along managing modest amounts of money, neither growing nor withering.

The switch to 401(k) plans has been be a mixed blessing for employees. Those whose defined benefit plans were replaced with 401(k) plans generally lost in the change. Whereas before they had a set pension benefit paid for entirely by the employer and guaranteed not only by the assets of the fund and the financial health of the employer, but also by the Pension Benefit Guaranty Corp., now they have an uncertain pension benefit for which they pay most of the cost. In addition, the size of their retirement income depends on how much they contribute each year and on their investment success with their 401(k) assets. Furthermore, there is no Pension Benefit Guaranty Corp. to help out if poor investment results leave them with an inadequate pension. Finally, employees often spend all or part of the assets in their 401(k) account when they change jobs, thus devouring part of their future retirement income. On the other hand, many employees who had no pension benefits when there were only defined benefit plans, now have some pension coverage through a 401(k) plan. Many employers who would not start a defined benefit plan because of its cost and complexity started 401(k) plans which are simpler and less expensive. In addition, the employees can take their 401(k) assets with them when they change jobs, whereas in a defined benefit plan they usually had to leave them behind, sometimes to be collected years later when they ultimately retired.

Foreign Competition

At the same time as the United States begins to feel the negative effect of this switch to 401(k) plans, other countries may be benefiting from a surge of retirement savings. Many countries are now revamping funded pension systems or are on the verge of building new ones where none existed. The United Kingdom is slowly adding defined contribution plans to its defined benefit structure. Japan is beginning to show some interest in defined contribution plans. Such plans might channel increasing amounts of Japan's high level of personal savings out of the low-interest Post Office Savings Scheme into the capital markets where it can help the economy more effectively. Defined contribution plans in Japan are unlikely to follow the U.S. model of high levels of employee choice. More of the investment responsibility is likely to remain in the hands of the employer. In addition, Japan has freed its corporate defined benefit plans from the investment regulations that kept the assets locked in low-return investments in captive trust banks and insurance companies that usually recycled them back to the parent or its subsidiaries, no matter how inefficient. By some measures, these policies were destroying capital. Now the funds have the freedom to invest as their U.S. counterparts do, even to using U.S.- and British-based money management firms. Only a few, however, have so far taken advantage of that freedom. If the developments in defined contribution and defined benefit plans in Japan continue to evolve as they seem to be doing, these plans will improve the efficiency of capital allocation in the Japanese market, with positive effects for the economy.

Germany and France, which have virtually no funded pension systems, appear to be on the verge of encouraging the development of defined contribution plans to supplement their overburdened and unfunded state plans. Similarly, Italy is developing a defined contribution pension system to supplement the virtually bankrupt government system. At present, the employers or unions sponsoring the new plans in Germany, France, and Italy will likely retain the investment control. The sponsor most likely will set the asset mix and hire the investment managers. If any investment choice is offered, it will be in the form of pre-mixed life-cycle or asset allocation funds. Therefore, the assets are likely to be invested more like U.S. defined benefit assets than U.S. defined contribution assets, and small amounts of the assets may be invested in venture capital, LBOs, and so on.

If, as seems likely, these plans take root, they will boost the capital markets in those countries, reducing the costs of investment just as investment becomes more costly in the United States. The burgeoning capital markets in these countries should not only boost investment and therefore growth, but should allocate capital more efficiently and make their economies more competitive with the U.S. economy, just as the improvement in U.S. economic efficiency begins to slow.

Solutions

What could offset the trend in the United States? First, the federal government could accept David Strauss's proposals to make defined benefit pension plans more attractive once again. A revival of defined benefit plans would be the best way to ensure the continuation of the money flood and the full benefits of the financial revolution it produced. However, even these proposals might not be enough, given the weakened state of defined benefit plans. The government might have to offer additional incentives, perhaps even tax credits, to spark a revival of such plans. When a patient is very weak, a blood transfusion is often needed to spur recovery. Tax credits might serve as a blood transfusion for defined benefit plans. Or the government could simply mandate a basic defined benefit plan as part of any pension mix for companies over a certain size. This seems unlikely because it might simply cause many companies to terminate all pension plans.

A second possible solution would be for the government to invest part of the Social Security surplus in the stock market, as President Clinton proposed in his 1999 State of the Union message. This would channel billions of additional dollars each year into the stock market. However, Mr. Clinton proposed having an independent board oversee the investment, probably through index funds. There is the danger, of course, that the investment of the assets would be politicized, with interest groups lobbying against investment in companies with nonunion workforces, or tobacco stocks, or arms makers, and so on. In addition, it would not allocate any of the assets to venture capital and thus would not replace the venture capital flow lost from defined benefit plans. Others have proposed letting each taxpayer invest part of his or her Social Security contribution, perhaps 2%, in stocks or bonds or other assets through mutual funds, much as they invest their 401(k) plan assets. This would eliminate the possible politicization of the investments. However, the individuals probably would invest in much the same way they invest their 401(k) assets and would thus do little to continue the asset flow to venture capital investing which has contributed so much to the U.S. economy.

Another approach would be to allow employees to set aside more for retirement in their 401(k) and other plans. At the beginning of 1999, the maximum employee tax-exempt contribution to a 401(k) plan was $10,000 per year. The maximum amount that can be contributed to a profit-sharing plan is $15,000. Given the projected federal budget surpluses, both of these arbitrary limits could be raised substantially, perhaps even doubled. This would allow all employees, particularly the post-baby boom generation, to save more for their own retirements. If they did defer more into these defined contribution plans, the flow of assets into the markets could help offset the withdrawals by the retiring baby boomers, keeping the cost of capital down and maintaining the U.S. advantage in competitiveness. In addition, more individuals could be allowed to establish individual retirement accounts (IRAs), and the limit on contributions to IRAs, now $2,500 per year, could be at least doubled. Besides helping to support the U.S. economy, such moves would allow the younger generations to save more for their own retirements. This in turn would make it more politically acceptable to scale back the level of Social Security benefits for upper income workers, preserving the system for many years into the future. However, this approach too, would do little to spur flows into venture capital except through the trickle down of capital as investors move from investments they regard as overvalued to those they regard as undervalued.

The best solution would be a revival of defined benefit plans, but this is unlikely. Therefore the second best solution is to encourage greater flows of assets into the stock market to keep the cost of capital low overall. Then assets will trickle down into venture capital, and so on, as investors more willing to take risk seek the higher returns options offer. Unless steps such as these are taken, the end of the economic revolution and boom generated by the money flood is in sight. And when it ends, the era of superior U.S. economic performance will end with it. The U.S. economy will become weaker, less dynamic, less flexible, and less competitive. The money flood from 1950 to 1998 lifted all boats. If it is allowed to recede, if no effort is made to develop new sources of liquidity for the capital markets, those boats will be deposited gently in the mud of mediocrity, perhaps never to rise again.

Appendix

Growth of U.S. Pension Fund Assets, Indexed Pension Equity Assets, and Pension Fund Equities

Growth of U.S. Pension Fund Assets
(Excludes Federal Employees Retirement System)

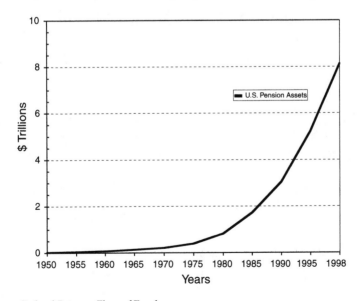

Source: Federal Reserve Flow of Funds
Employee Benefits Research Institute

Growth of Indexed Pension Equity Assets

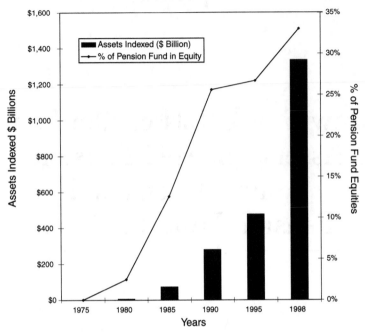

Source: Pensions Investments
Federal Reserve Flow of Fund Reports
* Not Material

Growth of Pension Fund Equities

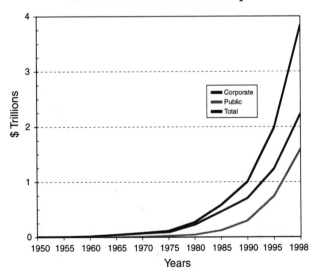

Source: Federal Reserve Flow of Funds

Notes

Chapter 1   Revolution

1. *Flow of Funds Accounts 1949–1978*, Board of Governors of the Federal Reserve System, p. 123.
2. *Flow of Funds Accounts of the United States*, Fourth Quarter 1998, Board of Governors of the Federal Reserve System, pp. 1 10–111.
3. Ibid.
4. Charles D. Ellis, *Winning the Losers' Game*, Third Edition (New York: McGraw-Hill, 1983), p. xviii.
5. *Flow of Funds Accounts 1949–1978*, Board of Governors of the Federal Reserve System, p. 123.
6. *Pensions & Investments*, January 25, 1999, p. 68.
7. *Flow of Funds Accounts 1949–1978*, Board of Governors of the Federal Reserve System, p. 123.
8. Ibid., p. 123.
9. Ibid., p. 124.
10. Ibid., p. 125.
11. *Pensions & Investments*, January 25, 1999, p. 25.
12. *Business Week*, April 5, 1999, p. 96.
13. *Pensions & Investments*, January 25, 1999, p. 25.
14. Ibid.
15. Ibid.
16. Interview with J. Twardowski, February 1998.

Chapter 2   The Way Things Were

1. Stephen A. Sass, *The Promise of Private Pensions*, (Cambridge, Mass.: Harvard University Press, 1997).
2. Ibid.

3. *Flow of Funds Accounts 1949–1978*, Board of Governors of the Federal Reserve System, p. 123.
4. Ibid.
5. Ibid.
6. Ibid.
7. Ibid.
8. Ibid.
9. Ibid.
10. Ibid.

Chapter 3   The Flood Begins

1. Interviews with Graham O. Harrison and Gary Glynn, the U.S. Steel & Carnegie Pension Fund, May 1998.
2. Ibbotson Associates, *Stocks, Bonds, Bills and Inflation*, 1999 Yearbook (Chicago: 1999).
3. Interview with Maury Maertens, Ford Motor Co., and New York University, June 1998.
4. Money Market Directories Inc., *The Money Market Directory* (Charlottesville, Va.: 1971).
5. Interviews with Gordon W. Binns Jr., and W. Allen Reed, General Motors Investment Management Co., June 1998.
6. Money Market Directories Inc., *The Money Market Directory* (Charlottesville, Va.: 1971).
7. Interview with W. Gordon Binns, June 1998.
8. Steven A. Sass, *The Promise of Private Pensions* (Cambridge, Mass., Harvard University Press, 1997).
9. Bell System Archives.
10. Ibid.
11. Ibid.
12. Money Market Directories Inc., *The Money Market Directory* (Charlottesville, Va.: 1971).
13. *Flow of Funds Accounts 1949–1978*, Board of Governors of the Federal Reserve System, p. 123.
14. Ibid.
15. Ibid.
16. Ibid.
17. Ibid.
18. William D. Ellis, and Nancy A. Schneider, *The Story Thus Far ... STRS at 75*, The Ohio State Teachers Retirement System, Columbus, Ohio, 1995. pp. 86–87.
19. *Pensions & Investments*, June 6, 1977, p. 22.

Chapter 4   The Rules Change

1. Peter L., Bernstein, *Capital Ideas* (The Free Press, New York, 1992).
2. Ibbotson Associates, *Stocks, Bonds, Bills and Inflation*, 1999 Yearbook (Chicago: 1999).
3. The National Foundation of Health, Welfare and Pension Plans, *Measuring and Reporting Investment Performance of Pension Funds*, 1966, p. 4.
4. Peter O. Dietz, *Measuring Investment Performance* (The Free Press, New York, 1966).

Chapter 5   New Players Enter

1. Natalie Grow, *The Putnam History*, Vol. 1, pp. 406–407.
2. Charles D. Ellis, *Winning the Losers' Game* (New York: McGraw-Hill, 1983).
3. *Pensions & Investments*, December 10, 1973, p. 19.
4. Ibid., February 11, 1974, p. 2.
5. *Pensions & Investments*, November 12, 1973, p. 21.
6. Harvard University Business School case study.

Chapter 6   Accelerated Change

1. *Money Market Directory*, 1971 and 1974 editions.
2. Ibid.
3. Ibid.
4. Ibid.
5. *Pensions & Investments*, January 1, 1974, p. 22.
6. Ibbotson Associates, *Stocks, Bonds, Bills and Inflation*, 1999 Yearbook (Chicago: 1999).
7. Ibid.
8. *Pensions & Investments*, October 29, 1973, p. 1.
9. Ibid., January 14, 1974, p. 1.
10. Ibid., September 9, 1974, p. 12.
11. Ibid., November 12, p. 3.
12. Ibid., December 10, 1973, p. 19.
13. Ibid., March 25, 1974, p. 4.
14. Ibid., p. 20.
15. Ibid., February 16, 1976, p. 19.
16. Ibid., March 1, 1976, p. 22.
17. Ibid., January 3, 1977, p. 10.
18. Ibid., March 11, 1974, p. 1.
19. Ibid.
20. *Flow of Funds Accounts 1949–1978*, Board of Governors of the Federal Reserve System.
21. Ibid.
22. *Pensions & Investments*, January 6, 1995, p. 1.
23. Ibid., March 3, 1975, p. 1.
24. Ibid., January 6, 1974, p. 24.

Chapter 7   Realty Revolution

1. *Flow of Funds Accounts, 1949–1978*, Board of Governors of the Federal Reserve System, p. 125.
2. Ibbotson Associates, *Stocks, Bonds, Bills and Inflation*, 1999 Yearbook (Chicago: 1999).
3. *Pensions & Investments*, July 15, 1974, p. 20.
4. Ibid., October 29, 1973, p. 2.
5. Ibid., July 29, 1974, pp. 1, 15, 34.
6. Ibid.
7. Ibid.
8. Ibid.
9. Ibid.

10. Ibid., August. 4, 1975, p. 3.
11. Ibid., July 29, 1974, p. 16.
12. Ibid.
13. Ibid., March 17, 1975, p. 35.
14. Ibid., April 14, 1975, p. 34.
15. Ibid., May 12, 1975, p. 6.
16. Ibid., p. 14.
17. Interview with G. Russell.
18. *Pensions & Investments*, September 23, 1974, p. 4.
19. Ibid., July 21, 1975, p. 1.
20. Ibid., December 8. 1975, p. 19.
21. Ibid., March 15, 1976, p. 1.
22. Bruno H. Solnik, "Why Not Diversify Internationally Rather Than Domestically," *Financial Analysts Journal*, July–August 1974, pp. 48–54.
23. *Pensions & Investments*, October 13, 1975, p. 1.
24. Ibid., February 6, 1976, p. 4.
25. Ibid., March 1, 1976, p. 4.
26. Ibid., November 28, 1976, p. 1.
27. Ibid., November 21, 1977, p. 11.
28. Ibid., April 4, 1978, p. 3.
29. Ibid., March 15, 1976, p. 22.
30. Ibid., August 4, 1975, p. 14.
31. Ibid., August 18, 1975, p. 18.
32. Ibid., September 15, 1975, p. 2.
33. Michael L., Costa, *Master Trust–Simplifying Employee Benefits Trust Administration*, © AMACOM, 1980.
34. *Pensions & Investments*, February 28, 1977, p. 2.
35. Ibid., August 15, 1977, p. 29.
36. Ibid., January 2, 1978, p. 1.
37. Ibbotson Associates, *Stocks, Bonds, Bills and Inflation*, 1999 Yearbook (Chicago: 1999).
38. *Flow of Funds Accounts*, Second Quarter 1992 Annual Revisions, Board of Governors of the Federal Reserve System, p. 95.
39. *Pensions & Investments*, April 14, 1975, p. 3.

Chapter 8   Profit Sharing

1. *Pensions & Investments*, April 24, 1977, p. 3.
2. Ibid., April 24, 1977, p. 2.
3. Ibid., May 23, 1977, p. 1.
4. Ibid, June 7, 1976, p. 1.
5. Ibid., July 5, 1976, p. 5.
6. Ibid., January 3, 1977, p. 9.
7. Ibbotson Associates, *Stocks, Bonds, Bills and Inflation*, 1999 Yearbook (Chicago: 1999).
8. Ibid.
9. *Pensions & Investments*, October 23, 1978, p. 1.
10. Ibid., November 26, 1973, p. 1.
11. Ibid., September 27, 1976, p. 8.
12. Ibid., January 28, 1974, p. 28.

13. Ibid., October 25, 1976, p. 23.
14. Ibid., December 6, 1976, p. 10.
15. Ibid., April 11, 1977, p. 23.
16. Ibid., May 8, 1978, p. 23.
17. Ibid., April 10, 1978, p. 11.
18. J. Rifkin and R. Barber, *The North Will Rise Again: Pensions, Politics and Power in the 1980s* (Beacon Press, Boston, 1978).
19. Ibid., January 6, 1975, p. 1.
20. Ibid., September 27, 1976, p. 3.
21. Ibid., November 8, 1976, p. 1.
22. Ibid., July 4, 1977, p. 1.
23. Ibid., April 11, 1977, p. 1.
24. Ibid., January 29, 1979, p. 3.
25. Ibid., September 13, 1976, p. 1.
26. Ibid., September 12, 1977, p. 3.
27. Ibbotson Associates, *Stocks, Bonds, Bills and Inflation*, 1999 Yearbook (Chicago: 1999).
28. *Pensions & Investments*, November 20, 1978, p. 16.
29. Ibid., August 27, 1979, p. 1.

Chapter 9   Inflationary Doldrums

1. *Pensions & Investments*, June 23, 1980, p. 12.
2. *Flow of Funds Accounts*, Second Quarter 1992, Board of Governors of the Federal Reserve System, p. 95.
3. Ibbotson Associates, *Stocks, Bonds, Bills and Inflation*, 1999 Yearbook (Chicago: 1999).
4. *Flow of Funds Accounts*, Second Quarter 1992, Board of Governors of the Federal Reserve System, p. 95.
5. Ibbotson Associates, *Stocks Bonds Bills and Inflation*, 1999 Yearbook (Chicago: 1999).
6. *Pensions & Investments*, January 21, 1980, p. 18.
7. Ibid., January 21, 1980, p. 19.
8. Ibid., p. 12.
9. Ibid., July 7, 1980, p. 2.
10. Ibid.
11. Ibid., December 22, 1980, p. 1.
12. Ibid., March 2, 1980, p. 6.
13. Ibid., August 18, 1980, p. 1.
14. Ibid., August 3, 1981, p. 3.
15. Ibid., September 19, 1983, p. 30.
16. Ibid., December 6, 1982, p. 1.
17. Ibid., March 29, 1982, p. 1.
18. Ibid., May 20, 1991, p. 3.
19. Ibid., January 24, 1983, p. 8.
20. Ibid., December 26, 1983, p. 1.
21. Ibid., May 17, 1993, p. 20.
22. Ibid., January 7, 1980, p. 1.
23. Ibid., March 31, 1980, p. 5.
24. Ibid., May 12, 1980, p. 14.
25. Ibid., May 26, 1980, p. 1.

26. Ibid., March 2, 1981, p. 1.
27. Ibid., September 19, 1981, p. 1.
28. Ibid., November 8, 1982, p. 3.
29. Ibid., December 31, 1983, p. 3.
30. Ibid., March 31, 1980, p. 5.
31. Ibid., July 4, 1980, p. 13.
32. Ibid., September 29, 1980, p. 2.
33. Ibid., December 27, 1980, p. 4.
34. Ibid., September 29, 1980, p. 1.
35. Ibid., July 4, 1980, p. 13.
36. Ibid., February 16, 1981, p. 15.
37. Ibid., March 2, 1981, p. 1.
38. Ibid., October 26, 1981, p. 1.
39. Ibid., p. 31.
40. Ibid., March 29, 1982, p. 1.
41. Ibid., August 2, 1981, p. 2.
42. Ibid., September 13, 1982, p. 1.
43. Ibid., November 14, 1983, p. 24.
44. Ibid., June 23, 1980, p. 15.
45. Ibid., July 7, 1980, p. 7.
46. Ibid., June 4, 1979, p. 3.
47. Ibid., February 18, 1980, p. 19.
48. Ibid., July 7, 1980, p. 22.
49. Ibid., March 16, 1981, p. 1.
50. Ibid., November 11, 1981, p. 2.
51. Ibid., December 12, 1981, p. 1.
52. Ibid., November 9, 1981, p. 1.
53. Ibid., December 7, 1981, p. 3.
54. Ibid., June 7, 1982, p. 1.
55. Ibid., February 2, 1982, p. 6.
56. Ibid., April 26, 1982, p. 3.
57. March 12, 1979, p. 3.
58. Ibid., October 13, 1980, p. 17.
59. Ibid., September 1, 1980, p. 1.
60. Ibid., December 20, 1980, p. 1.
61. Ibid., June 13, 1983, p. 1.
62. Ibid., October 13, 1980, p. 1.
63. Ibid., November 14, 1983, p. 1.
64. Ibid., June 23, 1980, p. 2.
65. Ibid., January 5, 1981, p. 2.

Chapter 10   Social Investing

1. *Pensions & Investments*, February 11, 1974, p. 5.
2. Ibid., July 1, 1974, p. 1.
3. Ibid.
4. Ibid., August 13, 1979, p. 1.
5. Ibid., September 2, 1985, p. 2.
6. Ibid., August 8, 1983, p. 3.

7. Ibid., February 17, 1986, p. 2.
8. Ibid., November 10, 1986, p. 3.
9. Ibid., March 14, 1977, p. 5.
10. Ibid., October 13, 1980, p. 2.
11. Ibid., October 8, 1980, p. 30.
12. Ibid., April 14, 1980, p. 11.
13. Ibid., June 8, 1981, p. 1.
14. Ibid., September 14, 1981, p. 19.
15. Ibid., January 4, 1982, p. 1.
16. Ibid., December 12, 1983, p. 43.
17. Ibid., September 13, 1982, p. 1.
18. Ibid., September 27, 1982, p. 1.
19. Ibid., November 8, 1982, p. 7.
20. Ibid., December 20, 1982, p. 1.
21. Ibid., March 21, 1983, p. 1.
22. Ibid., February 7, 1982, p. 1.
23. Ibid., April 4, 1983, p. 1.
24. Ibid.
25. Ibid., April 18, 1983, p. 1.
26. Ibid., May 2, 1983, p. 1.
27. Ibid., May 16, 1983, p. 1.
28. Ibid., July 11, 1983, p. 2.
29. Ibid., September 5, 1983, p. 1.
30. Ibid., September 14, 1983, p. 3.
31. Ibid., October 26, 1981, p. 1.
32. Ibid., December 21, 1981, p. 1.
33. Ibid., March 7, 1983, p. 1.
34. Ibid., October 26, 1981, p. 1.
35. Ibid., April 12, 1982, p. 3.
36. Ibid., October 21, 1981, p. 1.
37. Ibid., May 24, 1982, p. 1.
38. Ibid., September 27, 1982, p. 1.
39. Ibid., January 10, 1983, p. 3.
40. Ibid., May 30, 1983, p. 1.
41. Ibid., p. 3.
42. Ibid., August 8, 1983, p. 1.
43. Ibid., August 22, 1983, p. 3.
44. Ibid., October 17, 1983, p. 1.
45. Ibid., p. 1.
46. *Flow of Funds Accounts*, Second Quarter 1992, Board of Governors of the Federal Reserve System, September 28, 1992, p. 95.
47. *Pensions & Investments*, July 11, 1983, p. 9.
48. Ibid., October 11, 1982, p. 1.
49. Ibid., November 28, 1983, p. 1.

Chapter 11   Consolidation

1. *Flow of Funds Accounts*, Board of Governors of the Federal Reserve System, p. 95.
2. *Pensions & Investments*, Money Manager Profiles issues 1975, 1980, and 1985.

3. Ibid., May 17, 1999, p. 93.
4. Ibid., January 9, 1984, p. 2.
5. Ibid., September 3, 1984, p. 1.
6. Ibid., October 1, 1984, p. 1.
7. Ibid., May 14, 1984, p. 3.
8. Ibid., September 2, 1985, p. 1.
9. Ibid., October 29, 1984, p. 2.
10. Ibid., December 24, 1984, p. 1.
11. Ibid., February 4, 1985, p. 2.
12. Ibid., April 24, 1985, p. 4.
13. Ibid., June 9, 1986, p. 54.
14. Ibid., June 23, 1986, p. 1.
15. Ibid.
16. Ibid., September 29, 1986, p. 1.
17. Ibid., June 7, 1982, p. 22.
18. Ibid.
19. Ibid.
20. Ibid., January 10, 1983, p. 9.
21. Ibid., May 15, 1983, p. 48.
22. Ibid., May 15, 1985, p. 43.
23. Ibid., April 15, 1985, p. 35.
24. Ibid., November 12, 1984, p. 36.
25. Ibid., June 10, 1985, p. 3.
26. *Pensions & Investments*, March 15, 1982, p. 1.
27. Ibid., March 29, 1982, p. 20.
28. *Flow of Funds Accounts*, Board of Governors of the Federal Reserve System, p. 95.
29. Diana B. Henriques, *Fidelity's World* (New York: Simon & Schuster I., 1995), p. 199.
30. *Pensions & Investments*, April 15, p. 39.
31. Ibid., November 22, 1982, p. 1.
32. Ibid., January 9, 1984, p. 1.
33. Ibid., August 20, 1984, p. 1.
34. Ibid., December 10, 1984, p. 3.
35. Ibid., December 10, 1984, p. 1.
36. Ibid., October 15, 1984, p. 3.
37. Ibid., July 7, 1986, p. 1.
38. Ibid., September 15, 1986, p. 15.
39. Ibid., October 13, 1986, p. 8.
40. Ibid., April 15, 1985, p. 21.
41. Ibid., June 24, 1985, p. 13.
42. Ibid., July 8, 1985, p. 21.
43. Ibid., May 12, 1986, p. 88.
44. Ibid., August 4, 1986, p. 15.
45. Ibid., March 5, 1984, p. 2.
46. Ibid., February 4, 1985, p. 2.
47. Ibid., February 23, 1985, p. 6.
48. Ibid., January 20, 1986, p. 3.
49. Ibid., July 7, 1986, p. 6.
50. Ibid., September 15, 1986, p. 8.

51. Ibid., July 6, 1984, p. 54.
52. Ibid., August 6, 1984, p. 4.
53. Ibid., December 10, 1984, p. 8.
54. Ibid., February 20, 1984, p. 1.
55. Ibid., July 9, 1984, p. 2.
56. Ibid., August 6, 1984, p. 2.
57. Ibid., October 29, 1984, p. 3.
58. Ibid., May 14, 1984, p. 1.
59. Ibid., December 10, 1984, p. 2.
60. Ibid.
61. Ibid., October 14, 1985, p. 2.
62. Ibid., December 9, 1985, p. 41.
63. Ibid., April 14, 1986, p. 1.
64. Ibid., October 17, 1986, p. 1.
65. Ibid., March 2, 1986, p. 3.
66. Ibid., April 14, 1986, p. 2.
67. Ibid., July 8, 1985, p. 4.
68. Ibid., April 14, 1986, p. 6.
69. Ibid., December 10, 1984, p. 8.

Chapter 12   Portfolio Insurance

1. *Pensions & Investments*, July 6, 1981, p. 3.
2. Ibid., September 29, 1986, p. 3.
3. Ibid., January 26, 1987, p. 76.
4. Ibid., September 1, 1986, p. 44.
5. Ibid., June 9, 1986, p. 3.
6. Ibid., August 10, 1987, p. 2.
7. Ibid., September 7, 1987, p. 1.
8. Ibid., October 19, 1987, p. 70.
9. Ibid., October 19, 1987, p. 2.
10. Ibid., September 29, 1986, p. 3.
11. Ibid., February 9, 1987, p. 31.
12. Ibid., November 2, 1987, p. 50.
13. Peter L. Bernstein, *Capital Ideas* (New York: The Free Press, 1992).
14. Ibid., January 25, 1988, p. 2.
15. Ibid., November 2, 1987, p. 53.
16. Ibid., November 30, 1987, p. 1.
17. Ibid., February 8, 1988, p. 1.
18. Ibid., November 2, 1987, p. 6.
19. Ibid., September 5, 1988, p. 1.
20. Ibid., September 5, 1988, p. 1.
21. Ibid., May 18, 1998, p. 75.
22. Ibid., January 12, 1986, p. 14.
23. Ibid., January 26, 1987, p. 1.
24. Ibid., March 9, 1987, p. 1.
25. Ibid., March 23, 1987, p. 1.
26. Ibid., April 6, 1987, p. 1.

27. Ibid., April 20, 1987, p. 1.
28. Ibid., June 13, 1988, p. 1.
29. Ibid., March 7, 1988, p. 2.
30. Ibid., June 27, 1988, p. 1.
31. Ibid., January 11, 1988, p. 2.
32. Ibid., April 4, 1988, p. 6.
33. Ibid., July 11, 1988, p. 1.
34. Ibid., November 14, 1988, p. 3.
35. Ibid., December 12, 1988, p. 1.
36. Ibid., May 16, 1988, p. 2.
37. Ibid., June 27, 1988, p. 3.
38. Ibid., May 4, 1987, p. 2.
39. Ibid., May 23, 1988, p. 20.
40. Ibid., May 16, 1988, p. 1.
41. Ibid., July 25, 1988, p. 1.
42. Ibid., May 30, 1988, p. 3.
43. Ibid., September 5, 1988, p. 1.
44. Ibid., March 21, 1988, p. 1.

Chapter 13   Metzenbaum Wins

1. *Pensions & Investments*, November 15, 1990, p. 1.
2. *EBRI Databook on Employee Benefits*, Fourth Edition (Washington, D.C.: The Employee Benefits Research Institute), pp. 98, 116.
3. *Pensions & Investments*, May 17, 1993, p. 16.
4. Ibid., April 29, 1991, p. 1.
5. Ibid., May 27, 1991, p. 1.
6. Ibid., December 22, 1997, p. 1.
7. Ibid., August 5, 1991, p. 1.
8. Ibid., December 9, 1991, p. 2.
9. Ibid., June 10, 1991, p. 3.
10. Ibid., August 22, 1994, p. 1.
11. Ibid., July 12, 1993, p. 3.
12. Ibid., December 11, 1989, p. 37.
13. Ibid., May 15, 1989, p. 25.
14. Ibid., October 2, 1989, p. 33.
15. Ibid., June 26, 1989, p. 40.
16. Ibid., April 2, 1990, p. 32.
17. Ibid., May 14, 1990, p. 2.
18. Ibid., November 26, 1990, p. 26.
19. Ibid., August 6, 1990, p. 1.
20. Ibid., June 10, 1991, p. 1.
21. Ibid., February 17, 1992, p. 1.
22. Ibid., February 3, 1992, p. 3.
23. Ibid., August 31, 1992, p. 1.
24. Ibid., January 11, 1993, p. 1.
25. Ibid., November 23, 1992, p. 1.
26. Ibid., June 14, 1993, p. 29.

27. Ibid., May 16, 1994, p. 1.
28. Ibid., September 20, 1993, p. 21.
29. Ibid., October 18, 1993, p. 37.
30. Ibid., October 3, 1994, p. 17.
31. Ibid., October 2, 1995, p. 20.
32. Ibid., November 13, 1995, p. 2.
33. Ibid., January 22, 1990, p. 16.
34. Ibid., October 28, 1991, p. 2.
35. Ibid., January 22, 1990, p. 16.
36. Ibid., October 16, 1989, p. 43.
37. Ibid., April 29, 1991, p. 3.
38. Ibid., July 7, 1997, p. 18.
39. Ibid., July 9, 1990, p. 3.
40. Ibid., June 26, 1995, p. 1.
41. Ibid., September 28, 1992, p. 2.
42. Ibid., January 10, 1994, p. 1.
43. Ibid., May 2, 1994, p. 43.
44. Ibid., July 10, 1995, p. 2.
45. Ibid., July 8, 1996, p. 1.
46. Ibid., September 29, 1997, p. 1.
47. Ibid., November 24, 1997, p. 1.
48. Ibid., December 8, 1997, p. 1.
49. Ibid., April 20, 1998, p. 3.

Chapter 14   Pension Exports

1. *Pensions & Investments*, April 27, 1992, p. 1.
2. Ibid., February 9, 1998, p. 19.
3. Ibid., February 8, 1993, p. 1.
4. Ibid., May 31, 1993, p. 3.
5. Ibid., October 17, 1994, p. 4.
6. Ibid., April 3, 1995, p. 4.
7. Ibid., February 7, 1994, p. 27.
8. Ibid., June 9, 1997, p. 22.
9. Ibid., May 18, 1998, p. 24.
10. Ibid., April 18, 1994, p. 10.
11. Ibid., October 3, 1994, p. 2.
12. Ibid., December 26, 1994, p. 1.
13. Ibid., March 20, 1995, p. 26.
14. Ibid., April 28, 1997, p. 1.
15. Ibid., August 3, 2992, p. 1.
16. Ibid., August 23, 1993, p. 1.
17. Ibid., April 15, 1996, p. 2.
18. Ibid., November 11, 1996, p. 31.
19. Ibid., February 9, 1998, p. 1.
20. Ibid., January 25, 1999, p. 68.
21. Ibid., February 3, 1997, p. 1.
22. Ibid., December 23, 1996, p. 1.

23. Ibid., May 12, 1997, p. 1.
24. Ibid., September 1, 1997, p. 2.
25. Ibid., January 23, 1999, p. 50.
26. Ibid., p. 64.
27. Ibid., p. 30.
28. Ibid., p. 30.
29. Ibid., p. 36.
30. Ibid., p. 25.
31. Ibid., May 17, 1999, p. 26.   •

Chapter 15   Trouble Ahead

1. *EBRI Databook on Employee Benefits*, Fourth Edition (Washington, D.C.: The Employee Benefit Research Institute), p. 84.
2. *Pensions & Investments*, January 23, 1999, p. 1.
3. Ibid.
4. Steven C. Leuthold, *Perception for the Professional*, July 1999, p. 7.

Index